HUTChIsON'S
CANADIAN SEARCH
WARRANT MANUAL 2005

A Guide to Legal and Practical Issues Associated with Judicial Pre-Authorization of Investigative Techniques

by Scott C. Hutchison

Barrister and Crown Counsel
Crown Law Office – Criminal
Ministry of the Attorney General (Ontario)

THOMSON

™

CARSWELL

Library and Archives Canada has catalogued this publication as follows:

Hutchison, Scott C., 1962-
  Hutchison's Canadian search warrant manual : a guide to legal and practical issues associated with judicial pre-authorization of investigative techniques / Scott C. Hutchison. — 2nd ed.

1st ed. publ. under title: Canadian search warrant manual 2003.
Includes bibliographical references and index.
ISBN 0-459-24159-1

  1. Searches and seizures—Canada. 2. Warrants (Law)—Canada.
I. Title. II. Title: Canadian search warrant manual.

KE9270.H86 2004   345.71'0522
C2004-905996-3
KF9630.H88 2004

THOMSON
™
CARSWELL

One Corporate Plaza   Customer relations:
2075 Kennedy Road   Toronto 1-416-609-3800
Toronto, Ontario   Elsewhere in Canada/U.S. 1-800-387-5164
M1T 3V4   Fax 1-416-298-5082
                            E-mail: carswell.orders@thomson.com
                                      http://www.carswell.com

To Jack, Ally and Erika

Acknowledgments
to the 2005 edition

I am, once again, indebted to many people who have been good enough to have assisted me in the preparation of this practical guide to search warrants.

For almost 15 years I have been fortunate enough to participate in the education of police officers and justices of the peace in the province of Ontario and elsewhere. In the process I have learned much more than I have taught. I am grateful for the experience.

Justice of the Peace Opal Rosemond, and Sheilagh Stewart, counsel to the office of the Chief Justice of the Ontario Court, and Shelly Howell, now counsel with the Ministry of the Attorney General, each offered helpful comments on the draft of the 2003 edition, drawing on their extensive experience in judicial education in this area.

The prolific and proficient Justice Gilles Renaud of the Ontario Court of Justice provided words of encouragement and, just as important, offered a number of very helpful suggestions for this edition.

Three members of the police community deserve special mention. Michael Chevers, Coordinator for Criminal Investigation Training at the Ontario Police College and Det. Kim Gross of the Toronto Police Service provided their usual helpful comments and insights into the legal and practical challenges faced by police officers confronting search issues. Det. Insp. Michael Coughlin of the Ontario Provincial Police, a man of unparalleled integrity and policing skill, over the years has carried into action much of the advice set out here. He kindly reviewed an earlier draft and provided comments.

I am indebted as well to Det. Staff Sgt. Arni Stinnison and Sgt. Robert Gagnon of the E-Crime Unit of the Ontario Provincial Police who advised on computer searches and provided the model warrant used by that unit and recommended by them to officers around the province of Ontario.

I also benefited from the assistance of four valued colleagues and friends. Alex Smith (Director for Law and Technology, Ministry of the Attorney General (Ontario)), and Phil Downes and Robert Kelly (both Crown Counsel, Crown Law Office – Criminal) all provided valuable comments on earlier drafts. Fraser Kelly, of the London Crown Attorney's Office, took the time to provide a detailed review of an earlier version of the text bringing to bear the attention to detail and good sense that have made him one of the best trial lawyers in the Ontario prosecution service.

Jilean Bell, my (now promoted) editor at Carswell, has yet again distinguished herself as a friend and woman of tolerance and encouragement. I wish her well in her new position as Manager, Legal Product Development. Jennifer Hashimoto, responsible for just about everything right in this edition, proved to be the best technical editor I have had the pleasure to work with over the last decade with Thomson-Carswell. Her attention to detail and diligence border on the superhuman. She has been a pleasure and delight to work with.

Last, but by no means least, I am grateful to my spouse, Erika Chozik. I have, in the past, suggested that she is not by nature a patient person, but she has (again) proven me wrong. She is, and to that she adds a zest for life and energy that drives our family forward. She is in all things loving and supportive. This book is dedicated to her and to our daughter and son, Ally and Jack. They are all the centre of my life.

Preface

In *Nova Scotia (Attorney General) v. MacIntyre*, these observations were made about search warrants:

> A search warrant may be broadly defined as an order issued by a Justice under statutory powers, authorizing a named person to enter a specified place to search for and seize specified property which will afford evidence of the actual or intended commission of a crime. A warrant may issue upon a sworn information and proof of reasonable grounds for its issuance. The property seized must be carried before the Justice who issued the warrant to be dealt with by him according to law.

> Search warrants are part of the investigative pre-trial process of the criminal law, often employed early in the investigation and before the identity of all of the suspects is known. Parliament, in furtherance of the public interest in effective investigation and prosecution of crime, and through the enactment of s. 443 of the *Code*, has legalized what would otherwise be an illegal entry of premises and illegal seizure of property. The issuance of a search warrant is a judicial act on the part of the Justice, usually performed *ex parte* and *in camera*, by the very nature of the proceedings.

> The search warrant in recent years has become an increasingly important investigatory aid, as crime and criminals become increasingly sophisticated and the incidence of corporate white collar crime multiplies. The effectiveness of any search made pursuant to the issuance of a search warrant will depend much upon timing, upon the degree of confidentiality which attends the issuance of the warrant and upon the element of surprise which attends the search.

> As is often the case in a free society, there are at work two conflicting public interests. The one has to do with civil liberties and the protection of the individual from interference with the enjoyment of his property. There is a clear and important social value in avoidance of arbitrary searches and unlawful seizures. The other, competing, interest lies in the effective detection and proof of crime and the prompt apprehension and conviction of offenders. Public protection, afforded by efficient and effective law enforcement, is enhanced through the proper use of search warrants.

In this balancing of interests, Parliament has made a clear policy choice. The public interest in the detection, investigation and prosecution of crimes has been permitted to dominate the individual interest. To the extent of its reach, s. 443 has been introduced as an aid in the administration of justice and enforcement of the provisions of the *Criminal Code*.[1]

In the two decades since *MacIntyre*, the importance of search warrants has been underscored repeatedly by the Supreme Court. It is not unfair to suggest that the process whereby search warrants are obtained has been subject to more scrutiny than any other in this period. But little (if anything) has been written to deal with the difficult job of carrying the tide of judicial and statutory pronouncements into action.

This modest text aims to remedy this by providing practical advice on a variety of issues associated with the application for and issuance of search warrants.

It takes the form of a manual to be renewed annually, or as developments mandate. While the focus is on the practical, the law is discussed and hopefully explained in a way that makes obedience simpler and understandable.

I welcome any suggestions for improvement or additions, in particular suggestions for new improved precedents. I can be reached by e-mail at *scott.hutchison@jus.gov.on.ca.*

The views expressed here are, of course, my own and do not necessarily reflect the views of the Ministry of the Attorney General of Ontario, or of the many people who assisted in the preparation of this text.

---

[1] *Nova Scotia (Attorney General) v. MacIntyre* (1982), 65 C.C.C. (2d) 129, 26 C.R. (3d) 193 (S.C.C.) at pp. 141–142 [C.C.C.].

Table of Contents

    (g) DNA as Evidence v. DNA Data Bank
          Warrants and Orders 142
3. General Warrants and Assistance Orders – Sections 487.01 and
    487.02 142
    (a) Introduction and Background 142
        (i)   *Introduction* 142
        (ii)   *Rationale for the General Warrant* 143
            (A) *Background to Assistance Orders – Section*
                487.02 145
            (B) *Parliamentary Debates and Committee*
                Hearings 146
    (b) The Types of Techniques to be Authorized under Section
        487.01 147
        (i)   *Internal Limitations* 147
            (A) *Bodily Integrity (Section 487.01(2))* 147
            (B) *Video Surveillance* 149
            (C) *Covert Entry* 151
        (ii)   *"A Flexible Range of Investigative Procedures"* .. 151
        (iii) *Examples of Authorized Techniques* 154
    (c) The Types of Assistance Orders to be Authorized 159
    (d) Preconditions to Issuance of General Warrants 159
        (i)   *Introduction* 159
            (A) *Issuing Judicial Officer* 160
            (B) *Standard of Proof: "Reasonable grounds to*
                believe" 160
            (C) *Information Concerning the Offence Will Be*
                Obtained through the Technique 161
            (D) *The Best Interests of the Administration of*
                Justice 162
            (E) *No Other Provision That Would Provide for*
                a Warrant 163
    (e) Specific Issues 164
        (i)   *"Rolled-up" Approach* 164
        (ii)   *The "Confirm or Deny" Warrant* 165
        (iii) *Returns in General Warrant Cases* 166
        (iv) *Techniques with Scheduled Offences* 167
        (v)   *Cover-ups and Distractions: Terms and Conditions*
               168
    (f) No Provincial Offences 169
4. Special Locations 169
    (a) Law Offices after the Demise of Section 488.1 169
        (i)   *Introduction* 169
        (ii)   *The Post-*Lavallee *Law Office Search* 172
    (b) Media Outlets 173

Table of Cases

1

The Organizing Principles of Search and Seizure Law in Canada

1. Introduction – The Warrant Presumption and Its Significance

(a) The Central Role of Judicial Pre-Authorization

The enforcement of the criminal law depends upon efficient and knowledgeable police officers armed with the legal authority necessary to discover and demonstrate contraventions of the *Criminal Code* and other relevant statutes. Perhaps the most important body of legal authority available to such investigators is the power to search for and seize evidence of wrongdoing. As the Supreme Court of Canada said in the *Canadian Oxy Chemicals* case:

> [20] A primary, though not exclusive, purpose of the *Criminal Code*, and penal statutes in general, is to promote a safe, peaceful and honest society[.] This is achieved by providing guidelines prohibiting unacceptable conduct, and providing for the just prosecution and punishment of those who transgress these norms. The prompt and comprehensive investigation of potential offences is essential to fulfilling that purpose. The point of the investigative phase is to gather all the relevant evidence in order to allow a responsible and informed decision to be made as to whether charges should be laid.[1]

Against the need for such enforcement must be balanced the rights of individuals and businesses to be secure in their legitimate, private affairs. For generations, judicial officers – justices of the peace and judges – have guarded

---

[1] *Canadian Oxy Chemicals Ltd. v. Canada (Attorney General)* (1999), 133 C.C.C. (3d) 426, 23 C.R. (5th) 259 (S.C.C.) at p. 434 [C.C.C.].

these rights through the process of judicial pre-authorization.[2] These rights, long recognized (but only somewhat protected) by statute and the common law, were elevated to constitutional status in s. 8 of the *Charter of Rights and Freedoms*[3] in 1982. Section 8 of the *Charter* provides:

> **8.** Everyone has the right to be secure against unreasonable search or seizure.

Our Constitution also provides that where a search or seizure has been unreasonable, that is, where a search or seizure violates s. 8 of the *Charter*, evidence so obtained may be excluded from consideration at the accused's trial. Section 24 of the *Charter* provides:

> **24.** (1) Anyone whose rights or freedoms, as guaranteed by this Charter, have been infringed or denied may apply to a court of competent jurisdiction to obtain such remedy as the court considers appropriate and just in the circumstances.
>
> (2) Where, in proceedings under subsection (1), a court concludes that evidence was obtained in a manner that infringed or denied any rights or freedoms guaranteed by this Charter, the evidence shall be excluded if it is established that, having regard to all the circumstances, the admission of it in the proceedings would bring the administration of justice into disrepute.

The law related to search and seizure struggles to find the correct balance between the conflicting interests of the community as a whole (as represented by the police, other investigators and the Crown) on the one hand and individual rights on the other hand. Police officers responsible for the enforcement of the criminal law, indeed, all law enforcement officials, must be diligent in their efforts to ensure that their conduct conforms to the Constitution, that it is *lawful* and *reasonable*, at all times.

In the watershed decision in *Hunter v. Southam Inc.* (hereinafter *Hunter*),[4] the Supreme Court of Canada made it clear that the notion of *judicial pre-authorization* of search activity – most commonly by way of search warrant – is the key to this balancing effort. While other forms of lawful authority[5] may provide the legal basis for search activity without warrant, judicial pre-author-

---

[2] *Re Worrall* (1964), [1965] 2 C.C.C. 1, 44 C.R. 151 (Ont. C.A.) at p. 9 [C.C.C.] (per Roach J.A., dissenting on other grounds), leave to appeal refused [1965] S.C.R. ix (S.C.C.).

[3] *Canadian Charter of Rights and Freedoms*, Part I of the *Constitution Act, 1982*, being Schedule B of the *Canada Act 1982* (U.K.), 1982, c. 11.

[4] *Hunter v. Southam Inc.* (1984), 14 C.C.C. (3d) 97, 41 C.R. (3d) 97 (S.C.C.).

[5] There are a number of perfectly constitutional warrantless search and seizure powers. These include search incident to arrest, plain view, exigent circumstances (both at common law and pursuant to s. 487.11 of the *Criminal Code*), consent, and a range of special search powers given to law enforcement, in particular circumstances such as border crossings (*R. v. Simmons* (1988), 45 C.C.C. (3d) 296, 66 C.R. (3d) 297 (S.C.C.)) or to combat impaired driving (s. 254(3) of the *Criminal Code*).

ization in accordance with the *Hunter* standard remains the central measure against which the reasonableness of any form of legal authority to search or seize will be considered in the criminal law context.[6]

In *Hunter,* Chief Justice Dickson explained the centrality of judicial pre-authorization, saying:

> If the issue to be resolved in assessing the constitutionality of searches . . . were [whether] *in fact* the governmental interest in carrying out a given search outweighed that of the individual in resisting the governmental intrusion upon his privacy, then it would be appropriate to determine the balance of the competing interests *after* the search had been conducted. Such a *post facto* analysis would, however, be seriously at odds with the purpose of s. 8. That purpose is, as I have said, to protect individuals from unjustified State intrusions upon their privacy. That purpose requires a means of *preventing* unjustified searches before they happen, not simply of determining, after the fact, whether they ought to have occurred in the first place. This, in my view, can only be accomplished by a system of *prior authorization*, not one of subsequent validation.
>
> A requirement of prior authorization, usually in the form of a valid warrant, has been a consistent prerequisite for a valid search and seizure both at common law and under most statutes. Such a requirement puts the onus on the State to demonstrate the superiority of its interests to that of the individual. As such it accords with the apparent intention of the Charter to prefer, where feasible, the right of the individual to be free from State interference to the interests of the State in advancing its purposes through such interference.
>
> I recognize that it may not be reasonable in every instance to insist on prior authorization in order to validate governmental intrusions upon individuals' expectations of privacy. Nevertheless, where it is feasible to obtain prior authorization, I would hold that such authorization is a pre-condition for a valid search and seizure.[7] [emphasis in original]

There is, therefore, a presumption that, where feasible, judicial pre-authorization is the constitutionally mandated standard against which police powers are to be assessed.

---

[6] *Schreiber v. Canada (Attorney General)* (1998), 124 C.C.C. (3d) 129, 16 C.R. (5th) 1 (S.C.C.), reversing (1997), 114 C.C.C. (3d) 97, 6 C.R. (5th) 314 (Fed. C.A.). In this text the focus is on the warrant requirement as it operates in the context of police investigations into criminal offences. Clearly, different rules apply in determining whether a warrant is required (*Hunter v. Southam Inc.* (S.C.C.), *supra*, note 4; *R. v. Simmons* (S.C.C.), *supra*, note 5). However, much (if not all) of the law related to the formal and substantive requirements of search warrants is consistent across criminal, regulatory, administrative and civil schemes. Readers approaching these questions from the perspective of a non-criminal investigator would do well to keep in mind the special considerations which might mandate a more relaxed rule in the particular regulatory, administrative or civil regime.

[7] *Hunter v. Southam Inc.* (S.C.C.), *supra*, note 4, at p. 109 [C.C.C.].

The purpose of a constitutional protection which focuses on judicial pre-authorization is not to frustrate officers seeking evidence. As the United States Supreme Court observed many years ago:

> The point of the Fourth Amendment . . . is not that it denies law enforcement the support of the usual inferences which reasonable men draw from evidence. *Its protection consists in requiring that those inferences be drawn by a neutral and detached magistrate instead of being judged by the officer engaged in the often competitive enterprise of ferreting out crime* . . . . The right of officers to thrust themselves into a home is also a grave concern, not only to the individual but to a society which chooses to dwell in reasonable security and freedom from surveillance. *When the right of privacy must reasonably yield to the right of search is, as a rule, to be decided by a judicial officer, not by a policeman or Government enforcement agent.*[8] [emphasis added]

Constitutional "end-runs" by officers who know better (or who *should* know better) undermine the public's and the court's respect for law enforcement generally and colour any assessment related to the admission of evidence in a particular case. Just as good faith efforts to comply with the law will provide the Crown with a solid basis to advocate the admission of evidence under s. 24(2), the deliberate resort to "short-cuts" confines any effort to have evidence admitted. As the Ontario Court of Appeal observed in *R. v. Price*:

> [25] In their investigation, the police admittedly engaged in "short-cuts". The officer in charge was, of course, aware of the requirement of a search warrant. He ordered the warrantless search because he did not want to burden his officers with additional duties after having worked for a number of hours without sleep, given the difficulty of locating a Justice of the Peace on a Sunday. *In my view, these circumstances do not mitigate the seriousness of the breach. To the contrary, they lead one to conclude that the violation of s. 8 was deliberate, flagrant and one not committed in good faith.* The violation was not merely of a technical nature. It was not motivated by a situation of urgency or necessity. It would have been quite feasible for the police to secure the premises until a search warrant had been obtained.[9] [emphasis added]

It is important, therefore, that individual officers and law enforcement agencies endeavour at all times to *understand* the constitutional limitations on their powers, and strive to *conform* their conduct to that understanding. As well, police and regulatory agencies must make the necessary and appropriate in-

---

[8] *Johnson v. United States*, 333 U.S. 10, 68 S. Ct. 367 (U.S. S.C. 1948) per Jackson J. at p. 369 S. Ct.

[9] *R. v. Price*, 144 C.C.C. (3d) 343, 33 C.R. (5th) 278, 2000 CarswellOnt 837, [2000] O.J. No. 886 (Ont. C.A.) at pp. 352–353 [C.C.C.].

vestment in education to ensure that investigators are given the training that is essential to discharge their responsibilities in accordance with the fundamental law of the land. From the perspectives of the individual or the courts, it matters little whether the citizen's rights were violated because of a failing of the individual officer, or institutional neglect by the body responsible for training that officer: the state has failed in its constitutional mission in either case.[10]

(b) Asking the Right Question: "What Is My Legal Authority?"

The constitutional presumption that the police will obtain a warrant prior to search activity frames any consideration of search issues in individual cases. Rather than asking "*Do I need a warrant?*" officers should ask "*What is my legal authority for this investigative step?*" The first approach ("Do I need a warrant?") suggests that unless one can identify a reason to get a warrant, then one is not required. This, in effect, ignores the warrant presumption that should control any discussion of a search problem.

Approaching the inquiry from the other perspective – "What is my legal authority for this investigative step?" – obliges the officer to either identify some valid warrantless power or to look to judicial pre-authorization of the activity in question.

2. How Courts Analyze Search Problems

(a) Introduction

The analysis of a search issue normally requires the court to consider five questions:

1. Did the accused (or the party complaining about the police activity) have a reasonable expectation of privacy?
2. Did the investigative activity in issue interfere with the accused's reasonable expectation of privacy?
3. Was the investigative activity in issue authorized by law?
4. Is the law authorizing the investigative activity reasonable?
5. Was the investigative activity carried out or executed in a reasonable way?

---

[10] Indeed, a number of authorities have questioned whether institutional educational failures will cancel out a plea of good faith by an individual officer. If the officer's ignorance of constitutional norms reflects a lax attitude about the importance of in-service search warrant training, it might amount to "institutional bad faith," which would tend to suggest that evidence should be excluded. See C. Hill, S. Hutchison, L. Pringle, "Search Warrants: Protection or Illusion?" (1999) 28 C.R. (5th) 89–128; Law Reform Commission of Canada, *Police Powers – Search and Seizure in Criminal Law Enforcement (Working Paper 30)* (Ottawa: Queen's Printer, 1983) at pp. 84–85; S.C. Hill, "The Role of Fault in Section 24(2) of the *Charter*" in *The Charter's Impact on the Criminal Justice System*, J. Cameron, ed. (Toronto: Carswell, 1996) at pp. 69ff.

(b) Expectations of Privacy – Is There a Search or Seizure?

(i) *Introduction*

In *Hunter,*[11] the Supreme Court of Canada made it clear that s. 8 of the *Charter* was intended to protect the citizen's "reasonable expectation of privacy." Police activity (or other state investigative activity) that interferes with someone's reasonable expectation of privacy will be labelled as a "search" or "seizure." Identifying government conduct as a search or seizure is significant: once an investigative technique is labelled as a search or seizure the constitutional requirement of "reasonableness" applies. This carries with it the presumption – at least in respect of true criminal investigations – of judicial pre-authorization.

(ii) *Anyone's Expectation of Privacy Engages Section 8*

It is important to determine whether the proposed investigative action will interfere with *anyone's* reasonable expectation of privacy. In this regard one must keep in mind that the proper inquiry at this stage is not simply whether the *accused* or *subject of the investigation* has a privacy interest, but whether *anyone* has such an interest. After a charge has been laid the focus may shift to the question of whether the accused had an expectation of privacy, but it is not the proper inquiry when state actors are deciding whether to follow an investigative avenue. The Constitution requires the police to respect everyone's privacy in the investigation of crime, and not simply the privacy of targets. It is true that the accused will have to establish his or her own expectation of privacy to have "standing" to challenge a search at trial. The fact that it is someone other than the accused who enjoys an expectation of privacy is not, however, a basis for avoiding the warrant requirement imposed by s. 8 of the *Charter.*

Where a police investigative step will intrude on anyone's reasonable expectation of privacy, there must be some identifiable lawful authority for the intrusion. In the absence of some applicable warrantless authority (for example, the consent of a third party) or some other applicable legal power for the investigative activity, the police are obliged by the *Charter* to get a warrant.

Standing is a concept related to the notion of reasonable expectation of privacy. Before an accused can challenge police conduct in a particular case, he or she must demonstrate his or her "standing" to do so. The individual must show that his or her own "reasonable expectation of privacy" has been intruded

---

[11] *Hunter v. Southam Inc.* (S.C.C.), *supra*, note 4.

upon. It will not normally[12] be enough to show that someone else's expectation of privacy has been violated.

The similarity between the two questions: "Was there a 'search'?" and "Does the accused have 'standing' to challenge that search?" means that elements of the analysis overlap. The determination of whether there is any reasonable expectation of privacy will sometimes look very much like the "standing" analysis that the court engages in when it considers whether a person is entitled to bring a challenge to a particular search or seizure.

(iii) *Factors Determining Whether a Reasonable Expectation of Privacy Exists*

The *Charter* protects Canadians against unreasonable *searches* or *seizures*. If an investigative technique can be called a "search" or a "seizure," the standard of reasonableness (and the presumption of judicial pre-authorization) will ordinarily apply.[13]

Normally, it is not difficult to determine if an investigative technique amounts to a search or a seizure. An entry, inspection or physical taking of something real will almost always be a search (or seizure) for the purpose of analysis under the *Charter*.[14] More difficult questions, however, arise when the manifestations of an investigative practice are less concrete. Is it a search to ask a utility to produce someone's hydro billing records?[15] What about phone bills?[16] What about spying on someone's business from a high-rise building[17] or using an electronic device to track the movements of his or her

---

[12] In some exceptional cases it may be possible for an accused to point to police conduct not directly impacting on the particular accused (e.g., where the police conduct relates to a co-conspirator: *R. v. Sandhu* (1993), 82 C.C.C. (3d) 236, 22 C.R. (4th) 300 (B.C. C.A.), leave to appeal refused (1993), 84 C.C.C. (3d) vi, 25 C.R. (4th) 124 (note) (S.C.C.); or where the conduct in question is particularly egregious: *R. v. Harrer* (1995), 101 C.C.C. (3d) 193, 42 C.R. (4th) 269 (S.C.C.)).

[13] In the regulatory/administrative context, "reasonableness" may find a different definition, one more favourable to the position of an investigator taking advantage of warrantless search powers prescribed by provincial statute. Police officers investigating criminal activity that "overlaps" with regulated conduct should take care to observe the limits on their powers under the *Criminal Code* or other legislation they are enforcing.

[14] See *R. v. Potash* (1994), 91 C.C.C. (3d) 315, 21 C.R.R. (2d) 193 (S.C.C.), reversing (1992), 75 C.C.C. (3d) 367, 10 C.R.R. (2d) 335 (Que. C.A.).

[15] *R. v. Plant* (1993), 84 C.C.C. (3d) 203, 24 C.R. (4th) 47, [1993] 3 S.C.R. 281 (S.C.C.) (obtaining electricity records not a search).

[16] *R. v. Edwards*, 1999 CarswellOnt 3233, [1999] O.J. No. 3819 (Ont. S.C.J.) at pp. 33ff per LaForme J. (cell phone information not a search).

[17] *R. v. Elzein* (1993), 82 C.C.C. (3d) 455 (translation), 55 Q.A.C. 99 (Que. C.A.), leave to appeal refused (1993), 84 C.C.C. (3d) vi (note) (S.C.C.) (videotaping in public place not a search). See also the opinion of G. La Forest, retired Justice of the Supreme Court of Canada, for the privacy commissioner, "Opinion by Justice Gérard La Forest April 5, 2002: re Opinion – Video Surveillance" online at <www.privcom.gc.ca/media/nr-c/opinion__020410__e.asp> accessed September 1, 2004.

car on public roads?[18]

The law in this respect has taken a purposive approach to the question and, looking to the reasons for s. 8 and the sorts of interests protected there, concluded that s. 8 is intended to protect *reasonable expectations of privacy*. Accordingly, whenever agents of the state engage in investigative action that intrudes on a reasonable expectation of privacy, the law will consider that investigative step to be a search that must meet the constitutional test of reasonableness.

This step in the analysis is a helpful beginning in our approach to the question of whether an investigative technique is or is not a search. But this initial inquiry merely has the effect of moving the really hard work to a different question. The real question becomes: *When does someone have a reasonable expectation of privacy?* Early on in the life of the *Charter*, Canadian courts seemed inclined to adopt the American two-part test[19]: (1) Did the accused *subjectively* have an expectation of privacy? and (2) Is that an expectation of privacy that *society* is prepared to recognize as reasonable and legitimate? Some Canadian cases had questioned whether the first part of the test was relevant to the analysis under the Canadian *Charter*.

The controversy was resolved by the Supreme Court of Canada decision in *R. v. Wong*, where Mr. Justice La Forest, for the majority, held that video surveillance in a hotel room was a search (even though the accused had made an open invitation to the public, through a number of leaflet and poster advertisements, to come to the room to engage in illegal gambling):

> [12] . . . *R. v. Sanelli* approached the problem of determining whether a person had a reasonable expectation of privacy in given circumstances by attempting to assess whether, by the standards of privacy that persons can expect to enjoy in a free and democratic society, the agents of the state were bound to conform to the requirements of the *Charter* when effecting the intrusion in question. This involves asking *whether the persons whose privacy was intruded upon could legitimately claim that in the circumstances it should not have been open to the agents of the state to act as they did without prior judicial authorization.* To borrow from Professor Amsterdam's reflections . . . the adoption of this standard invites the courts to assess whether giving their sanction to the particular form of unauthorized surveillance in question would see the amount of privacy and freedom remaining to citizens diminished to a compass inconsistent with the aims of a free and open society.[20] [emphasis added]

---

[18] *R. v. Wise* (1992), 70 C.C.C. (3d) 193, 11 C.R. (4th) 253 (S.C.C.) (use of tracking device is a search, albeit one based on intrusion into limited area of privacy).

[19] *Katz v. United States*, 389 U.S. 347, 88 S. Ct. 507 (U.S. S.C. 1967).

[20] *R. v. Wong* (1990), 60 C.C.C. (3d) 460, 1 C.R. (4th) 1 (S.C.C.) at p. 9 [C.R.].

What has developed in Canada then is a purely *objective* test that will be applied by the courts as to whether or not they will tolerate particular investigative techniques without prior judicial authorization. That is, it is not determinative if the particular party did or did not have an expectation of privacy – the question to be asked and answered is whether the *reasonable* person would expect that the investigative technique in question so trenched on personal privacy that it should only be available to agents of the state with some form of judicial pre-authorization.[21]

The assessment of whether a reasonable expectation of privacy exists takes place having regard to all the factual circumstances of the case and when measured against common understandings, is related to what *innocent* citizens would understand in respect of a particular constellation of factors. Consider the different areas surrounding a multi-unit dwelling such as an apartment building. While one might not have an expectation of privacy in relation to smells travelling into the hallways used by other residents (and so could not complain if the police gained information by virtue of smells coming from one's apartment), an apartment dweller might reasonably expect that the police could not engage in a close-up perimeter search by walking up to the window of their apartment and looking into the unit.[22]

In *Edwards,*[23] the Supreme Court of Canada considered the issue of "standing" and observed that, "A reasonable expectation of privacy is to be determined on the basis of the totality of the circumstances." *Edwards* suggests a number of factors to be considered as part of the "totality of the circumstances" in this inquiry. This non-exhaustive list includes:

1. presence at the time of the search;
2. possession or control of the property or place searched;
3. ownership of the property or place;
4. historical use of the property or item;
5. the ability to regulate access, including the right to admit or exclude others from the place;
6. the existence of a subjective expectation of privacy; and
7. the objective reasonableness of the expectation.

---

[21] Often the question that drives a case is whether there was any reasonable expectation of privacy. For example, in *R. v. M. (M.R.)* (1998), 129 C.C.C. (3d) 361, 20 C.R. (5th) 197 (S.C.C.), affirming (1997), 7 C.R. (5th) 1, 159 N.S.R. (2d) 321 (N.S. C.A.), the issue was whether students have a reasonable expectation that they will not be subjected to drug searches by school officials (apparently, they do not).

[22] *R. v. Laurin* (1997), 113 C.C.C. (3d) 519, 6 C.R. (5th) 201 (Ont. C.A.) (even though the area outside the window was not private or reserved for the use of the occupant).

[23] *R. v. Edwards* (1996), 104 C.C.C. (3d) 136, 45 C.R. (4th) 307 (S.C.C.) at p. 150 [C.C.C.], para. 45. See also *R. v. Polashek* (1999), 134 C.C.C. (3d) 187, 25 C.R. (5th) 183 (Ont. C.A.) per Rosenberg J.A, where weaknesses in police statement education were described as "a serious systemic failure within the police community." (at p. 201 [C.C.C.], para. 30)

No one of these considerations is controlling.[24] The assessment to be made is based on all of the facts, with no single element being required or dominating. Part of this assessment involves a consideration of how a free and democratic society *should* approach the privacy question in issue.

(iv) Pure "Informational Searches"

In *R. v. Plant*,[25] the Supreme Court considered whether police could access a public utility's electricity billing records for a particular address. If such warrantless access was an unreasonable search, then it could not be considered in determining whether a warrant in relation to the house should have been issued. Assessing the correct avenue to approach the release of *information* about a person, the Court observed:

> The purpose of s. 8 is to protect against intrusion of the state on an individual's privacy. The limits on such state action are determined by balancing the right of citizens to have respected a reasonable expectation of privacy as against the state interest in law enforcement: . . . *Hunter*. Section 8 protects people and not property. It is, therefore, unnecessary to establish a proprietary interest in the thing seized: see *Hunter* . . .; *Dyment* . . .; *Katz v. United States.*
>
> . . .
>
> While this court has considered the possibility of violations of s. 8 in relation to informational privacy . . . , we have not previously considered whether state inspection of computer records implicates s. 8 of the Charter.
>
> Some indication of the parameters of the protection afforded by s. 8 with respect to informational privacy can be derived from the following passage from the reasons of La Forest J. in *Dyment, supra*, at p. 256, commenting on the Report of the Task Force on Privacy and Computers:
>
> > In modern society, especially, retention of information about oneself is extremely important. We may, for one reason or another, wish or be compelled to reveal such information, but situations abound where the reasonable expectations of the individual that the information shall remain confidential to persons to whom, and restricted to the purposes for which it is divulged, must be protected.
> >
> > *Consideration of such factors as the nature of the information itself, the nature of the relationship between the party releasing the information and the party claiming its confidentiality, the place where the information was obtained, the*

---

[24] But control of access would seem to have some more significant role in assessing *Charter* s. 8 interests in a place.

[25] *R. v. Plant* (S.C.C.), *supra*, note 15.

manner in which it was obtained, and the seriousness of the crime being investigated, allow for a balancing of the societal interests in protecting individual dignity, integrity and autonomy with effective law enforcement.[26] [emphasis added]

This "contextual approach" guides assessments of search conduct which involves informational privacy questions. The circumstances to be considered by the court may be summarized as follows:

1. *The Nature of the Information*
    Is it highly personal information (e.g., health billing records), information related to the operation of a purely commercial enterprise, or is it information that would not ordinarily be considered particularly private (CPIC)?
2. *The Nature of the Relationship Between the Party That Releases the Information and the Person Now Claiming That There Has Been a Violation of His or Her Right to Privacy*
    Was the relationship commercial, professional or personal, long-term or transient, compulsory or optional? Does any sort of legislation promise privacy in relation to the information?
3. *The Place Where the Information Was Obtained*
    Was there any sort of physical intrusion of a place in any sense related to the person asserting that there has been an unreasonable search associated with the information obtained?
4. *The Manner in Which the Information Was Obtained*
    Was the information obtained by exercise of police authority on the third-party custodian of the information, by some standing arrangement, with the consent of the third-party custodian, or by positive action by the third-party custodian?
5. *The Seriousness of the Crime Under Investigation*
    Is the offence a true crime, is it a real and pressing problem for the community, how heavily does society's need for effective enforcement weigh in the constitutional scales?

Working through the first two elements of this standard with regard to the electricity billing information in question in *Plant,* Mr. Justice Sopinka for the Supreme Court of Canada concluded:

[I]n order for constitutional protection to be extended, the information seized must be of a *"personal and confidential"* nature. In fostering the underlying values of dignity, integrity and autonomy, it is fitting that s. 8 of the Charter should seek to *protect a biographical core of personal information which individuals in a free and democratic society would wish to maintain and control from dissemination*

---

[26] Ibid., at pp. 211–212 [C.C.C.].

to the state. This would include information which tends to reveal intimate details of the lifestyle and personal choices of the individual. The computer records investigated in the case at bar while revealing the pattern of electricity consumption in the residence cannot reasonably be said to reveal intimate details of the appellant's life since electricity consumption reveals very little about the personal lifestyle or private decisions of the occupant of the residence. [27] [emphasis added]

In general, the focus of any consideration of "informational searches" will be the nature of the relationship between the individual and the holder of the information and the nature of the information itself. In *Plant,* both factors told in favour of a very low expectation of privacy. [28]

R. v. Lillico [29] offers another common fact situation raising *Plant*-type "informational search" issues. The police, acting on a complaint from a victim, contacted the corporate security officer at the accused's bank and inquired whether a particular cheque had been negotiated at the bank, what account it had been deposited to, and whether there had been any activity on the account since that deposit. The corporate security officer confirmed the transactions. He testified that the call from the officers investigating Lillico was fairly typical of the types of calls received and answered by bank officers. The practice, testified the corporate security officer, is to "check the records and either confirm or deny the fact of the deposit and whether there has been subsequent activity, but never to provide the police with more specific information without a search warrant." [30] Lillico complained that by obtaining this information from the bank without any judicial pre-authorization the officers had, for the purposes of constitutional analysis, conducted a warrantless search. On this basis, he argued, the information from the bank officer should not have been used in the warrant application.

---

[27] Ibid., at pp. 213–214 [C.C.C.].

[28] See, though, *R. v. Makwaychuk* (1993), 81 C.C.C. (3d) 186, 22 C.R. (4th) 103 (Man. C.A.) where the Manitoba Court of Appeal found that such "hydro searches" amounted to an invasion of a person's reasonable expectation of privacy because provincial legislation limited the circumstances for disclosure.

[29] *R. v. Lillico* (1994), 92 C.C.C. (3d) 90 (Ont. Gen. Div.), affirmed (1999), 1999 CarswellOnt 131, [1999] O.J. No. 95 (Ont. C.A.). Consider also *R. v. Edwards* (Ont. S.C.J.), *supra*, note 16, holding that name and address information for a cell user is not private. In *R. v. Eddy* (1994), 370 A.P.R. 91, 119 Nfld. & P.E.I.R. 91 (Nfld. T.D.), the Court held that there was a "substantially greater expectation of privacy relating to the records of an individual's personal financial position, and the pattern of the individual's operating on his or her bank account." (at p. 126, para. 176) The Court in *Eddy* found that warrantless inquiries by the police at a bank regarding the identity of a bankbook holder and about a major transaction which took place on that account *did* interfere with a reasonable expectation of privacy. In part because of this privacy interest, the relationship between a customer and his or her bank is characterized at common law by a duty of confidentiality and secrecy (see M.H. Ogilvie, "Banker and Customer Revisited" (1986) 65 Can. Bar Rev. 3–36 at p. 6).

[30] *R. v. Lillico* (Ont. Gen. Div.), *supra*, at p. 93.

The Court declined to follow this line of reasoning, though it did properly recognize that *Plant* and the related cases made it clear that such action might be categorized as a search in the right case. In his conclusion, the trial judge held that "a balance must be struck between the customer's right to confidentiality and the public's right to effective law enforcement." The balance would not include confirmation of certain limited information that "does not threaten the 'biographical core of personal information' which is inherent in the meaning of the phrase 'private and confidential'." This conclusion was upheld in the Court of Appeal.[31]

It also appears to be consistent with some cases that had considered other privacy/informational search issues prior to *Plant*.[32] *Lillico* likely represents the "outer limit" for the release of this kind of banking information. It is important to note that on the facts of the case the police were confirming information they already had from another source, and that they only received "general information" about the particular account (as opposed to receiving, for example, a detailed review of all transactions). Indeed, other cases suggest that *Lillico* goes too far in extending the scope of warrantless police power.[33]

In *R. v. Tessling*, the leading case on what constitutes an expectation of privacy, the Supreme Court of Canada looked at a challenge to the use of heat profiling technology that allowed police to detect "hot spots" on houses and thereby confirm (or refute) possible marijuana "grow-ops." The court noted the need to balance privacy and law enforcement in assessing whether police activity invaded a "reasonable expectation of privacy." Justice Binnie, for a unanimous court, repeated the court's many pronouncements about the importance of privacy in a democratic society and the need for the courts to guard against state intrusions, and then said:

> [S]ocial and economic life creates competing demands. The community wants privacy but it also insists on protection. Safety, security and the suppression of crime are legitimate countervailing concerns. Thus s. 8 of the *Charter* accepts the validity of *reasonable* searches and seizures. A balance must be struck . . . .[34]

The limited information obtained from the gross heat profile measurement device did not tip the balance too far and was thus acceptable.

---

[31] Ibid. (Ont. Gen. Div.), at p. 95; (Ont. C.A.), *supra*, note 29, at para. 2.

[32] Consider, for example, *R. v. Dersch* (1993), 85 C.C.C. (3d) 1, 25 C.R. (4th) 88, [1993] 3 S.C.R. 768 (S.C.C.), where the Court, in an obiter comment, suggested that hospitals might provide general information (the fact that a person was/is a patient) to police even though release of medical information would be prohibited.

[33] The courts are not, however, unanimous on this point. In *R. v. Eddy*, *supra*, note 29, the Newfoundland Supreme Court (Trial Division) reached the opposite conclusion on similar facts.

[34] *R. v. Tessling* (2004), 2004 CarswellOnt 4351, 2004 SCC 67 (S.C.C.), reversing (2003), 171 C.C.C. (3d) 361, 9 C.R. (6th) 36 (Ont. C.A.), at para. 17 (emphasis in original).

(c) Examples of When Reasonable Expectation of Privacy Does (and Does Not) Exist

While every case must be analyzed on its own particular facts, it is useful to review some situations in which reasonable expectations of privacy have, and have not, been found:

Cases Finding a Reasonable Expectation of Privacy Does Exist

1. Individual's body and bodily fluids "harvested" from the individual;[35]
2. Home;[36]
3. Hotel rooms – even when there has been an invitation to strangers to enter or permission from the management of the hotel to enter;[37]
4. Passenger in vehicle, interest in personal articles in vehicle (but not in vehicle *per se*);[38]
5. Information held by a doctor or hospital as a result of medical treatment;[39]
6. In an open field where the occupier had put up "no trespassing" signs;[40]
7. The area around a house ("curtilage") and any trespass associated with "peeking" in windows;[41]
8. The general-use area or stalls of a public washroom;[42]
9. Any detailed banking information;[43]

---

[35] *R. v. Dyment* (1988), 45 C.C.C. (3d) 244, 66 C.R. (3d) 348 (S.C.C.); *R. v. Stillman* (1997), 113 C.C.C. (3d) 321, 5 C.R. (5th) 1 (S.C.C.) (seizure of buccal swabs, hair, dental impressions from detainee).

[36] *R. v. Feeney* (1997), 115 C.C.C. (3d) 129, 7 C.R. (5th) 101 (S.C.C.), reconsideration granted [1997] 2 S.C.R. 117 (S.C.C.); *R. v. Sutherland* (2000), 150 C.C.C. (3d) 231, 39 C.R. (5th) 310 (Ont. C.A.) (dwelling house place with "highest degree of privacy expected").

[37] *R. v. Wong* (S.C.C.), *supra*, note 20 (hotel room used as gaming house – private); *R. v. Mercer* (1992), 70 C.C.C. (3d) 180, 11 C.R. (4th) 325 (Ont. C.A.), leave to appeal refused (1992), 74 C.C.C. (3d) vi, 143 N.R. 396 (note) (S.C.C.) (permission from hotel manager to enter hotel room after cleaning staff found drugs).

[38] *R. v. Belnavis* (1997), 118 C.C.C. (3d) 405, 10 C.R. (5th) 65 (S.C.C.) (search of passenger compartment and trunk in car lawfully borrowed).

[39] *R. v. Dersch* (1991), 65 C.C.C. (3d) 252, 35 M.V.R. (2d) 86 (B.C. C.A.), reversed (1993), 85 C.C.C. (3d) 1, 25 C.R. (4th) 88 (S.C.C.) (blood sample taken and results provided to police by doctor).

[40] *R. v. Lauda* (1999), 136 C.C.C. (3d) 358, 25 C.R. (5th) 320 (Ont. C.A.) (police entering onto private but "open" field).

[41] *R. v. Kokesch* (1991), 61 C.C.C. (3d) 207, 1 C.R. (4th) 62 (S.C.C.) (so-called "perimeter searches").

[42] *R. v. LeBeau* (1988), 41 C.C.C. (3d) 163, 62 C.R. (3d) 157 (Ont. C.A.), affirmed (1990), 149 N.R. 236, 60 O.A.C. 320 (S.C.C.) (surveillance of washroom facilities).

[43] *R. v. Eddy* (Nfld. T.D.), *supra*, note 29 (police call to bank to get name and information related to account where they have discovered account book).

10. Articles stolen and reported to the police;[44]
11. Inmates' interest in outgoing telephone calls using prison phones.[45]

Cases Finding an Expectation of Privacy, But a Reduced One[46]

12. Motor vehicle on public roadway;[47]
13. Information obtained using "sniffer-dogs" at a bus station to detect drugs in a locker or luggage;[48]
14. A day locker rented at a bus station;[49]
15. Offices, workplaces;[50]
16. Border crossings;[51]
17. Tracking devices;[52]
18. Prison inmates' cells;[53]
19. The public area outside an apartment window;[54]
20. Courthouses;[55]
21. Suitcases checked on a *domestic* common carrier.[56]

---

[44] *R. v. Law* (2002), 160 C.C.C. (3d) 449, 48 C.R. (5th) 199 (S.C.C.) at pp. 457–458 [C.C.C.] (police breached *Charter* s. 8 when they carefully scrutinized apparently innocent items located in a safe that had been stolen from accused).

[45] *R. v. Hansen*, 2003 CarswellBC 3419, 2003 BCSC 927, [2003] B.C.J. No. 3112 (B.C.S.C.).

[46] Even a reduced expectation of privacy may be sufficient to require a s. 8 analysis: *R. v. Buhay* (2003), 174 C.C.C. (3d) 97, 10 C.R. (6th) 205 (S.C.C.).

[47] *R. v. Wise* (S.C.C.), *supra*, note 18 (use of tracking device in vehicle); *R. v. Caslake* (1998), 121 C.C.C. (3d) 97, 13 C.R. (5th) 1, [1998] 1 S.C.R. 51 (S.C.C.) (search of vehicle incident to arrest). Note that the driver (if driving with permission of the owner) will enjoy a greater expectation of privacy in the various compartments of the vehicle than a passenger, who will normally have no control over such spaces: *R. v. Belnavis* (S.C.C.), *supra*, note 38.

[48] *R. v. Lam* (2003), 178 C.C.C. (3d) 59, 11 C.R. (6th) 58, 2003 CarswellAlta 911, [2003] A.J. No. 811 (C.A.).

[49] *R. v. Buhay*, *supra*, note 46.

[50] *R. v. Rao* (1984), 12 C.C.C. (3d) 97, 40 C.R. (3d) 1 (Ont. C.A.), leave to appeal refused (1984), 40 C.R. (3d) xxvi, 57 N.R. 238n (S.C.C.) (search of office).

[51] *R. v. Simmons* (S.C.C.), *supra*, note 5 (border search under *Customs Act*).

[52] *R. v. Wise* (S.C.C.), *supra*, note 18, at p. 218 [C.C.C.] (planted beeper on vehicle unauthorized search).

[53] *R. v. Rodney* (1991), 65 C.C.C. (3d) 304, 5 C.R. (4th) 393 (B.C. S.C.); *Royer v. Canada (Procureur général)* (2001), 215 F.T.R. 45 (translation), 2001 CarswellNat 2991, [2001] F.C.J. No. 1869 [reversed on other grounds (2003), 172 C.C.C. (3d) 403, 2003 CarswellNat 99 (Fed. C.A.)], where an inmate's expectation of privacy in an institution was described by the trial judge as "basically almost nil" (p. 51 [F.T.R.], para. 24). See also *Weatherall v. Canada (Attorney General)*, [1993] 2 S.C.R. 872, 83 C.C.C. (3d) 1, 23 C.R. (4th) 1 (S.C.C.).

[54] *R. v. Laurin*, *supra*, note 22 (police putting faces up to window to look into ground floor apartment).

[55] *R. v. Lindsay*, 26 C.R. (5th) 62, 1999 CarswellMan 213, [1999] M.J. No. 562 (Man. Q.B.), reversed (1999), 141 C.C.C. (3d) 526, 29 C.R. (5th) 386 (Man. C.A.).

[56] *R v. Matthiessen* (1999), 133 C.C.C. (3d) 93, 1999 CarswellAlta 73 (Alta. C.A.), leave to appeal to S.C.C. refused (1999), 62 C.R.R. (2d) 376 (note), 243 N.R. 195 (note) (S.C.C.).

Cases Finding No Expectation of Privacy[57]

22. Information learned by the use of specialized surveillance equipment (e.g., FLIR);[58]
23. Basic banking information from banker,[59] including the physical location of banking records;[60]
24. Subscriber information related to cell phones;[61]
25. Marijuana being cultivated by accused on farm where he or she was trespasser[62] or in plain sight on Crown land;[63]
26. Some generic information from hospitals (e.g., confirming that patient is in hospital) without any medical information;[64]
27. Things in plain view in place where public ordinarily invited;[65]
28. People being surreptitiously photographed in public places;[66]
29. Use of infrared overhead technology;[67]
30. Stolen vehicles (*vis-à-vis* the thief);[68]
31. Garbage[69]
    (a) left at the roadside for pickup;[70]

---

[57] It is important to note that these cases often turn on a detailed review of the facts and that not every case involving similar situations will result in the same finding.

[58] *R. v. Tessling*, *supra*, note 34. See also *Kyllo v. United States*, 533 U.S. 27, 121 S. Ct. 2038 (U.S.S.C. 2001). But see *R. v. Federink*, 2003 CarswellBC 3296, [2003] B.C.J. No. 3026 (B.C.S.C.).

[59] *R. v. Lillico* (Ont. C.A.), *supra*, note 29 (basic banking information confirming one transaction).

[60] *Re Canada (Department of National Revenue)*, [1998] O.J. No. 3517 (Prov. Div.).

[61] *R. v. Edwards* (Ont. S.C.J.), *supra*, note 16, at para. 33ff. (subscriber information from cell phone used by accused).

[62] *R. v. Lauda* (1998), 129 C.C.C. (3d) 225, 20 C.R. (5th) 316 (S.C.C.), affirming (1998), 122 C.C.C. (3d) 74, 13 C.R. (5th) 20 (Ont. C.A.).

[63] *R. v. Boersma* (1993), [1993] B.C.J. No. 2748, 62 W.A.C. 310 (B.C. C.A.), affirmed 31 C.R. (4th) 386, [1994] 2 S.C.R. 488 (S.C.C.) (marijuana grown on Crown land).

[64] *R. v. Dersch*, *supra*, note 32, at p. 13 [C.C.C.] (comment by Court on possible information doctors could give out).

[65] *R. v. Fitt* (1996), 103 C.C.C. (3d) 224, 46 C.R. (4th) 267 (S.C.C.), affirming (1995), 96 C.C.C. (3d) 341, 38 C.R. (4th) 52 (N.S. C.A.) (gaming devices at taxi stand); and *R. v. Kouyas* (1994), 26 C.R.R. (2d) 354, 136 N.S.R. (2d) 195 (N.S. C.A.) (games room), affirmed (1996), 103 C.C.C. (3d) 224, 46 C.R. (4th) 267 (S.C.C.).

[66] *R. v. Bryntwick* (2002), 2002 CarswellOnt 3106, [2002] O.J. No. 3618 (Ont. S.C.J.) (police photographing accused in public place to compare to surveillance video from bank). See also *R. v. Elzein*, *supra*, note 17.

[67] *R. v. Tessling*, *supra*, note 34. See also *R. v. Evans* (1996), 104 C.C.C. (3d) 23, 45 C.R. (4th) 210 (S.C.C.) at p. 36 [C.C.C.] (alternatives suggested to illegal "knock and sniff").

[68] *R. v. Spinelli* (1995), 101 C.C.C. (3d) 385, 1995 CarswellBC 2523 (B.C. C.A.), leave to appeal refused (1996), 105 C.C.C. (3d) vi (note), 35 C.R.R. (2d) 187 (note) (S.C.C.).

[69] For the American position on garbage see *California v. Greenwood*, 486 U.S. 35, 100 L. Ed 2d 30 (1988).

[70] *R. v. Krist* (1995), 100 C.C.C. (3d) 58, 42 C.R. (4th) 159 (B.C. C.A.); see also *R. v. Tam* (1993), 19 W.C.B. (2d) 357 (B.C. S.C.).

(b) in a common dumpster in an apartment building;[71]
(c) dropped at the roadside;[72]
32. Utility billing records (where no special contractual provisions);[73]
33. Welfare records given to police to investigate fraud on welfare agency;[74]
34. Smells in the common areas (hallway) of an apartment;[75]
35. A trespasser on land;[76]
36. Cigarette butts left behind at police station by *non-detained* interviewee;[77]
37. The outside of articles seized or surrendered when a detainee is booked into a pre-trial detention facility;[78]
38. One does not have standing to challenge a search merely because one is the target of an investigation;[79]
39. Sealing, but not taking custody of, medical blood samples (this may be a "seizure" but not an "unreasonable search or seizure");[80]
40. Bedrooms occupied by children in their parents' homes (where parent or other adult consents);[81]
41. *Non-surreptitious* police attendance at door consistent with implied invitation to attend at door of dwelling to converse with residents;[82]
42. Visitor at a home has no expectation that owner will not invite police to enter and arrest him or her.[83]

---

[71] *R. v. Kennedy* (1996), 3 C.R. (5th) 170, 95 O.A.C. 321 (Ont. C.A.), affirming (1992), 1992 CarswellOnt 1913 (Ont. Gen. Div.).

[72] *R. v. Caslake, supra*, note 47, where the accused tried to abandon a quantity of marijuana at the roadside after being discovered.

[73] *R. v. Plant* (S.C.C.), *supra*, note 15, at p. 214 [C.C.C.]. But note that in some provinces local rules respecting the disclosure of such information might create a reasonable expectation: *R. v. Makwaychuk* (Man. C.A.), *supra*, note 28.

[74] *R. v. D'Amour* (2002), 166 C.C.C. (3d) 477, 4 C.R. (6th) 275, 2002 CarswellOnt 2603, [2002] O.J. No. 3103 (Ont. C.A.) (welfare authorities providing documents to police where welfare is victim of fraud).

[75] *R. v. Laurin, supra*, note 22.

[76] *R. v. Lauda* (S.C.C.), *supra*, note 62.

[77] *R. v. F. (D.M.)* (1999), 139 C.C.C. (3d) 144, 1999 CarswellAlta 872 (Alta. C.A.).

[78] *R. v. Blais* (2004), 182 C.C.C. (3d) 39, 2004 CarswellOnt 37 (Ont. C.A.).

[79] *R. v. Pugliese* (1992), 71 C.C.C (3d) 295, 1992 CarswellOnt 1461 (Ont. C.A.) at pp. 302–303 [C.C.C.].

[80] *R. v. Gettins* (2003), 181 C.C.C. (3d) 304, 2003 CarswellOnt 4872, [2003] O.J. No. 4758 (Ont. C.A.).

[81] This area is very fact-driven. See *R. v. F. (D.M.), supra*, note 77 – no privacy expectation; *R. v. Rai*, 1998 CarswellBC 2147, [1998] B.C.J. No. 2187 (B.C.S.C.) – privacy expectation subject to father's consent to police; *R v. Figueroa* (2002), 2002 CarswellOnt 2564, [2002] O.J. No. 3188 (Ont. S.C.J.).

[82] *R. v. Tricker* (1995), 96 C.C.C. (3d) 198, 21 O.R. (3d) 575 (Ont. C.A.) at p. 579 [O.R.]; but see *R. v. Evans* (S.C.C.), *supra*, note 67, for limits on this rule.

[83] *R. v. Guiboche* (2004), 183 C.C.C. (3d) 361, 2004 CarswellMan 38 (Man. C.A.), leave to appeal refused, 2004 CarswellMan 354 (S.C.C.).

(d) Did the *Police* Activity in Question Interfere with the Expectation of Privacy?

The *Charter* only applies to the conduct of the *police* or other persons acting on behalf of the *state*; it does not apply to the actions of private citizens. Before s. 8 will be engaged, there must be some showing that it is the conduct of the police (or other state actor) that has infringed the citizen's expectation of privacy. If the police conduct does not interfere in any meaningful way with someone's expectation of privacy, there has been no search or seizure (and the warrant presumption is not controlling). For example, if a private citizen were to record a conversation or telephone call with a suspect before coming to the police, no *Charter* issue is engaged: the police, in simply receiving the tape from the citizen, have not done anything to interfere with the privacy of the citizen.[84] It is important to note that private citizens acting on the *direction* or *suggestion* of the police will often be found to be "agents of the state" and their activity will be tested as though it were done by police directly.[85]

In *Buhay*,[86] the Supreme Court held that in general private security guards are not agents of the state, but that they might become agents if asked by police to assist in a specific case:

> [30] Volunteer participation in the detection of crime by private actors, or general encouragements by the police authorities to citizens to participate in the detection of crime, will not usually be sufficient direction by the police to trigger the application of the *Charter*. Rather, the intervention of the police must be specific to the case being investigated . . . .[87]

---

[84] *R. v. Fegan* (1993), 80 C.C.C. (3d) 356, 21 C.R. (4th) 65 (Ont. C.A.).

[85] The issue of when a person becomes a "state agent" and thus restrained by the *Charter* is not always obvious. Where someone has his or her own motive and authority to act independently of police involvement, the court will be less likely to find an agency relationship. See *R. v. M. (M.R.)* (S.C.C.), *supra*, note 21, where the actions of a school vice-principal who searched a student for drugs and handed them over to a police officer who was present at his request were held not to make the vice-principal an agent of the police. See also *R. v. Shafie* (1989), 47 C.C.C. (3d) 27, 68 C.R. (3d) 259 (Ont. C.A.). On a similar note, where a citizen is given specific search powers by statute, the statute must be reasonable: *R. v. Lerke* (1986), 24 C.C.C. (3d) 129, 49 C.R. (3d) 324 (Alta. C.A.).

[86] *R. v. Buhay, supra,* note 46. See also *R. v. Chang* (2003), 180 C.C.C. (3d) 330, 2003 CarswellAlta 1473, [2003] A.J. No. 1281 (C.A.), leave to appeal refused (2004), 114 C.R.R. (2d) 188 (note) (S.C.C.).

[87] *R. v. Buhay, supra,* note 46, at p. 111 [C.C.C.], citing *R. v. Fitch* (1994), 93 C.C.C. (3d) 185, 1994 CarswellBC 1003 (B.C.C.A.); and *R. v. Caucci* (1995), 43 C.R. (4th) 403, 1995 CarswellQue 146 (Que. C.A.).

3. "Reasonableness" of a Search

The test from *Collins*[88] requires the court to assess the validity of a search from three different perspectives:

> A search will be reasonable if it is authorized by law, if the law itself is reasonable and if the manner in which the search was carried out is reasonable.

Each of these three tests involves a separate inquiry. The first measures the search against the statutory or common law authority claimed by the police. The second tests that law against the constitutional standard articulated in s. 8 of the *Charter*. The third evaluates the execution of the search power against both constitutional and common law standards.

This analysis is not, of course, normally part of the warrant-granting process. Rather, it is engaged when someone challenges a particular search, asserting that the conduct of the state does not conform to the *Charter*.

(a) Was the Search Authorized by Law?

A search or seizure must be authorized by law. The police are subject to the normal rules related to trespass and theft.[89] In the absence of some identifiable legal authority, police entry onto, or seizure of, property will be characterized as a trespass or possibly even theft. In *Caslake*, the Supreme Court of Canada identified three ways in which a search or seizure might fail to meet this requirement:

> [12] . . . There are three ways in which a search can fail to meet this requirement. *First, the state authority conducting the search must be able to point to a specific statute or common law rule* that authorizes the search. If they cannot do so, the search cannot be said to be authorized by law. *Second, the search must be carried out in accordance with the procedural and substantive requirements the law provides.* For example, s. 487 of the *Criminal Code*, R.S.C., 1985, c. C-46, authorizes searches, but only with a warrant issued by a justice on the basis of a sworn information setting out reasonable and probable grounds. A failure to meet one of these requirements will result in a search which has not been authorized by law. *Third, and in the same vein, the scope of the search is limited to the area and to those items for which the law has granted the authority to search.* To the extent that a search exceeds these limits, it is not authorized by law.[90]

In other words:

---

[88] *R. v. Collins* (1987), 33 C.C.C. (3d) 1, 56 C.R. (3d) 193 (S.C.C.) at p. 14 [C.C.C.].
[89] *R. v. Campbell* (1999), 133 C.C.C. (3d) 257, 24 C.R. (5th) 365 (S.C.C.).
[90] *R. v. Caslake, supra*, note 47, at pp. 105–106 [C.C.C.].

1. What was the legal power the police relied upon?
2. Was that legal power available in the circumstances of the case (i.e., were the preconditions for its use present)?
3. Was the scope of the search within that authorized by the power? Did the police do more than they were allowed to do?

(b) Is the Law Reasonable?

Section 8 of the *Charter* limits the powers that Parliament (or the provincial legislatures) can give to those responsible for law enforcement. Warrant-granting provisions must meet the *Hunter* standards: they must ensure that the warrant issues only following a showing that the state's interest in gathering evidence has become superior to the individual's interest in privacy. This is normally achieved when reasonable grounds exist to believe that the investigative step in question will provide evidence or information relevant to the offence (though in some exceptional cases a lower threshold may suffice[91]). If a statute authorizes the issuance of a warrant on some relaxed basis (for example, by allowing a non-neutral party to issue the warrant,[92] by removing any discretion to issue the warrant,[93] or by failing to require reasonable grounds related to an important precondition[94]), then the law itself is unreasonable. Even if the police have followed the law, the state has nonetheless breached the Constitution.

Statutory and common law warrantless search powers are similarly subject to interrogation against the *Hunter* standards. If a statute or long recognized common law power would permit the police to search without warrant in the absence of a compelling reason, then the rule authorizing the search runs contrary to s. 8 and should be struck down (or if a common law rule, modified).[95]

(c) Was the Search Executed in a Reasonable Manner?

A search that has been lawfully justified may become unconstitutional if the police act unreasonably in carrying out the search so authorized. For example,

---

[91] For example, in *R. v. Wise*, *supra*, note 18 (per Cory J. for the majority) the Supreme Court of Canada held that a simple "beeper" device used to track a car on public highways might be authorized on the basis of a lower standard such as "a 'solid ground' for suspicion." This in turn has found statutory expression as s. 492.1 of the *Criminal Code* authorizing a tracking device warrant on the basis of "reasonable grounds to suspect" that information relevant to the offence will be obtained by using such a device.

[92] Which was the case in *Hunter v. Southam Inc.* (S.C.C.), *supra*, note 4.

[93] *R. v. Baron* (1993), 78 C.C.C. (3d) 510, 18 C.R. (4th) 374 (S.C.C.).

[94] *R. v. Hurrell* (2002), 166 C.C.C. (3d) 343, 4 C.R. (6th) 169 (Ont. C.A.), leave to appeal abandoned (April 26, 2004), Doc. 29376 (S.C.C.).

[95] For example, the common law power to enter a dwelling house to give effect to a power of arrest (*R. v. Landry* (1986), 25 C.C.C. (3d) 1, 50 C.R. (3d) 55 (S.C.C.)) was struck down as contrary to s. 8 in *R. v. Feeney* (S.C.C.), *supra*, note 36.

an officer is obliged to have a search warrant with him or her if feasible and to produce it upon reasonable request. A failure to do so does not invalidate the warrant, but does render the search unreasonable and may lead to the exclusion of evidence.[96] The use of force beyond that necessary to give effect to the terms of the warrant would be considered under this heading.[97] Notifying the media in advance with a view to "currying favour" with particular journalists is improper,[98] as is inviting media representatives to join a "ride-along" to execute a warrant.[99] Similarly, executing a properly issued warrant at nighttime might be unreasonable.[100]

4. Regulatory Searches

The conduct of regulatory inspectors and investigators is subject to a modified version of the analysis set down in *Hunter*.[101] For the purposes of ensuring compliance (that is, inquiries directed at civil or administrative remedies) regulators are given a number of "super powers" to engage in search and seizure activities. Where their conduct is instead directed at quasi-criminal sanctions intended to result in charges under a regulatory statute, however, even regulators are expected to conform as closely as possible to the *Hunter* standard of judicial pre-authorization.[102]

5. Meaningful Judicial Pre-Authorization

Meaningful judicial pre-authorization requires that the police investigation be assessed by a neutral third party capable of acting judicially. The purpose of this examination is to determine if the state of the investigation to date justifies the intrusion the police propose. This requires an assessment of both the quantity and quality of the evidence that causes the police to think that the investigative step in issue will yield the additional information or evidence they are seeking.

---

[96] *R. v. Bohn* (2000), 145 C.C.C. (3d) 320, 33 C.R. (5th) 265 (B.C. C.A.). But see *R. v. B. (J.E.)* (1989), 52 C.C.C. (3d) 224, 247 A.P.R. 312 (N.S. C.A.); and *R. v. Pettit* (2003), 179 C.C.C. (3d) 295, 307 W.A.C. 246 (B.C.C.A.).

[97] *R. v. Wong,* [1997] O.J. No. 1379, 35 O.T.C. 321 (Ont. Gen. Div.).

[98] *Uni-Jet Industrial Pipe Ltd. v. Canada (Attorney General)* (2001), [2002] 1 W.W.R. 287, 198 D.L.R. (4th) 577 (Man. C.A.) (where subject of search successfully sued police for damages).

[99] *R. v. West* (1997), 122 C.C.C. (3d) 218, 12 C.R. (5th) 106 (B.C.C.A.). The same view was taken in the United States: *Wilson v. Layne*, 526 U.S. 603 (1999).

[100] *R. v. Sutherland, supra*, note 36.

[101] *Hunter v. Southam Inc.* (S.C.C.), *supra*, note 4.

[102] *R. v. Inco Ltd.* (2001), 155 C.C.C. (3d) 383, 83 C.R.R. (2d) 189 (Ont. C.A.), leave to appeal refused (2002), 45 C.E.L.R. (N.S.) 5, 90 C.R.R. (2d) 376 (note) (S.C.C.).

This requirement drives most of the important drafting rules. As we will see later, the neutrality of judicial pre-authorization defines the role of the issuing judicial officer.

6. Remedies for Constitutional Breaches – *Charter* Section 24(2)

While every unreasonable search will be a breach of s. 8 of the *Charter*, not every unreasonable search will lead to the exclusion of evidence. Section 24 of the *Charter* provides for an inquiry into whether the exclusion or admission of the evidence seized in any given case will tend to bring the administration of justice into disrepute. The test under this section is remarkably subtle and involved, turning largely (but by no means exclusively) on the nature of the evidence seized and the seriousness of the breach.[103]

The fact that evidence may be admitted notwithstanding a breach of s. 8 is not, however, relevant to an assessment of whether a warrant is required or whether reasonable grounds exist. The police – as much if not more than other citizens – are obliged to obey the law. The Constitution is nothing less than the first and most fundamental law of the land. A belief that constitutional "short cuts" might be acceptable because no s. 24 remedy is likely to be available is as unacceptable as any other illegal activity by the police. A conscious decision not to obey the *Charter* casts a long and dark shadow over a police investigation and jeopardizes all of the evidence gathered in that matter.

---

[103] *R. v. Stillman* (S.C.C.), *supra*, note 35.

2

The Roles and Responsibilities of Participants in the Warrant Process: Understanding the Nature of Judicial Pre-Authorization

1. The Constitutional Standards – *Hunter v. Southam Inc.*

As already noted, *Hunter v. Southam Inc.*[1] set down the "bedrock" principles related to search and seizure. At the core of those principles is the concept of judicial pre-authorization as the key protection against unjustified state intrusions *before* they happen. Meaningful judicial pre-authorization requires a neutral third party capable of acting as a true intermediary between the interests of the state and the individual.

The Australian High Court has captured this important role in its judgment in *Parker v. Churchill*.[2] The process is "not some quaint ritual of the law, requiring a perfunctory scanning of the right formal phrases, perceived but not considered, and followed by an inevitable signature." The judicial officer must "stand between the police and the citizen to give real attention to the question whether the information proffered by the police does justify the intrusion they desire to make into the privacy of the citizen and the inviolate security of his personal and business affairs."

Most of the substantive and constitutional rules related to Informations to Obtain and warrant drafting arise from the function of the independent judicial officer. At the core of these requirements is the insistence that the justice be placed in a position to *independently* determine how persuasive the evidence already gathered is. This requires the search warrant applicant to set out his or her sources of information and evidence. In those cases where the source cannot

---

[1] *Hunter v. Southam Inc.* (1984), 14 C.C.C. (3d) 97, 41 C.R. (3d) 97 (S.C.C.).
[2] *Parker v. Churchill* (1985), 9 F.C.R. 316 (Aust. H.C.).

be named (tipsters and confidential informers), the Information to Obtain must put the judicial officer in a position to make an assessment of the source before any weight can be attached to that evidence.

2. The Nature of Judicial Review of Warrant Applications

Dealing with the review of search warrant application after issuance, Mr. Justice Hill of the Superior Court of Ontario has identified the following guidelines for judicial officers:

> In addition, in considering the facial validity of search warrants and search warrant informations, there exists a judicially created subset of review guidelines, including the following:
>
> 1. *Quality of drafting*
> Search warrants are statutorily authorized investigative aids issued most frequently before criminal proceedings have been instituted. Almost invariably a peace officer prepares the search warrant and information without the benefit of legal advice. *The specificity and legal precision of drafting expected of pleadings at the trial stage is not the measure of quality required in a search warrant information . . . .*
>
> 2. *Review of the whole document*
> The appropriate approach for judicial review of a search warrant information is *scrutiny of the whole of the document, not a limited focus upon an isolated passage or paragraph.* Reference to all data within the four corners of the information provides the fair and reasonable context for the assertions in question . . . .
>
> 3. *Drawing reasonable inferences*
> A search warrant information draftsperson or affiant is obliged to state investigative facts sufficient to establish reasonable grounds for believing that an offence has been committed, that the things to be searched for will afford evidence, and, that the things in question will be discovered at a specified place. *An issuing justice is entitled to draw reasonable inferences from stated facts and an informant is not obliged to underline the obvious . . . . In this regard, some deference should be paid to the ability of a trained peace officer to draw inferences and make deductions which might well elude an untrained person . . . .* Probable cause does not arise, however, from purely conclusory narrative. A search warrant information is not a Crown brief and the affiant is not obliged to record every minute step taken in the course of the investigation . . . .[3] [emphasis added]

---

[3] *R. v. Sanchez* (1994), 93 C.C.C. (3d) 357, 32 C.R. (4th) 269 (Ont. Gen. Div.) at pp. 364–365 [C.C.C.].

Reading warrant applications is an exercise that requires both scrutiny and understanding. It must hold the applicant to the constitutional standard in each case if the promise of a secure society made in s. 8 of the *Charter* is to be honoured. However, it must equally do so recognizing the realities of policing and the various duties police have.

The review of a search warrant should not be a microscopic analysis of the affidavit:

> [15] . . . It would be impractical to expect of an officer swearing an information in these circumstances the precise prose of an Oxford grammarian, the detailed disclosures of a confessional and the legal knowledge of a Rhodes scholar.[4]

It should be a good faith reading which is based on a genuine effort to discover what the writer intended to convey (and not a quest to tease out every conceivable ambiguity):

> [21] It is not appropriate, when testing the validity of a warrant, to parse and microscopically examine words, phrases or paragraphs in isolation, as the appellants urge us to do. The warrant must be read in its entirety in order to arrive at the meaning that the person exercising it would attribute to it.[5]

3. The Role of the Justice of the Peace

(a) The Constitutional Standard

Hunter did not require that a *judicial* officer be responsible for all preauthorization, but did dictate that the authorizing person be capable of acting *judicially* and therefore must be neutral and impartial as between the competing interests to be weighed before the granting or withholding of an authorization:

> The purpose of a requirement of prior authorization is to provide an opportunity, before the event, for the conflicting interests of the State and the individual to be assessed, so that the individual's right to privacy will be breached only where the appropriate standard has been met, and the interests of the State are thus demonstrably superior. For such an authorization procedure to be meaningful it is necessary for the person authorizing the search to be able to assess the evidence as to whether that standard has been met, in an entirely neutral and impartial manner.[6]

---

[4] *R. v. Melenchuk* (1993), 24 B.C.A.C. 97, 40 W.A.C. 97 (B.C. C.A.) at p. 101 [B.C.A.C.] per Gibbs J.A.

[5] *Simonyi-Gindele v. Sliter* (1991), 2 B.C.A.C. 73, 5 W.A.C. 73 (B.C. C.A.) at p. 79 [B.C.A.C.] per Gibbs J.A.

[6] *Hunter v. Southam Inc., supra,* note 1, at p. 110 [C.C.C.].

Included in this requirement is the ability to exercise discretion with respect to whether to authorize the search activity sought by investigators. Warrant-granting provisions which *mandate* the issuance of a warrant, rather than *permitting* the issuance, improperly constrain the judicial discretion of the issuing justice and therefore fall short of the *Hunter* standards for pre-authorization.[7]

The important role of the issuing judicial officer, and the need for impartiality in the warrant-granting process, was not only a function of the constitutionalization of the rights in s. 8. Earlier common law and statutory provisions had stressed the need for the issuing justice to act judicially with a recognition of the importance of that role:

> [The *Criminal Code*] confers upon a Justice of the Peace a grave and extraordinary power which can and should be exercised only if and when the requirements for its exercise as set out in that section are clearly fulfilled. The reason, of course, is that this statutory right to search is a derogation from common law rights which protect the subject's home and property from intrusion by any one.[8]

As a practical matter, almost all modern pre-authorization regimes look to members of the judiciary (justices of the peace and judges) to provide this function.[9]

(b) Practical Implications of the "Neutrality" Requirement

It is important that the authorizing officer *in fact* be independent of the executive arm of government. In several cases the courts have been invited to look behind the superficial independence of the issuing justice of the peace to determine whether the justice was, in fact, sufficiently impartial (either in the particular case or by virtue of his or her institutional position) to satisfy the constitutional requirement of an independent decision-maker acting impar-

---

[7] *R. v. Baron* (1993), 78 C.C.C. (3d) 510, 18 C.R. (4th) 374 (S.C.C.) holding unconstitutional certain *Income Tax Act* warrant sections because they removed judicial discretion by providing that a warrant "shall" issue upon the demonstration of certain preconditions, thereby removing any judicial discretion. See as well *R. v. Langer* (1995), 97 C.C.C. (3d) 290, 40 C.R. (4th) 204 (Ont. Gen. Div.), leave to appeal refused (1995), 100 C.C.C. (3d) vi, 42 C.R. (4th) 410n (S.C.C.).

[8] *Re Worrall* (1964), [1965] 2 C.C.C. 1, 44 C.R. 151 (Ont. C.A.) at p. 9 [C.C.C.] per Roach J.A., dissenting on other grounds, leave to appeal refused [1965] S.C.R. ix (S.C.C.).

[9] Indeed, if anything, there is a tendency in more recent legislation to err in favour of more senior members of the judicial branch, looking more and more to provincially and federally appointed judges (as opposed to justices of the peace) as authorizing officers (*An Act to Amend the Criminal Code, the Crown Liability and Proceedings Act and the Radiocommunications Act*, S.C. 1993, c. 40 and *An Act to Amend the Criminal Code and the Young Offenders Act (Forensic DNA Analysis)*, S.C. 1995, c. 27 (though this phenomenon may be a function of the more serious forms of intrusion generally mandated by newer provisions).

tially.[10] This involves the reviewing court following the calling of evidence in an assessment of the practices and procedures actually followed by the issuing authority.

In 1993, in the case of *R. v. Gray*,[11] the Manitoba Court of Appeal condemned the practices of the justices of the peace in that province as they existed at that time. The Winnipeg police force and the local judiciary had developed a procedure whereby they submitted a "draft" Information to Obtain to the justice to determine if the grounds set out in the document were sufficient to persuade the justice to issue the warrant. If the justice considered the Information to be wanting he or she would assist the officer in re-drafting an Information more to the justice's liking, sometimes going so far as to dictate appropriate language to the officer, or even typing the Information out for the officer. The Information was only sworn after the suggestions of the justice had been incorporated into the document.

This process of judicial "assistance" in the drafting of the Information was condemned by the Court as a "serious violation of section 8 of the Charter,"[12] which left the warrant fundamentally flawed:

> [T]he impugned practice disclosed by the evidence resulted in the failure of the judicial officer to properly exercise her detached independent function. Where direction is given by a judicial officer respecting the contents of the information to obtain on a material point going to the merits of the application, he/she simply becomes an agent or arm of the police. It is not proper for the police to present a judicial officer with an unsigned or incomplete information to obtain and, after receiving inappropriate direction with respect not only to the technical language but also the substance of the document, to then swear it in its altered form before the same judicial officer.
>
> It is of course open to a magistrate hearing an application for a warrant and considering the evidence presented to identify deficiencies and to reconsider the application when these deficiencies have been remedied by the police. But that was not what took place in this case.[13]

The justice presented with an Information to Obtain must, like any judicial officer, scrutinize the document and determine if it satisfies him or her of the existence of the necessary preconditions for the issuance of the warrant or authorization sought. If the document is wanting there is certainly nothing to prevent the justice from declining to issue the warrant and giving reasons for

---

[10] *R. v. Baylis* (1988), 43 C.C.C. (3d) 514, 65 C.R. (3d) 62 (Sask. C.A.); *R. v. Gray* (1993), 81 C.C.C. (3d) 174, 22 C.R. (4th) 114 (Man. C.A.); *Campbell v. Clough* (1979), 23 Nfld. & P.E.I.R. 249, 61 A.P.R. 249 (P.E.I. S.C.).

[11] *R. v. Gray, supra*, note 10; see also *R. v. Magee*, [1988] 3 W.W.R. 169, 57 Alta. L.R. (2d) 247 (Alta. Q.B.).

[12] *R. v. Gray, supra*, note 10, at p. 181 [C.C.C.].

[13] Ibid., at p. 182 [C.C.C.].

that decision, even if only informally indicating the nature of the deficiencies to the search warrant applicant, either orally, or by way of a short note written directly on the returned material. Indeed, it is a fundamental part of adjudication to provide reasons for decision.[14] The officer can then make a subsequent application to that justice (or another) with whatever improvements are available in answer to the deficiencies identified. Such a second application (disclosing, of course, the first application[15]) should be considered as a fresh application.[16]

The process cannot, however, be allowed to become anything more than a judicial officer indicating reasons for refusing an application for a particular court order. If the exchange turns into something beyond this, then the issuing justice runs the risk of becoming, or of being seen as, a *collaborator* in the Information. Such a role is inconsistent with the justice's responsibilities as a neutral judicial officer and cannot be maintained.[17]

Prior to making a determination with respect to the issuance (or denial) of the warrant, the best practice has, for some time, been for the applicant and the judicial officer to engage in *no additional communication* beyond swearing the Information to Obtain and conversation necessary to deal with any purely administrative issues related to the warrant application.

This relative formality is in the officer's interest as well: any additional discussion raises the possibility of material from outside the four corners of the warrant being placed before the justice, and invites speculation about

---

[14] *Re Criminal Code* (1997), [1997] O.J. No. 4393, 44 O.T.C. 350 (Ont. Gen. Div.) (sometimes cited as *Re A.G.O. 55/97*).

[15] *R. v. Colbourne* (2001), 157 C.C.C. (3d) 273, [2001] O.J. No. 3620 (Ont. C.A.).

[16] *R. v. Eng*, 56 B.C.A.C. 18, 1995 CarswellBC 1702, [1995] B.C.J. No. 329 (B.C. C.A.); see also the related case, *R. v. Eng*, 1995 CarswellBC 1193, [1995] B.C.J. No. 2959 (B.C. S.C.). See also *R. v. Chan*, [2003] O.J. No. 188 (S.C.J.).

[17] More often than not the courts have found particular examples of impugned interaction between officer and justice to be acceptable: *R. v. Haley* (1995), 407 A.P.R. 107, 142 N.S.R. (2d) 107 (N.S. C.A.) and the review of the authorities therein. See also *R. v. Pedersen*, 2 M.V.R. (5th) 1, 2004 CarswellBC 232, [2004] B.C.J. No. 229 (B.C.C.A.); *R. v. Kelly* (1995), 105 W.A.C. 144, 64 B.C.A.C. 144 (B.C. C.A.). The proper role of a judicial officer considering an application for a search warrant – or other judicial pre-authorization – was considered by Mr. Justice Hill in *Re Criminal Code*, supra, note 14, where His Honour wrote:

> [13] I think it important to state that the role of the court, in those cases where an application is dismissed, is to provide those reasons which animated the court's decision. Such reasons or observations may have the incidental effect of the authorities retooling a failed application in order to make a successive application to the court upon appropriate material. Although this may be an incidental effect of the delivery of reasons for judgment by the court, it is important to understand that the court is not to be co-opted into partnership with the government in the drafting of further and better materials. That approach oversteps the confines of judicial neutrality: *R. v. Gray* (1993), 81 C.C.C. (3d) 174 (Man. C.A.) at pp. 179–184 per Scott C.J.M.; *R. v. Howe* (1994), 52 B.C.A.C. 271 (C.A.) at paras. 8, 12–13, 17, 20–25 per Cumming J.A. and at paras. 37–39 per Prowse J.A.

whether the applicant improperly influenced the justice. In *Gordon*,[18] the Manitoba Court of Appeal cautioned against any communication outside the four corners of the Information to Obtain between a warrant applicant and the issuing justice. The accused challenged a warrant on a variety of fronts, including the fact that there had been certain unrecorded oral communications between the warrant applicant and the issuing judge. While not quashing the particular warrant on this basis, the Court recommended a "paper only" process:

> [49] However, the process the police followed in obtaining the warrant in this case can and should be improved so as to eliminate any opportunity to challenge the function of an authorizing justice as an independent, impartial quasi-judicial officer.
>
> [50] When making an application for a search warrant, police officers should present to the authorizing justice a completed package, with the affidavit executed. The package should be left with the justice to review and to render a decision. The contents of the package should not be discussed, no further information should be given to the justice, and there should be no interaction between the affiant and the authorizing justice. If the affidavit is properly drawn and all the information is placed before the authorizing justice, there is no need for any conversation or discussion between the police and the judicial officer.[19]

Since *Gordon*, other cases have indicated that communication between the affiant and judicial officer, while perhaps not recommended, is not fatal to a warrant. Indeed, in *Araujo*,[20] the Supreme Court of Canada indicated that it would be appropriate for a judge considering another form of judicial pre-authorization (a wiretap authorization) to discuss the application with the officer. The Court suggested that the judge "should not be reluctant to ask questions from the applicant, to discuss or to require more information or to narrow down"[21] the authorization sought. Similarly, there is authority to support the suggestion that it is legitimate for a justice to refuse a warrant and then recommend to police an application under a different statutory provision[22] or

---

[18] *R. v. Gordon* (1997), 139 C.C.C. (3d) 239, 28 C.R. (5th) 168 (Man. C.A.).

[19] Ibid., at p. 252 [C.C.C.].

[20] *R. v. Araujo* (2000), 149 C.C.C. (3d) 449, 38 C.R. (5th) 307 (S.C.C.).

[21] Ibid., at p. 464 [C.C.C.], para. 29. Other cases have suggested that oral communications might "top up" the Information to Obtain (for example, *R. v. Coull* (1986), 33 C.C.C. (3d) 186, 1986 CarswellBC 681 (B.C. C.A.) at pp. 189–190 [C.C.C.]) but the better view, even after *Araujo*, is that the best approach is to have a single affiant who presents all evidence through a written Information to Obtain prepared in accordance with the form in the *Criminal Code*.

[22] *R. v. Krist* (1998), 130 C.C.C. (3d) 347, 113 B.C.A.C. 176 (B.C. C.A.), leave to appeal refused (1999), 243 N.R. 194 (note), 132 B.C.A.C. 170 (note) (S.C.C.), where a justice of the peace refused a warrant under s. 487, but suggested (at p. 351 [C.C.C.]) that an application under the

to seek clarification and possible minor amendment to an Information to Obtain.[23]

The substantive question that the courts will ask in these situations is whether the interaction between the officer and the justice raised a concern that the justice's impartiality has been compromised.

Thus, where officers met with a justice of the peace to seek his advice on whether grounds existed for a search *before* preparing their Information to Obtain, the Court held the justice was tainted by an appearance of partiality.[24]

(c) Dealing with Possible Constitutional Violations Apparent in the Warrant Application

How should a judicial officer deal with a warrant application that appears to rely upon evidence obtained as a result of some earlier constitutional violation?[25]

---

firearms provisions might be appropriate:

> [8] . . . I am not able to accede to that submission. In my view, the justice of the peace was entitled, having an application before him, to indicate to the police that he thought that the process was wrong and should be brought under the other section; nor do I think there was anything wrong with the justice of the peace advising the officers what further information, if any, he needed in order to issue a warrant; so I would not give effect to that submission.

[23] *R. v. Howe*, [1994] B.C.J. No. 2731, 52 B.C.A.C. 271 (B.C. C.A.). See also *R. v. Araujo, supra*, note 20, at p. 464 [C.C.C.], where, without further discussion, LeBel J. suggested (albeit in the context of a wiretap authorization):

> [29] . . . The judge should not view himself or herself as a mere rubber stamp, but should take a close look at the material submitted by the applicant. He or she *should not be reluctant to ask questions from the applicant, to discuss or to require more information or to narrow down the authorization requested if it seems too wide or too vague*. The authorizing judge should grant the authorization only as far as need is demonstrated by the material submitted by the applicant. [emphasis added]

Perhaps the point is that if conversation happens and anything of substance comes of it, this must be made part of the formal Form 1 record. See *R. v. Rowbotham* (1988), 41 C.C.C. (3d) 1, 63 C.R. (3d) 113 (Ont. C.A.) at p. 46 [C.C.C.] where the Court says:

> It was first said that, since the cross-examination of the applicant revealed that questions had been put to the officer by the authorizing judge, the authorization was no longer valid as it was not based exclusively upon the affidavit. That contention cannot be sustained. It is quite reasonable and proper, for example, for a justice of the peace to question a police officer on his or her affidavit submitted in support of an application to obtain a search warrant. It must be assumed that if the answers to the questions had any significant bearing upon the application that a record of them would have been made and a reference to them given by the judge granting the authorization.

[24] *R. v. Malik* (2002), 2002 CarswellBC 3634, 2002 BCSC 1731 (B.C.S.C.).

[25] The problem of unconstitutionally obtained evidence is dealt with from the perspective of a warrant applicant in Chapter 9, "Specific Drafting Challenges," under heading 4, "Dealing with Earlier Constitutional Errors." In general, if, after consultation with Crown counsel, a warrant applicant is concerned that there has been some constitutional misstep in the investi-

There is no clear authority guiding a judicial officer who is at first instance confronting a warrant application where, on the basis of the Information to Obtain, the judicial officer is concerned that the applicant may be *relying* upon evidence obtained as a result of some earlier constitutional breach.[26]

In this situation three options appear to be available to the judicial officer considering the warrant, depending on the role the questioned material plays in the application:

1. *The Warrant Application Is Sufficient Without the Questioned Evidence*
   The justice should identify the evidence in the Information to Obtain that may be constitutionally tainted and consider whether the warrant could issue on the basis of the remainder of the evidence. If there is sufficient remaining evidence to justify the issuance of the warrant, and it is otherwise appropriate, the justice should issue the warrant. The issuing justice may wish to give short reasons indicating briefly which paragraphs have been disregarded and why.

2. *The Warrant Application Is Insufficient Even if the Questioned Evidence Is Included*
   The justice should identify the evidence in the Information to Obtain that may be constitutionally tainted and consider whether the warrant could issue even if the suspect evidence is included. If the warrant would not issue even with the questioned portions of the Information to Obtain, then the warrant application should, of course, be refused in the normal course. The refusing judicial officer may or may not advert to the possible constitutional problem in his or her reasons for refusal.

3. *The Warrant Application Is Sufficient Only if the Questioned Evidence Is Included*
   Where the questioned evidence is essential to establish reasonable grounds (in the sense that it is the questioned evidence that "tips the balance" in favour of issuance), the judicial officer has two options.
   The first option is for the judicial officer to refuse the warrant and give reasons indicating what material was thought to be constitutionally tainted, noting that the refusal is without prejudice to the applicant to re-apply.

---

gation, the applicant should disclose the circumstances which gave rise to the possible violation, and indicate clearly that he or she does not rely upon such information in support of the application. See the model language for a warrant applicant to deal with this issue in Chapter 14, "Possible Language for Specific Situations," under heading 4, "Language to Deal with Unconstitutionally Obtained Evidence."

[26] This is different from the situation where a warrant applicant explicitly disclaims any reliance on possibly constitutionally tainted evidence. (See the discussion in Chapter 9 under heading 4, "Dealing with Earlier Constitutional Errors.") Where the applicant does not rely on doubted material, the judicial officer need not resolve possible breach at the reasonable grounds stage: they will or will not exist without reference to the doubted material. The facts related to the possible breach will, however, be relevant to the judicial officer's exercise of discretion.

This permits the justice to dispose of the particular application while allowing the warrant applicant to address the problem in a subsequent application if appropriate.

Alternatively, the justice may reserve decision on the warrant application and invite the warrant applicant to attend with counsel (who may be the Crown or other counsel) and make any relevant and appropriate submissions on the legal issues associated with the possible breach or evidence flowing from it.[27] Such an invitation should be made in a formal way, normally in writing, and should identify for the applicant the specific issue that is of concern for the judicial officer considering the application. Care should be taken to ensure that any subsequent hearing is limited to submission on legal issues and does not become a forum to improperly supplement the factual record. The object of the hearing is not to "improve" the existing application, but to provide legal submissions that will assist the judicial officer in considering the original materials.

It is well established that a reviewing court considering a subsequent *inter partes* challenge (either at trial or in an application for prerogative relief) should edit out those portions of an Information to Obtain that can be shown to be based on evidence that was obtained through some constitutional breach. For example, if a warrant to search a house is based on an informer's report, some proper surveillance, and an illegal perimeter search, the court will edit out or "redact" the evidence acquired from the illegal perimeter search and consider whether the warrant could have issued on the remaining information.[28] The decision to remove such material from consideration is made after a full hearing where the parties' minds are directed to the issue of whether a violation has taken place or not. The party challenging the warrant specifies the nature of the breach alleged. The Crown can call additional evidence to ensure that the record speaks to whether or not a violation has taken place and the party challenging the warrant has an opportunity to respond.

Clearly, a judicial officer considering a warrant application cannot simply ignore an obvious and well established breach, such as a warrantless perimeter search. It should be emphasized, however, that the justice's role is *not* to tease out every possible constitutional breach that may or may not be sustainable: the constitutional law governing police conduct is subtle and complex, often turning on delicate questions of reasonableness and context.[29] It might be that the warrantless perimeter search was somehow authorized by law (plain view, exigent circumstances, third-party consent) and that the applicant has not included that in the Information to Obtain believing it not to be material. It is

---

[27] See *Re Criminal Code (Warrant)*, [2002] O.J. No. 3804 (Ont. C.J.).

[28] *R. v. Plant* (1993), 84 C.C.C. (3d) 203, 24 C.R. (4th) 47 (S.C.C.).

[29] As to the duty of trial judges to deal with constitutional problems not raised by the parties, see *R. v. Tran* (2001), 156 C.C.C. (3d) 1, 44 C.R. (5th) 12 (Ont. C.A.); and *R. v. Arbour* (1990), 4 C.R.R. (2d) 369, 1990 CarswellOnt 892 (Ont. C.A.).

important to always have in mind that the warrant application process is *not* the place where constitutional complaints are litigated in any normal sense. It is only where the possible breach "leaps out" from the face of the Information to Obtain that the issuing judicial officer should consider raising these issues.

(d) Systemic or Institutional Independence

Justices of the peace must, as judicial officers, be independent of government. This includes a degree of administrative and organizational independence.[30] A "court services justice of the peace" (who is paid and supervised essentially like clerical staff, and who enjoys no security of tenure) lacks such independence and cannot be said to be an independent judicial officer.[31]

4. The Roles of the Police Investigator and Crown Counsel

(a) Introduction

Police officers are expected to master a wide range of skills in order to function as effective investigators. They must understand everything from forensic sciences to how to physically subdue an arrestee, to the law governing statements (s. 10(b) of the *Charter*, as well as voluntariness) and search and seizure. On the topic of search and seizure they are expected to understand relatively subtle notions ranging from when a "reasonable expectation of privacy" exists to whether "exigent circumstances" arise on a given set of facts. Beyond this we expect every officer to be able to draft a search warrant and supporting Information to Obtain. The increasing complexity of search and seizure law places a significant burden on police officers.

At the same time, the potential for the exclusion of evidence as a remedy for constitutional breaches makes it critical that police officers strive at all times to know and obey the law governing their evidence-gathering powers. The result of these two trends has been an increased premium on legal advice during the search warrant drafting process. Police officers now regularly consult with Crown counsel with respect to search issues generally and warrants in particular. And Crown counsel are, in general, ready and willing to assist – they recognize that time invested in advising an officer on a search warrant issue will almost always pay dividends later by avoiding unnecessary *Charter* litigation.

While this sort of collaboration is to be encouraged, there should be a clear understanding of the different roles and responsibilities of officers and advising

---

[30] *Ell v. Alberta*, [2003] 1 S.C.R. 857, 11 C.R. (6th) 207.
[31] *R. v. Do* (2001), 2001 CarswellBC 1863, 2001 BCSC 1088 (B.C.S.C.). See also *R. v. Federink*, 2003 CarswellBC 3296, [2003] B.C.J. No. 3026 (B.C.S.C.); and *R. v. Pomerleau* (2003), [2004] R.J.Q. 83, 2003 CarswellQue 3448, [2003] Q.J. No. 19020 (Que. C.A.).

Crown counsel. This ensures that Crown and police understand and perform their respective functions and serves to preserve their mutual independence.

(b) Role of the Police

(i) *Division of Labour*

The officer is, and remains, the *applicant* (the party formally and practically seeking the order of the court) and the person ultimately responsible for the decision to seek a search warrant and for the contents of the Information to Obtain.[32] In this, as in a number of other pre-charge decisions, the officer as applicant has the final say.[33]

In addition, the fact-driven nature of this process means that the officer must remain as the drafter while the Crown's function is limited to legal review and advice. Only the officer can ultimately determine whether the warrant application makes the necessary full, frank and fair disclosure of all material facts. The Crown's role is to ensure that the officer understands and applies the proper legal test and, to the extent possible from outside the investigation, to attempt to apply that test to the disclosure that is made in the Information to Obtain.

Courts have repeatedly acknowledged that documents prepared during the investigative phase of a criminal prosecution are not to be held to the same

---

[32] There are some exceptions to this general rule, for example, some of the proceeds of crime provisions make the Attorney General the applicant (see, for example, the Special Search Warrant provided in s. 462.32 and the Restraint Order set out in s. 462.33). In these cases the role of the Crown is different, with the Crown having responsibility for all final decisions related to the form and content of the application, as well as the decision on whether to seek such an order in the first place.

In the context of wiretaps, for example, it is clear that the Crown, and not the officer, is the applicant and that the materials will be assessed on that basis: "The Attorney General of Canada, as the applicant for the authorization under s. 186 . . . was, ultimately, responsible for the contents of Detective Cavanaugh's affidavit." See *R. v. B. (G.)*, 146 C.C.C. (3d) 465, 2000 CarswellOnt 2750 (Ont. C.A.) at p. 479 [C.C.C.], para. 41, leave to appeal refused (2001), 271 N.R. 200 (note), 149 O.A.C. 391 (note) (S.C.C.).

[33] In Canada the police have control over almost all investigative decisions taken before a charge is before the courts. In most, but not all jurisdictions, the police are responsible for the decision to lay a charge. Once a charge is before the courts the Crown has carriage of the prosecution and may direct further investigative decisions supportive of the Crown's case: *Attorney General's Advisory Committee on Charge Screening, Disclosure and Resolution Discussions* (Toronto: Queen's Printer, 1993) (known widely as the "Martin Report") at p. 117. See also *R. v. Regan* (2002), 161 C.C.C. (3d) 97, 49 C.R. (5th) 1 (S.C.C.), affirming (1999), 137 C.C.C. (3d) 449, 28 C.R. (5th) 1 (N.S. C.A.). (Of course, where Crown counsel have provided pre-charge legal advice which is ignored or not followed by the officer, the officer does so at his or her peril.)

standard of precision as those created for use at trial.[34] An Information to Obtain is not held to the same standard as an indictment or other formal pleading. Firstly, at the investigative phase it is impossible for the state to achieve the same degree of precision – indeed, the very purpose of the investigation is to allow the police to gather the evidence necessary to allow precision later in the process. Secondly, documents prepared at the pre-trial stage are acknowledged to be largely the product of lay drafters – police officers – who should not be held to the same standard as is applied to documentation prepared by counsel.

While the Crown may be involved – in some cases intimately involved – with the drafting, in reality the officer is the applicant. The officer is, of course, responsible for the physical production of the Information to Obtain in a form that is acceptable to the court. Again, the Crown may provide legal advice in this area, but it is ultimately the officer who must carry that advice into action.

(ii) Duty to Make Full, Frank and Fair Disclosure to the Judicial Officer

Officers are constantly reminded of their duty to make "full, frank and fair" disclosure of all material facts to the issuing justice.[35] This requires the officer to present all of the relevant and material evidence gathered to date as well as outlining all of the significant investigative steps taken in relation to the case that gives rise to the warrant request. The duty arises from the *ex parte* nature of a search warrant application. Since the other side is not present, the court expects that the officer will provide it with all the information that it needs to make a *fair decision* on the application – even if that evidence is not relied upon by the officer, or may run counter to the officer's theory.

As the Supreme Court said in one case:[36]

> [46] Looking at matters practically in order to learn from this case for the future, what kind of affidavit should the police submit in order to seek permission to use wiretapping? The legal obligation on anyone seeking an *ex parte* authori-

---

[34] In *R. v. Hunter* (1987), 34 C.C.C. (3d) 14, 57 C.R. (3d) 1 (Ont. C.A.) at p. 27 [C.C.C.], Cory J.A. (as he then was) observed for the Court:

> It must be remembered that the search warrant is an important investigative tool. The affidavits used in support of an application for a warrant are often prepared in a hurry, frequently by persons who have little or no legal training. Detailed perfection should not be required at this stage of the investigative process.

See also *Re Times Square Book Store* (1985), 21 C.C.C. (3d) 503, 48 C.R. (3d) 132 (Ont. C.A.) at p. 513 [C.C.C.] and the comments in *Lubell v. R.* (1973), 11 C.C.C. (2d) 188 (Ont. H.C.) at p. 189.

[35] *R. v. Araujo, supra,* note 20, at pp. 469–470 [C.C.C.], para. 46; *R. v. Church of Scientology (No. 6)* (1987), 31 C.C.C. (3d) 449, 30 C.R.R. 238 (Ont. C.A.) at p. 528 [C.C.C.], leave to appeal refused [1987] 1 S.C.R. vii, 33 C.R.R. 384 (note) (S.C.C.).

[36] *R. v. Araujo, supra,* note 20.

zation is *full and frank* disclosure of *material facts* . . . . So long as the affidavit meets the requisite legal norm, there is no need for it to be as lengthy as *À la recherche du temps perdu*, as lively as the *Kama Sutra*, or as detailed as an automotive repair manual. All that it must do is set out the facts fully and frankly for the authorizing judge in order that he or she can make an assessment of whether these rise to the standard required in the legal test for the authorization. Ideally, an affidavit should be not only full and frank but also *clear and concise*. It need not include every minute detail of the police investigation over a number of months and even of years.

[47] A corollary to the requirement of an affidavit being full and frank is that it should never attempt to trick its readers. At best, the use of boiler-plate language adds extra verbiage and seldom anything of meaning; at worst, it has the potential to trick the reader into thinking that the affidavit means something that it does not. Although the use of boiler-plate language will not automatically prevent a judge from issuing an authorization (there is, after all, no formal legal requirement to avoid it), I cannot stress enough that judges should deplore it. There is nothing wrong — and much right — with an affidavit that sets out the facts truthfully, fully and *plainly*. Counsel and police officers submitting materials to obtain wire-tapping authorizations should not allow themselves to be led into the temptation of misleading the authorizing judge, either by the language used or strategic omissions.[37] [emphasis in original]

Ideally the Information to Obtain will include reference to any material witness interviews, surveillance, forensic reports, earlier searches (or electronic surveillance), statements made by the accused or target, exculpatory evidence from other sources, and the background, if relevant, of the target.

(iii) *Duty to Present the Information to Obtain in a Comprehensible Form*

Officers are also obliged to present the evidence and information they have amassed in a fashion that can be reasonably understood by the judicial officer considering the application. In *Re Criminal Code*, Mr. Justice Casey Hill explained the duty in these terms:

[9] . . . [T]he application affidavit/information must be reasonably comprehensible. This factor engages a consideration of such sub-factors as organization of the document, spelling, grammar, punctuation and language, including word choice. As with the text of any document, meaning and understanding can be impaired by defects in these respective subject areas. In some instances, the number and severity of such defects may render the document confusing and incomprehensible. The court should not find itself in a position of endlessly re-reading the application document in order to discover whether the statutory pre-conditions are

---

[37] Ibid., at pp. 469–470 [C.C.C.].

satisfied. I accept that in some cases the complexity of the investigation and the relevant quantity of investigative data will contribute to a lengthy application document. However, the creation of undue complexity and unnecessary length in the application document can obscure, even for sophisticated readers, the presence of all necessary pre-requisites. The inherent danger is that one or more of the orders sought will issue despite the absence of a valid supporting record.[38]

This will often be a challenging task, particularly in complex or lengthy investigations.[39] Nonetheless, the duty of the drafting officer is to "separate the wheat from the chaff" and thereby distill for the justice the necessary material, taking care, however, not to leave out anything that is material.

These seemingly conflicting duties – the need to reduce and decant versus the duty to make full, frank and fair disclosure – should normally be reconciled by inclusion rather than removal of material.

(iv) *Draft Warrant or Order*

Technically, the Information to Obtain is the warrant applicant's document. The warrant itself, however, is the judicial officer's document. Though it is not formally required anywhere, the universal practice is for the officer to prepare a *draft* warrant to be considered in tandem with the Information to Obtain submitted to the justice. The justice is, of course, free to modify the draft warrant by deleting, adding or amending any element of the draft warrant, or by starting over and preparing a new warrant without reference to the draft. Indeed, there is no legal impediment that would prevent the justice from starting from scratch and preparing a new warrant entirely.

(c) Crown Counsel's Function in Warrant Applications

Crown counsel's function in most search warrant applications, while important, is limited. The police are ultimately responsible for investigative decisions – whether to seek a warrant, when to execute it, etc. – and the Crown cannot usurp this function prior to a charge being before the courts.

The Crown's role is to provide legal advice to the police to ensure they understand the legal framework within which their investigation is being conducted. This includes advising the police as to whether a particular investigative course is lawful and what the legal implications are if that investigative course is followed.[40]

---

[38] *Re Criminal Code, supra,* note 14 (sometimes cited as *A.G.O. 55/97*).
[39] In Chapter 4 there is a discussion of techniques that may assist a warrant drafter in organizing and presenting material.
[40] *R. v. Regan, supra,* note 33.

Crown counsel asked to provide advice on a warrant in a complex case can, and often should, require the officer to prepare an investigative brief. This ensures that the Crown has adequate knowledge of the facts, provides a record of the factual basis upon which any advice may have been based, and will inevitably assist the officer in the Information to Obtain preparation.

The Crown's function is not to "re-write" draft material provided by the search warrant applicant. The core function of the Crown is to identify legal issues or deficiencies in the material and to instruct the applicant on how to repair the document.

Crown counsel should normally ensure that an accurate record of his or her advice is created for future reference and to avoid misunderstanding or conflicts at a later time. This can be done by:

1. providing the advice in writing;
2. making detailed comments in writing on draft material setting out legal issues and identifying possible avenues of repair;
3. instructing the officer to note in his or her notebook the advice given to ensure there cannot be any later misunderstanding of the substance of the advice; or
4. where it is the only practical option, taking careful, detailed and contemporaneous notes of any advice given orally.

Legal advice given to the police by the Crown is protected by a form of solicitor-client privilege. Officers and Crowns alike should take care to preserve the privilege by ensuring that the content of advice is not provided to third parties who are not part of the investigative team (i.e., to the accused or to witnesses) even as part of the disclosure process.[41]

(d) When Should the Crown Be Brought In?

While the Crown is consulted far more today than in the past, it is still the case that most warrants are prepared and submitted without the assistance of the prosecutor.[42] In which circumstances should a police officer involve the Crown in the warrant process? In general, the answer is: whenever the officer is unsure of what the legal rules are that govern a situation, or of the effect of

---

[41] *R. v. Campbell* (1999), 133 C.C.C. (3d) 257, 24 C.R. (5th) 365 (S.C.C.). In some cases the Court may order disclosure of Crown/police communications, but only where they have become relevant to the particular case. In general, such material should not be disclosed.

[42] In some jurisdictions there is a practice of requiring the Crown to review all warrants before submission where feasible. In Ontario some judicial protocols (such as the one in place in Toronto) require that the Crown review a warrant before submission to a provincial judge, though not before submission to a justice of the peace (see below in the Appendix to Chapter 3).

those rules on the particular facts. Common situations in which warrant advice is sought are:

1. *Do I Have Reasonable Grounds to Obtain a Warrant?* The application of this standard to a body of evidence is a legal issue. It is appropriate for an officer to seek the advice of Crown counsel on whether the evidence gathered to date can reasonably support a warrant application.
2. *Can I Obtain a Warrant to Do This? What Warrant Should I Be Seeking?* The *Charter* considers any police activity that interferes with an individual's expectation of privacy to be a search or seizure. This does not mean that the police cannot engage in the questioned activity, only that they must obtain some sort of judicial pre-authorization (or be able to point to a valid warrantless search power) for such activity. In the last 15 years there has been an explosion of warrant-granting powers under the *Criminal Code*. Crown counsel can assist officers in identifying which warrant power is legally available and in identifying the best avenue by which to pursue authorization.
3. *Is There a Warrantless Search Power Available in this Situation?* It is legitimate for police officers to first exhaust whatever warrantless search powers apply to a particular situation before resorting to judicial pre-authorization. In many cases the police will wish to advance their investigation using warrantless powers because they are still at the stage of generating reasonable grounds for belief, which grounds will be the basis for subsequent applications.
4. *I Am Using this Warrant Power for the First Time – Can You Assist?* The myriad of search warrant powers in the *Criminal Code* mean that it is not possible to expect every officer to have experience with every warrant. In many cases there are a number of substantive and procedural pitfalls that await the uninitiated lay drafter. Crown counsel can assist in identifying the preconditions for issuance and pointing up any procedural or technical issues that the officer will need to address.
5. *How Can I Best Protect My Source or the Integrity of My Investigation?* There are different legal avenues available to ensure the integrity of a police investigation. Whether the answer is a sealing order, a non-publication order, careful drafting to remove identifying detail, or other technique, consultation with the Crown can ensure that the process used is the most effective and most appropriate for the situation.
6. *I Need to Search a (i) Media Outlet, (ii) Psychiatric Hospital, (iii) Law Office or (iv) Other Place with Special Privacy Interests.* Some places enjoy special protection because they are related to special privacy interests. Media outlets (newspaper offices, radio and television stations, website offices) are associated with freedom of expression; law offices are linked to solicitor-client privilege; psychiatric hospitals necessarily con-

tain mental health records (which may enjoy special statutory status);[43] other locations may exist that have similar special concerns. Warrants in relation to each of these locations attract intense scrutiny from the courts. Even very experienced officers applying for such warrants will almost always seek out the advice of Crown counsel before submitting a warrant application to a court.

In addition, this sort of warrant frequently generates complex and hotly contested pre-trial litigation. Media outlets, for example, routinely challenge search warrants on principle: they perceive their first duty to be to protect the flow of information to the public through them. Because such warrants normally provide for modified execution (seize, seal and permit an *inter partes* challenge to the warrant before the police are permitted to examine the objects of seizure), the police will want to take every step to ensure a speedy resolution of this warrant litigation.

7. *I Have Already Seized this Evidence Without Warrant – Has My Conduct Been Lawful?* The nature of law enforcement is such that it will not always permit careful reflection before action is required. Police sometimes question whether an investigative decision may have led to a possible unconstitutional search. Crown counsel is well placed to assist in identifying if there has been a misstep and, more importantly, in identifying the best way to repair any damage done to the case by such a misstep.

8. *My Search Warrant Application Has Been Refused and I Am Not Sure Why or What I Should Do Now.* The refusal of a warrant can frustrate an investigation. Crown counsel can identify what legal basis there may have been for the refusal and assist the officer in addressing whatever deficiency led to the refusal.

(e) Who to Call

There are a number of possible legal resources available to police officers: the local provincial Crown Attorney; Crown counsel at the provincial Ministry of the Attorney General (such as the Crown Law Office – Criminal, in the Ontario Attorney General's Ministry); the local federal Crown agent; Department of Justice counsel in Ottawa, Toronto and Vancouver; counsel to the particular police service (if such exists). Where to call depends in part on the nature of the inquiry.

(i) *Inquiries Arising in a Particular Investigation*

Normally the most appropriate avenue is to consult with the Crown office most likely to have carriage of any prosecution arising out of the particular investigation. For example, in a murder investigation the proper source of

---

[43] See, for example, the Ontario *Mental Health Act*, R.S.O. 1990, c. M.7, ss. 35–36.

advice would be the provincial Crown Attorney's office most likely to have carriage of any charges.

(ii) General Policy or Procedure

Most large police agencies today have policies in place that instruct officers on how to deal with specific search and seizure issues. For example, when should a police officer strip search an arrestee? The courts have set down general principles to guide such searches,[44] but police service policy will often provide more concrete direction to the officer. Where the issue relates to an interpretation of service policy or position on a particular issue, counsel within the service is usually the best source of advice and information.

(iii) Where No Identified Charging Jurisdiction

When there is no identified charging jurisdiction (where, for example, the location of the offence is not known, or where the offence was committed in a variety of jurisdictions), it may be appropriate to approach counsel at a centralized ministry office. In Ontario, for example, the Crown Law Office – Criminal in Toronto, provides advice to police officers involved in multi-jurisdictional investigations.

(iv) No "Crown Shopping"

Some officers will ask multiple Crowns for their opinions on a legal problem associated with a warrant. They then choose from among the opinions the view that they prefer. This sort of "Crown shopping" taints the process of advice. It is wrong for police officers to "shop" for a Crown who will provide them with favourable advice. Indeed, an officer who goes "Crown shopping" is not really seeking "advice" but rather simply confirmation of his or her pre-existing views. Crown counsel rightly look at such conduct with suspicion and may be reluctant to deal with a "shopping" officer in the future.

"Crown shopping" makes it seem like the Crown's advice is only valued if it confirms the officer's pre-determined preferred course of action. It is wasteful of scarce Crown resources and, if done without notice, it is disrespectful of the first Crown's opinion. Moreover, it will appear to the court that the officer sought advice not as part of a legitimate, bona fide effort to conform to the law but as an exercise to avoid compliance. Defence counsel will be quick to bring to the judge's attention "Crown shopping" with a view to casting a shadow over everything done by that officer.

---

[44] R. v. Golden (2001), 159 C.C.C. (3d) 449, 47 C.R. (5th) 1 (S.C.C.).

3

Understanding Warrant Provisions: The Conventional Warrant – Section 487

1. Preconditions to Issuance and Scope of Authority

Every search warrant provision can be understood in terms of both the *preconditions to issuance* and the *scope of authority* given by virtue of the warrant.

(a) Preconditions

The preconditions to issuance identify what set of circumstances must be demonstrated by the warrant applicant before the judicial officer has the authority to issue the warrant in question. An understanding of the preconditions to a particular warrant will necessarily involve appreciating (a) the applicable standard of proof, as well as (b) the elements of a valid warrant application.

The *standard* of proof normally required is a showing of "reasonable grounds to believe"[1] – although this is not always the case. In some uncommon situations the law permits a warrant to issue where the elements of the warrant are demonstrated on a "reasonable grounds to suspect" standard.

The *elements* of a valid warrant are, like the elements of an offence, the particular facts or circumstances which must exist before the warrant can issue. For example, before a s. 487 warrant can issue, there must be reasonable grounds to believe (the standard of proof) that the following elements are present:

1. An offence (or offences) against the *Criminal Code* or other federal statute has been committed.[2]

---

[1] Discussed below under heading 2(d), "Reasonable Grounds to Believe."

[2] Sections 487(1)(a) and (c) suggest intended or suspected commission, but these powers are constitutionally suspect and only rarely necessary. See also *R. v. Branton* (2001), 154 C.C.C. (3d) 139, 44 C.R. (5th) 275 (Ont. C.A.).

2. The things to be seized are in an identified building, receptacle or place at the time the warrant is being issued.
3. The things to be seized have a physical existence.
4. The things to be seized:
    (a) will afford evidence with respect to the commission of the offence;
    (b) are something on or in respect of which the offence was committed;
    (c) will reveal the whereabouts of a person who is believed to have committed the offence; or
    (d) are any offence-related property.

A warrant application must address each of these "elements" by setting out the evidence that shows that there are reasonable grounds to believe in the "element."

(b) Scope of Authority

A search warrant provision in a statute gives the judicial officer the power to make an order authorizing only very specific investigative techniques. If the proposed investigative action involves the use of techniques not contemplated by the warrant-granting section, then even if the necessary preconditions can be shown to exist, the warrant cannot issue. For example, s. 487 does not authorize a warrant to make a dental impression of a suspect. This investigative technique falls outside the straightforward, though common, type of investigative action that can be authorized under a conventional warrant. It is important therefore to take care to ensure not simply that the police obtain a warrant, but that they obtain the *right* warrant.[3]

2. Common Language and Its Meaning

(a) Introduction

In the absence of a specific statutory authorization, a justice of the peace has no power to issue a warrant to search. Section 487 of the *Criminal Code* provides the most frequently used example of such authority, although there are other Code provisions that authorize search (or search-like) investigative techniques. There are also a number of other federal and provincial statutes that make provision for judicial pre-authorization of search and seizure. These other statutes provide for the issuance of warrants in circumstances specific to the regulatory enforcement regime created by the particular statute and will often invite authorization of searches or inspections not covered by s. 487. A warrant under s. 487 is only available to authorize certain investigative tech-

---

[3] In this situation, s. 487.092 authorizes an "impression warrant."

niques. Other investigative activity will have to look to other provisions of the Code if they are to be authorized.

Such specific warrant provisions will apply in their own terms. Investigators should be familiar with the particular forms of legal authority they purport to invoke in seeking some form of judicial pre-authorization. This involves an understanding of both the *powers* granted by the statute, and the *legal preconditions* to the exercise of those powers. Section 487 of the *Criminal Code* authorizes a justice of the peace to issue a warrant in the prescribed form when presented with evidence, on oath, supporting the application for such a warrant. The section reads:

> **487.** (1) **Information for search warrant** – A justice who is satisfied by information on oath in Form 1 that there are reasonable grounds to believe that there is in a building, receptacle or place
>
> > (a) anything on or in respect of which any offence against this Act or any other Act of Parliament has been or is suspected to have been committed,
> > (b) anything that there are reasonable grounds to believe will afford evidence with respect to the commission of an offence, or will reveal the whereabouts of a person who is believed to have committed an offence, against this Act or any other Act of Parliament,
> > (c) anything that there are reasonable grounds to believe is intended to be used for the purpose of committing any offence against the person for which a person may be arrested without warrant, or
> > (c.1) any offence-related property,
>
> may at any time issue a warrant authorizing a peace officer or a public officer who has been appointed or designated to administer or enforce a federal or provincial law and whose duties include the enforcement of this Act or any other Act of Parliament and who is named in the warrant
>
> > (d) to search the building, receptacle or place for any such thing and to seize it, and
> > (e) subject to any other Act of Parliament, to, as soon as practicable, bring the thing seized before, or make a report in respect thereof to, the justice or some other justice for the same territorial division in accordance with section 489.1.

The language of the section provides a useful framework within which to consider a number of questions related to the issuance of search warrants and the sections of the *Criminal Code* available to investigators seeking to ensure that their conduct falls within the limits established by the Constitution and the *Criminal Code*.

(b) "Satisfied by Information on Oath"

(i) *The Requirement for Sourcing*

The single most important substantive requirement in relation to search warrants is the requirement that they set out the warrant applicant's *sources of information*. This requirement is driven by the judicial officer's role in the process. The issuing judicial officer is expected to independently assess whether the applicant's belief is a reasonable one. This requires a weighing of the evidence that gives rise to the police officer's belief.

It is clear that in order to pass constitutional muster, a statutory provision authorizing the granting of a search warrant must require that the issuing justice of the peace be satisfied by sworn evidence. As was said in *Hunter*:

> The purpose of a requirement of prior authorization is to provide an opportunity, before the event, for the conflicting interests of the State and the individual to be assessed, so that the individual's right to privacy will be breached only where the appropriate standard has been met, and the interests of the State are thus demonstrably superior. *For such an authorization procedure to be meaningful it is necessary for the person authorizing the search to be able to assess the evidence as to whether that standard has been met,* in an entirely neutral and impartial manner.
>
> . . .
>
> The State's interest in detecting and preventing crime begins to prevail over the individual's interest in being left alone at the point where credibly-based probability replaces suspicion. . . . *In cases [where the state seeks evidence of criminal acts], reasonable and probable grounds, established upon oath, to believe that an offence has been committed and that there is evidence to be found at the place of the search, constitutes the minimum standard,* consistent with s. 8 of the Charter, for authorizing search and seizure.[4] [emphasis added]

Such evidence can include hearsay, but where hearsay evidence is used it must be presented in a way that will allow the issuing justice to make up his or her own mind about how trustworthy the original source of the evidence really is.

---

[4] *Hunter v. Southam Inc.* (1984), 14 C.C.C. (3d) 97, 41 C.R. (3d) 97 (S.C.C.) at pp. 110, 114–115 [C.C.C.], referred to as *Hunter* or *Hunter v. Southam* below.

(ii) *Information from Other Investigators: "Police Investigation Has Revealed"*

The most common example of hearsay involves information coming from colleagues involved in the investigation. These parties should be named and their source of knowledge identified. For example, the statement in an Information to Obtain, *"My investigation has revealed that the records of the business were at the location to be searched in July 2004,"* would be of almost no value to the justice; the justice cannot weigh this evidence without more information. The "source" of the information ("my investigation") is such that it is all but impossible for the issuing justice to make any independent evaluation of the "evidence" – it could be a rumour for all the justice knows. On the other hand, consider the statement:

> I reviewed the transcript of an interview of John Smith (conducted by P.C. Allen on August 21, 2004) who worked at the location to be searched until July 12, 2004. He told police that there were stand-alone personal computers at the location to be searched until that date and that he saw these computers used for record-keeping. John Smith also reports that hard copies of these records were made and kept at the location to be searched.

This identifies the source of the hearsay and provides the justice with a reasonable opportunity to consider whether that piece of evidence can contribute to the satisfaction of the "reasonable ground" test for the issuance of the warrant.[5]

The Information must avoid using phrases such as "police investigation has revealed. . . " or "based on my investigation I have concluded" as these or similar statements reveal *nothing* that would allow the judicial officer to consider whether such information should be believed.[6] In *Restaurant le Clémenceau Inc. v. Drouin*, the Supreme Court of Canada stated:

---

[5] In some cases the court has taken a relatively generous view of what can be implied from the language used by the officer: *R. v. Day* (1998), 1998 CarswellOnt 4182, [1998] O.J. No. 4461 (Ont. C.A.), leave to appeal refused (1999), 130 O.A.C. 199 (note), 250 N.R. 195 (note) (S.C.C.). Officers should not count on this type of inference-drawing, however, when a modest degree of effort can ensure the explicit statement of all investigative resources.

[6] *R. v. Grant* (1999), 132 C.C.C. (3d) 531, 117 O.A.C. 345, 1999 CarswellOnt 408, [1999] O.J. No. 327 (Ont. C.A.), leave to appeal refused (2001), 146 O.A.C. 199 (note), 266 N.R. 399 (note) (S.C.C.), though in a limited number of cases it may be possible for this form of language to support a reasonable inference of the ultimate source of the information. Consider *R. v. Day*, *supra*, note 5, where the Court, in a moment of generosity, said:

> [2] Given that the allegation set out in the information was impaired driving and arose out of an accident on a public highway that resulted in the hospitalization of the seriously injured appellant, the Justice of the Peace could reasonably infer that the informant, who was a police officer, gained his information concerning the accident and the surrounding circumstances from reliable standard police sources.

He [the Informant] further asserted that this belief was reasonable and rested on an investigation he had undertaken, though he did not disclose its nature, and during which he had discovered certain facts. *In order to perform his duty of supervision, the judge had to determine whether the facts on which the informant's belief was based were such that his belief was indeed reasonable.* None of these facts are disclosed by the information. The judge then had a duty to ask for further information, which he elected not to do. In the case at bar, in view of what was before the judge, he could not and in fact did not verify the reasonableness of the informant's belief . . . . [7] [emphasis added]

It is not enough that the investigator swearing the Information to Obtain has satisfied himself or herself that a warrant should issue; the Information must put the issuing justice in a position to consider the question independently and weigh whether there are reasonable grounds for believing that the prerequisites for the issuance of the warrant are made out.

Accordingly, an investigator must outline in the Information the nature of the investigation. For example, the Information should include such aspects of the investigation as physical surveillance of premises, interviews with witnesses, forensic analysis, the results of any previous search, statements made by the target, etc.

(iii) *Use of Hearsay*

The central inquiry in a warrant application is the determination of whether the officer's belief is reasonable – the insertion of the judicial officer's independent, objective review of the officer's belief based on evidence and information provided to him or her. The officer's belief can reasonably be based on his or her own observations, things the officer has been told directly by witnesses, or evidence relayed to him or her through one or more police or other sources. In short, hearsay (evidence that is related to the officer and the justice secondhand) can be considered, though its reliability must be assessed.

The key to the effective and lawful presentation of hearsay information will be found by reference to the justice's role. The justice is expected to assess the probative value of hearsay information – to what degree could this hearsay source be the basis for a reasonable belief? For example, the statement "Officer Smith tells me that Leslie Jones, the manager of the bank, reports that her staff have confirmed that the target of the search signed a signature card to open a bank account three weeks ago" is, all things being equal, a reliable statement, even though it is triple hearsay.

There is a need to go to the "root" of hearsay rather than simply presenting the latest or last repetition of secondhand information. As the Quebec Court

---

[7] *Restaurant le Clémenceau Inc. v. Drouin*, 35 C.C.C. (3d) 381, [1987] 1 S.C.R. 706 (S.C.C.) at p. 384 [C.C.C.].

of Appeal has stated: "Hearsay is not prohibited . . . but [it is allowed] on the condition that it is accompanied by sufficient evidence which can reassure the issuing judge of the reliability of the information: the [warrant applicant] must be able to answer for it."[8]

(iv) *Privileged Informers and Tipsters*

Some sources cannot be identified for the judicial officer considering a warrant application. Anonymous tipsters and confidential informers (whose identity may be known to the officer, but is protected by informer privilege) cannot be named or described for the judicial officer. They present special drafting problems that are addressed later in this text.[9]

(v) *Expert Evidence*

If the Information to Obtain relies in part on evidence that involves an expert opinion, the foundation for the opinion must be set out. For example, if an officer wants to seize bed linens to secure hair samples for hair/fibre analysis or DNA testing, the Information to Obtain should set out the nature of the testing to be done and, in general terms, the scientific process that will allow the justice to conclude that, in fact, there is reason to believe that such material will afford evidence of an offence.[10]

(vi) *Criminal Records*

Many of the exclusionary rules of evidence that operate at trial do not limit the use of evidence in a search warrant application. Evidence of an investigative target's criminal past is often relevant and can be included to show his or her propensity to commit the sort of crime being investigated (and thus assists in demonstrating reasonable grounds to believe that the offence under investigation has been committed and that the target is involved).[11] In this context the

---

[8] *R. v. Future Électronique Inc.* (2000), 151 C.C.C. (3d) 403 (translation), 42 C.R. (5th) 132 (Que. C.A.) at p. 412 [C.C.C.], para. 27, quashed (2002), 2002 CarswellQue 440 (S.C.C.). See also *R. v. Cheecham* (1989), 51 C.C.C. (3d) 498, 80 Sask. R. 74 (Sask. C.A.).

[9] See Chapter 9, "Specific Drafting Challenges."

[10] *R. v. Kesselring* (2000), 145 C.C.C. (3d) 119, 74 C.R.R. (2d) 286 (Ont. C.A.) at p. 126ff [C.C.C.], para. 21ff, on when an expert may be required with respect to electric consumption patterns. It is not necessary to qualify the science behind the proposed evidence to the same standard as is used during a trial – it should be sufficient to show that it is reasonable to believe that the science in question will yield evidence.

[11] *R. v. Debot* (1986), 30 C.C.C. (3d) 207, 54 C.R. (3d) 120 (Ont. C.A.) at pp. 220–221 [C.C.C.], affirmed (1989), 52 C.C.C. (3d) 193, 73 C.R. (3d) 129 (S.C.C.); *R. v. Storrey* (1990), 53 C.C.C. (3d) 316, 75 C.R. (3d) 1 (S.C.C.) at pp. 319, 324 [C.C.C.].

"similar act rule" (sometimes called the "other discreditable conduct" rule[12]) does not prevent consideration of this sort of evidence. This is not, however, a licence to unjustifiably sully the character of the target of the search in the warrant application. Charges that have been withdrawn or stayed or resulted in acquittal are all the same for legal purposes. These should be omitted, or if they must be included,[13] there should be full disclosure to the issuing justice of what happened with the charges, and why the warrant applicant has elected to include them.[14]

(c) "Information on Oath *In Writing*": The Form and the Four Corners Rule

The language used in s. 487 (and most other warrant-granting provisions) requires that a search warrant application be supported exclusively by written materials.[15] Indeed, the wording of s. 487 goes further and requires that the written materials follow a specific written form, Form 1, which is in turn prescribed by s. 849.[16] Pre-printed forms that include additional language that does not alter the substance of the averments required by Form 1 and s. 849 are acceptable (but any pre-printed provisions must be in English and French). By its own terms, s. 849(1) permits forms "varied to suit the case, or forms to

---

[12] See, generally, *R. v. B. (L.)* (1997), 116 C.C.C. (3d) 481, 9 C.R. (5th) 38 (Ont. C.A.).

[13] For example, if they demonstrate knowledge by the target of the search.

[14] *R. v. Sismey* (1990), 55 C.C.C. (3d) 281, 1 C.R.R. (2d) 381 (B.C. C.A.) at pp. 283–284 [C.C.C.].

[15] Section 487.1 and the telewarrant regime permit a relaxation of this general writing requirement to recognize the potential for oral telecommunications (i.e., a telephone) to provide a medium for the authorization of search activity.

[16] Section 849, as amended by S.C. 2002, c. 13, s. 84, provides a very simple version of the s. 487 Information to Obtain:

INFORMATION TO OBTAIN A SEARCH WARRANT
Canada,
Province of .... ,
(*territorial division*).
    This is the information of A.B., of ...., in the said (*territorial division*), (*occupation*), hereinafter called the informant, taken before me.
    The informant says that (*describe things to be searched for and offence in respect of which search is to be made*), and that he believes on reasonable grounds that the said things, or some part of them, are in the (*dwelling-house, etc.*) of C.D., of ...., in the said (*territorial division*). (*Here add the grounds of belief, whatever they may be.*)
    Wherefore the informant prays that a search warrant may be granted to search the said (*dwelling-house, etc.*) for the said things.

Sworn before me this .... day of .... , A.D. .... , at ....

                                    (*Signature of Informant*)

....
A Justice of the Peace in and for ....

the like effect." Section 32 of the federal *Interpretation Act*[17] provides that "[w]here a form is prescribed, deviations from that form, not affecting the substance or calculated to mislead, do not invalidate the form used." (Even if a warrant provision only makes reference to a justice considering "information," there is an argument that it should be in writing and that the writing should follow Form 1.[18] Given the flexibility permitted in this area, the best course is to attempt to follow Form 1 (varied to suit the case) as much as possible.

Any additional evidence or information provided to the judicial officer in oral comments made at the time of the application do not form part of the record in support of the warrant application. It is therefore critical that anything important related to the application be recorded within the four corners of the written application.[19]

Sometimes a judicial officer considering a warrant application will ask questions that elicit from the officer additional clarifying – but nonetheless important – information related to the application that is not in the written material. In these circumstances, if time permits, the best course is for the officer to thank the judicial officer for identifying the factual gap and to ask for leave to withdraw the application so as to be able to amend the written material to accord with the points raised by the justice. The revised materials can be resubmitted, and care should be taken to disclose the fact of the earlier withdrawn application. Alternatively, it is legally sufficient for the officer to use a pen to interlineate into the existing documents modest additions, corrections or clarifications to the original written Information to Obtain. Such additions must be sworn to as part of the application and should be initialled by both the officer and the person swearing the officer's amended affidavit.

(d) "Reasonable Grounds to Believe"

The constitutional standard set down in *Hunter v. Southam* for criminal searches was one of reasonable belief based on sworn evidence. The concept of "reasonable grounds for belief," while a commonplace of the criminal process, remains difficult to articulate. The United States Supreme Court said in one case that the equivalent American standard (probable cause) was "a fluid concept – turning on the assessment of probabilities in particular factual

---

[17] *Interpretation Act*, R.S.C. 1985, c. I-21.

[18] See below, the discussion of *Re Magar* (1998), 1998 CarswellOnt 2429 (Ont. Prov. Div.) at note 56, under heading 5, "Who Swears an 'Information'?"

[19] *R. v. Silvestrone* (1991), 66 C.C.C. (3d) 125, 2 B.C.A.C. 195 (B.C. C.A.) at p. 133 [C.C.C.]. In *R. v. Araujo* (2000), 149 C.C.C. (3d) 449, 38 C.R. (5th) 307 (S.C.C.) the Supreme Court of Canada suggested that the judicial officer might consider questioning the officer about the contents of the Information to Obtain, but this advice is contrary to long-settled practice and should not be seen as a licence to supplement the written application requirement provided for in s. 487 and elsewhere.

contexts – not readily, or even usefully, reduced to a neat set of legal rules."[20] In *Maryland v. Pringle*, the U.S. Supreme Court said that:

> The probable cause standard is incapable of precise definition or quantification into percentages because it deals with probabilities and depends on the totality of the circumstances.[21]

In *Debot*, the Supreme Court of Canada stated:

> The question as to what standard of proof must be met in order to establish reasonable grounds for a search may be disposed of quickly. I agree with Martin J.A. that the appropriate standard is one of "reasonable probability" rather than "proof beyond a reasonable doubt" or "prima facie case". The phrase "reasonable belief" also approximates the requisite standard.[22]

How much evidence must the justice of the peace have presented to him or her? What is the standard against which the evidence will be measured? The *Criminal Code* calls for "reasonable grounds to believe"[23] but there is little authority in Canada on the exact meaning of this phrase. This is a modest, but legally irrelevant,[24] modification of the language used before 1985 which spoke of "reasonable *and probable* grounds to believe."[25] As noted already, *Hunter*[26] considered the constitutional standard to be "where credibly-based probability replaces suspicion." The Information to Obtain a search warrant must, therefore, give the justice of the peace sufficient weighable evidence to allow the justice independently to find the officer could reasonably find a *credibly based probability* that all of the preconditions for the issuance of the warrant exist.

The notion of "reasonable grounds" as set out in s. 487 of the *Criminal Code*, or "reasonable and probable grounds" or "probable cause" (as the Americans call it) or the constitutional standard described as "credibly based prob-

---

[20] *Illinois v. Gates*, 462 U.S. 213, 103 S. Ct. 436 (1983).

[21] *Maryland v. Pringle*, 124 S. Ct. 795 (2003) at p. 799.

[22] *R. v. Debot* (S.C.C.), *supra*, note 11, at p. 213 [C.C.C], affirming (1986), 30 C.C.C. (3d) 207, 54 C.R. (3d) 120 (Ont. C.A.). Some authorities suggest that the standard is a more formal "balance of probabilities," but later cases like *Debot* make it clear that what is intended is a practical non-technical probability that should not be equated with the balance of probabilities standard: *Re Times Square Book Store* (1985), 21 C.C.C. (3d) 503, 48 C.R. (3d) 132 (Ont. C.A.) at pp. 507, 514 [C.C.C.].

[23] *Hunter v. Southam Inc.*, *supra*, note 4, at pp. 114–115 [C.C.C.]. A lower threshold might prevail when the state's interest in gathering evidence is related to national security, or in the context of regulatory searches.

[24] *R. v. Baron* (1993), 78 C.C.C. (3d) 510, 18 C.R. (4th) 374 (S.C.C.); *Kourtessis v. Minister of National Revenue* (1988), 44 C.C.C. (3d) 79, 30 B.C.L.R. (2d) 342 (B.C. S.C.), affirmed (1989), 50 C.C.C. (3d) 201, 72 C.R. (3d) 196 (B.C. C.A.), reversed (1993), 81 C.C.C. (3d) 286, 20 C.R. (4th) 104 (S.C.C.).

[25] *Criminal Code*, R.S.C. 1970, c. C-34, s. 443.

[26] *Hunter v. Southam Inc.*, *supra*, note 4, at pp. 114–115 [C.C.C.].

ability" in *Hunter* does not require proof beyond a reasonable doubt or indeed proof to the standard of a *prima facie* case. A practical, reasonable and non-technical probability that evidence is available is all that is required. In determining whether such a likelihood exists, the neutral judicial officer (the justice) can consider hearsay evidence. In assessing whether the issuing judicial officer could conclude that such evidence is entitled to any weight, a reviewing court must, like the judicial officer at first instance, have regard to the *"totality of the circumstances."*[27]

In *Hunter*, Dickson J. stated:

> Section 443 [now s. 487] of the *Criminal Code* authorizes a warrant only where there has been information upon oath that there is "reasonable ground to believe" that there is evidence of an offence in the place to be searched. The American *Bill of Rights* provides that "no warrants shall issue but upon probable cause, supported by oath or affirmation . . . ". *The phrasing is slightly different but the standard in each of these formulations is identical.*[28] [emphasis added]

Because of the fact that the court has indicated that the two standards are the same, the American cases construing "probable cause " become important. Those authorities underscore the modest, common-sense threshold created by this standard. For example, in *Illinois v. Gates*, the United States Supreme Court stated:

> [T]he term "probable cause", according to its usual acceptation, means less than evidence which would justify condemnation . . . It imports a seizure made under circumstances which warrant suspicion". More recently, we said that "the quanta . . . of proof " appropriate in ordinary judicial proceedings are inapplicable to the decision to issue a warrant . . . Finely-tuned standards such as proof beyond a reasonable doubt or by a preponderance of evidence, useful in formal trials, have no place in the magistrate's decision. While an effort to fix some general, numerically precise degree of certainty corresponding to "probable cause" may be helpful, it is clear "that only the probability, and not a *prima facie* showing of criminal activity is the standard of probable cause."[29]

[27] *R. v. Church of Scientology (No. 6)* (1987), 31 C.C.C. (3d) 449, 30 C.R.R. 238 (Ont. C.A.) at p. 494 [C.C.C.], leave to appeal refused [1987] 1 S.C.R. vii, 33 C.R.R. 384 (note) (S.C.C.); *Hunter v. Southam Inc., supra*, note 4, at p. 114 [C.C.C.] per Dickson C.J.C.; *Illinois v. Gates, supra*, note 20, at p. 2328 per Rehnquist, J. (as he then was); *Texas v. Brown*, 103 S. Ct. 1535, 460 U.S. 730 (U.S. Tex. 1983) at p. 1543 [S. Ct.] per Rehnquist J. (as he then was); *R. v. Debot* (1986), 30 C.C.C. (3d) 207, 54 C.R. (3d) 120 (Ont. C.A.) at pp. 218–219 [C.C.C.] per Martin J.A., affirmed (1989), 52 C.C.C. (3d) 193, 73 C.R. (3d) 129 (S.C.C.) at p. 213 [C.C.C.] per Wilson J.; *R. v. Canadian Broadcasting Corp.* (1992), 77 C.C.C. (3d) 341, 17 C.R. (4th) 198 (Ont. Gen. Div.).
[28] *Hunter v. Southam Inc., supra*, note 4, at p. 114 [C.C.C.].
[29] *Illinois v. Gates, supra,* note 20.

Similarly, in *Texas v. Brown,* the United States Supreme Court stated:

> [I]t does not demand any showing that such a belief be *correct* or *more likely true* than false. A "practical, nontechnical" probability that incriminating evidence is involved is all that is required.[30] [emphasis added]

In *R. v. Debot,* the Supreme Court of Canada approved of the standard described by Martin J.A. in the Ontario Court of Appeal where he stated:

> The standard of "reasonable ground to believe" or "probable cause" is not to be equated with proof beyond a reasonable doubt or a *prima facie* case. The standard to be met is one of reasonable probability.[31]

It is important also to keep in mind that the test is not whether the judicial officer *agrees* with the particular conclusion or belief – the test is whether the belief of the warrant applicant is reasonable. If it is reasonable, it does not matter whether the issuing justice agrees with that belief. The purpose of the prior judicial authorization regime is to ensure a neutral consideration of the reasonableness of the government's basis for acting. If there is a reasonable basis for the investigative step in question then it can properly be authorized.

The importance of the exact nature of this standard can be seen in the problem of simultaneous searches. There are circumstances where investigators have grounds to believe that an item they wish to seize may be in one of a number of different locations. For example, suppose an investigator has learned that the owner of a business keeps a secret set of records with the true affairs of the company in a notebook computer which he or she moves between two business locations and the home, but nowhere else. The investigator may wish (or more likely, need) to obtain three different search warrants to search simultaneously these three separate locations for the notebook. If the requirement of reasonable grounds means that the investigator had to be at least 51% satisfied that the notebook was at one of these locations as opposed to the others, the investigator would probably not be able to get even one warrant, let alone successive warrants, as there is simply no evidence suggesting that it is any more likely that the secret records are at one location over the others. However, as noted, the weight of the authorities to date states that reasonable and probable grounds does not require this type of certainty or probability. All that is required is "reasonable probability." Accordingly, if it is reasonably probable that the subject left the notebook in any one of the three locations (as would appear), then the requirement has been satisfied. For practical reasons an investigator in such circumstances would want to be able to move on all locations within a fixed and limited span of time to ensure that the execution of one warrant

---

[30] *Texas v. Brown, supra,* note 27, at p. 1543 [S. Ct.].
[31] *R. v. Debot* (S.C.C.), *supra,* note 11, at p. 219 [C.C.C.]. See also *R. v. Storrey, supra,* note 11.

did not "tip the hand" of the investigation, providing the target with an opportunity to destroy evidence.

The American authorities have recognized that simultaneous search warrants in such circumstances comports with the constitutional standard of probable cause.[32] Presumably these authorities would apply in Canada, because the courts have been clear in their conclusion that the constitutional standard is the same in both countries.[33]

(e) "Reasonable Grounds to Suspect"

This lower standard of proof is used in circumstances where either the authorized intrusion is very modest (because the expectation of privacy is limited) or where the state interest is particularly pressing or important (such as where individual safety is said to be at stake). Several search warrant provisions authorize the issuance of a warrant upon a showing of reasonable suspicion. These include *Number Recorder Warrants* (s. 492.2) and *Tracking Device Warrants* (s. 492.1).[34]

When these or other statutory provisions occasionally speak of "reasonable suspicion" or "reasonable grounds to suspect," they refer to the same relatively modest standard. In respect of this "statutory threshold," the Ontario Court of Appeal has said:

> [36] The statutory threshold of suspicion based on reasonable grounds must be based on something more than a mere suspicion and something less than a belief based on reasonable and probable grounds: *R. v. Simmons, supra; R. v. Monney* (1999), 133 C.C.C. (3d) 129 (S.C.C.); *R. v. Oluwa* (1996), 107 C.C.C. (3d) 236 (B.C. C.A.); *R. v. Gladstone* (1985), 22 C.C.C. (3d) 151 (B.C. C.A.). It is important that care be taken to ensure that persons are not gratuitously detained on mere suspicion or for arbitrary reasons at this country's borders. There must be a constellation of objectively discernible facts that give the officer reasonable grounds to suspect: *R. v. Jacques*, [1996] 3 S.C.R. 312 at 326, 110 C.C.C. (3d) 1.[35]

---

[32] *United States v. Hendershot*, 614 F.2d 648 (U.S. 9th Cir. Cal. 1980); *United States v. Melvin*, 596 F.2d 492 (U.S. 1st Cir. Mass. 1979); *United States v. Heldt*, 668 F.2d 1238 (U.S. D.C. Cir. Ct. 1981).

[33] *Hunter v. Southam, supra,* note 4.

[34] In *R. v. Wise* (1992), 70 C.C.C. (3d) 193, 11 C.R. (4th) 253 (S.C.C.), the Court invited authorization of tracking devices on a lower threshold. The limited information obtained by a telephone number recorder would seem to support a lower threshold also: *R. v. Fegan* (1993), 80 C.C.C. (3d) 356, 21 C.R. (4th) 65, 1993 CarswellOnt 92 (Ont. C.A.). However, some courts have held that this standard is too low: *R. v. Nguyen* (2004), 2004 CarswellBC 279, 2004 BCSC 76 (B.C.S.C.), additional reasons to *R. v. Nguyen*, 2004 CarswellBC 280 (B.C.S.C.).

[35] *R. v. Granston* (2000), 146 C.C.C. (3d) 411, 77 C.R.R. (2d) 131 (Ont. C.A.) at p. 423 [C.C.C.].

A "constellation of objectively discernable facts" requires that the officer be able to identify and articulate those circumstances that caused him or her to suspect the subject of the search. These must be more than a "hunch," "experience" or "just good police work." If the officer cannot *say* what exactly animated this suspicion, then it is impossible to ask the court to find that that suspicion was reasonable.[36]

(f) "That There *Is*" (the Present Tense Requirement)

Section 487 and other warrant provisions[37] require a showing that the preconditions for the issuance of the warrant exist at the time the warrant is issued. That is, they do not permit a warrant to issue in anticipation that the object of the seizure will be there by the time the warrant is executed even though it may not be there at the time of the application. This "present tense requirement" means that anticipatory warrants are not permitted pursuant to provisions with this wording.[38]

This requirement does not prevent resort to s. 487.01, the general or residual warrant power, which can authorize any "investigative technique" including anticipatory warrants that might have been unlawful under s. 487.[39]

(g) "Anything That Will Afford Evidence"

The question of whether the thing to be seized "will afford evidence" of the offence is to be answered with a view to the nature of the warrant application as an *investigative* step. In *R. v. Canadian Broadcasting Corp.*,[40] the Court considered this issue. Mr. Justice Moldaver restated and applied the statement of the law in an earlier case:

> [39] The proper interpretation was set out many years ago by Chief Justice McRuer in the case of *Re Bell Telephone Co. of Canada* . . . [T]he Chief Justice said:

---

[36] *R. v. Simpson* (1993), 79 C.C.C. (3d) 482, 20 C.R. (4th) 1 (Ont. C.A.); *Brown v. Durham Regional Police Force* (1998), 131 C.C.C. (3d) 1, 21 C.R. (5th) 1 (Ont. C.A.), leave to appeal granted (1999), 252 N.R. 198 (note), 133 O.A.C. 200 (note) (S.C.C.); *R. v. Jacques* (1996), 110 C.C.C. (3d) 1, 1 C.R. (5th) 229 (S.C.C.) at p. 11 [C.C.C.].

[37] See, for example, the *Controlled Drugs and Substances Act*, S.C. 1996, c. 19, s. 11(1).

[38] *R. v. Fleet Aerospace Corp.*, 19 C.C.C. (3d) 385, 1985 CarswellOnt 1413 (Ont. H.C.); *R. v. Cameron* (1984), 16 C.C.C. (3d) 240, 15 C.R.R. 282 (B.C. C.A.); *R. v. Church of Scientology (No. 6)*, *supra*, note 27.

[39] See *R. v. Noseworthy* (1997), 116 C.C.C. (3d) 376, 43 C.R.R. (2d) 313 (Ont. C.A.), reversing (1995), 101 C.C.C. (3d) 447 (Ont. Gen. Div.), confirming that s. 487 will not authorize the issuance of an anticipatory warrant, but holding that a s. 487.01 general warrant could authorize an anticipatory warrant.

[40] *R. v. Canadian Broadcasting Corp.* (1992), 77 C.C.C. (3d) 341, 17 C.R. (4th) 198 (Ont. Gen. Div.).

As I view it, the object and purpose of these sections is to assist the administration of justice by enabling the constable or other properly designated person to go upon the premises indicated for the purpose of procuring things that will in some degree afford evidence of the commission of an alleged crime. *It is not necessary that the thing in itself should be evidence of the crime, but it must be something either taken by itself or in relation to other things, that could be reasonably believed to be evidence of the commission of the crime.* [emphasis by Moldaver J.]

[40] Applying that interpretation to the case at hand, I am satisfied that the information did contain reasonable grounds which could satisfy the issuing judge that the material sought would, *not taken by itself but in relation to other things,* afford evidence with respect to the commission of at least some of the specified offences.[41] [emphasis in original]

If the thing sought depends for its relevance on other evidence, of course, the Information to Obtain should set out the context within which the thing to be seized can be said to "afford evidence" of the offence under investigation. Where it is not obvious from the balance of the Information how the thing to be seized will help prove the case as alleged (as will sometimes be the case in investigations driven by uncommon or novel forensics or complex circumstantial evidence), that should be made clear, either from the officer's own knowledge and training or from other expert evidence appropriately referenced.

(h) "Information Concerning the Offence"

The expression "information concerning the offence" does not appear in s. 487. Indeed, prior to the addition of s. 487.01 of the *Criminal Code* in 1993, this expression was unknown to search and seizure law. Its inclusion in s. 487.01 signals a broader scope for the warrant, permitting techniques that do not directly afford evidence, but which nonetheless advance an investigation. It suggests a broader scope for investigative activity and invites the authorization of investigations that will permit the police to advance their cause without necessarily providing "evidence."[42] The language now appears in several other sections[43] but does not seem to have received any judicial consideration.

---

[41] Ibid., at p. 209 [C.R.], quoting from *Re Bell Telephone Co.* (1947), 89 C.C.C. 196, 4 C.R. 162 (Ont. H.C.) at p. 198 [C.C.C.].

[42] R. Pomerance, *"Criminal Code* Search Warrants: A Plea for a New Generic Warrant" 382–405 in D. Stuart et al., *Towards a Clear and Just Criminal Law: A Criminal Reports Forum* (Toronto: Carswell, 1999) at p. 405.

[43] Sections 83.28(4) re: order for investigative hearing into terrorism offence; 184.2(2) re: one-party consent interception of private communications; 487.092(1) re: impression warrant.

3. *Ex Parte* Nature of the Application

The normal process for the consideration of an application for search warrant (or other similar order) is *"ex parte,"* or with only one side present. There is no need for an explicit statement in the legislation creating the warrant power that application is to be made *ex parte* as such a procedure is implicit in the language of s. 487 and other warrant provisions by virtue of the nature of search warrant applications.[44]

It will sometimes occur, however, that counsel for the target of a proposed search will seek notice of an application with a view to getting standing before the judicial officer who is to consider the search warrant application. It is not unusual, for example, for an arrested accused in a sexual assault case to know that a DNA warrant application is coming, or for a media outlet to be aware from interviews with the police that a warrant will be sought. In such a case the proper approach for the officer seeking the warrant is to (a) alert prosecution counsel that counsel for the subject of the search has sought notice of the warrant application, (b) unless prosecution counsel indicates otherwise, inform counsel for the subject that the officer does not intend to give them notice of the application *but* will (c) bring the fact of their request to the attention of the judicial officer considering the application and include any correspondence or other documentation on the subject they wish to provide. In unusual cases the judicial officer considering the application may make a special order to permit the target of the search to attend and make submissions before any decision is made on the issuance of the warrant.[45]

4. Which Judicial Officer Is Authorized to Issue?

(a) Generally

There is no inherent or common law authority for any judicial officer to issue any form of judicial pre-authorization. Any power to issue a search warrant must therefore find its origin in some specific statutory provision. Each warrant-granting power identifies which judicial officers are authorized to grant the warrant in question. The first practical step in any warrant application is therefore to determine which judicial officers can provide the pre-authorization sought.

---

[44] *R. v. Canadian Broadcasting Corp.* (2001), 42 C.R. (5th) 290, [2001] O.J. No. 706 (Ont. C.A.) at p. 299 [C.R.], para. 29, leave to appeal refused (2001), 276 N.R. 398 (note), 154 O.A.C. 199 (note) (S.C.C.). On the implicit *ex parte* nature of search warrant applications, see also *R. v. Hurrell* (2002), 166 C.C.C. (3d) 343, 4 C.R. (6th) 169, [2002] O.J. No. 2819 (Ont. C.A.) at p. 355 [C.C.C.], para. 26, leave to appeal to S.C.C. abandoned (April 26, 2004) (S.C.C.).

[45] *R. v. F. (S.)* (2000), 141 C.C.C. (3d) 225, 32 C.R. (5th) 79 (Ont. C.A.).

In making this determination it is important to recall that federal and provincial legislation often provides that one class of judicial officers may enjoy the powers of another. For example, in most provinces the statute creating the office of "justice of the peace" provides that all provincial, superior and appeal court judges are also *ex officio* (by virtue of their office) justices of the peace.[46] Similarly, s. 2 of the *Criminal Code* provides that " 'justice' means a justice of the peace or a provincial court judge. . ."[47]

Superior court judges, however, are not necessarily vested with all the powers of provincial judges. Therefore, where a warrant by the terms of the creating legislation can be granted only by a "provincial judge" (and not a justice of the peace), there is no jurisdiction in a superior court judge to issue the warrant.[48]

There is, in general, a preference that warrant applications should be made to the most "junior" judicial officer legally authorized to entertain the application. Thus, for example, most s. 487 search warrant applications should be made to a justice of the peace. This preference is embodied in some informal practice directions that see provincial judges decline to entertain search warrant applications unless the Crown confirms that the particular application is appropriate for consideration by a judge (as opposed to a justice of the peace).

---

[46] In Ontario, the *Justices of the Peace Act*, R.S.O. 1990, c. J.4, s. 5, as amended by S.O. 2002, c. 18, s. 1(1), Sched. A, s. 11(13), provides:

> 5. Every judge of the Supreme Court of Canada, the Federal Court of Canada, the Court of Appeal, the Superior Court of Justice and every provincial judge is by virtue of his or her office a justice of the peace and also has power to do alone whatever two or more justices of the peace are authorized to do together.

See also similar provisions: British Columbia: *Provincial Court Act*, R.S.B.C. 1996, c. 379, s. 30(3); Alberta: *Provincial Court Act*, R.S.A. 2000, c. P-31, s. 9.2(d), as enacted by R.S.A. 2000, c. 16 (Supp.), s. 6; Quebec: re: superior court judges – *Courts of Justice Act*, R.S.Q. c. T-16, s. 70, as amended to S.Q. 1995, c. 42, s. 46 (Fr.); *Provincial Court Act*, R.S.N.B. 1973, c. P-21, s. 8(1), as amended by S.N.B. 1988, c. 36.

[47] *Criminal Code*, R.S.C. 1985, c. C-46, s. 2 "justice."

[48] This is the case for DNA warrants under s. 487.05 of the *Criminal Code* – they can only be issued by provincial court judges. The only exception for this would be if the provincial legislation creating the courts provided that judges of the superior court *ex officio* had the authority of a provincial judge.

(b) Ancillary Orders

Related orders, such as sealing orders,[49] assistance orders,[50] and extra-provincial execution endorsements,[51] are normally granted by the same judicial officer (or another member of the same judicial rank). Such orders – like any court order – must be based upon a proper factual foundation. That is, there must be evidence to demonstrate the preconditions for the making of the order requested. This will often be done under a separate heading in the Information to Obtain identifying the nature of the order sought and setting out the evidentiary basis for the request. For example, if the officer sought an assistance order, the Information to Obtain should include a heading such as "Assistance Order – Computer Experts" and then set out the needed expertise of the required assisting party, his or her willingness or unwillingness to assist and any terms or conditions that the warrant applicant would suggest to ensure fairness to the assisting party.

(c) Table of Judicial Officers

The following table sets out search warrant powers and the judicial officers authorized to grant them:

Warrant-Granting Power	Judicial Officers Authorized to Issue
Conventional Warrant (s. 487)	"justice"*
Authorization or Warrant to Enter Dwelling House (s. 529 and s. 529.1) ("*Feeney* Warrants")	"justice"*
Tracking Device Warrant (s. 492.1)	"justice"*
Number Recorder Warrant (s. 492.2)	"justice"*
Bodily Impression Warrant (s. 487.092)	"justice"*
Production Order (s. 487.012)[52]	"justice or judge"

---

[49] *Criminal Code*, s. 487.3.
[50] *Criminal Code*, s. 487.02.
[51] *Criminal Code*, s. 487(2) and s. 487.03.
[52] *Criminal Code*, s. 487.012, as enacted by S.C. 2004, c. 3, s. 7, in force September 15, 2004.

Warrant-Granting Power	Judicial Officers Authorized to Issue
Production Order (Financial or Commercial Information) (s. 487.013)[53]	"justice or judge"
Drink and Drive "Blood Warrant" (s. 256)	"justice"*
Firearms Warrants (s. 117.04)	"justice"*
CDSA[54] Warrant (s. 11)	"justice"*
DNA Warrant (s. 487.05)	"provincial court judge"**
General Warrant (s. 487.01)	provincial court judge; superior court judge; a judge as defined in s. 552
Consent Intercept of Private Communications (s. 184.2)	provincial court judge; superior court judge; a judge as defined in s. 552
Non-consent Intercept of Private Communications (s. 185)	superior court judge; a judge as defined in s. 552
Special Search Warrant (s. 462.32 – Proceeds of Crime)	a judge as defined in s. 552; superior court judge

* Includes provincial court judge by virtue of s. 2 of *Criminal Code* and most other judges by virtue of provincial justices of the peace legislation.

** It should be noted that superior court judges are not given *ex officio* status as provincial judges. As such, superior court judges are *not* authorized to issue DNA warrants.

5. Who Swears an "Information"?

It is the practice in many areas for counsel to commission the Information (i.e., have the informant swear or affirm the Information as an affidavit) before submission of the Information to Obtain to the justice of the peace or other judicial officer. Such an approach would certainly comply with the constitutional requirement that a warrant application be based on "sworn evidence." This process would be perfectly appropriate for any other form of application for relief in either criminal or civil proceedings.

There would, however, seem to be a basis to question whether this process complies with the technical requirements of the *Criminal Code*, at least with

---

[53] *Criminal Code*, s. 487.013, as enacted by S.C. 2004, c. 3, s. 7, in force September 15, 2004.

[54] *Controlled Drugs and Substances Act, supra*, note 37.

respect to the swearing of Informations to Obtain.[55] Some authorities take the view that the nature of an "Information" is different from that of a mere affidavit or statutory declaration. In *Re Magar,* Mr. Justice Fairgrieve suggested only a "justice" could commission an Information to Obtain:

> [2] Pursuant to s. 1(1) of the *Commissioners for Taking Affidavits Act,* R.S.O. 1990, c. C.17, a barrister and solicitor entitled to practise law in Ontario is a commissioner for taking affidavits in the province. In my opinion, however . . . I do not think it follows that [Crown counsel] has been authorized to swear such an information under the *Criminal Code.*
>
> [3] The *Criminal Code* appears to distinguish between affidavits, as referred to in s. 185(1), for example, and informations, as referred to in such provisions as s. 504, s. 487, and s. 487.01. Section 504, for example, provides that a person may lay "an information in writing and under oath before a justice". While the phrase "before a justice" could conceivably relate to the laying of the information rather than to the oath, it has been authoritatively held that an information must be sworn before a justice . . . .
>
> [4] The most obvious argument against this position would seem to be simply that administering an oath to an affiant or informant is an entirely administrative act, and that the significance of pledging one's oath should not vary according to the occupation of the person performing this administrative function. On the other hand, without wishing to denigrate the role of lawyers, it may be that the involvement of an independent judicial officer conveys a degree of solemnity and ensures appropriate compliance with the formalities of administering an oath . . . .
>
> [5] I appreciate as well that there may be some potential ambiguity in the use of the word "information", which can presumably describe either a document itself or simply data that might be recorded or repeated. The provision in s. 487.01(1)(a) that the judge be satisfied "by information on oath in writing" arguably imposes no requirements concerning the document or who is authorized to swear it, but I think that there are compelling reasons to conclude that Parliament intended a procedure consistent both with search warrant applications and with the specialized meaning that "information" has acquired elsewhere in the criminal law context.[56]

The textual argument is certainly more compelling for s. 487 warrants than for s. 487.01 or the other warrants.

---

[55] This process, while perhaps inconsistent with the interpretation of s. 487 provided by Justice Fairgrieve in *Re Magar,* 1998 CarswellOnt 2429 (Ont. Prov. Div.), as discussed below, would be sufficient for constitutional purposes because it is based on sworn evidence: see *Hunter v. Southam Inc., supra,* note 4.

[56] *Re Magar,* 1998 CarswellOnt 2429, [1998] O.J. No. 2495 (Ont. Prov. Div.) at paras. 2–5 per Fairgrieve Prov. J. As to other warrant provisions where there is no statutory form, but a reference to "information on oath," the same judge has indicated that no different approach is justified: *Re Magar,* 1998 CarswellOnt 3419, 56 C.R.R. (2d) 145, [1998] O.J. No. 3517 (Ont. Prov. Div.).

While there is certainly support for this conclusion in the text of the *Criminal Code*, it is, with respect, difficult to see what significant substantive advantage is obtained by inserting an unnecessary hurdle between the police and a possible warrant. No additional penalty would attach to a false Information sworn before a justice and the solemnity attached to attending before a justice to swear such an Information is, with respect, only marginally (if at all) greater than that associated with swearing before a commissioner for taking oaths.

6. Judicial Protocols

Many jurisdictions have put in place "protocols" of greater or lesser formality to ensure the orderly presentation of search warrant applications to justices and judges. Normally these protocols require the applying officer to seek out the "least senior" judicial officer legally authorized to issue the warrant in question (for example, a protocol will require all s. 487 warrant applications to be made to a justice of the peace in the absence of extraordinary considerations). Such administrative regimes, if properly structured, can provide a transparent and helpful method for the identification of where and how officers should seek warrants.[57]

The courts should take care, however, to preserve a degree of flexibility to recognize that no administrative protocol can anticipate every scenario. Protocols work best when they prescribe a general practice and at the same time permit case-by-case exceptions.

As well, such protocols or practices should not frustrate legitimate "rolled-up" applications which might require a more senior judicial officer to consider a package of judicial authorizations that includes a warrant that might otherwise have been issued by a less senior judicial officer.[58] Thus, for example, it should be possible for an officer to submit to a provincial judge an application for a s. 487 warrant in conjunction with a s. 487.01 general warrant on the basis of a single Information to Obtain even though a justice of the peace might have considered the s. 487 portion of the application.[59]

---

[57] See the Ontario protocol in the Appendix at the end of this chapter.

[58] In *Re Criminal Code*, [1997] O.J. No. 4393 (Ont. Gen. Div.) the Court approved of the practice of rolled-up applications including different forms of warrant authorizations.

[59] The need for balance in this area was captured nicely by Halderman Prov. J. of the Saskatchewan Provincial Court in *Re Application for a General Warrant pursuant to S. 487.01 of the Criminal Code*, 2002 CarswellSask 70, [2002] S.J. No. 54, 2002 SKPC 11 (Sask. Prov. Ct.):

> [26] In my view a judge has an obligation to deal with every application for a General or DNA warrant in a timely and serious fashion, and as quickly as judicial resources will allow. Additionally, it is not the function of the judge to expect or insist on a perfect Information, devoid of surplusage or niggling deficiency, nor to impose unreasonable or unnecessary procedural hoops through which busy police forces must jump.
>
> [27] It is not, on the other hand, appropriate for the warrant applicant to carelessly

One might also question the authority or propriety of a judicially created requirement that the police obtain the approval of all warrant applications from Crown counsel before submission. While this is likely a good policy for the police to adopt, the court should be slow to tell any party that they can only bring an application if it has been approved by another quasi-judicial officer (the Crown) or if they have sought legal advice first.

7. To Whom Is the Warrant Directed?

Prior to 1999, a s. 487 warrant could issue to anyone. The section was amended in that year to provide that a s. 487 warrant could only issue to:

> a peace officer or a public officer who has been appointed or designated to administer or enforce a federal or provincial law and whose duties include the enforcement of this Act or any other Act of Parliament and who is named in the warrant. . .[60]

This only requires the individual naming of the *public* officer: the warrant can continue to issue to "peace officers" generally or described by sub-class, such as the "peace officers in the province of Ontario."[61] In order to fall into the second category of officials responsible for the execution of s. 487 warrants, the designated executing party must be:

(i)   a public officer;[62]

(ii)   appointed or designated to administer or enforce a federal or provincial law;

(iii)   a person whose duties include the enforcement of the *Criminal Code* or any other federal statute; and

(iv)   personally named in the warrant.[63]

---

      put together an inadequate Information, in the expectation that the judge will do the legal legwork, point out the deficiencies, and ultimately authorize the warrant.

[60] S.C. 1999, c. 5, s. 16.

[61] *Re Den Hoy Gin*, 47 C.R. 89, 1965 CarswellOnt 19 (Ont. C.A.); *R. v. Benz* (1986), 27 C.C.C. (3d) 454, 51 C.R. (3d) 363 (Ont. C.A.).

[62] Section 2 of the *Criminal Code* provides that the term "public officer" includes

    (a) an officer of customs or excise,

    (b) an officer of the Canadian Forces,

    (c) an officer of the Royal Canadian Mounted Police, and

    (d) any officer while the officer is engaged in enforcing the laws of Canada relating to revenue, customs, excise, trade or navigation.

This is a non-exhaustive definition. The language of s. 487 obviously intends to include individuals not covered by this definition.

[63] Where a statute requires the naming of an individual in a warrant, the failure to do so is a significant defect: *R. v. Genest* (1989), 45 C.C.C. (3d) 385, 67 C.R. (3d) 224 (S.C.C.).

Where a civilian is required to assist in the execution of a warrant, the appropriate course is to seek an assistance order under s. 487.02. Such an order will authorize the participation of non-peace officers whose conduct might otherwise be a trespass (or other breach of the property or privacy rights of the target of the search).

Some warrant provisions specifically require the naming of the executing peace officers (or some of them). Even in these cases it is still permissible for the named officer to call upon others to assist him or her, provided the named officer remains responsible for the search activity of unnamed officials.[64]

8. Amending, Extending, Modifying Warrants after Issuance

Search warrants are court orders. Once made they cannot be altered or amended except by the court and then only in very limited circumstances. It is not open to an officer to amend even an obvious typographical error on a warrant that has issued. Even the issuing justice is limited in what can be done to "repair" a defective warrant that has issued. If a warrant is to be amended, any change must be justified by evidence that would have been sufficient to deal with issuance in the first place. In two cases, *Jamieson*[65] and *Sieger*,[66] the courts considered whether a justice could amend commonly requested changes – the date for execution or the address on a warrant – after the officer re-attended and orally explained why the change was needed. In both cases the amendments, even when made by the justice, rendered the warrant invalid.

The better course in any such case is to swear a new Information to Obtain which briefly explains why a new warrant (which incorporates the requested amendment) is required, and which appends as an exhibit the first warrant and Information to Obtain.

APPENDIX

In Toronto, the Ontario Court of Justice has implemented a protocol to be used whenever a warrant application is made to a provincial court judge.[67]

Ontario Court of Justice
Toronto Region

Protocol and Procedure for Obtaining General Warrants, DNA Warrants and Other Warrants Normally Issued By This Court

---

[64] *R. v. Fekete* (1985), 17 C.C.C. (3d) 188, 44 C.R. (3d) 92 (Ont. C.A.).

[65] *R. v. Jamieson* (1989), 48 C.C.C. (3d) 287, 1989 CarswellNS 293, [1989] N.S.J. No. 158 (N.S. C.A.).

[66] *Sieger v. R.* (1982), 65 C.C.C. (2d) 449, 27 C.R. (3d) 91 (B.C. S.C.).

[67] See also *Re Application for a General Warrant pursuant to S. 487.01 of the Criminal Code,* supra, note 59.

1. These guidelines apply to all warrant and wiretap applications made to a "provincial court judge".
2. All application materials are to be reviewed in advance by Crown counsel. An endorsement confirming such review must accompany every application. The Crown endorsement should include the date of the review and the name and telephone number of Crown counsel to contact with respect to the application.
3. Three copies of the application materials must be presented at the Judges' Office. These materials must include a sworn "Information to obtain" together with a draft warrant or Order.
4. The "Information to obtain" must be sworn *in advance*; this will usually allow the issuance of the warrant without the necessity of any attendance in chambers.
5. If it is necessary for Crown counsel to attend for the purpose of making submissions, such submissions must be based strictly on the sworn materials filed. If Crown counsel wish to appear on an application, an appointment may be made at the time that the material is left with the Judges' Office. In any event, the affiant, usually the officer seeking the warrant, should not attend in chambers.
6. These applications are always considered by the Court to be a high priority. If an application is particularly urgent, Crown counsel should note this on their endorsement and bring this to the attention of the Judges' Office so that consideration of the application can be expedited.
7. The Judges Office will advise the applicant as soon as the endorsed warrant is available for pick up. The warrant will be provided by the Judges' Office to the crown or police officer involved. The Court will retain the original Information to obtain together with a copy of the warrant.
8. When a sealing Order is made, a copy of the warrant and the Information to obtain will be placed in an envelope and sealed with the date and signature of the Judge together with an endorsement to the effect that "The contents herein are ordered sealed until further order of the Court". The Clerk of the Court will retain the sealed envelope.
9. A Judge who declines to issue a warrant will endorse the face of the Information accordingly and/or attach separate written reasons. All of the application materials will then be returned to the applicant.
10. If an application is refused, any subsequent applications must include a statement in the Information to obtain as to the fact of the prior refusal and a recitation or copy of the reasons for refusal.

September 5, 2000

4

General Drafting Approaches

1. Introduction

The task of actually preparing a search warrant application (the draft warrant and, more importantly, the Information to Obtain or supporting affidavit) can appear deceptively simple. While the law recognizes that such documents are prepared by police officers and not by counsel, this will not justify or excuse sloppy or misleading drafting.[1] Care should be taken to ensure that the document is clear, accurate, succinct and complete. Equally important is the fact that the Information or affidavit is, at least in part, an act of advocacy intended to persuade the judicial reader (first the issuing justice and later, possibly a reviewing court) that reasonable grounds exist. The document should be prepared with this in mind also.

2. Empirical Studies of Warrant Drafting

We know a little about how warrants are drafted and why they tend to be refused from some empirical studies in recent years. First, in a 1999 review of a sample of warrants from the Old City Hall Court House in Toronto, a superior court judge, a defence lawyer, and a Crown identified a number of facial validity concerns.[2] Other studies had identified similar concerns,[3] finding roughly 40 to 50% of the warrants that those studies considered turned out to be facially invalid.[4] But the 1999 study examined the reviewed warrant application materials to attempt to identify problem areas more precisely. It found, among other things, that:

---

[1] *Re Criminal Code* (1997), [1997] O.J. No. 4393 (Ont. Gen. Div.).

[2] S.C. Hill, S. Hutchison, L. Pringle, "Search Warrants: Protection or Illusion?" (1999) 28 C.R. (5th) 89–128.

[3] *Police Powers – Search and Seizure in Criminal Law Enforcement (Working Paper 30)*, Law Reform Commission of Canada (Ottawa: Queen's Printer, 1983) at pp. 84–85; S.C. Hill, "The Role of Fault in Section 24(2) of the *Charter*," c. 3, 57–74, in *The Charter's Impact on the Criminal Justice System*, J. Cameron, ed. (Toronto: Carswell, 1996) at pp. 69–74.

[4] "Facial invalidity" is a fatal flaw apparent from a review of the warrant application materials (as opposed to, for example, a flaw that only becomes apparent when one examines evidence or information not included in those materials).

- 35% of the warrants contained a substantive defect in the description of things to be seized (principally problems of vagueness, overbreadth and impermissible basket clauses).
- 20% of the warrants contained substantive defects in the description of the offence under investigation (providing no real identification of the trans-action, often simply indicating the offence-creating section of the *Criminal Code* and nothing more).
- The grounds for belief were wanting in a mix of situations – in 20% of the Informations to Obtain there were not grounds to believe the things to be seized were at the place to be searched. In 10% of the Informations there were insufficient grounds to believe the things to be seized would afford evidence, and in 10% of the cases there were no grounds to believe that an offence had been committed (there was overlap between these, partic-ularly in cases where the defect was with respect to an overall failure to source appropriate investigative resources).
- In 23% of the overall sample the warrants authorized night searches with-out the necessary grounds being shown.[5]

Looking beyond facial validity, the review suggested that almost 40% of the warrants examined had been prepared by police officers that lacked an appro-priate understanding of the demands of the warrant application process. While disappointing, these results are consistent with those found in earlier studies. These significant failings are troubling.

On another front, in 1997, the Ontario Court of Justice established a tele-warrant centre to provide a facility to consider warrant applications under s. 487.1 of the *Criminal Code*. As part of this effort the Court set out to collect statistical information related to the number of warrant applications received, the numbers granted and refused, and the reasons for those refusals. In the 360 weeks ending August 1, 2004, there had been 20,017 telewarrant applications, of which some 11,428 (or 57%) had been issued.[6] While the number of appli-cations may fluctuate from week to week, the refusal/issuance ratio has been relatively stable.

The reasons for refusal are instructive. The boldface entries note the more common reasons for refusals:

---

[5] Section 488 requires *Criminal Code* warrants to be executed by day (6 a.m. to 9 p.m.) unless specially endorsed. In most cases where there was a defect under this heading, no reason for the endorsement was apparent on the record and it may have been added by the issuing judicial officers on their own motions.

[6] I am once again grateful to Warren Dunlop, with the Program Development Branch of the Court Services Division of the Ministry of the Attorney General of Ontario for these statistics. It should be noted that in some cases a warrant subject to multiple refusals might appear more than once in the statistics. As well, a warrant might have been refused for multiple reasons and therefore might appear in more than one category in Table 1.

Table 1

Ontario Telewarrant Refusal Statistics After 360 Weeks (Ending August 1, 2004)		
Reason for Refusal	Total Since Inception	% Since Inception
Abandoned	162	2.0
Address discrepancies	103	1.2
Address not provided	32	0.4
Address obscure	67	0.8
Application for a general warrant	6	0.1
Application withdrawn	29	0.4
Conflicting information	62	0.8
Description of items - Too broad	63	0.8
Errors *Criminal Code*	37	0.4
Failure to follow telewarrant protocol	**383**	**4.6**
Format	6	0.1
Forms – improper	**668**	**8.1**
Forms – incomplete	**292**	**3.5**
General warrant	46	0.6
Illegible	12	0.1
Impracticability test not met 487.1(4)(a)	**315**	**3.8**
Incomplete transmission	126	1.5
Incorrect statement on Information	15	0.2
Informant's name missing	8	0.1
Information illegible	7	0.1
Information not signed	**827**	**10.0**
Information not sworn	44	0.5
Information unclear	72	0.9
Insufficient disclosure	190	2.3
Insufficient grounds	**2,285**	**27.7**
Invalid signature	9	0.1
Lack of credibility of Information	112	1.4

Ontario Telewarrant Refusal Statistics After 360 Weeks (Ending August 1, 2004)		
Reason for Refusal	Total Since Inception	% Since Inception
Lacking details	119	1.4
Location of search obscure	109	1.3
Missing appendix	108	1.3
Multiple search warrant – same application	21	0.3
Nexus (evidence not tied together)	58	0.7
Night-time grounds not met	**444**	**5.4**
No charge indicated	10	0.1
No date of offence	16	0.2
No endorsement	101	1.2
No evidence of indictable offence	43	0.5
No *Firearms Act* jurisdiction	8	0.1
No independent corroboration	149	1.8
No indication of items to be seized	16	0.2
No Information to Obtain	29	0.4
No jurisdiction	162	2.0
No oath statement	21	0.3
No offence stated on Information to Obtain	96	1.2
No person named	4	0.0
No *Provincial Offences Act* jurisdiction	8	0.1
No specific location	43	0.5
No statement of previous application	159	1.9
Not enough evidence	99	1.2
One application for two warrants	12	0.1
Prior knowledge	47	0.6
Reliability of Information	56	0.7
Section 103 Firearms Warrant request	2	0.0
Warrant incomplete	**175**	**2.1**
Warrant sought after the fact	47	0.6

Ontario Telewarrant Refusal Statistics After 360 Weeks (Ending August 1, 2004)		
Reason for Refusal	Total Since Inception	% Since Inception
Warrant to search not submitted	26	0.3
Wording discrepancies	156	1.9
TOTAL	8,248	100.0

Purely formal defects seem unacceptably common:

Information not signed	827	10.0
Failure to follow telewarrant protocol	383	4.6
Forms – improper	668	8.1
Forms – incomplete	292	3.5

Whatever debate there may be about the standard applied by the judicial officer considering a warrant, it is clear that if, for example, the Information to Obtain is not signed (fully 10% of the refusals, more than 630 applications) the judicial officer has no option but to refuse.

Interestingly, almost a third of the refusals (28%) were based on the conclusion by the justice of the peace that the Information to Obtain did not contain sufficient grounds to support the application. This statistic confirms the important role of judicial pre-authorization in controlling unreasonable searches. It also points out the need for officers to be better trained in the preparation of warrant applications.[7]

3. Falsehoods in an Information to Obtain

The *ex parte* nature of a warrant application requires scrupulous honesty and candour by the swearing officer. If an officer fails to disclose material information in an Information to Obtain, the reviewing court will consider this in assessing whether the balance of the remaining evidence meets the reason-

---

[7] In Ontario, in part in response to the empirical reviews noted above, the Ministry of the Attorney General and the Ministry of Public Safety (formerly the Ministry of the Solicitor General) had established a week-long course on warrant preparation ("Preparing Search Warrant Materials"), which was offered annually, for warrant writers around the province. The program was last offered in 2003.

able grounds standard.[8] Where, however, an officer has included a deliberate falsehood in respect of a material element of the case, the warrant is fatally tainted. To put it another way, the court will ask: after we take away the lies, and take into account that the affiant is a liar, what could really be left to support the warrant? Ultimately, "a search warrant must be quashed if it is shown that the police in applying for the warrant engaged in a deliberate deception . . . . "[9] with respect to a material fact bearing on the issuance of the warrant.

4. Using Precedents

Precedents, when used appropriately, can provide a warrant-drafter with a useful start to a warrant-writing project. But precedents can be as dangerous as they are helpful. The danger, of course, is that the precedent will take the place of the unavoidable hard work of thinking through each individual warrant application. The uncritical use of precedents assumes – often without any basis – that the drafter of the precedent document had some particular skill or insight. This is not necessarily the case.

A precedent can preserve and perpetuate *bad writing* just as effectively as it can good writing. Courts are quick to pick up on a warrant application that has mindlessly mimicked a precedent. Statements made by officers in such documents are now viewed with an element of scepticism – how much of this is correct, and how much is simply present as part of the officer's efforts to parrot the precedent?

The case of *R. v. Branton*[10] offers a helpful example of how excessive reliance on a precedent can lead a warrant applicant into error. In the case, the swearing officer used an earlier Information to Obtain as a "template" for his own. Unknown to the officer, however, the "template" Information to Obtain had been held to be defective in *two* earlier cases. As well, significant passages from the template had no relevance to the investigation at hand: the officer simply included them without assessing whether they were relevant to his case.

---

[8] *R. v. Monroe* (1997), 8 C.R. (5th) 324, 1997 CarswellBC 923 (B.C .C.A.). See also *R. v. Pratas* (2000), 133 O.A.C. 350, [2000] O.J. No. 2286 (Ont. C.A.), at pp. 351–352, leave to appeal refused (2001), 267 N.R. 198 (note), 147 O.A.C. 199 (note) (S.C.C.):

> [5] As the Supreme Court of Canada has held in *R. v. Bisson (J.) et autres* [*sub nom. Bisson v. Canada (Attorney General)*], [1994] 3 S.C.R. 1097; 173 N.R. 237; 65 Q.A.C. 241; 94 C.C.C. (3d) 94, even where material nondisclosure has been demonstrated, there is no per se rule that a search warrant must be quashed where the unaffected portions of the affidavit in support disclose reasonable grounds to sustain the issuance of the search warrant.

[9] *R. v. Kesselring* (2000), 145 C.C.C. (3d) 119, 74 C.R.R. (2d) 286, 2000 CarswellOnt 1413, [2000] O.J. No. 1436 (Ont. C.A.) at p. 127 [C.C.C.], para. 31. See also *R. v. Donaldson* (1990), 58 C.C.C. (3d) 294, 48 B.C.L.R. (2d) 273 (B.C. C.A.).

[10] *R. v. Branton* (2001), 154 C.C.C. (3d) 139, 44 C.R. (5th) 275 (Ont. C.A.).

This approach (the uncritical regurgitation of precedent material) was condemned by the Ontario Court of Appeal:

> [30] Language in a search warrant that is so careless, filled with inaccuracies, or reliance on ritualistic phrases that it masks the true state of affairs and deprives a judicial officer of the opportunity to fairly assess whether the requirements for the issuance of a warrant have been met strikes at the core of the administration of justice. . . .[11]

The use of precedents tempts the writer into using formulaic language that is not appropriate or justified in the context of his or her particular case. In *Sutherland,*[12] the Court considered the use of frequently repeated language relating to unnamed informers – language no doubt learned by rote by many officers through thoughtless repetition from precedent to precedent. Criticizing the practice of simply reciting such language rather than actually explaining to the issuing justice the particular circumstances of the case, the Court stated:

> [12] . . . The familiar words "proven reliable informant" were probably inserted because they were jargon – words that a Justice of the Peace is accustomed to seeing. When this is combined with [other defects in the warrant], the overall appearance is that truly important police work lay elsewhere. The suggestion is that warrants can be obtained by going through the motions. . . .[13]

Similarly, in *Araujo,*[14] Mr. Justice LeBel of the Supreme Court of Canada was deprecating in his condemnation of reliance on precedents or "boiler plate" language, saying:

> [47] . . . At best, the use of boiler-plate language adds extra verbiage and seldom anything of meaning; at worst, it has the potential to trick the reader into thinking that the affidavit means something that it does not. *Although the use of boiler-plate language will not automatically prevent a judge from issuing an authorization (there is, after all, no formal legal requirement to avoid it), I cannot stress enough that judges should deplore it. There is nothing wrong — and much right — with an affidavit that sets out the facts truthfully, fully, and plainly.* Counsel and police officers submitting materials to obtain wiretapping authorizations should not allow themselves to be led into the temptation of misleading the authorizing judge, either by the language used or strategic omissions.[15] [emphasis added]

---

[11] Ibid., at p. 153 [C.C.C.], citing *R. v. Hosie* (1996), 107 C.C.C. (3d) 385, 49 C.R. (4th) 1 (Ont. C.A.) at pp. 398–400 [C.C.C.].

[12] *R. v. Sutherland* (2000), 150 C.C.C. (3d) 231, 39 C.R. (5th) 310 (Ont. C.A.).

[13] Ibid., at pp. 237–238 [C.C.C.].

[14] *R. v. Araujo* (2000), 149 C.C.C. (3d) 449, 38 C.R. (5th) 307 (S.C.C.).

[15] Ibid., at p. 470 [C.C.C.]

The bottom line is that the appropriate use of precedents is limited to assisting the drafter to identify the issues to be addressed in the materials and suggesting – but not dictating – some of the ways of approaching those issues. The drafter must engage in a critical assessment of the precedent document. Contrary to the popular expression, the wheel must indeed be reinvented each time.

5. Avoiding Archaic or Legalistic Language

There is a temptation to use archaic or legalistic language which adds little or nothing to the quality of the warrant application. Such language is seen in some circles as carrying additional weight because of the official and elevated tone it suggests. Usually, however, this sort of writing involves officers attempting to capture the "flamboyance from another age."[16] Common examples include the warrant writer referring to himself or herself in the third person as "Your Informant" and the insistence on beginning each paragraph with the declarative "That. . . ." Some Informations conclude with obsolete and ornate prayers for relief ("Wherefore your Informant prayeth that a warrant may issue under your hand. . .") that are unnecessary. There are any number of other examples common to most bad writing (or certainly common to bad writing in the legal world).[17] This sort of prose rarely impresses anyone and is more likely to suggest to the reader that the document is deserving of a second look because of its out-of-date approach.

6. Avoiding the Passive Voice

Sentences can have "active" ("P.C. Smith found evidence") or "passive" ("evidence was found") structures. Using passive tenses – writing with a "passive voice" – may be appropriate in some writing, but it is almost never helpful in a warrant application. While this is technically a grammatical or stylistic point, it has potential legal ramifications. Writing in the passive voice makes it more likely that a warrant drafter will fail to properly source assertions in the Information to Obtain. It is not impossible to write a proper warrant application using the passive voice, but it is very difficult.[18]

In an active sentence it is clear who is doing what. The structure of an active sentence usually follows a basic construction:

---

[16] W. A. Bablitch, *Writing to Win*, The Compleat Lawyer (quoted in T. Perrin, *Better Writing for Lawyers* (Toronto: Law Society of Upper Canada, 1990) at p. 139).

[17] In his masterful book, *Better Writing for Lawyers*, *supra*, note 16, Tim Perrin offers up a compelling and helpful critique of this "old school" writing. Though written for lawyers, his book remains one of the best texts available to anyone who wishes to become a better writer.

[18] Most writing manuals and guides discourage the use of the passive voice in persuasive or legal writing. See, for example, C. Rooke, *A Grammar Booklet for Lawyers* (Toronto: Law Society of Upper Canada, 1991); R. D. Wydick, "Plain English for Lawyers" (1978) 66 Calif. L. Rev. 727.

Active Voice:
Someone [the subject] ***did some act*** [the action] ***to someone or something*** [the object].

This structure is the most common and natural form of expression, and lends itself to proper sourcing. Writing in the active voice makes proper sourcing easy:

Examples of Active Sentences:
1. P.C. Smith [subject] interviewed [action] the accountant [object].
2. The accountant [subject] explained [action] how the fraud worked [object].
3. P.C. Smith [subject] seized and reviewed [action] the documents [object].
4. The documents [subject] contained [action] the following statements . . . [object].

An Information to Obtain, indeed, any document that uses the active voice, will be "stronger, briefer, and clearer."[19] Whenever possible a warrant drafter should try to use the active voice.

The use of passive tenses or the passive voice reverses the natural structure of a sentence so that the thing acted upon appears at the beginning of the sentence:

Passive Voice:
Something [the object] ***had some act done to it*** [the action] ***by someone*** [the subject].

The passive voice tends to hide, or at least obscure, the source of information. Indeed, the passive voice is often used by writers or speakers who *wish* to be vague. There is a tendency to leave the subject of the sentence out or to have it implied. "Mistakes were made" (a favourite of politicians) is a good example. It is easy to say but does not identify who made the mistakes. The speaker's goal in using this structure is to discuss the mistakes without giving away who is responsible for them.

An Information to Obtain using the passive tense, which tends to imply rather than state the subject of the sentence, may not clearly convey the source of the information:

Examples of Passive Sentences:
1. The accountant [object] was interviewed [action]. (by whom?)
2. The fraud's operation [object] was explained [action]. (by whom?)
3. The documents [object] were seized and reviewed [action]. (by whom, how?)
4. False statements [object] were located [action]. (by whom?)

---

[19] R. D. Wydick, "Plain English for Lawyers," *supra*, note 18, at p. 747.

Good, direct writers avoid the passive voice. This does not mean that it can never be used. It can be used occasionally where the subject of the sentence can genuinely be inferred from the surrounding active text and where the object of the sentence is what the writer wants to emphasize:

> P.C. Smith reviewed the documents with the accountant. They examined them carefully. *False statements were found.*

The last sentence is clearly in the passive voice, but it is equally clear what the subject of the sentence was: P.C. Smith and the accountant are doing the finding. It is also an appropriate case for using the passive voice because what the writer wants to emphasize or highlight is the false statements found by Smith and the accountant.

There is nothing *per se* inadequate about the passive voice. However, it is very difficult to write a proper Information to Obtain using this form of language.

7. "Write (or Read) to the Section"

The first step in the preparation or review of a search warrant is the identification of the statutory authority for the warrant sought. Warrants are creatures of statute and their availability is limited to those situations described in the warrant provision authorizing the particular warrant. This will instruct as to which judicial officers can entertain an application for the particular warrant and will prescribe the standard for issuance and preconditions to be met by the application materials. A warrant writer or judicial officer considering a warrant should analyze the enabling statutory provision and identify the preconditions for issuance.

In Chapter 15, I have provided a number of checklists for most of the frequently used warrant provisions (and some statutory warrantless powers), which identify the basic procedural requirements, as well as the elements of a valid application.

(a) Standard for Issuance

The standard for issuance will ordinarily be easy enough to ascertain: it will be described as either "reasonable grounds to believe" or "reasonable grounds to suspect." The legal test used to determine whether a particular warrant meets the standard is discussed in Chapter 3.[20] A warrant application should be prepared and reviewed with the applicable standard and the "totality of the circumstances" test in mind.[21]

---

[20] See Chapter 3, heading 2, "Common Language and Its Meaning."
[21] *R. v. Debot* (1989), 52 C.C.C. (3d) 193, 73 C.R. (3d) 129 (S.C.C.).

(b) Preconditions

Identifying the preconditions or elements for a valid warrant application requires one to break down the authorizing statutory provision into discrete requirements or prerequisites. The easiest way to do this is to dissect the language of the section itself and draw up a checklist based on that language. The warrant application should hone in on the key issues that are of concern in respect of the particular species of warrant.

8. The "Rule Against Narrative"

There is a natural temptation on the part of every writer to tell a story and a desire in every reader to be told a tale. Narrative is the most natural way to present information. Warrant writers are not infrequently drawn into telling the tale of the crime they are investigating and in so doing end up neglecting their real purpose: explaining what evidence they have gathered to date to cause them to believe that evidence of the offence will be found by the use of the investigative technique for which they are seeking authority. A warrant application that simply sets out a narrative of the offence is fundamentally flawed. This is known as "the rule against narrative."

The "three questions approach" described below will ensure that a warrant application is prepared and reviewed in such a way that the temptation to narrate the offence (rather than summarize the investigation) is avoided or detected.

9. Telling the Story of the Investigation

The "rule against narrative" does not mean that all narrative is to be shunned. On the contrary: a savvy warrant applicant will often choose to structure his or her Information to Obtain as a narrative of the investigation to date. There are a number of advantages to telling the story of the investigation.

First, an Information to Obtain which tells the story of the investigation will necessarily be appropriately sourced. The process of investigating is the process of finding and scrutinizing sources of information and evidence. It necessarily parallels in many important respects the function of the warrant application. A narrative of the investigation is necessarily a source-based review of the evidence gathered to date.

Second, in complex or prolonged investigations involving multiple warrants sought at different times, the "story of the investigaton" structure facilitates an evolving Information to Obtain. As new steps are taken in the investigation they can be readily integrated into the earlier Information. This process is also complementary to most major case management regimes used by police agencies to organize large and complex investigations.[22]

10. The "Three Questions Approach" for the Warrant Writer and the Judicial Officer

Another technique to ensure that supporting materials have been prepared in a way that serves the central purpose of a search warrant application is to return to the three key questions that have to be addressed in any such application: First, **what does the officer know?** Second, **how does the officer know it?** And third, **why does it matter?** By repeatedly returning to these three questions the warrant applicant or judicial officer will be sure to address the important elements of the warrant. Warrant applicants and judicial officers should have these three questions running through their minds as they undertake their respective functions in the warrant process.

(a) What Does the Officer Know?

First and foremost the purpose of the Information to Obtain is to place before the judicial officer the evidence that the officer and his or her colleagues have gathered to date. This requires that the Information to Obtain set out in reasonable detail the information that has been amassed by investigators. What have police learned to cause them to believe that the investigative technique in question will provide them with evidence related to the offence they are inquiring into?

(b) How Does the Officer Know It?

It is not enough to summarize the information accumulated to date; the officer must take care to identify the *sources* of the material presented in the Information to Obtain, i.e., how did the officer come to possess the information in question? This involves the officer reciting the various investigative resources that have been identified, including witness interviews, physical evidence gathered, intelligence, criminal indices searches, surveillance, previous warranted or warrantless searches, wiretaps or other investigative techniques, as well as forensic or expert reports received.

In this sense, the officer must ask "Is this my knowledge or something I have been told?" If it is information provided by some other source, how does that source know? Each layer of hearsay is permitted, provided it is set out, until the root of the information is clear.

---

[22] For examples in Ontario, see the procedure mandated by the Ministry of Public Safety in *Ontario Major Case Management Manual*, Version 1.0 (11/2001).

(c) Why Does It Matter?

Often it will not be obvious to a judicial officer why information is signifi-cant. If there are factual links to be drawn either directly or by inference, these may be pointed out to the judicial officer. If a piece of evidence plays a significant role in a circumstantial case it is proper – indeed, preferable – for the warrant applicant to point out to the judicial officer how this item fits into the broader picture and the applicant's theory of the case.

11. Organizational Tips

Organization is key when approaching anything but the simplest of warrant applications. A well organized Information to Obtain is more likely to address the statutory preconditions for the order in question and, equally important, is more likely to convey the existence of such preconditions effectively. Further, a well organized Information to Obtain is easier to defend should a challenge arise in a subsequent prosecution or attack on the warrant.

A number of simple techniques can assist the search warrant applicant in preparing warrant materials that will effectively and efficiently present the officer's grounds for belief.

(a) Overview and Introduction

While an officer's task in preparing an Information to Obtain is to set out the evidence gathered to date to substantiate his or her belief, it is legitimate and indeed appropriate to also provide the officer's theory of the case and an introduction at an overview level. Such an introduction places the evidence in context and serves a function similar to the opening statement of the Crown to the jury: it is not evidence itself, but permits the reader to assimilate the evidence with a reasonable preview of what will be important and how the case fits together.

(b) Cast of Characters

In many cases officers will be obliged to present relatively complex factual situations involving numerous individuals, corporations, locations and agen-cies. For the drafting officer these names will often have been ingrained on his or her brain. For the reader being introduced to the case, however, it may not be such a simple matter to remember who plays which role. A list of the participants in the investigation and the offence, together with a short summary of their part in the play, can assist the reader in following even the most involved warrant application.

(c) Headings

Headings provide a useful guide for both the writer and the reader. They serve as a checklist for the warrant applicant and, if carefully prepared, ensure that the Information to Obtain speaks to each of the statutory preconditions for issuance.

For example, a simple Information to Obtain a conventional search warrant might include the following headings:

A. Introduction and Background
B. Cast of Characters and Locations
C. Grounds to Believe an Offence Has Been Committed
D. Grounds to Believe the Things to be Seized Will Afford Evidence of that Offence
E. Grounds to Believe that the Things to be Seized are at the Location to be Searched
F. Conclusion and Order Requested.

Beginning with these headings on the computer screen will force the drafter to turn his or her attention to each of the enumerated statutory preconditions (headings C, D and E) and will introduce those areas cleanly and explicitly for the judicial officer considering the application.

(d) Formatting and Paragraph/Page Numbering

Any persuasive document is improved by pleasant and consistent formatting. Search warrants that move inexplicably between fonts, change spacing and margins, or which use unconventional or haphazard formats, will inevitably appear hurried, unprofessional and unreliable. Judicial officers considering warrant applications cannot help but be unconsciously influenced by the appearance of a document, an influence that will operate both to the benefit and detriment of the application. While formatting cannot replace content, it is unrealistic to think that presentation might not make a difference in a warrant application that sits particularly close to the line.

Something as simple as the inclusion of paragraph and page numbering can increase the "ease of use" of a search warrant document. It permits the writer to provide easy references between different portions of the material. If the judicial officer wishes to ask questions prior to issuance,[23] it allows for the quick identification of whatever passage is of concern. Should the warrant be challenged later, numbering can make it easier for all users of the document to navigate through it. With the ease of paragraph and page numbering in even

---

[23] As to the best way to deal with such inquiries, see Chapter 2, under heading 3(b), "Practical Implications of the 'Neutrality' Requirement."

rudimentary word-processing software, there is no reason not to provide this benefit to readers of every warrant application.

(e) Using Exhibits and Appendices

While the drafter of search warrant materials is obliged to reduce, organize and summarize, it will not always be enough to simply distill the evidence: sometimes it will be appropriate to reproduce as an exhibit or appendix a piece of evidence (for instance, a photograph, a transcript of an interview, a key document in a transaction). It will be appropriate to include such evidence as an exhibit to the Information to Obtain if (a) describing evidence in the text of the warrant would be unnecessarily involved, (b) if the document included a potentially exculpatory interpretation that deserved to be placed before the judicial officer directly, or (c) if the exhibit simply makes the point more effectively than any textual summary of its contents could. Including an exhibit in a warrant application does not prevent the applicant from summarizing it and highlighting for the judicial officer the probative value the applicant says the exhibit has.

The latitude traditionally shown to warrant materials will normally permit any reasonably clear reference for inclusion of an exhibit. At a minimum the Information to Obtain should refer to the document, assign it some designation and indicate the source of the exhibit. For example, in a case involving a stock fraud an Information might adopt the language used in general affidavits and state, "Now shown to me and marked as 'Exhibit H' is a true copy of the offering prospectus issued to clients and provided to me by Joan Smith." Alternatively, the writer might simply say "I have attached a copy of the offering prospectus provided to me by Joan Smith and marked it as 'Exhibit 8.'"

There is, of course, no need to attach every document touching on the investigation (for example, one would not normally reproduce notes or transcripts of every interview). The key is to reproduce anything that cannot be safely or fairly summarized without risk of omission by the warrant applicant.

(f) Proofreading

Ideally, applications should be reviewed by a reader not familiar with the file before being submitted to the judicial officer. It will seem trite to seasoned warrant drafters to suggest that proofreading is an important stage in any warrant application. But a skilled writer always asks someone else to review any significant document to ensure its coherence and to make sure it reads well. Lawyers preparing important written arguments will usually have colleagues go over the materials looking for substantive and cosmetic points that invite suggestions for improvement. A second set of eyes will invariably identify aspects that may be readily repaired before the document is submitted to the judicial officer.

As well, most current word-processing software is quite willing to step in and check the spelling and basic grammar for writers who may be less confident in these areas, although such programs cannot detect, for example, improper usage. There is simply no reason for a warrant application to be submitted with spelling or basic grammatical errors. Documents with such errors, even if substantively adequate, leave the reader wondering if the author takes the task seriously. A warrant writer who is careless in this regard "digs a deep hole" for himself or herself, and for the Crown later, should the warrant be challenged.

12. A Word About Pre-Printed Forms[24]

Before the widespread use of computers, pre-printed forms issued by a government agency or the police agency provided a helpful tool for officers preparing search warrant applications. With the arrival of computers and word processing, however, pre-printed forms have become far less common.

There are several dangers involved in using pre-printed forms. First, with the pace of development in the law, pre-printed forms can become out of date. Judicial decisions identifying defects in the language of a form do not always reach the desk of those responsible for stocking the stationery stores at a police agency.[25] Second, the pre-printed forms can themselves be unintentionally deceiving. For example, the pre-printed form for a s. 487 Information to Obtain used in Ontario leaves only a small space (about two centimetres) for the statement of the officer's "Grounds for Belief." Pre-printed forms can also lead officers into error. In *Colbourne*,[26] an officer inexperienced in the preparation of search warrant applications used a pre-printed form without any appendices:

> [23] . . . He used a pre-printed form and was unaware of the practice of attaching appendices to the pre-printed form which, among other things, set out the inform-ant's reasonable and probable grounds for believing that the material to be seized would afford evidence of the commission of a criminal offence. [The officer] put his grounds for believing that the appellant's blood could afford evidence of the commission of a crime in the one-inch space provided in the pre-printed form.[27]

The universal practice is to use an appendix to set out the grounds. Even in recent years, however, it happens from time to time that an officer takes this

---

[24] See also the discussion above in Chapter 3, under heading 2(c), " 'Information on Oath *In Writing*': The Form and the Four Corners Rule."

[25] See *R. v. Branton, supra*, note 10.

[26] *R. v. Colbourne* (2001), 157 C.C.C. (3d) 273, 2001 CarswellOnt 3337, [2001] O.J. No. 3620 (Ont. C.A.).

[27] Ibid., at p. 282 [C.C.C.].

to mean that it should be possible for him or her to set out all the grounds in such a small space.[28]

In *Branton*, mentioned above, the Court noted that the pre-printed form used by the officer was defective on its face, purporting to authorize the search and seizure of:

> [35] . . . "[T]hings . . . that are being sought as evidence in respect of the commission, *suspected commission or intended commission* of an offence against the *Radiocommunication Act* . . ." [emphasis added] The warrant was issued pursuant to s. 487(1)(*b*) of the *Criminal Code*. That section limits a search to "evidence with respect to the commission of an offence". In authorizing a search for evidence of the "suspected or intended commission" of an offence, the warrants exceeded the authority prescribed in s. 487.[29] [emphasis in *Branton*]

---

[28] Difficult as it may be to believe, as recently as 1996 officers were claiming that they did not appreciate that an Information to Obtain could require more than a few lines to set out their grounds. See *R. v. Colbourne*, *supra*, note 26.

[29] *R. v. Branton*, *supra*, note 10, at p. 156 [C.C.C.].

5

Describing the Things to be Searched for and Seized

1. Introduction – The "Fellow Officer Test"

While the Information to Obtain and the warrant are usually prepared and considered as a package, it is important to keep in mind that a search warrant is intended to be a free-standing judicial order that must be able to exist independently of the Information. It must be sufficiently specific that a person having reference only to the warrant will know what actions *are* and, of equal importance, what actions *are not*, authorized. The face of the warrant must therefore describe the things to be seized with sufficient particularity that:

    (i)   the issuing judicial officer,
    (ii) the executing officers,
    (iii) the subject of the search, and
    (iv) any reviewing court

will all be able to determine whether the things to be seized (or investigative steps taken) were, or were not, within the scope of the warrant. Simply put, the warrant, as a judicial order, must be prepared in such a way that the maker of the order – the issuing justice – does not simply delegate his or her discretion to the executing officer. The warrant cannot be prepared in such a way as to leave it completely to the executing officer to determine what should or should not be seized.[1]

It should be remembered that the justice is authorizing a specific search for specific things; a reasonably specific description of the investigative action authorized is an important part of the constitutional protection mandated by *Charter* s. 8 and the *Hunter*[2] standards. The warrant will authorize a search for the things identified in it and the taking of those things once they are found. The scope or intrusiveness of the search and validity of any consequent seizure

---

[1] *Shumiatcher v. Saskatchewan (Attorney General) (No. 2)* (1960), 129 C.C.C. 270, 34 C.R. 154 (Sask. Q.B.); *R. v. Solloway Mills & Co.*, 53 C.C.C. 261, [1930] 1 W.W.R. 779 (Alta. C.A.).
[2] *Hunter v. Southam Inc.* (1984), 14 C.C.C. (3d) 97, 41 C.R. (3d) 97 (S.C.C.).

will be measured against the description of the things to be seized. It is essential, therefore, that the warrant set out, in a fashion appropriate to the search activity authorized, what is to be seized.

The substance of this requirement is usually captured in the so-called "fellow officer test." This yardstick offers a convenient and relatively easy-to-apply standard that permits the officer to quickly test whether a draft warrant meets this facial threshold. The test asks:

> Would another police officer unfamiliar with the rest of the investigation be able to execute the warrant without reference to the Information to Obtain or other material? Would such an officer know from the warrant (and nothing else) what to seize, and what to leave behind?

If the question can be answered in the affirmative, this element of the warrant is facially valid.

2. Limit on "Things" That May be Seized

It is important to ensure that the warrant being issued is legally capable of authorizing the investigative step that is anticipated. Section 487, the most commonly invoked of the search powers, provides the authority for the issuance of conventional search warrants. The section[3] limits such warrants to cases where the officer seeks to seize:

(a) *anything* on or in respect of which any offence against [the *Criminal Code* or other federal law] has been or is suspected to have been committed,

(b) *anything* that there are reasonable grounds to believe will afford evidence with respect to the commission of an offence, or will reveal the whereabouts of a person who is believed to have committed an offence, against [the *Criminal Code* or other federal law],

(c) *anything* that there are reasonable grounds to believe is intended to be used for the purpose of committing any offence against the person for which a person may be arrested without warrant, or

(c.1) any offence-related property,[4] . . . [emphasis added]

---

[3] Section 487(1)(a)–(c.1) (s. 487 as amended to S.C. 1999, c. 5, s. 16).

[4] "Offence-related property," as amended to S.C. 2001, c. 32, s. 1, is defined in s. 2 to mean "any property, within or outside Canada,

(a) by means or in respect of which an indictable offence under [the *Criminal Code*] is committed,

(b) that is used in any manner in connection with the commission of an indictable offence under [the *Criminal Code*], or

(c) that is intended for use for the purpose of committing an indictable offence under [the *Criminal Code*.] . . . ."

The "anything" requirement limits these warrants to seizure of things having a physical existence at the time of the warrant's issuance. A s. 487 warrant cannot issue to authorize the seizure of "intangibles."[5] (This does *not* mean that no form of judicial authorization is available for such investigative techniques. Section 487.01 – the general warrant provision – is available to authorize such "intangible search/seizures" as a technique not authorized elsewhere which would otherwise be a breach of s. 8.)

Similarly, a person cannot be "seized" pursuant to this section. A person is not "anything"[6] (nor, for that matter, is a person a "building, receptacle or place"[7]).

This limitation on the "things to be searched for" under a *Criminal Code* s. 487 warrant has been held not to authorize a search for or seizure of "intangible" things. Thus one cannot obtain a s. 487 warrant to take videotaped images of persons in a place where they have a reasonable expectation of privacy. Nor can one obtain a warrant to seize incorporeal property, such as funds in a bank account.[8] Similarly, prior to the enactment of s. 487(2.1),[9] one could not use a s. 487 warrant to authorize the copying of computer records or the inspection or review of computerized files. If officers wanted to seize such material, the appropriate course then was to seize the hardware related to the record or program needed to advance their investigation. With the addition of s. 487(2.1) it is now possible to engage in copying or review of computer files.

There is some uncertainty as to whether fixtures (things attached to real property like doors and windows) can be seized under such a warrant, even if named. An early case, the 1938 decision in *R. v. Munn*,[10] suggested that such articles, technically real property, could not be seized because, as real property, they were not "anything" (a term denoting personal property). In a slightly more recent case, *R. v. Spitzer*,[11] the Court held that a warrant could authorize the removal and seizure of such articles provided the Information to Obtain properly identified such things and set out the necessary grounds to demonstrate the basis for such seizure.

---

[5] *Quebec (Attorney General) v. Royal Bank* (1985), 18 C.C.C. (3d) 98, 44 C.R. (3d) 387 (Que. C.A.), leave to appeal refused (1985), 18 C.C.C. (3d) 98n, 59 N.R. 239n (S.C.C.) holding that a s. 487 warrant could not authorize the seizure of "intangibles" such as a credit balance in a bank account.

[6] See C. Hill, S. Hutchison & L. Pringle, "Search Warrants: Protection or Illusion?" (1999) 28 C.R. (5th) 89–128, at p. 93.

[7] *Laporte v. R.* (1972), 8 C.C.C. (2d) 343, 18 C.R.N.S. 357 (Que. Q.B.).

[8] *R. v. Wong* (1987), 34 C.C.C. (3d) 51, 56 C.R. (3d) 352 (Ont. C.A.), affirmed (1990), 60 C.C.C. (3d) 460, 1 C.R. (4th) 1 (S.C.C.) (videos); *Quebec (Attorney General) v. Royal Bank, supra,* note 5 (incorporeal property).

[9] S.C. 1997, c. 18, s. 41.

[10] *R. v. Munn* (1938), 71 C.C.C. 139, 13 M.P.R. 181 (P.E.I. S.C.).

[11] *R. v. Spitzer* (1984), 15 C.C.C. (3d) 98, 36 Sask. R. 146 (Sask. Q.B.).

Offence-related property, a new class of seizable things which was added in 1997, is defined in s. 2 of the *Criminal Code*.[12]

3. Describing Classes of Things

(a) Generally

In *R. v. Church of Scientology (No. 6)*,[13] the Ontario Court of Appeal considered the issue of class descriptions at some length. In this case the warrant described broad classes of documents and things for seizure in relation to times and persons. The subjects of the seizure (the church and certain individuals) argued that the class descriptions were overbroad and that they therefore failed to meet the *Hunter* standard of a specific pre-authorization. Rejecting these complaints the Court emphasized the need to assess each warrant, and each description of things to be seized, in the context of the particular circumstances of the case.[14] This approach found support in a number of cases, including *R. v. Print Three Inc.*[15] In *Print Three*, MacKinnon A.C.J.O. had observed:

> The warrants describe distinct categories of items to be searched for depending on the specific company or individual; they are restricted to specific years; the descriptions conclude with the words "relating to or necessary for the determination of taxable income and tax payable . . ." for specific years. As counsel for the Attorney General pointed out, because of the extent and complexity of business affairs made possible by modern technology and merchandising methods, it is impossible to define with exact precision the documents sought in cases involving fraud or tax evasion. Zuber, J.A. pointed out in *Re Lubell and The Queen* (1973), 11 C.C.C. (2d) 188 at p. 189:

>> The second ground upon which it is moved to quash both search warrants is that the materials sought to be found at the premises are too vaguely described. I think one has to remember that at this stage the authorities are still at an investigative stage in their procedure and by virtue of that fact are likely not able to name the things for which they are looking with precision. A search warrant is not intended to be a *carte blanche*, but at the same time the applicants must be afforded a reasonable latitude in describing the things that they have reasonable ground to believe they might find.

---

[12] See note 4, *supra*.

[13] *R. v. Church of Scientology (No. 6)* (1987), 31 C.C.C. (3d) 449, 30 C.R.R. 238 (Ont. C.A.), leave to appeal refused [1987] 1 S.C.R. vii, 33 C.R.R. 384 (note) (S.C.C.).

[14] Ibid., at p. 510 [C.C.C.].

[15] *R. v. Print Three Inc.* (1985), 20 C.C.C. (3d) 392, 47 C.R. (3d) 91 (Ont. C.A.), leave to appeal refused 18 C.R.R. 192 (note), [1985] S.C.R. x (S.C.C.).

In our view, having regard to the nature of the offence, there is sufficient specificity and particularity in the warrants, and they do not, in that regard, breach s. 8 of the Charter. Any necessary inferences could be properly drawn by the justice of the peace from the informations and there was no jurisdictional error that would warrant *certiorari*.[16]

The passage from *Lubell*[17] (quoted by the Court of Appeal above) emphasizes another important point: the warrant is an investigative tool and as such the application of forms of analysis designed for other circumstances may not be appropriate.

The following are cases where the manner in which the things were to be seized was attacked on review and held to be satisfactory:[18]

• *Worrall*:
"... oil paintings, records and documents of all descriptions, art books, artists' supplies, paints and restoration materials, and correspondence ..."[19]

• *Pink Triangle Press*:[20]
corporate records, invoices and documents pertaining to the business operations of a publication known as Body Policies.

• *Thames Valley*:[21]
books of account, financial statements, tax files, bank documents, cancelled cheques, deposit slips, payroll records, telephone and utility bills, purchase and sales records, vehicle maintenance and expense records, expense vouchers and receipts and correspondence relating to Thames Valley Ambulance Limited and Thames Valley Medic-Aid Limited between January 1, 1978, and December 31, 1979.

---

[16] Ibid., at pp. 397–398 [C.C.C].

[17] *Lubell v. R.* (1973), 11 C.C.C. (2d) 188 (Ont. H.C.) at p. 189, quoted in the passage from *Print Three*. It should be noted that the Court in *Scientology, supra*, note 13, at p. 511 [C.C.C.] commented of this passage: "We note in passing that the last line in the passage quoted from *Lubell* probably should read: " '... things that they have reasonable grounds to believe they *will* find' rather than 'they *might* find'." [emphasis in *Scientology*]

[18] It must be noted that, as in all issues surrounding the issuance of warrants, the particular circumstances of the case must be considered; language adequate in one set of circumstances may be deficient in another.

[19] *Re Worrall* (1964), [1965] 2 C.C.C. 1, 44 C.R. 151 (Ont. C.A.) at p. 16 [C.C.C.], leave to appeal refused [1965] S.C.R. ix (S.C.C.).

[20] *R. v. Pink Triangle Press* (1978), 2 W.C.B. 228 (Ont. H.C.), affirmed (April 14, 1978) (Ont. C.A.), leave to appeal to S.C.C. refused (June 5, 1978).

[21] *R. v. Thames Valley* (May 8, 1980), Reid J. (Ont. S.C.).

- *Lubell*:[22]
  financial records, cheques, statements of account and similar financial documents for Moviematic Limited and/or Peter Joseph Santangelo.

  all company records, minute books, financial statements, books of account, ledgers, journals and correspondence relative to Federal Periodicals, Capital Distributing Company Ltd. and A.B.C. News.

- *Times Square Book Store*:[23]
  The Magazine Mistress Magenta's Phonebook, No. 1, and other similar obscene material located in the area for the display of "adult" magazines and which has covers depicting obscene acts similar to those portrayed in the named magazine.

For an example of a deficient description of things to be seized, consider the *Harris* case.[24] There investigators identified the things to be seized, in the following terms:

- Obscene video tapes, TABOO, TIGRESS and other obscene video cassette tapes; and
- Any business documents relating to the sale, purchase, or rental of the video cassettes to be seized; and
- Any monies relating to the sale, purchase, or rental of the video cassette tapes to be seized; and
- Any documents that link the employees to the company; and
- Any documents that indicate who the owners or operators of the company are; and
- Any other thing that may assist in the prosecution of the offence.

The first group of things to be seized was isolated by the Court of Appeal as deficient because it offered no real limits on what was to be seized and, in effect, delegated to the searchers the task of deciding whether an offence had been committed (i.e., whether the tapes were obscene). The problematic language in the balance of the bullet points is self-evident.[25]

[22] *Lubell v. R.*, *supra*, note 17.
[23] *Re Times Square Book Store* (1985), 21 C.C.C. (3d) 503, 48 C.R. (3d) 132 (Ont. C.A.).
[24] *R. v. Harris* (1987), 35 C.C.C. (3d) 1, 57 C.R. (3d) 356 (Ont. C.A.), leave to appeal refused (1987), 38 C.C.C. (3d) vi, 61 C.R. (3d) xxix (S.C.C.).
[25] In *Re Times Square Book Store*, *supra*, note 23, the Ontario Court of Appeal observed at pp. 511–512 [C.C.C.]:

> In this country, as in the United States, a warrant should be reasonably specific in the description of a book or magazine that is to be seized because of the concepts it expresses. However, I am in general agreement with the conclusion reached by the minority in *Guarino*, *supra*, as to the validity of a warrant describing a named magazine

In complex cases necessitating intensive documentary reviews, it will be, almost by definition, difficult if not impossible to describe with complete precision the things sought by investigators. However, even though broad or potentially broad classes of things might be described as the things to be seized, it is important that the Information to Obtain speak to the entire class of things to be seized. In cases where the Information, though otherwise sufficient, fails to provide grounds to believe that everything reasonably falling into the class described is subject to seizure on the *Hunter* standard, the warrant may be quashed, or the offending, unsupported portion quashed.[26]

(b) "Basket Clauses"

A "basket clause" is, when used properly, a legitimate description of a group or class of things to be seized. It is an acceptable practice that is perfectly consistent with the constitutional and statutory limits on warranted searches. The use of proper descriptions of classes of documents permits the applicant and issuing justice to "categorize in a summary fashion" the things to be seized.[27]

There is a temptation, however, to fall into what have been called "scoop shovel methods"[28] in which the officer seeks authority to seize everything with a view to sorting it out later. This clearly is not permissible.[29]

---

and other similar obscene material. I would add the proviso that the "other similar obscene material" should be further identified by their location in the store and by describing their covers as depicting obscene acts similar to those portrayed in the named magazine.

[26] *R. v. B. (J.E.)* (1989), 52 C.C.C. (3d) 224, 94 N.S.R. (2d) 312 (N.S. C.A.).

[27] *Dare To Be Great of Canada (1971) Ltd. v. Alberta (Attorney General)*, 6 C.C.C. (2d) 408, [1972] 3 W.W.R. 307 (Alta. T.D.) at p. 414 [C.C.C.].

[28] Ibid., at p. 411 [C.C.C.].

[29] In *R. v. Church of Scientology (No. 6)* (1985), 21 C.C.C. (3d) 147, 15 C.R.R. 23 (Ont. H.C.) at pp. 177–178 [C.C.C.], affirmed (1987), 31 C.C.C. (3d) 449, 30 C.R.R. 238 (Ont. C.A.) (leave to appeal refused at [1987] 1 S.C.R. vii, 33 C.R.R. 384 (note) (S.C.C.)), Osler J. observed that some balance had to be struck between precision in description and execution on the one side and reasonable expedition in the carrying out of the warrant's mandate:

I wish to add one word regarding the "search then seize", not "seize then search" argument. I have stated that the seizure resulted in the removal of something like 2,000,000 documents, or individual pages. The search was perforce carried out by a number of people, channelling thousands of documents through some six supervisory officers. It occupied little more than 20 hours' time. Quite obviously, no detailed analysis of the searched material could be made under those circumstances in such a way as to afford the officers complete certainty that what they were seizing came within the authorized description. Indeed, partly due to the exigencies of these and related proceedings, I am told that the analysis of the material is not yet complete.

The result was that approximately 30% of the entire contents of the Scientology office was removed. Their inability to retain this material quite obviously might cause grave difficulty to the occupants of the office in carrying on their daily legitimate

The authorities accept[30] that "basket clauses" can be used to capture a group or class of documents or things to be seized so long as:

- *First,* the "basket" is written in such a way that a reasonable person, unfamiliar with the investigation or the Information to Obtain, would be able to identify what things were included in the "basket" and what were excluded; *and*

- *Second,* the Information to Obtain sets out the reasonable grounds to believe that all the things falling within the "basket" meet the standard for seizure (i.e., that they will afford evidence of the offence under investigation).

(i) *Legitimate Basket Clauses*

As noted, a legitimate basket clause must reasonably define what things are authorized for seizure under the warrant. There is no "magic formula" for such clauses. Normally, however, a legitimate basket clause will identify examples of the class of things to be covered by the clause, and then authorize seizure of "similar documents [or things]" and attempt to put some parameters around the class. For example:

> Cheques, money orders, bills of exchange, electronic funds transfer confirmations, promissory notes, and other similar documents and instruments drawn, executed or negotiated between June 1, 2004, and June 30, 2004, by any of John Smith, Jane Smith, Bill Jones, and/or Wendy Jones.

This involves the initial examples of the sorts of documents making up the class: *"Cheques, money orders, bills of exchange, electronic funds transfer confirmations, promissory notes,"* followed by a description of the class by reference to the examples: *"and other similar documents and instruments,"* together with an appropriate bracketing of the class by reference to a time period and to the transactions or individuals involved (*"drawn, executed or*

---

activities. On the other hand, the continued presence for days, weeks and possibly even months of a large number of searchers in the office would cause even greater disruption.

Provided that the seizing body, the Ontario Provincial Police, act in good faith and continue to set aside for return to the applicants that material that is found, on more careful examination, not to be included within the things authorized by reason of the fact that it will not afford evidence, I am satisfied that the rule of search first and then seize has been and is being followed as well as it reasonably can be in the circumstances.

[30] *R. v. Church of Scientology (No. 6), supra,* note 29; *Dare To Be Great of Canada (1971) Ltd. v. Alberta (Attorney General), supra,* note 27; *R. v. Marlboro Manufacturing Ltd.,* 16 C.R.N.S. 338, [1971] 5 W.W.R. 534 (Man. Q.B.).

negotiated between June 1, 2004, and June 30, 2004, by any of John Smith," etc.).

(ii) *Unacceptable Basket Clauses*

An unacceptable basket clause is open-ended or vague in a way that allows the officer to seize things without meaningful judicial control.[31] Notwithstanding a number of judicial pronouncements on this point a recent study found a number of indefensible basket clauses including:

> "any other pertinent items"
> "any property that may have been left behind by the culprits"
> "any other related paraphernalia"
> "any other pertinent documents/records relating to this address"
> "and any other relevant item which may afford evidence to the offence of possession for the purpose."[32]

These clauses amount to open-ended authorizations to seize without meaningful judicial control.

It should be noted that most of these unconstitutional basket clauses were probably unnecessary in light of s. 489 and the broad plain view powers given to officers executing search warrants or otherwise acting in the course of their duties.[33]

(iii) *Setting Parameters*

One relatively easy way to ensure that a "basket clause" is properly limited is to set parameters for the scope of the basket. This is readily done in the context of financial or documentary searches. In such cases a basket clause will routinely be limited by reference to:

---

[31] *R. v. PSI Mind Development Institute Ltd.* (1977), 37 C.C.C. (2d) 263 (Ont. H.C.).

[32] Hill, Hutchison & Pringle, "Search Warrants: Protection or Illusion?", *supra*, note 6, at p. 92.

[33] Section 489 provides statutory authority confirming the common law power of everyone who executes a warrant or any peace officer, and every public officer who is lawfully present in a place (pursuant to a warrant or otherwise in the execution of duties) to seize without warrant any thing that they believe on reasonable grounds:

> (a) has been obtained by the commission of an offence against this or any other Act of Parliament;
>
> (b) has been used in the commission of an offence against this or any other Act of Parliament; or
>
> (c) will afford evidence in respect of an offence against this or any other Act of Parliament. [as amended to S.C. 1997, c. 18, s. 48]

This would seem to serve as a kind of statutory "basket clause" that permits seizures, provided the officer can justify to a "reasonable grounds to believe" standard his or her conclusion that the thing seized was evidence or obtained by an offence.

- *Dates* (from earliest relevant date, to latest, perhaps even the date the warrant was issued);
- *Parties* (which companies and individuals are implicated in the affairs giving rise to the warrant such that documents involving them might be seized); and
- *Transactions* (are there particular transactions that might be identified so that any document touching on that transaction is relevant to the inquiry at hand).

When assessing the parameters imposed on a search of documents especially, the words of *Lubell* are helpful:

> The second ground upon which it is moved to quash both search warrants is that the materials sought to be found at the premises are too vaguely described. I think one has to remember that at this stage the authorities are still at an investigative stage in their procedure and by virtue of that fact are likely not able to name the things for which they are looking with precision. A search warrant is not intended to be a *carte blanche*, but at the same time the applicants must be afforded a reasonable latitude in describing the things that they have reasonable ground to believe they might find. In both instances the documents have been described with reasonable particularity. In the case of the information of Mitchell, the documents are described as "company records, Minute Books, Financial Statements, Books of Account" and so forth which gives a fairly accurate delineation of the class of documents that are being sought and, secondly, they are ascribed to three businesses, Federal Periodicals, Capital Distributing Co. (Canada) Ltd. and A.B.C. News, so obviously the police are not entitled to go into the office of this accountant and look for things blindly. They are confined in the case of the search warrant founded on the Mitchell information to a certain class of documents and further restricted to three of the apparent clients of Mr. Lubell. The same things can be said of the warrant founded on the information of Murden. Again the class of documents is spelled out with reasonable particularity and those that are attributable to Moviematic Limited and Peter Joseph Santangelo, so again there is reasonable particularity ascribed to the things that the police are seeking.[34]

In *PSI Mind Development Institute*, the Court condemned an open-ended basket clause while accepting that the description of the things to be seized was otherwise acceptable:

> The second main issue is the sufficiency of the particulars describing the things to be seized. The objection is substantially that the words "and other materials of every nature" are too vague, general and a "basket or catch-all" term of description. Such wording of the search warrants demonstrated that the police officers were

---

[34] *Lubell v. R., supra*, note 17, at p. 189.

seeking evidence to establish an alleged offence but could not more specifically describe the things that would be such evidence until they had made the searches. In the case of *Re Lubell and The Queen* (1973), 11 C.C.C. (2d) 188 at p. 189, Zuber, J., stated that:

> A search warrant is not intended to be a *carte blanche*, but at the same time the applicants must be afforded a reasonable latitude in describing the things they have reasonable ground to believe they might find.

That is, the items to be searched for — particularly where there are many documents referring to various individuals and money transactions — need not be described in the warrants "with precision". . . . Accordingly, the principal group of specified "things" in the warrant may stand.

It was submitted that the description of the things to be seized unduly left to the discretion of the peace officers conducting the search the determination of those things which in their opinion and judgment should be seized. This objection only applied to the apparently offending words "and other materials of every nature" and to that extent I am in agreement. In *Re Laborde and The Queen* . . . ; it was held that the words "and others" were [too] indefinite for a peace officer to act upon and were severable and accordingly that part of the search warrant was quashed. . . .[35]

Similarly, in *Scientology*, the description of the things to be seized included the following parameters:

> The above described documents to be searched for are to relate to the time period January 1, 1976, to February 15, 1983, with the exception of the documents described in paragraphs 7 and 8 which are to relate to the time period January 1, 1972, to February 15, 1983. . . .[36]

(c) "Will Afford Evidence" Requirement

One of the statutory preconditions for the issuance for a s. 487 warrant is a showing in the Information to Obtain that the objects of seizure "will afford evidence with respect to the commission of an offence." As noted earlier,[37] whether something "will afford evidence" is to be considered bearing in mind the investigative nature of the warrant procedure. It is not necessary that the thing in itself be evidence of the crime, but it must be something either taken by itself, or in relation to other things, that could be reasonably believed to be

---

[35] *R. v. PSI Mind Development Institute Ltd., supra,* note 31, at pp. 270–271.
[36] *R. v. Church of Scientology (No. 6), supra,* note 13, at p. 513 [C.C.C.].
[37] See above, Chapter 3.

evidence of the commission of the crime.[38] The Information to Obtain must explain the relationship between the things sought and the proof (or disproof) of material facts related to the transaction under investigation.

The language "with respect to the commission of an offence" has received a similarly generous interpretation. In *Canadian Oxy Chemicals Ltd.*,[40] the Court held that this phrase:

> is a broad statement, encompassing all materials which might shed light on the circumstances of an event which appears to constitute an offence. The natural and ordinary meaning of this phrase is that *anything relevant or rationally connected to the incident under investigation, the parties involved, and their potential culpability falls within the scope of the warrant.*[41] [emphasis added]

This very broad language makes it clear that the statute authorizes the seizure of any evidence relevant to the issues in the case, including known or possible *defences* that the accused or target of the investigation might raise.

Recent amendments added "offence-related property" in s. 487(1)(c.1) and reference to evidence tending to reveal the whereabouts of a fugitive (language added to s. 487(1)(b)). These are discussed in more detail below.

Even where another "Act of Parliament" includes a discrete federal investigative regime with a warrant-granting power (as, for example, the *Bankruptcy Act*[42] does) this section is nonetheless available to authorize the granting of a warrant.[43] Of course, s. 487 only applies to the investigation of federally created offences. Authorities investigating provincially created offences must look to the local provincial offence statute, or the relevant regulatory statute, either or both of which may set out warrant powers.[44]

4. Other Bases of Seizure: Offence-Related Property, Location of Fugitive

Two other bases for seizure were added to the *Criminal Code* in the 1990s. Section 487(1)(b) was amended to provide for the search for evidence that "will reveal the whereabouts of a person who is believed to have committed

---

[38] *Re Bell Telephone Co.* (1947), 89 C.C.C. 196, 4 C.R. 162 (Ont. H.C.).
[40] *Canadian Oxy Chemicals Ltd. v. Canada (Attorney General)* (1999), 133 C.C.C. (3d) 426, 23 C.R. (5th) 259 (S.C.C.).
[41] Ibid., at p. 433 [C.C.C.], para. 15.
[42] R.S.C. 1985, c. B-3, renamed the *Bankruptcy and Insolvency Act*, S.C. 1992, c. 27.
[43] *R. v. Multiform Manufacturing Co.* (1990), 58 C.C.C. (3d) 257, 79 C.R. (3d) 390 (S.C.C.).
[44] For example, see the Ontario equivalent to *Criminal Code* s. 487, the warrant created by s. 158 of the *Provincial Offences Act*, R.S.O. 1990, c. P.33. (Note that s. 158 will be amended by S.O. 2002, c. 18, Sched. A, s. 15(2), upon proclamation of the latter section.) Some provinces have, by local *Summary Conviction Acts*, incorporated the *Criminal Code* procedures for enforcement.

an offence."[45] As well, as part of the various anti-biker/anti-organized crime initiatives s. 487(1)(c.1) was added in 1997[46] to authorize the seizure of any "offence-related property" (a term of art defined in s. 2 of the *Criminal Code*[47]). These other bases of seizure do not relieve in any way the need to describe the things to be seized in a way that will meet the fellow officer test.

5. Banking Records: Originals v. Copies

Section 29 of the *Canada Evidence Act*[48] with the admission into evidence of copies of banking documents. In essence it mandates that in most situations copies of banking records are sufficient to prove the transactions recorded there. Subsection 29(7), however, makes it clear that originals can be seized, but only if the warrant is endorsed to permit such seizure. The subsection says that:

> *unless the warrant is expressly endorsed by the person under whose hand it is issued as not being limited by [s. 29(7)]*, the authority conferred by any such warrant to search the premises of a financial institution and to seize and take away anything in it shall, with respect to the books or records of the institution, be construed as limited to the searching of those premises for the purpose of inspecting and taking copies of entries in those books or records, . . .[49] [emphasis added]

The result is that where a warrant is intended to authorize the seizure of *original bank records* the warrant must have an endorsement. This can be as simple as adding the words "This warrant shall not be limited by s. 29(7) of the *Canada Evidence Act*" anywhere on the warrant.[50]

Where copies are seized under the authority of a warrant without a s. 29(7) endorsement the closing words of the provision remove the normal s. 490 requirement that the officer seek detention orders (though an original report to a justice mandated by s. 489.1 is still required).

---

[45] S.C. 1994, c. 44, s. 36.

[46] S.C. 1997, c. 23, s. 12.

[47] See note 4, *supra*.

[48] *Canada Evidence Act*, R.S.C. 1985, c. C-5, s. 29(7).

[49] As amended by S.C. 1994, c. 44, s. 90(2).

[50] If such an endorsement is sought, officers should also add to the Information to Obtain the reasons said to justify the seizure of originals rather than copies. For example, if a signature card is sought for the purpose of handwriting analysis and the forensic examiner has said that an original is better for such analysis (as will normally be the case) that should be included in the warrant.

6

Describing the Location to be Searched

1. Introduction – The Importance of the Rule

Search warrants are generally location-specific documents, authorizing a physical intrusion into a defined space.[1] The scope of the intrusion is limited by the description of the place set out in the face of the warrant. And the scope of the intrusion on the face of the warrant must be justified by the reasonable grounds set out in the Information to Obtain. That is, the Information to Obtain must describe the basis for the applicant's belief that the degree of intrusion to be authorized is reasonable in light of the evidence marshalled to date and the evidence to be sought during the search in question. There is reason to believe that this aspect of warrant preparation is relatively well understood and carried out by those responsible for drafting and issuing warrants.[2]

This being said, even the relatively simple element of warrant preparation presents challenges for the inexperienced or untrained officer. The failure to set out the place to be searched in the warrant is fatal, even if it is properly described in the Information to Obtain and properly executed otherwise.[3]

2. Building, Receptacle or Place

Section 487 of the *Criminal Code of Canada* authorizes a physical entry and search of a "building, receptacle or place." It does not authorize a search

---

[1] This is certainly true of s. 487 warrants. More recently created warrant provisions do not focus in the same way on physical intrusions, but on privacy breaches (e.g., s. 487.01). Nonetheless, temporal privacy – the right to control who has physical access to space under our control or use – remains an important element of *Charter* s. 8 protection and a key feature of warrant authority.

[2] C. Hill, S. Hutchison & L. Pringle, "Search Warrants: Protection or Illusion?" (1999) 28 C.R. (5th) 89–128, at p. 95 concluding 95% of the warrants examined in a study were at least facially valid in their description of the place to be searched.

[3] *R. v. Parent* (1989), 47 C.C.C. (3d) 385, 41 C.R.R. 323 (Y.T. C.A.).

for evidence on a person's body or the taking of bodily samples[4] or a forced surgical procedure to seize a bullet in an accused's body following a shoot-out;[5] a person is not a "building, receptacle or place." Similarly (at least prior to recent amendments), a s. 487 warrant would not have authorized a "cyber-search" of a website or computer by way of a modem. If such investigative steps were to be pursued they would have had to have found their legal authorization elsewhere. With the addition of s. 487(2.1), it is now possible to have a s. 487 warrant endorsed to include a "computer system" as within the scope of the place to be searched.[6]

3. Outbuildings

Normally a warrant will identify the location of the place to be searched by reference to the municipal address. In such a case, the question arises as to what authority has been given in respect of a building, receptacle or place not obviously within the dwelling house (or identified business) referenced by the address. What of the garage, or the shed? Such "outbuildings" are not included automatically in a warrant[7] and if they are to be searched they should probably be named in the warrant.

While specifically identifying outbuildings in the warrant is clearly the safest course, some structures may be included by virtue of the language of the *Criminal Code*. Section 2 of the Code defines a "dwelling-house" as follows:

> "dwelling-house" means the whole or any part of a building or structure that is kept or occupied as a permanent or temporary residence, *and includes*
>
> > (a) a building within the curtilage of a dwelling-house that is connected to it by a doorway or by a covered and enclosed passage-way, . . .[8] [emphasis added]

Thus, a warrant that authorized the search of a "dwelling-house" at a particular municipal address would include authority to search an attached garage or shed.

If outbuildings are to be included they should be described in such a way that searchers unfamiliar with the property will know which of such buildings

---

[4] *R. v. Mutch* (1986), 26 C.C.C. (3d) 477, 22 C.R.R. 310 (Sask. Q.B.); *R. v. Legere* (1988), 43 C.C.C. (3d) 502, 89 N.B.R. (2d) 361 (N.B. C.A.), leave to appeal refused 96 N.B.R. (2d) 180 (note), [1989] 2 S.C.R. viii (S.C.C.); *R. v. Miller* (1987), 38 C.C.C. (3d) 252, 62 O.R. (2d) 97 (Ont. C.A.); *R. v. Tomaso* (1989), 70 C.R. (3d) 152, 47 C.R.R. 372 (Ont. C.A.).

[5] *Laporte v. R.* (1972), 8 C.C.C. (2d) 343, 18 C.R.N.S. 357 (Que. Q.B.).

[6] See s. 487(2.1), enacted by S.C. 1997, c. 18, s. 41.

[7] *R. v. Laplante* (1987), 40 C.C.C. (3d) 63, 33 C.R.R. 15 (Sask. C.A.). See also *R. v. Hall*, 2003 CarswellBC 2336, 2003 BCSC 1433 (B.C.S.C.).

[8] *Criminal Code*, s. 2 "dwelling-house."

they are authorized to search. In some cases this can be done by a general identification of "all outbuildings, sheds, and other structures on or directly associated with the dwelling house," assuming that the grounds for belief would justify a search of this scope.

4. Rural Properties

Rural properties test the principled approach to the description of the place to be searched. Municipal addresses often do not exist for such properties. In the absence of any readily identifiable municipal description of the property, some other reasonably specific description is needed. Reference to the county concession and a description of the dwelling might suffice, for example:

> Lot 3, concession 14, North Umberton county, the large white, two-storey farm house on the small rise of land about 250 metres back from the road.

With the advent of readily available global positioning system (GPS) technology, reference might include reference to the longitude and latitude of the location of the search.[9]

The degree of specificity required may vary depending on the area of the search. In a small community some latitude may be permitted. Thus, in one case,[10] the description "premises and/or buildings, vehicles, storage receptacles, under the control of Gould's Fisheries Limited" was sufficient.

5. Multi-Unit Dwellings and Offices

As in all things related to search warrants, reasonableness is the watchword for the description of a location involving multi-unit dwellings or office buildings. Clearly a simple municipal address will not be sufficient as that would potentially authorize searching an entire office tower.

Offices and apartments should be identified by unit number and, in the case of large office complexes with many employees within a single "suite," reference can be made to the designation and general location of the office or room to be searched, for example, "the offices of XYX Corp, located at 22 Bay Street, Suite 1800, the office ordinarily occupied by Scott Hutchison in the southwest corner, and the lunch room across the hall from that office."

The degree of precision required will be a function of the grounds for belief and the nature of the things to be seized.

---

[9] *R. v. Large* (2002), 2002 SKQB 152, 2002 CarswellSask 212 (Sask. Q.B.), affirmed (2003), 2003 CarswellSask 88, 2003 SKCA 12 (Sask. C.A.).

[10] *R. v. Gould's Fisheries Ltd.*, 2002 CarswellNfld 126, [2002] N.J. No. 135 (Nfld. Prov. Ct.) at paras. 14–20.

6. Motor Vehicles

Vehicles present a peculiar challenge in search law because they can be both "places" to be searched[11] as well as "things" to be seized. Whether a vehicle is a place or an object of seizure will depend on the particular case. It is important, however, that warrant materials properly identify what role or roles the vehicle plays in the search. Is the vehicle the thing the officers want to seize, or is it a place or receptacle containing the evidence the police seek?

The authorities are divided on whether a search warrant authorizing police to enter and search a house (or other location) includes implicitly the authority to search a motor vehicle parked on or near the property.[12] Where there is no reference to vehicles in a warrant directed at a residence, it would seem difficult to find a textual basis for such an implied power. Indeed, the standard wording would suggest the opposite. The better practice is, of course, to include a reference to vehicles known or unknown in the warrant in the first place (assuming that there are reasonable grounds to believe that there will be evidence in such vehicles).

7. Computer Searches and Section 487(2.1)[13]

(a) Describing Computer Hardware Seizures

In the context of the seizure of computerized records it is often advisable, having regard to the exigencies of the particular investigation, to seize physically the entire operating platform (if this is practicable) and any related manuals or paraphernalia. The decision to engage in this sort of invasive seizure should be taken only after investigators have considered whether some less intrusive search or seizure might accomplish the same investigative end.[14] If

---

[11] *R. v. Rao* (1984), 12 C.C.C. (3d) 97, 40 C.R. (3d) 1 (Ont. C.A.), leave to appeal refused (1984), 40 C.R. (3d) xxvi, 57 N.R. 238n (S.C.C.).

[12] The leading case supporting such an implied power is *R. v. Haley* (1986), 27 C.C.C. (3d) 454, 51 C.R. (3d) 363 (Ont. C.A.). See also *R. v. Laplante, supra,* note 7 (per Wakeling J.A. in dissent). A contrary position is expressed in *R. v. Nguyen* (2004), 184 C.C.C. (3d) 545, 2004 CarswellBC 903 (B.C.C.A.); *R. v. Brown* (1995), 1995 CarswellBC 680, [1995] B.C.J. No. 2642 (B.C. S.C.); *R. v. Brennen* (2000), 2000 CarswellOnt 3858, [2000] O.J. No. 3257 (Ont. S.C.J.); *United States v. Dunn,* 480 U.S. 294, 107 S. Ct. 1134 (U.S. Tex. 1987).

[13] Issues related to computer searches are dealt with in more detail in Chapter 8, below.

[14] Consider, for example, whether the execution of a conventional warrant with a s. 487(2.1) endorsement to seize data might accomplish the same end. In the case of innocent third-party custodians of evidence this will almost always be the case. On the other hand, if it is suggested that the equipment in question has been an instrumentality of the offence (as, for example, in the pirating of software, or the intentional distribution of pornography) it should be seized as the equipment itself is evidence, independent of any documentary value there may be in the machine-readable data.

COMPUTER SEARCHES AND SECTION 487(2.1)

no such reasonable alternative exists, then the "things to be seized" clause might be worded as follows:

> Computer and word-processing equipment including magnetic or other machine-readable storage equipment, programs or software associated with the said equipment, manuals or other documentation associated with either the equipment or software, or any other device and associated software and manuals, used or capable of being used to create, store or manipulate documents or records related to the business, persons and time frame in question.

As is always the case, however, this language can be (and, indeed, should be) modified to ensure that it applies to the facts of the case as detailed in the Information to Obtain.

The *Criminal Code* was amended in the mid-1990s[15] to provide specific authority to allow for electronic searches as part of the execution of a s. 487 warrant. Now s. 487(2.1) (and companion s. 487(2.2)) make it clear that a warrant authorizing a search of a computer for electronic information may also authorize the making of copies and the seizure of same. As well, these provisions make it clear that any person at the scene is required to permit the use of the computer. Further, if necessary, an assistance order under s. 487.02 may be sought to address any issues related to conscripting the aid of persons with expertise at the place to be searched. The new sections provide:

487. (2.1) Operation of computer system and copying equipment – A person authorized under this section to search a computer system in a building or place for data may

(a) use or cause to be used any computer system at the building or place to search any data contained in or available to the computer system;

(b) reproduce or cause to be reproduced any data in the form of a print-out or other intelligible output;

(c) seize the print-out or other output for examination or copying; and

(d) use or cause to be used any copying equipment at the place to make copies of the data.

(2.2) **Duty of person in possession or control** — Every person who is in possession or control of any building or place in respect of which a search is carried out under this section shall, on presentation of the warrant, permit the person carrying out the search

(a) to use or cause to be used any computer system at the building or place in order to search any data contained in or available to the computer system for data that the person is authorized by this section to search for;

---

[15] S.C. 1997, c. 18, s. 41.

(b) to obtain a hard copy of the data and to seize it; and

(c) to use or cause to be used any copying equipment at the place to make copies of the data.

(b) Wording the Warrant – Section 487(2.1)

A warrant which is to be used to gather "data" evidence on the authority of s. 487(2.1) should identify the "place to be searched" as including the computer systems that are to be searched (e.g., "The office of ABC Co. at 123 Main and the computer systems located there") as well as identifying the data to be seized in the "things to be seized" portion of the warrant.

7

Describing the Offences Under Investigation

1. Introduction

A central precondition to the issuance of a search warrant is a showing that there is a specific instance of possible criminal activity that is being investigated. The warrant and Information to Obtain must set out the offence in such a way that the person searched has a reasonable idea of what the criminal inquiry is:

> The person whose premises are to be searched who is entitled to see the warrant would have no knowledge of the reason of the search. . . . [I]t seems to me it should disclose the offence to enable such person to learn that much, at least, of the object of the search. [1]

The search warrant must identify the transaction and offence in such a way that the issuing judicial officer can assess the "nexus" between the evidence being sought and the grounds demonstrated in the Information to Obtain. In *PSI Mind Development Institute,* the Court said:

> The offence should be sufficiently described on the face of the search warrant to reasonably inform the person in charge of the premises to be entered and searched of the nature of the offence and the object of the search. In addition to conforming to the *Criminal Code* and the case-law, one must apply common sense to the factual situation when the peace officer presents himself armed with a search warrant. [2]

The failure to properly state a transaction or offence being investigated is potentially fatal to a warrant application. This requires an appreciation of the

---

[1] *R. v. Solloway Mills & Co.*, 53 C.C.C. 261, [1930] 1 W.W.R. 779 (Alta. C.A.) at pp. 262–263 [C.C.C.].

[2] *R. v. PSI Mind Development Institute Ltd.* (1977), 37 C.C.C. (2d) 263 (Ont. H.C.) at p. 268.

elements of the offence being investigated and some reasonable basis, articulated in the Information to Obtain, to believe that each of those elements is present.[3] If there is no underlying offence properly requiring investigation then there is no basis for a warrant.[4]

2. Approaches to Wording

While not held to the particularity of charging documents,[5] the search warrant and Information to Obtain must describe the transaction being investigated in a way that permits the justice to consider whether there is a reasonable basis to conclude that the objects of seizure bear the necessary relationship to the offence being inquired into. Merely identifying the offence created by the Code will not suffice (it is not enough to simply allege "fraud over $5,000" even if the reading of the Information to Obtain might make it clear what fraud is being investigated.[6] There is, in this context, no magic to the charging language used in the recommended form of charge included in the annotated codes.[7] It provides, however, a good start and a useful structure with the advantage of being flexible. Using the language normally employed in a charging document will ensure that the statement of the offence in the warrant and Information to Obtain include all the key allegations.[8]

3. Dealing with "Unknowns"

The law recognizes that a search warrant is an *investigative* tool and tests the adequacy of the offence described in the warrant with this in mind.[9] This

[3] *R. v. Dombrowski* (1985), 18 C.C.C. (3d) 164, 44 C.R. (3d) 1 (Sask. C.A.).
[4] *R. v. Branton* (2001), 154 C.C.C. (3d) 139, 44 C.R. (5th) 275 (Ont. C.A.) where the Court of Appeal concluded that the activity of the targets of the search, even if proven beyond reasonable doubt, would not be an offence and as such, no warrant should have issued. But note that the substantive question – the illegality of grey market decoders – was subsequently decided differently by the Supreme Court of Canada: see *Bell ExpressVu Ltd. Partnership v. Rex*, 93 C.R.R. (2d) 189, 2002 CarswellBC 851, 2002 SCC 42 (S.C.C.).
[5] *Re Times Square Book Store* (1985), 21 C.C.C. (3d) 503, 48 C.R. (3d) 132 (Ont. C.A.) at p. 512 [C.C.C.]; see as well *R. v. Dombrowski, supra*, note 3, where the Information to Obtain and warrant failed to name any offence.
[6] C. Hill, S. Hutchison & L. Pringle, "Search Warrants: Protection or Illusion?" (1999) 28 C.R. (5th) 89–128.
[7] *Tremeear's Annotated Criminal Code*, D. Watt & M. Fuerst, eds. (Toronto: Carswell (annual)) and *Martin's Annual Criminal Code*, E.L. Greenspan & M. Rosenberg, eds. (Aurora: Canada Law Book).
[8] It is not unheard of for a warrant to fail to allege some important element of the offence under investigation. Where such a failure is present the warrant is fatally flawed: *R. v. Levesque* (1918), 30 C.C.C. 190, 42 D.L.R. 120 (N.B. C.A.) (failure to state *any* offence); *R. v. Solloway Mills & Co., supra*, note 1 (failure to state *any* offence); *R. v. Dombrowski, supra*, note 3.
[9] *R. v. Stockton Financial Services Corp.* (1990), 60 C.C.C. (3d) 527, 68 Man. R. (2d) 233 (Man. C.A.) per Huband J.A.

means that in many cases the police will not know or even suspect certain details of an offence. Such "unknowns" can be reasonably incorporated into the description of the transaction under investigation. For example, in a riot where police seek evidence in respect of an offence where they do not yet have a suspect, the warrant could track the language of the normal charging provision referencing "a person or persons unknown" as the subject of the investigation.[10]

In one case, the Court noted that something more than a statement of the statutory charging section was required:

> [38] Having regard to the draft orders provided to the court, in my view, the offences under investigation ought to be described other than in a summary and generic fashion such as "robbery, contrary to section 344 of the *Criminal Code*." In order to ensure adequate direction to those operating under investigative orders of the variety applied for here, and to reduce the potential for over-seizure or an impermissibly broad exercise of discretion, the offences should, as circumstances permit, be more particularly described.[11]

The central test is to link the investigative step to a *transaction* that is said to constitute a criminal (or other) offence. Only in this way can the proper and necessary nexus or connection be established between the offence under investigation and the evidence being sought. For example, it is not enough to write "attempted murder" in the Information to Obtain or the warrant. The proper description would be:

> That a person or persons unknown did, on or about the 12th day of September, 2004, at the City of Toronto, in the Toronto Region, in the Province of Ontario attempt to kill Jason Smith by stabbing him, and did thereby commit the crime of attempted murder.

This description identifies a transaction and allows the judicial officer to relate the investigation to that transaction.

---

[10] For example, "that a person or persons unknown did, on the 5th day of June, 2004, at the City of Toronto, in the Province of Ontario, attempt to murder Jane Smith by stabbing her contrary to s. 239 of the *Criminal Code*."

[11] *Re Criminal Code* (1997), [1997] O.J. No. 4393 (Ont. Gen. Div.).

8

Computers and Search Warrants

1. Introduction — The Medium v. the Message

(a) Introduction

Computers present particular challenges to the law governing search warrants. Warrants have, historically, been directed at a particular thing or documents located at clearly identifiable physical locations. Computer technology frees evidence and information from such physical limits and allows data to reside in various places, on different media with no version representing an obvious "original." Inexpensive mass storage devices permit even unsophisticated computer users to store huge amounts of data on a single physical medium. The search warrant scheme in the *Criminal Code* is a regime originally designed to deal with physical manifestations of privacy. As such, it does not always blend easily with the world of "virtual evidence."[1]

Section 487 of the *Criminal Code*, for example, did not – until recently – authorize the taking of copies of data. Parliament offered some relief to this doctrinal dilemma in 1997 when it added s. 487(2.1) and (2.2) to the *Criminal Code*.[2] These provisions, reproduced below, are among only a few technology-specific investigative provisions in the *Criminal Code*. Section 487(2.1) provides as follows:

---

[1] There are a variety of useful resources for the computer crime investigator. Among the most useful is the United States Department of Justice (USDOJ) website and two documents that, while designed for an American audience, are useful to Canadian investigators. The first is the well known *Searching and Seizing Computers and Obtaining Electronic Evidence in Criminal Investigations* prepared by the Computer Crime and Intellectual Property Section of the Criminal Division of the USDOJ. It is available online at <www.usdoj.gov/criminal/cybercrime/s&smanual2002.pdf> (accessed on September 1, 2004). The second is a practical document for first responders who may not be experts in the execution of computer warrants, *Electronic Crime Scene Investigation: A Guide for First Responders*, published by the National Institute of Justice and available online at <www.ojp.usdoj.gov/nij/pubs-sum/187736.htm> (accessed on September 1, 2004). Finally, *Best Practices for Seizing Electronic Evidence (version 2.0)* can be found at the U.S. Secret Service website <www.secretservice.gov/electronic__evidence.shtml> (accessed on September 1, 2004).

[2] Sections 487(2.1) and (2.2) were added in June 1997 (S.C. 1997, c. 18, s. 41).

487. (2.1) **Operation of computer system and copying equipment** – A person authorized under this section to search a computer system in a building or place for data may

(a) use or cause to be used any computer system at the building or place to search any data contained in or available to the computer system;
(b) reproduce or cause to be reproduced any data in the form of a print-out or other intelligible output;
(c) seize the print-out or other output for examination or copying; and
(d) use or cause to be used any copying equipment at the place to make copies of the data.

This section provides a powerful tool to permit the reasonably expeditious seizure of evidence in electronic form.

New s. 487(2.2) seems to impose special duties on anyone "in possession or control of any building or place in respect of which a search is carried out":

(2.2) **Duty of person in possession or control** – Every person who is in possession or control of any building or place in respect of which a search is carried out under this section shall, on presentation of the warrant, permit the person carrying out the search

(a) to use or cause to be used any computer system at the building or place in order to search any data contained in or available to the computer system for data that the person is authorized by this section to search for;
(b) to obtain a hard copy of the data and to seize it; and
(c) to use or cause to be used any copying equipment at the place to make copies of the data.

(b) Informational Searches

The significance of the legal issues associated with computer evidence was magnified by the judgment of the Supreme Court of Canada in *Plant*.[3] In that case,[4] the Court held that extracting information from a data base might amount to a "search" (depending on, among other things, the nature of the information and the status of the data source). The result is that information drawn from computers must be approached like any other evidence-gathering and must be preceded by an assessment of whether anyone has a reasonable expectation of privacy in the information being accessed. If they do, some lawful authority (a warrantless power, or a properly authorized search warrant of some kind) must be identified before the police can access the data in question.

---

[3] *R. v. Plant* (1993), 84 C.C.C. (3d) 203, 24 C.R. (4th) 47 (S.C.C.).
[4] Discussed in Chapter 1, under heading 2, "How Courts Analyze Search Problems."

(c) Distinguishing Between the "Medium" and the "Message"

Computer programmers have worked hard to make information on computers appear as simple as possible through a number of real world metaphors or analogies. Data is presented as "documents" in "folders" and "filing cabinets," complete with icons that look like their namesakes. It is easy to confuse these visual aids with the reality of what is going on with the physical medium upon which the actual evidence is written. The message – the substance of the data contained on the computer – is sometimes all the police want or need. On other occasions the police will need the "best evidence" – the actual physical medium, complete and intact. The *Criminal Code* provides them with the tools they need to acquire either form of evidence, the key being for officers to identify exactly which investigative technique they want to perform and to then find the appropriate warrant to authorize that technique. One issue to be canvassed in any medium versus message debate is the evidentiary value of copies versus the original medium. This engages a range of forensic and legal issues.[5]

2. Seizing Hardware

(a) Deciding to Seize Hardware

There are a number of reasons for the police to seize hardware (the computer, including the hard drive). Ordinarily care should be taken in the decision to seize a computer, especially where the role of the subject of the seizure is not clear. Computers are not simply giant store-houses of evidence – they are important business tools; their seizure can seriously impair the ability of a legitimate (or illegitimate) business to carry on. In general it will be appropriate to seize the computer (as opposed to engaging s. 487(2.1)) where:

- the computer is being used for the ongoing commission of an offence (e.g., in a child pornography case);
- the computer was itself obtained by the commission of an indictable offence (i.e., it was stolen or obtained by fraud);
- the computer would be left with the accused or a party affiliated with the accused such that it might not be available at a later time;
- the nature of the investigation requires or would benefit from a forensic examination of the data involved (a proper forensic examination requires access to "the box" to permit experts to test the system and guarantee that any of the data they retrieve is not an artifact created by testing or copying.

---

[5] Some of these legal issues are resolved by the recent changes to the *Canada Evidence Act*, and the addition of ss. 31.1–31.8, enacted S.C. 2000, c. 5, s. 56, which create a mini-code for dealing with electronic evidence issues.

(b) Peripherals

Where a warrant authorizes the seizure of a computer it will also often authorize the seizure of all related peripherals. The devices (keyboard, monitor, mouse, external drives, etc.) impact on the operation of the overall system; it is impossible to know for certain how the absence of a particular device might affect the booting-up of the system or the way the system operates once booted.

3. The Innocent Third Party – Using Section 487(2.1) to Seize Copies

(a) When and Why to Seize Copies of Data

Sometimes copies of data will be enough to satisfy the standards of the *Canada Evidence Act* and will be the preferable way for investigators to proceed. Section 487(2.1) now makes such a procedure relatively easy. The new *Canada Evidence Act* provisions[6] may be satisfied by a copy or printout in some circumstances.

---

[6] The *Canada Evidence Act* provides now in ss. 31.2 and 31.3, enacted S.C. 2000, c. 5, s. 56, as follows:

> **31.2 (1) Application of best evidence rule — electronic documents** — The best evidence rule in respect of an electronic document is satisfied
>
>> (a) on proof of the integrity of the electronic documents system by or in which the electronic document was recorded or stored; or
>> (b) if an evidentiary presumption established under section 31.4 applies.
>
> . . . .
>
> **31.3 Presumption of integrity** — For the purposes of subsection 31.2(1), in the absence of evidence to the contrary, the integrity of an electronic documents system by or in which an electronic document is recorded or stored is proven
>
>> (a) by evidence capable of supporting a finding that at all material times the computer system or other similar device used by the electronic documents system was operating properly or, if it was not, the fact of its not operating properly did not affect the integrity of the electronic document and there are no other reasonable grounds to doubt the integrity of the electronic documents system;
>> (b) if it is established that the electronic document was recorded or stored by a party who is adverse in interest to the party seeking to introduce it; or
>> (c) if it is established that the electronic document was recorded or stored in the usual and ordinary course of business by a person who is not a party and who did not record or store it under the control of the party seeking to introduce it.

(b) Drafting the Section 487(2.1) Warrant

A warrant seeking to take advantage of the authority under s. 487(2.1) must adhere to the language of that provision. It authorizes a "person authorized under this section to search a computer system in a building or place for data . . . ." Clearly then, if the officer executing the warrant intends to take advantage of the powers granted under s. 487(2.1), the warrant itself must:

1. authorize the search of a computer system at the place being searched (an extension of the place to be searched portion of the warrant); *and*
2. authorize the search for data[7] (an extension of the things to be searched for).

Thus, for example, the description of the place to be searched might read:

> The business offices of XYZ Corp, located at 182 Dundas St. West, Suite 1202 and any computer system located in that place.

And the description of the things to be seized might read:

> Memoranda, correspondence, notes, and other similar documents (including e-mail) whether recorded on paper or as data stored on or available to a computer system at the place to be searched, created between June 1, 2004 and September 2, 2004, related to the affairs of the company and its dealings with ABC Corp.

4. Expert or Network Administrator Assistance

Section 487(2.2) seems to create a duty to cooperate, but this is probably misleading. The section appears to have been copied from other federal administrative legislation which was the "template" for s. 487(2.1).[8] While this subsection would be necessary to ensure non-resistance to regulatory execution of a computer search, it is not needed for police execution.

If it is expected that a network administrator or civilian computer expert will be needed to assist in the execution of the warrant, the appropriate course is to have them named in an assistance order (under s. 487.02) that sets out their duties in clear and unambiguous language.

---

[7] A term defined in *Criminal Code* s. 342.1(2) in these terms:

> "data" means representations of information or of concepts that are being prepared or have been prepared in a form suitable for use in a computer system.

[8] *Canadian Environmental Protection Act*, R.S.C. 1985, c. 16 (4th Supp.), ss. 101(5) and (6); see now the *Canadian Environmental Protection Act, 1999*, S.C. 1999, c. 33, s. 220(6) and (7).

5. Overseizure and Computer Media

One challenge peculiar to electronic media is that of overseizure. A warrant authorizes the seizure of certain identifiable things. The seizure of those things is justified by the grounds in the Information to Obtain. The warrant will be properly challenged if it authorizes the seizure of things beyond those justified by the grounds.[9]

Computers, however, condense onto a single physical medium a wide range of information about a person. A warrant to seize a computer hard drive authorizes the seizure of a mass of information about the target. For example, a perfectly valid warrant might authorize the seizure of a hard drive of a child pornographer to permit the police to have the best evidence for court and to ensure that the contraband images are not left with the accused (for to do so would be to permit a continuing offence). However, that hard drive may well have on it other information not related to the accused's pornographic effort, but related to, for example, a credit card fraud otherwise unknown to the police.

In such a situation the concepts of plain view would seem to provide the police with a legitimate justification for their conduct. There is, however, good reason to question whether this approach will survive.

The search and seizure of mass storage devices tests the "reasonableness" of plain view when applied to the context of computer crime investigations. Justifiable searches will often require sweeping examinations of all data on a hard drive. Where the circumstances of the particular investigation justify such a wide-ranging search (for example, where evidence suggests that the target of the search has used "counter measures" to secrete seizable data in, or disguised as, other files), then no issues should arise.

Where, however, police routinely seize and review all material on a hard drive, even if they know only a small percentage is likely to be responsive to their warrant, then constitutional issues are engaged. At present these issues remain unresolved but it is likely that police use of software such as Encase will be challenged as "overseizure."

6. Sample Warrant Where Seizure of Computer Otherwise Justified

The Electronic Crime Section (E-Crime) of the Ontario Provincial Police has been on the cutting edge of legal and technical developments related to the investigation of crime where computers are involved. They offer the following language to assist officers drafting warrant applications where it is proposed to seize a computer with a view to subjecting it to forensic examination:

---

[9] See S.W. Brenner & B.A. Frideriksen, "Computer Searches and Seizures: Some Unresolved Issues" (2002) 8 Mich. Telecomm. Tech. L. Rev. 39 at p. 89, <www.mttlr.org/voleight/brenner.pdf> (accessed on September 1, 2004).

SUGGESTED APPENDIX "A"[10]
(Items To Be Seized)

- a computer system,* and its peripherals and related devices, including the video monitor, any input or output devices, and associated communication equipment, cables and connectors
- devices or media capable of storing data**
- devices, media and documents containing computer passwords
- operating systems and computer programs
- computer system or software manuals and reference materials

Suggested Reasonable Grounds To Believe Things Seized Will Afford Evidence Of Offence

NOTE: Please remember to modify this section (especially paragraphs 1, 2, 6 & 7) to suit your individual warrant.

1. On [*insert date*], I spoke with [*insert rank & name of e-Crime member*] of the Electronic Crime Team, Ontario Provincial Police. He is a member of this Section, which investigates computer crime and specialises in the search, seizure and analysis of computer systems.

2. [*insert rank & name of e-Crime member*] told me that members of their Section could forensically analyse a computer system and retrieve a wide variety of information from it. This information includes, but is not limited to:

- copies of web pages created on the computer or downloaded from the Internet;
- copies of electronically created documents (e.g. letters and journals);
- copies of e-mails received and sent from the computer system;
- records of instant messaging and chat conversions (e.g. ICQ, MSN Messenger).

3. The forensic analysis can retrieve data that may be hidden or previously deleted, including prior drafts of web pages, documents and e-mails. Further, it may assist in identifying when a web page or document was created or modified, when an e-mail was sent or received, or when a chat conversation occurred.

4. Deleted files or file fragments may exist for an extended period of time (e.g. weeks or months) on the computer system, due to the design of most common computer operating systems (e.g. Microsoft Windows). Files that have been deleted by the user are not physically erased. Rather, the operating system merely marks the area of the storage disk where the file was stored as available to be re-

---

[10] Provided by Sgt. Robert Gagnon of the Ontario Provincial Police. I am grateful to Sgt. Gagnon, Det. Staff Sgt. Arni Stinnison and the Ontario Provincial Police for their kind permission to reproduce this helpful example.

used in the future. If that space is not re-used prior to seizure, forensic programs can retrieve these deleted files or file fragments.

5. Typically, the data sought is found on the hard disk drive(s) contained within the seized computer system – the primary data storage device of a personal computer. The Electronic Crime Section analyst will make an exact copy, called an "image", of the entire hard disk drive, and conduct all subsequent analysis on that image. The original hard disk drive is reinstalled in the seized computer and dealt with through the provisions of section 490 of the *Criminal Code*.

6. The analysis will include searching the entire hard disk drive and any seized storage media for electronic copies of the web page [see attached], draft copies of it, or graphic images that appear on the web page. The analysis can also determine whether it was possible to create the web page in question and transmit it over the Internet using the target computer.

7. Further, the analysis will include examining any e-mail or the various forms of instantaneous correspondence (e.g. MSN Messaging) that have been saved on the hard disk drive or other storage media to ascertain if the suspect has canvassed assistance from others (e.g. advice on how to build a web page or suggestions for what to put on it) in committing the offence under investigation.

8. There are a wide variety of techniques available to even novice computer users to disguise or resist casual examination of data saved on the hard disk drive. Electronic files that constitute evidence can be easily renamed to appear as otherwise innocuous system files, and/or be moved into directories housing unrelated programs. Files can also be password protected, encrypted, or compressed by the user, with widely available, free software or using features included in popular office suites (e.g. Microsoft Office). In addition, it is also possible to hide one type of file (e.g. a Word document) inside another, much larger file (typically, a large photograph). When opened, the larger file (in this example, a photograph) appears unchanged, exactly the same as it did before the "insertion". This technique is known as *steganography*.

9. It requires time, experience and computer resources to defeat these and other techniques. Accordingly, it is necessary to examine the entire hard disk drive, including the directory structure, program files, and – in varying degrees – each and every file to complete a comprehensive search for electronic evidence.

10. Passwords can be used by computer systems and computer programs to protect data. Several computer manufacturers offer password protection on computer laptop hard disk drives. The user is prompted for a password when the computer is first turned on. If the correct password is not provided, the hard disk drive will not operate and the data on it is unreadable. Presently, there exists no technique to defeat this "lock-out" feature. In addition, widely available encryption programs (e.g. Entrust, Pretty Good Privacy) are capable, with a sufficiently robust password, of providing nearly absolute protection of data from viewing by other users. It simply may be impossible to "crack" the password. Without the password, the encrypted file cannot be read. Users sometimes store passwords electronically or reduce them to writing in areas near the computer. Accordingly, it is necessary

to search for and seize any devices, media or documents that contain passwords for the computer system, computer programs or data files stored on it or other storage media.

11. Storage media (e.g. floppy diskettes, removable hard drives, CD-ROM) found at the scene may contain copies of web pages, documents, e-mails or other information that was originally created on a computer system and subsequently saved on to the media. If the original data cannot be located or retrieved from the computer system, it may nevertheless exist on the media. The storage media may, therefore, be required to fully analyse information created by the computer system.

12. In addition to the computer system itself, it may be necessary to seize the accompanying peripherals for several reasons. First, it may not be possible to properly assess the system without its constituent parts. If the computer system is dated or novel in design or construction, the peripheral devices, cables and hardware may not be commercially or otherwise available to investigators. Thus, the analysis may require the components that are found with the computer system.

13. For the same reasons, it may be necessary to seize copies of software and manuals found at the scene. Some data may only be displayed in intelligible form when viewed through the software program used to create them. If the computer system utilises software programs that are dated or novel, the software programs that created them may not be commercially or otherwise available to investigators. Thus, the analysis may require the software programs and manuals that are found at the scene.

14. Finally, some computer peripheral devices (e.g. printers) have separate memory chips that are capable of storing data that has been sent to them. Accordingly, these peripherals may contain further data that corroborates or supplements data retrieved from the computer system.

15. Members of the Electronic Crime Section will be present at the search, and will assess, based on the aforementioned reasoning, whether it is necessary to seize the computer system's various peripherals. Items that are not required to conduct the analysis will not be seized.

---

* Defined in section 342.1(2) of the *Criminal Code*, R.S.C. 1985, Chap. C-46 as:

> . . . a device that, or a group of interconnected or related devices one or more of which,
>
> (a) contains computer programs or other data, and
> (b) pursuant to computer programs,
>   (i) performs logic and control, and
>   (ii) may perform any other function.

** *Ibid.*, defined as:

> . . . representations of information or of concepts that are being prepared or have been prepared in a form suitable for use in a computer system.

9

Specific Drafting Challenges

1. Introduction

This chapter looks at some specific warrant-drafting challenges.

2. The Complex Warrant Application

Modern warrants and Informations to Obtain are consistently lengthier and more complex than similar documents would have been in comparable pre-*Charter* or early *Charter* investigations. This is a function of (a) more thorough investigations by police, (b) a more sophisticated and demanding judiciary, (c) the emphasis on, and importance of, making full, frank and fair disclosure to the issuing justice, and (d) a better trained and more sophisticated police community. This increased complexity presents special challenges for the warrant writer. It is not sufficient for the writer to simply "dump" all the raw investigative data into the form of an Information to Obtain and hope that the judicial officer can "figure it out." In *Re Criminal Code*, the Court underscored the duty on the warrant writer to present a comprehensible and comprehensive document saying:

> [9] . . . [T]the application affidavit/information must be reasonably comprehensible. This factor engages a consideration of such sub-factors as organization of the document, spelling, grammar, punctuation and language, including word choice. As with the text of any document, meaning and understanding can be impaired by defects in these respective subject areas. In some instances, the number and severity of such defects may render the document confusing and incomprehensible. The court should not find itself in a position of endlessly re-reading the application document in order to discover whether the statutory pre-conditions are satisfied. I accept that in some cases the complexity of the investigation and the relevant quantity of investigative data will contribute to a lengthy application document. However, the creation of undue complexity and unnecessary length in the application document can obscure, even for sophisticated readers, the presence

of all necessary pre-requisites. The inherent danger is that one or more of the orders sought will issue despite the absence of a valid supporting record.[1]

The complex warrant requires the writer to dedicate significant effort to the task of organizing the evidentiary record. Indeed, in most cases, organizing the material in an accessible and orderly way is as challenging, if not more challenging, than the act of writing.

The writer must remain focused on the theory of the case that animates the warrant and the goal of explaining that theory to the court within the rules of warrant-drafting.

In such cases the usual tools of organization – use of an overview, cast of characters, and regular, descriptive headings – become mandatory. The physical presentation of the document takes on greater significance. Page and paragraph numbering are essential to make it possible to navigate through the document.

3. The Informer and the Tipster

(a) The Challenge of Anonymous Sources

Colleagues and other conventional investigative resources are the most common sources of information in a warrant application. This material is readily presented to the judicial officer in a way that permits easy assessment. A police officer or named civilian witness can be evaluated, and his or her evidence weighed, using the normal techniques of any judicial proceeding. A more problematic situation arises where the warrant applicant seeks to present evidence from an informer or tipster who either has not revealed himself or herself to the investigator (the "tipster") or who does not want the investigator to disclose information tending to identify him or her (the "confidential informer").

The nature of the judicial pre-authorization requires that the judicial officer be placed in a position to independently assess the value or weight to be given to the tipster or confidential informer's information, but circumstance and legal duty prevent the warrant applicant from disclosing who the tipster/confidential informer is, or how they have knowledge of the case. There are ways to deal with the seeming conundrum created by these conflicting imperatives.

(b) Nomenclature: Informant, Anonymous Tipster and Confidential Informer

The language used in this area is confusing and overlapping. It is made more confusing because some police agencies have developed internal practices that

---

[1] *Re Criminal Code* (1997), [1997] O.J. No. 4393 (Ont. Gen. Div.).

suggest other meanings for these words. In this text (and in most, but not all of the cases[2]), the following terminology will be used:

- An *Informant*, in accord with the language of Form 1 and the other provisions of the *Criminal Code*, is the officer swearing the Information to Obtain, sometimes also called the warrant applicant.
- The *Tipster* (or *Anonymous Tipster*) is a civilian who has provided information to the police without revealing to the police his or her identity. Such information might be provided in anonymous calls to the police or through privately operated programs such as Crimestoppers.[3]
- The classic *Confidential Informer* is someone who has given the police information or evidence on the understanding that his or her identity will not be disclosed. They enjoy "informer privilege," an important legal right which police and the courts have a duty actively to protect.

(c) The Challenge for the Warrant Applicant and Judicial Officer

In the Information to Obtain a search warrant, the investigator is entitled to outline the hearsay information received from a tipster/confidential informer, if it is presented in a way that permits meaningful judicial consideration of that evidence. The justice must be able *to satisfy himself or herself* that the information from the tipster/confidential informer is to some extent reliable, and is not based on idle gossip or rumour.

This assessment is done by reference to all the circumstances related to the tipster/confidential informer and how his or her information fits in to the rest of the case as presented to the judicial officer.

In *R. v. Debot,* Mr. Justice Martin stated:

> [A] mere statement by the informant that he or she was told by a reliable informer that a certain person is carrying on a criminal activity or that drugs would be found at a certain place would be an insufficient basis for the granting of the warrant. *The underlying circumstances disclosed by the informer for his or her conclusion must be set out, thus enabling the justice to satisfy himself or herself that there are reasonable grounds for believing what is alleged. I am of the view that such a mere conclusory statement made by an informer to a police officer would not constitute reasonable grounds for conducting a warrantless search or for making an arrest without warrant. Highly relevant to whether information supplied by an informer constitutes reasonable grounds to justify a warrantless search or an arrest without warrant are whether the informer's "tip" contains sufficient detail to ensure that it is based on more than mere rumour or gossip, whether the informer*

---

[2] *R. v. Leipert* (1996), 106 C.C.C. (3d) 375, 47 C.R. (4th) 31 (B.C. C.A.), affirmed (1997), 112 C.C.C. (3d) 385, 4 C.R. (5th) 259 (S.C.C.).
[3] *R. v. Leipert* (S.C.C.), *supra*, note 2.

discloses his or her source or means of knowledge and whether there are any
indicia of his or her reliability, such as the supplying of reliable information in
the past or confirmation of part of his or her story by police surveillance. I do not
intend to imply that each of these relevant criteria must be present in every case,
provided that the totality of the circumstances meets the standard of the necessary
reasonable grounds for belief.[4] [emphasis added]

This standard will apply both to (a) the pre-authorization stage of the warrant,
and (b) cases involving warrantless searches dependent on the investigator's
"reasonable grounds." This position was reaffirmed by the Supreme Court of
Canada decision in *R. v. Greffe*, where Lamer C.J.C. stated:

> [A] conclusion that the police had reliable information about the appellant's
> attempt to import heroin must be based on more than the fact of a subsequent
> recovery of the drugs. *There must be an independent inquiry into the source and*
> *reliability of the confidential information in order to determine whether, in the*
> *totality of the circumstances, there existed reasonable and probable grounds to*
> *believe the appellant was carrying the heroin or whether there was mere suspicion.*
> Relevant to this inquiry is whether the information received contains sufficient
> detail to ensure that it is based on more than mere rumour or gossip, whether the
> source or means of knowledge is revealed and whether there is any *indicia* of the
> reliability of the source of the information, such as the supplying of reliable
> information in the past. . . .[5] [emphasis added]

It is therefore not enough for the officer to "vouch" for the anonymous source,
saying that the officer believes the source and restating the source's conclusion
respecting the involvement of the target in crime, or the presence of evidence
at the place to be searched.

(d) Assessing the Anonymous Source – The "Three Cs"

The classic statement of the standard from *Debot*[6] provides a structure to
the totality of the circumstances test and invites a review of the tipster/confi-
dential informer evidence from three perspectives, easily remembered as the
"Three Cs": looking at the totality of the circumstances, to what extent is the
information (a) compelling, (b) credible, or (c) corroborated or confirmed:

> First, was the information predicting the commission of a criminal offence com-
> pelling? Second, where that information was based on a "tip" originating from a

---

[4] *R. v. Debot* (1986), 30 C.C.C. (3d) 207, 54 C.R. (3d) 120 (Ont. C.A.) at pp. 218–219 [C.C.C.],
affirmed (1989), 52 C.C.C. (3d) 193, 73 C.R. (3d) 129 (S.C.C.).

[5] *R. v. Greffe* (1990), 55 C.C.C. (3d) 161, 75 C.R. (3d) 257 (S.C.C.) at pp. 176–177 [C.C.C.].

[6] *R. v. Debot* (S.C.C.), *supra*, note 4, at p. 215 [C.C.C.].

source outside the police, was that source credible? Finally, was the information corroborated by police investigation prior to making the decision to conduct the search?[7]

Compelling: Where possible, the warrant applicant should include whatever detail can be disclosed without tending to reveal the identity of the tipster/ confidential informer. Detail, a statement of the informer's source of knowledge (how they know what they have told police), evidence that the source was first-hand rather than local rumour, a story that is internally consistent and which "makes sense" when measured against normal experience; these will all make the information from the confidential source more compelling.

Credible: In the case of confidential informers, the police know who the source is, even if they cannot disclose that source to the judicial officer. If the source is credible (in the sense that they are personally believable and trustworthy when providing information to the police), the officer can say so, but must set out why he or she reaches that conclusion. The officer can do so by including statements that the informer has provided accurate information in the past, that they are paid for their information but only for accurate information, that the source has a criminal record, but not for offences of dishonesty (theft, fraud, perjury, etc.), or that they have no motive known to the officer to lie about the particular target. This must be done, of course, in a way that (a) does not mislead the judicial officer, and (b) does not tend to disclose the identity of the source.

Often this is the most challenging area around which to draft. The officer wishes to provide an accurate picture of the source without identifying him or her. As well, the officer cannot leave out detail that might, if omitted, give an unduly favourable picture of the source. This challenge can sometimes be met by providing vague but accurate information about the informer in a way that does not falsely inflate his or her credibility.

Corroborated (Confirmed): The best way for an officer to bolster the value of tipster/confidential informer evidence is to find other material, either in the existing file or from further investigation, that corroborates material elements of what the informer has told the police. This is the one aspect of the informer's evidence that the officer has any control over – the officer cannot make the source more credible or make the information more compelling, but investigation can begin to confirm what the source has said.

Corroboration in this context must be confirmation of something more than innocent details (or publicly available information) in the context of an anonymous tip. For example, if the police received a tip that John Smith would be travelling by plane to Toronto on a particular flight and that he would have

---

[7] Ibid.

drugs with him, it would not be enough to confirm that such a passenger was on the flight. There must be confirmation of something more than innocent facts which might be readily known. This is not to say that there must be other directly inculpatory evidence, but it does mean that something beyond super-ficial confirmation is needed.[8] The question is whether the police confirmation is sufficient to remove or displace the possibility of innocent coincidence, mistake or fabrication.

Totality of the Circumstances: There is no requirement that the grounds demonstrate that a source is all three of the Cs (credible, compelling and corroborated). Rather, the test is based on all the circumstances. Tipster infor-mation (where the credibility of the source is unknown even to the officer) can be the basis for a warrant if it is compelling and corroborated in some material way. Equally, detailed information from a known credible source may provide a sufficient basis for a warrant even though the information is not confirmed.

An example of the test in operation can be seen in the Supreme Court of Canada case of *R. v. Wiley.*[9] In the case, the Supreme Court considered whether an informer's tip could provide investigators with a sufficient basis for a warrant to search for marijuana plants believed to be growing in the subject's basement. Looking at the evidence from the paid informer and the surrounding circumstances as detailed in the Information to Obtain, Mr. Justice Sopinka said:

> In the case at bar, the two tips of an informant which were received by police formed important components of the information sworn to obtain the search warrant. To decide whether these tips properly contributed to the reasonable grounds asserted by police, it is necessary to assess their reliability. In *R. v. Debot. . .* , this court determined that the reliability of the tip of an informant depends on an assessment of the totality of the circumstances and specified three areas of concern (at p. 215):

>> First, was the information predicting the commission of a criminal offence compelling? Secondly, where that information was based on a "tip" origi-nating from a source outside the police, was that source credible? Finally, was the information corroborated by police investigation prior to making the decision to conduct the search?

> The first tip received by police indicated that the appellant was engaged in a hydroponic marijuana growing operation in his residence. The tip was rendered more *compelling* by the informant's detailed description of the residence and its location and a statement which indicated that the informant had seen 60 marijuana

---

[8] *R. v. Lewis* (1998), 122 C.C.C. (3d) 481, 13 C.R. (5th) 34 (Ont. C.A.).
[9] *R. v. Wiley* (1993), 84 C.C.C. (3d) 161, 24 C.R. (4th) 34 (S.C.C.).

plants growing in a lab in a concrete bunker below a hot tub attached to the house. The second tip, obtained just a few days prior to issuance of the search warrant, from the same informant, indicated that the informant had detected the smell of marijuana emanating from the appellant's premises. Both of these tips contained information with sufficient detail and accuracy to categorize them as *compelling*.

The source of the two tips was *credible*. The police knew the identity of the informant and indicated that he or she had been a reliable source of information in the past. Thus, the *credibility* of the informant was established without the need to infer it from the fact that the tip given proved accurate on subsequent inspection by police.

The tips were *corroborated* in subsequent police reconnaissance. The police were able to confirm from the road outside of the appellant's residence that a low, vented concrete structure was located at the back of the house. Not only was this consistent with the description offered by the informant in the first tip, the police were able to confirm from past experience that the existence of the vents was in keeping with a hydroponic marijuana growing operation, thereby supporting the second tip with respect to the odour of marijuana emanating from the premises.

On this basis, I would conclude that the tips were relevant and reliable and properly taken into account by the issuing justice in determining whether the officers had reasonable grounds to believe that an illicit narcotic was contained in the appellant's residence in contravention of the *NCA*. . . . Given that the tips meet the test set out by this court in *Debot, supra*, and ought not to be excised from the information on the basis of wrongdoing by the police, the issuing justice properly relied on the facts derived from the tips in the information sworn to obtain the search warrant.

In addition, other information was also available. As previously indicated, the police had conducted a reconnaissance of the premises which confirmed the existence of the vented concrete bunker attached to the appellant's residence which was consistent with the existence of a hydroponic marijuana growing operation. Finally, the police could also rely on inquiries made at the station-house which revealed that the house was the residence of the appellant, which was important for the purposes of identifying the suspect in the information sworn to obtain the search warrant.[10]

(e) The Nature and Scope of Informer Privilege

(i) *What Is Informer Privilege?*

Informers play an important role in the criminal justice system. They provide the police with vital information, which in turn permits the police to preserve the safety of the community. The law recognizes this and through the rule of

---

[10] Ibid., at pp. 170–171 [C.C.C.].

informer privilege prevents the disclosure of information tending to identify an informer. The privilege:

> is an ancient and hallowed protection which plays a vital role in law enforcement. It is premised on the duty of all citizens to aid in enforcing the law. The discharge of this duty carries with it the risk of retribution from those involved in crime. The rule of informer privilege was developed to protect citizens who assist in law enforcement and to encourage others to do the same.[11]

The courts appreciate the role that informers play, and the rule of informer privilege and its high standing in the law of evidence and procedure is based the importance of this role:

> The value of informers to police investigations has long been recognized. As long as crimes have been committed, certainly as long as they have been prosecuted, informers have played an important role in their investigation. It may well be true that some informers act for compensation or for self-serving purposes. Whatever their motives, the position of the informer is always precarious and their role is fraught with danger.
>
> The role of informers in drug-related cases is particularly important and dangerous. Informers often provide the only means for the police to gain some knowledge of the workings of drug trafficking operations and networks. . . . The investigation often will be based upon a relationship of trust between the police officer and the informer, something that may take a long time to establish. The safety, indeed the lives not only of the informers but also of the undercover police officers, will depend on that relationship of trust.[12]

The rule prohibits the police from disclosing information tending to identify a person who has provided them with information on the basis of an explicit or implicit promise that his or her identity would remain secret. While technically a privilege belonging to the Crown, informer privilege can only be waived with consent of the informer. The police, the Crown and the court are all under an affirmative duty to ensure that the privilege is honoured.

(ii) *Who Is an Informer?*

In order for informer privilege to attach there must be some sort of explicit or implicit request by the source for the police to keep the source's identity confidential, and a corresponding promise by the police (either explicit or implicit) to do so. There are no magic words and no requirement for the

---

[11] *R. v. Leipert* (S.C.C.), *supra*, note 2, at p. 390 [C.C.C.], para. 9; see also *Bisaillon v. Keable* (1983), 7 C.C.C. (3d) 385, 37 C.R. (3d) 289 (S.C.C.).

[12] *R. v. Scott* (1990), 61 C.C.C. (3d) 300, 2 C.R. (4th) 153 (S.C.C.) at pp. 313–314 [C.C.C.].

informer to justify to the police or the court the reason for the requested confidentiality.[13] Once the request is made and the police agree to keep the confidence (even if the promise of confidentiality is only implied), the rule attaches and the police are duty-bound to protect the informer.

(iii) Limits on Police Dealing with Informer Information

The privilege here exists for the benefit, and is under the control of, the informer. The police are not simply allowed to withhold information identifying the informer – they are under an *affirmative legal duty to actively protect the secrecy of the informer*. Even if the police wish to disclose the identity of the informer, or use information that might tend to identify him or her, they cannot.

(f) Special Challenges Raised by Tipsters

Tipsters (sources who provide information to investigators without providing their identity to even the police) present special challenges for warrant applicants and judicial officers. These sources present challenges to officers in two ways: *First*, the officer is not normally in a position to vouch for the credibility of a tipster – by definition the officer does not know the identity of the source and cannot relate the current information to any history of prior accuracy. *Second*, because the source is not known to the officer, special safety concerns arise. Since the officer does not know who the source is, the officer cannot say whether any particular bit of information in the "tip" will tend to identify the source.[14]

In respect of the first challenge, the only acceptable response is to present only the absolutely necessary information respecting material obtained from the tipster, and then only if the officer is confident that it can be done without compromising the source. The judicial officer should be told that because the information is from a tipster the warrant applicant is including few or no details.

(g) How to Protect Informers

It is important to remember that the warrant applicant's first duty is to protect the privilege of the tipster/confidential informer. There are a number of ways this can be done:

---

[13] *R. v. 4-12 Electronics Corp.* (1996), 47 C.R. (4th) 20, 108 Man. R. (2d) 32 (Man. Q.B.) at pp. 26–27 [C.R.]; *R. v. Brown*, 74 C.R.R. (2d) 164, 1999 CarswellOnt 4704, [1999] O.J. No. 4870 (Ont. S.C.J.) at pp. 169–170 [C.R.R.], para. 4.

[14] *R. v. Leipert, supra*, note 2.

1. Do not quote the informer directly; paraphrase, and then only as absolutely necessary.
2. Avoid modifiers or explanations that might tend to identify the informer.
3. When setting out the background of the informer, present the information in a way that avoids specifics but at the same time makes full, frank and fair disclosure to the judicial officer.
4. Consider sealing the warrant application, and write the warrant application with a view to later editing (including decribing the position of the informer in an appendix which contains any material that would be edited out of any disclosed warrant).

(h) The Only Exception to the Rule

The only time an informer's identity will be ordered disclosed by the court is if the accused can demonstrate that his or her innocence is at stake. This "innocence at stake" exception might arise if the accused can show:

1. The informer was a material witness to the offence (especially if he or she was the *only* material witness);
2. The informer was an *agent provocateur* who in fact was an important participant in the offence, or acted to induce the accused to commit the crime (usually at the request of the police);
3. The accused seeks to show that there were no reasonable grounds for the search.

With respect to the third situation, the accused will succeed only if he or she can show that successfully attacking the warrant is his or her only defence and that the only way to attack the warrant involves the discovery of information tending to disclose the identity of the informer.[15]

4. Dealing with Earlier Constitutional Errors

In their efforts to demonstrate that reasonable grounds exist, investigators *cannot* rely upon information obtained as a result of unconstitutional investigative activity.[16] This is not to say that such material should not be included in an Information to Obtain a search warrant. On the contrary, because the application for a search warrant is an *ex parte* proceeding (the subject of the search is not there), the investigator seeking the warrant is under *a special duty to bring all relevant information to the attention of the issuing justice of the peace.* This will include reference to any inappropriate investigative steps taken prior to seeking the warrant. If it should happen that such information is

---

[15] *R. v. Leipert* (S.C.C.), *supra*, note 2, at pp. 394–397 [C.C.C.], paras. 21–28.
[16] *R. v. Plant* (1993), 84 C.C.C. (3d) 203, 24 C.R. (4th) 47 (S.C.C.).

available, the informant should include the fact of the unconstitutional step and indicate that he or she does not rely upon the information obtained as a result of the step in support of the application for a warrant and should make clear that the information is included only to provide the justice with a full and fair disclosure of how the investigation has proceeded. If such material is included and is relied upon by the issuing justice, the court will, in any subsequent review, consider whether the warrant would have issued without the tainted evidence. That is, the court will consider what is left over after the unconstitutionally obtained material is excised from the information.[17]

In general, unconstitutionally obtained evidence should not be used to support the issuance of a search warrant. Where unconstitutionally obtained evidence is included and the warrant issues, the court that reviews the warrant will ignore the tainted evidence in assessing whether the warrant should have issued. The warrant will only be upheld if it can be shown that it could have issued on the basis of the properly obtained evidence described in the Information to Obtain.[18]

5. Multiple Warrants Based on One Information to Obtain – The "Roll-Up"

It is lawful for a search warrant applicant to seek multiple warrants on the basis of a single sworn document. Such "rolled-up" applications normally provide an efficient and reasonable way for a single judicial officer to consider a range of investigative steps at one time. However, care must be taken to ensure that (a) all the orders sought are within the jurisdiction of the judicial officer considering the rolled-up application, and (b) the supporting materials meet the different statutory preconditions to issuance for the different judicial orders sought.[19]

6. Regulators and Earlier Seizures

The community has a number of different interests represented by the different enforcement arms of the state. As already noted, the interests of the community in the effective enforcement of regulatory regimes and the limited

---

[17] *R. v. Grant* (1993), 84 C.C.C. (3d) 173, 24 C.R. (4th) 1 (S.C.C.).
[18] *R. v. Garofoli* (1990), 60 C.C.C. (3d) 161, 80 C.R. (3d) 317 (S.C.C.); *R. v. Grant, supra*, note 17; and *R. v. Plant, supra*, note 16, as good examples of this rule in action. There the Court refused to consider evidence gathered during illegal perimeter searches in deciding whether there was a basis for the various warrants to issue.
[19] *Re Criminal Code, supra*, note 1; *Re Canada (Attorney General)*, [1997] O.J. No. 1314.

privacy interests generally associated with such enterprises invites departures from the *Hunter*[20] standard of presumed judicial pre-authorization.

The nature of criminal activity and modern enforcement practices are such that the criminal activity often overlaps with, and is first discovered in, the context of regulatory wrongdoing: the stockbroker's fraud is discovered when his or her monthly reports to the TSE are questioned; thefts from a Legion account are uncovered when regulators audit to see whether a new bingo licence should be granted; failure to provide the necessities of life is discovered by the CAS worker; the coroner's investigation reveals foul play. In these cases, great care should be taken by all concerned to ensure that every representative of the community acts within his or her scope of authority. The law is clear that criminal investigations ought not to be advanced by tools crafted for use in regulatory enforcement.

As a practical matter, there are two ways in which criminal investigations overlap with regulatory/civil/administrative inquiries. Either the regulatory investigation *evolves* into a criminal investigation (the regulatory investigators, looking for regulatory violations, discover evidence leading them to conclude that there has been a violation of the criminal law and they notify police authorities of that fact) or regulatory authorities and criminal investigators act *concurrently*, investigating the same set of events with a view to action under different legal regimes.

In either case the criminal investigator should take care to ensure that all investigative steps, or the fruit of all investigative steps, are taken or obtained following some procedure that would comply with the *Hunter* standard. That is, where information or evidence flow from an administrative investigation to a criminal investigation, the process whereby the representatives of the community responsible for the enforcement of the criminal law come to possess the evidence should *"criminalize"* the process.

One particularly sensitive class of investigation often involving an "evolution" from administrative to criminal law is the *Coroners Act*[21] inquiry. These investigations are often conducted on behalf of the coroner by senior police officers to take advantage of their experience and familiarity with difficult, forensically intensive investigations. It is not uncommon for such investigation, however, to evolve (sometimes quickly and sometimes over time) into criminal investigations looking to assign criminal liability for a death under consideration. In these cases especially, the investigator must take care to ensure that, as the investigation evolves, the standard of "reasonableness" (against which investigative steps are measured) also evolves. In *R. v. Colarusso*, Mr. Justice La Forest stated, for the majority of the Court:

---

[20] *Hunter v. Southam Inc.* (1984), 14 C.C.C. (3d) 97, 41 C.R. (3d) 97 (S.C.C.).

[21] In *R. v. Colarusso*, discussed below, the Court looked at the Ontario *Coroners Act*, and the civil search powers given to the coroner in that province.

[S]o long as the evidence (or the information derived from the evidence) is in the possession of the state (*i.e.*, the coroner or the criminal law enforcement branch), the following would hold true: (1) while the evidence is being used by the coroner for valid non-criminal purposes within the scope of the *Coroners Act*, the seizure is reasonable and not caught by s. 8 of the Charter; and (2) when the evidence, or the information derived from the evidence, is appropriated by the criminal law enforcement arm of the state for use against the person from whom it was seized, the seizure will become unreasonable and will run afoul of s. 8 of the Charter. *In other words, the criminal law enforcement arm of the state cannot rely on the seizure by the coroner to circumvent the guarantees of* Hunter, supra, *as any seizure by the coroner pursuant to s. 16(2) is valid for non-criminal purposes only.*[22] [emphasis added]

Officers involved in death investigations must ensure that seizures associated with the investigation comply with the form of the investigation they are genuinely conducting and should be constantly reassessing whether the stage has been reached where the investigation has become a criminal, and not a coroner's, investigation. Once that stage is reached, *the entire investigation (what has been done and what will follow) must be made to conform to the requirements of a criminal investigation by judicial authorization if the evidence so gathered is to be used to advance a criminal investigation or prosecution.*[23]

This is not intended to suggest that there must be an impermeable wall between criminal and non-criminal investigators. On the contrary, administrative/regulatory investigators may often provide, without constitutional taint, useful information or evidence to advance criminal investigations. The central point is that the police should not indirectly take advantage of non-criminal investigative "super powers" enjoyed by regulators.[24]

---

[22] *R. v. Colarusso* (1994), 87 C.C.C. (3d) 193, 26 C.R. (4th) 289 (S.C.C.) at p. 222 [C.C.C.].

[23] At least one pre-*Colarusso* white-collar investigation has come to grief because of a too-friendly relationship between criminal and regulatory investigators: *R. v. Williams* (1994), 130 N.S.R. (2d) 8, 367 A.P.R. 8 (N.S. S.C.). For a discussion of the case see: "*R. v. Williams* – Section 8 violation by Secondary Use of 'Fruits of Investigation' " (1994) 3 S.S.L.R. 163. See also *R. v. Ouaida* (1996), 1996 CarswellOnt 929, [1996] O.J. No. 962 (Ont. Gen. Div.) in which an arson investigation faltered because of the activities of the authorities acting under the auspices of the *Fire Marshals Act*, R.S.O. 1990, c. F.17 (since repealed and replaced by the *Fire Protection and Prevention Act, 1997*, S.O. 1997, c. 4).

[24] For example, if a civil investigator with the Ontario Securities Commission interviewed a number of investors/victims without the exercise of any special authority enjoyed by the Commission, the information obtained from those interviews might properly pass over to a criminal investigation. If, however, the Commission's investigation went on to invoke any of the warrantless demand/production powers or the compelled interviews of potential targets, that material could not pass over to the criminal side without some judicial intervention (and even then there might be constitutional problems).

10

Observations on Some Specialized Warrants

1. Introduction – Entering "the Thicket"

Over the course of the last 15 years there has been a steady growth in the volume and complexity of the law governing search and seizure generally, and the law related to search warrants in particular. The law in this area has accumulated more than it has developed. That is, a veritable maze of warrant-granting powers now exists, each power with its own idiosyncratic statutory regime and slowly developing body of jurisprudence. Officers who recognize the need to "get a warrant" may have only begun their legal inquiries. Which warrant to obtain, and how to obtain it, are often equally challenging questions. This "thicket" of warrant powers can be daunting.[1] This chapter examines some issues related to particular "specialized" warrants.

2. DNA Warrants[2]

In 1995 it was doubtful whether police could use any warrant power to seize DNA evidence from the person of an accused or target of an investigation. Conventional warrants could not issue to search a person. General warrants under s. 487.01 could not (and still cannot) issue to authorize a technique that would "interfere" with the "bodily integrity" of an individual. It was hardly clear whether this limit on s. 487.01 warrants prevented the harvesting of modest amounts of biological material in the form of pulled hair, buccal swabs of the mouth, or a few drops of blood drawn using a sterile lancet.

In an effort to remove the cloud of doubt cast over this important investigative technique, Bill C-104 was introduced and passed in one day in the House

---

[1] Renee Pomerance has called for the simplification and rationalization of search warrant powers in the *Criminal Code*. Her article "*Criminal Code* Search Warrants: A Plea for a New Generic Warrant" 382–405 in D. Stuart, R. J. Delisle & A. Manson, eds., *Towards a Clear and Just Criminal Law: A Criminal Reports Forum* (Toronto: Carswell, 1999) at p. 405 presents a clear and compelling call for reform in this area.

[2] For a checklist related to the issuance of DNA warrants, see below, Chapter 15.

of Commons. Three weeks later, on July 13, 1995 (after passage by the Senate and a speedy Royal Assent), the amendments adding new ss. 487.03 to 487.09 were in force.[3]

This regime[4] has three important features: the authorization process, conditions related to execution, and post-execution privacy safeguards. They are all important to the warrant applicant.[5]

(a) Authorization

The conditions for authorization for the DNA warrant are found in s. 487.05, which provides the statutory authority for a warrant in the following terms:

487.05 (1) Information for warrant to take bodily substances for forensic DNA analysis – A provincial court judge who on *ex parte* application made in Form 5.01 is satisfied by information on oath that there are reasonable grounds to believe

  (a) that a designated offence has been committed,
  (b) that a bodily substance has been found or obtained
    (i) at the place where the offence was committed,
    (ii) on or within the body of the victim of the offence,
    (ii) on anything worn or carried by the victim at the time when the offence was committed, or
    (iv) on or within the body of any person or thing or at any place associated with the commission of the offence,
  (c) that a person was a party to the offence, and
  (d) that forensic DNA analysis of a bodily substance from the person will provide evidence about whether the bodily substance referred to in paragraph (b) was from that person

and who is satisfied that it is in the best interests of the administration of justice to do so may issue a warrant in Form 5.02 authorizing the taking, from that person, for the purpose of forensic DNA analysis, of any number of samples of one or

---

[3] S.C. 1995, c. 27.

[4] The original 1995 scheme has been modified in several ways by later legislation creating a national DNA data bank: S.C. 1998, c. 37; S.C. 2000, c. 10. For a discussion of the new regime see as well R. Pomerance, "A Practical Guide to the New DNA Warrants" (1995) 39 C.R. (4th) 224–245.

[5] It is important to note that these provisions describe one way to get a DNA sample. It is the only way for the police to forcibly obtain a sample extracted directly from the accused. However, abandoned samples can be seized if cast off by an out-of-custody suspect. Equally, a suspect can consent to provide a DNA sample. And, of course, it is still possible to obtain a s. 487 warrant to seize cast-off or ambient DNA from things worn or used by the suspect.

more bodily substances that is reasonably required for that purpose, by means of the investigative procedures described in subsection 487.06(1).[6]

Subsection 487.05(2) provides this additional guidance to the judicial officer considering an application for this warrant:

> (2) **Criteria** – In considering whether to issue the warrant, the provincial court judge shall have regard to all relevant matters, including
>
> > (a) the nature of the designated offence and the circumstances of its commission; and
> > (b) whether there is
> > > (i) a peace officer who is able, by virtue of training or experience, to take samples of bodily substances from the person, by means of the investigative procedures described in subsection 487.06(1), or
> > > (ii) another person who is able, by virtue of training or experience, to take, under the direction of a peace officer, samples of bodily substances from the person, by means of those investigative procedures.[7]

The section on its face provides for authorization by only provincial court judges.[8] Interestingly, the section does not make reference to s. 552 judges or judges of courts of superior jurisdiction.[9]

(b) What Is Authorized?

The investigative process authorized under a s. 487.05 DNA warrant is carefully delineated in s. 487.06, reproduced below:

> **487.06** (1) **Investigative procedures** – A peace officer or another person under the direction of a peace officer is authorized to take samples of bodily substances from a person by a warrant under section 487.05 or an order under section 487.051 or 487.052 or an authorization under section 487.055 or 487.091, by any of the following means:

---

[6] Section 487.05, as amended to S.C. 1998, c. 37, s. 16.

[7] Section 487.05, as amended to S.C. 1998, c. 37, s. 16.

[8] Section 487.04 defines "provincial court judge" to include, in relation to a young person, a judge of the youth justice court within the meaning of s. 2(1) of the *Youth Criminal Justice Act*, S.C. 2002, c. 1.

[9] The rationale for this exception is not readily apparent, and leaves the law in an unusual state. Most s. 552 judges and judges of superior jurisdiction, as well as provincial judges, are justices of the peace by virtue of their offices. Their exclusion from s. 487.05 means that while such judges might issue s. 487 warrants as justices, and may issue s. 487.01 warrants in their own right, they have no authority to issue DNA warrants.

(a) the plucking of individual hairs from the person, including the root sheath;

(b) the taking of buccal swabs by swabbing the lips, tongue and inside cheeks of the mouth to collect epithelial cells; or

(c) the taking of blood by pricking the skin surface with a sterile lancet.

(2) **Terms and conditions** – The warrant, order or authorization shall include any terms and conditions that the provincial court judge or court, as the case may be, considers advisable to ensure that the taking of the samples authorized by the warrant, order or authorization is reasonable in the circumstances.

(3) **Fingerprints** – A peace officer, or any person acting under a peace officer's direction, who is authorized to take samples of bodily substances from a person by an order under section 487.051 or 487.052 or an authorization under section 487.055 or 487.091 may take fingerprints from the person for the purpose of the *DNA Identification Act*.[10]

As authorities in this area have noted,[11] these three techniques for the harvesting of biological samples had been made (before this section was enacted) attempted under the authority of s. 487.01, though the legality of that approach has been doubted.

The closing language of s. 487.05(1) describes the warrant to be issued to the applying peace officer. It indicates that the warrant, in writing, is to be directed to a peace officer and authorizes the officer or someone acting under his or her authority to obtain a biological sample in one of the three investigative procedures noted above (and found in s. 487.06(1)).

In one case, *R. v. F. (S.)*, the Court summarized the various elements of the scheme that serve to protect the privacy rights of individuals who might be tested:

a) The jurisdiction to issue a DNA warrant is reserved for provincial court judges, and may not be exercised by justices of the peace (s. 487.05(1)).

b) DNA warrants are only available to further the investigation of the specific offences enumerated in s. 487.04.

c) Section 487.05 imposes highly specialized reasonable grounds requirements, which are carefully designed to address the unique issues arising in this context.

---

[10] As amended to S.C. 2000, c. 10, s. 19.

[11] R. Pomerance, " 'Body' of Evidence: Section 487.01 of the *Code*, Bodily Integrity, and the Seizure of Biological Samples" (July 1995) 2 Crown's Newsletter 1–54.

d) The issuing judge is expressly required to advert to certain relevant factors, including the qualifications of the person who is to collect the bodily substance (s. 487.05(2)).

e) The issuing judge must be satisfied that the warrant is in the best interests of the administration of justice (s. 487.05(1)).

f) Section 487.06(2) requires the issuing judge to impose any terms and conditions which are necessary to ensure that the seizure of a bodily substance authorized by the warrant will be reasonable in the circumstances. A number of such conditions were imposed in the case in appeal.

g) Pursuant to s. 487.06, a warrant under s. 487.05 may only authorize certain designated procedures.

h) Section 487.07 imposes a number of explicit requirements governing execution of the DNA warrant. Section 487.07(3) imposes an overarching requirement that the executing officer ensure that the privacy of the suspect is respected in a manner that is reasonable in the circumstances.

i) Sections 487.08 and 487.09 create a comprehensive and rigorous scheme governing disposition of bodily substances and results obtained under a DNA warrant. These provisions not only maximize the protection of privacy in biological and genetic material; they also place clear limits on the extent to which evidence obtained under DNA warrant can be used to incriminate the suspect.[12]

(c) Preconditions for Authorization

The DNA warrant follows the conventions of *Hunter*[13] and s. 487 by requiring that the issuing judicial officer be "satisfied by information on oath that there are reasonable grounds to believe" in the factual circumstances that constitute the preconditions for authorization. The collection of preconditions for authorization established by s. 487.05 embraces the facts of the most common DNA-assisted investigations, but clearly does not authorize the seizure of such samples in all of the circumstances in which the state may be said to have a compelling interest in obtaining such evidence.

---

[12] *R. v. F. (S.)* (2000), 141 C.C.C. (3d) 225, 32 C.R. (5th) 79 (Ont. C.A.) at p. 239 [C.C.C.], para. 26, reversing in part (1997), 120 C.C.C. (3d) 260, 11 C.R. (5th) 232 (Ont. Gen. Div.). See also *R. v. Brighteyes* (1997), 43 C.R.R. (2d) 55, 54 Alta. L.R. (3d) 347 (Alta. Q.B.).

[13] *Hunter v. Southam Inc.* (1984), 14 C.C.C. (3d) 97, 41 C.R. (3d) 97 (S.C.C.).

(i) *Designated Offence*

As it has done in other areas,[14] Parliament has limited the availability of the DNA warrant to investigations of certain offences. Broadly speaking, the offences involve most serious crimes against the person.[15] The significance of identifying the designated offence under investigation is apparent if you consider the limitations placed on the use of the evidence post-execution.[16]

Understandably, the warrant will only issue when the offence has been committed, and as such will not authorize seizure for offences not yet completed.[17] This makes sense when one considers the nature of the evidence and the unlikelihood of DNA being relevant to investigations of inchoate offences (besides attempt) against the person.

(ii) *The Forensic Sample*

Logically enough, the material filed on the application must demonstrate that there are reasonable grounds to believe that there exists a forensic sample associated with the offence. More specifically, the section demands grounds to believe a bodily substance[18] has been found at the place where the offence was committed, on or within the body of the victim, on anything worn by the victim at the time of the offence, or "on or within the body of any person or thing or at any place associated with the commission of the offence." This last basket clause would seem to cast a fairly broad net for the source of the forensic sample. By virtue of s. 487.05(1)(d), the forensic sample must be capable of being subjected to DNA analysis such that it will provide evidence about whether the forensic sample originated with the person identified in the warrant.[19] The belief that the crime scene sample is capable of providing a DNA profile does not require a formal report from the laboratory – a verbal report from an analyst is sufficient.[20]

---

[14] Consider the limitations on electronic surveillance (s. 183) and proceeds of crime authorizations (s. 462.3).

[15] The term "designated offence" is defined in s. 487.04 by reference to a number of current Code provisions. The definition also embraces several sex- or arson-related offences which have come and gone over the years, including the old crime of rape. Some offences that one might expect to find are not included, for example, criminal harassment.

[16] As noted below, the biological substance seized from the person and the results from any analysis can only be used to advance the investigation of the designated offence identified in the warrant: s. 487.08.

[17] Though the definition of designated offence includes attempts.

[18] A term not defined in the legislation, but necessarily meaning a substance from a human being containing some DNA component suitable for analysis.

[19] The language used in the new provisions is somewhat sloppy, but it is clear, upon a reading of s. 487.05 as a whole, that the warrant must identify a person from whom a sample is to be taken, and that the evidence must be used to include that person.

[20] *R. v. Feeney* (2001), 152 C.C.C. (3d) 390, 41 C.R. (5th) 326 (B.C.C.A.) at p. 401 [C.C.C.], para. 30.

An interesting issue arises as to whether s. 487.05 would recognize genetic material that is included in the genetic make-up of a child, produced by a criminal act (incest or sexual assault), or from fetal material recovered from a hospital, as "a bodily substance . . . found or obtained" at a place associated with the offence. In other words, does the section contemplate paternity/maternity testing? While the language of the section suggests otherwise, high authority confirms that fetal material, and presumably other genetic material created as a result of illegal acts of intercourse, are valid "crime scene" samples.[21]

(iii) *The Best Interests of the Administration of Justice*

The judge called upon to issue the warrant must be satisfied that its issuance is in the best interests of the administration of justice. This language is found in s. 487.01(1) and in the provisions in Part VI of the Code related to interceptions of private communications.[22] It imports a balancing, weighing the nature of the intrusion contemplated against the seriousness of the offence under investigation and the potential of the evidence in question to contribute to the determination of the party responsible for that offence (though one would think that this was part of the residual discretion enjoyed by every judicial officer called upon to consider any warrant application[23]). Thus, a judge might decline to issue a warrant even where all the other statutory preconditions are present, if the offence under investigation is not serious and the value of the DNA evidence is limited.

Subsection 487.05(2) offers a partial catalogue of considerations for the issuing judge, all of which one would have expected to see considered under the head of the "best interests of the administration of justice" (the nature and seriousness of the offence, and the availability of a properly qualified person to take the sample).

(d) Conditions Related to Execution

Section 487.07 sets out a strict regime for the execution of the DNA warrant and establishes a particular scheme to deal with DNA seizures from young offenders.[24]

---

[21] See *R. v. B. (S.A.)* (2003), 178 C.C.C. (3d) 193, 14 C.R. (6th) 205 (S.C.C.) at pp. 204–205 [C.C.C.], para. 23.

[22] See *R. v. Finlay* (1985), 23 C.C.C. (3d) 48, 48 C.R. (3d) 341 (Ont. C.A.), leave to appeal refused, 50 C.R. (3d) xxv, [1986] 1 S.C.R. ix (S.C.C.).

[23] *R. v. Baron* (1993), 78 C.C.C. (3d) 510, 18 C.R. (4th) 374 (S.C.C.); *Canadian Broadcasting Corp. v. New Brunswick (Attorney General)* (1991), 67 C.C.C. (3d) 544, 9 C.R. (4th) 192 (S.C.C.).

[24] In *R. v. F. (S.)* (Ont. Gen. Div.), *supra*, note 12, at pp. 318–319 in endnote 1, reversed in part (2000), 141 C.C.C. (3d) 225, 32 C.R. (5th) 79 (Ont. C.A.), Mr. Justice Hill recounted some of

The executing officer is obliged[25] to inform the subject of the seizure of the contents of the warrant, the nature of the s. 487.06(1) investigative procedure to be used (blood, hair, buccal swab), the reason for the seizure, the possible use of the DNA results in evidence, and the authority of the officer and any person acting to execute the warrant to use as much force as is necessary to carry out the investigative procedure identified in the warrant. The executing officer is authorized by s. 487.07(2) to detain the subject of the seizure for a reasonable time to make the execution of the warrant feasible and to require the subject to accompany him or her to some other location. In all of this, the officer and anyone acting on the authority of the officer under the DNA warrant shall take reasonable care to protect the privacy of the subject of the seizure. Subsections 487.07(4) and (5) provide for seizures from young persons and set up a regime similar to that related to the taking of statements found in s. 146 of the *Youth Criminal Justice Act.*[26]

In Ontario, it is common for warrants to include additional terms and conditions requiring that the procedure be videotaped, that the target be given his or her right to counsel, that the individual be offered an opportunity to exercise that right, that the individual be told he or she is under no obligation to make any statement, and that the collection be in accordance with provincial forensic laboratory guidelines (which are normally included in the Information to Obtain).

(e) Delay Pending Challenge

It sometimes happens that defence counsel will learn of a DNA warrant that has been issued and will indicate to the police, or to the Crown, that they intend to bring an application to quash the warrant. Often they will urge the Crown and the police to delay execution of the DNA warrant pending the hearing of the application to quash.

---

the terms included in the warrant there scrutinized:

> The taking of blood samples. This will be done by first asking [(F. (S.)] to lay his arm on a table and to provide free access to his hand and fingers. One of his fingers will then be cleansed with alcohol and then the surface of one of his finger tips will be pricked with a small sharp sterile lancet. About six (6) drops of blood from the fingerprick will be collected on a square sterile gauze to give a continuous stain the size of a one dollar coin. The gauze will then be air dried and packaged for the purpose of forensic DNA analysis, and to report thereon to the clerk of the court as soon as practicable, but within a period not exceeding seven days after the execution of the warrant.

[25] By s. 487.07(1).
[26] See note 8, *supra.* The language tracks important portions of s. 56 of the former *Young Offenders Act*, R.S.C. 1985, c. Y-1, which was repealed and replaced by the *Youth Criminal Justice Act* ("YCJA"), and so cases decided in relation to former s. 56 and YCJA s. 146 will be useful in measuring compliance with ss. 487.07(4) and (5).

There would appear to be no legal obligation that the police delay such an application. Indeed, there is a compelling argument that the order to gather DNA evidence is operative unless and until another court orders otherwise. This will, of course, sometimes occur if there is an application before the superior court to quash. But until such a stay has been ordered, the DNA warrant is operative and the police can and should act to carry out the investigative technique authorized by the warrant.[27]

(f) Post-Execution Conditions

The new DNA warrant comes with some of the most Draconian post-execution provisions ever witnessed. Under s. 487.08 it is a summary conviction offence for anyone to use the sample obtained for any purpose other than "for the purpose of forensic DNA analysis in the course of an investigation of a designated offence."[28] Equally, it is a summary offence to

> use the results of forensic DNA analysis . . . [for any purpose other than]
>
> (a) in the course of an investigation of the designated offence or any other designated offence in respect of which a warrant was issued or a bodily substance found in the circumstances described in paragraph 487.05(1)(b) or in paragraph 196.12(1)(b) of the *National Defence Act*; or
> (b) in any proceeding for such an offence.[29]

The language in this latter provision is almost incoherent. It is not clear whether investigations into other offences not identified in the warrant, but related to the same transaction, might be advanced without further judicial intervention.

The final aspect of the post-execution privacy-protecting regime set up by the section is found in the mandatory destruction of evidence following the subject being cleared by the forensic comparison, the acquittal of the subject on the designated offence, or any other termination of proceedings in favour of the subject.[30] A saving provision[31] allows for an application to a provincial court judge to delay the destruction of the evidence.

This mandatory destruction of evidence, while clearly intended to benefit individuals subject to DNA seizures, will necessarily come into conflict with the Crown's disclosure obligations. Individuals ultimately charged with offences will want to know who had been investigated and whether and how they were cleared. The Crown will be obliged to disclose what it knows about such other suspects. It will be impossible, however, for the prosecution to make

---

[27] *R. v. Campbell*, [1996] O.J. No. 5447 (Ont. Gen. Div.).
[28] Section 487.08(1), as amended to S.C. 2000, c. 10, s. 22.
[29] Section 487.08(2), as amended to S.C. 2000, c. 10, s. 22.
[30] Section 487.09(1)(c), which deals with cases in which no indictment goes forward after a discharge, committal, or stay.
[31] Section 487.09(2).

disclosure of the destroyed evidence and this may provide the basis for a complaint by the accused under s. 7 of the *Charter*.

(g) DNA as Evidence v. DNA Data Bank Warrants and Orders

DNA data bank orders and samples should be distinguished from DNA evidence warrants (s. 487.05 warrants). The data bank regime is intended to serve as an investigative resource. It is not a substitute for the use of a s. 487.05 DNA warrant to obtain an evidence sample in a particular case.

DNA data bank samples cannot be used as evidence by virtue of the *DNA Identification Act*.[32]

3. General Warrants and Assistance Orders – Sections 487.01 and 487.02[33]

(a) Introduction and Background

(i) *Introduction*

The procedures for judicial pre-authorization of search activity by the state in criminal proceedings have become, to say the least, Byzantine.[34] The *Criminal Code* has, in the last two decades, exploded with new search provisions. Where the 1982 *Criminal Code* included perhaps four principal warrant provisions occupying some 7.5 pages in the 1982 *Martin's Annual Criminal Code*, the same core provisions ballooned by a factor of 10 to almost 70 pages in the 2004 edition.[35] In place of the four core provisions (what would now be ss. 487, 488, 489, and 490), we now have ss. 487, 487.01, 487.012, 487.013, 487.02, 487.03, 487.04, 487.05, 487.06, 487.07, 487.08, 487.09, 487.091, 487.092, 487.1, 487.11, 487.2, 487.3, 488, 488.1, 489, 489.1, 490, 492.1 and 492.2, as the core warrant and warrant-related provisions. This, of course, ignores the plethora of special warrant provisions in the *Criminal Code* (impaired driving blood warrants; firearms) and in the *Controlled Drugs and Substances Act* and a variety of other federal statutes.

---

[32] *DNA Identification Act*, S.C. 1998, c. 37; see s. 6(1).

[33] This discussion of general warrants is a modestly reworked version of a paper presented at the Third Symposium on Issues in Search and Seizure Law in Canada (Osgoode Hall Professional Development, September 20, 2003). I am grateful to my colleague and co-author of this paper, Sarah Gray, for her kind permission to use this material here.

[34] This is not the first such indictment of the present regime: R. Pomerance, "*Criminal Code* Search Warrants," *supra*, note 1.

[35] E. Greenspan, ed., *Martin's Annual Criminal Code, 1982* (Aurora: Canada Law Book, 1981), contrasted with E. Greenspan & M. Rosenberg, eds., *Martin's Annual Criminal Code, 2004* (Aurora: Canada Law Book, 2003) at pp. CC/811 to CC/878.

Most of this mass of detail is the product of Parliament's effort to respond to judicial pronouncements which have narrowly interpreted existing legal authority to search and seize. Parliament has endeavoured to identify specifically when and how police and other state actors may invade privacy with judicial pre-authorization, or under the authority of an appropriate warrantless search power. This degree of precision has the benefit of ensuring that specific techniques are authorized by carefully customized warrant-granting powers which articulate Parliament's effort to balance private and public interests.

But a legislative approach that is based on very precise, narrowly drawn provisions runs the risk of leaving behind important search powers. The myriad of circumstances which can arise in the context of criminal investigations effectively defies such efforts at precision. Section 487.01 and the general warrant-granting power it creates are intended to provide a legislative "failsafe" that ensures that an appropriate legal authority will be in place to deal with cases that might otherwise have escaped more focused legislative provisions.

(ii) Rationale for the General Warrant

Through s. 487.01 (and s. 487.02), Parliament has provided a broad, plenary warrant-granting power intended to ensure that judicial authorization is legally available for virtually any investigative technique that can be brought within the *Hunter*[36] conditions for judicial pre-authorization.

The general warrant[37] and assistance order provisions of the *Criminal Code* were enacted as part of Parliament's 1993 overhaul of a number of search powers.[38] The new provisions were a response to a variety of Supreme Court

---

[36] *Hunter v. Southam Inc.*, *supra*, note 13, which first, required that, where practical, a judicial officer pre-authorize investigative intrusions on reasonable expectations of privacy; and second, set "reasonable grounds to believe" that evidence of the offence under investigation would be discovered as the presumptive standard for issuance of such a judicial order.

[37] The marginal note to s. 487.01 describes the warrant simply as a "general warrant," though it is also known as a "general investigative warrant." The term "general warrant" is not entirely helpful and has an unhappy history (see *Entick v. Carrington* (1765), 95 E.R. 807, [1558-1774] All E.R. Rep. 41 (Eng. K.B.)). Indeed, historically general warrants denoted a very different sort of instrument, similar to a writ of assistance. The historic general warrant was described by Lord Camden as subversive of "all the comforts of society" (p. 817 [E.R.]) and "contrary to the genius of the law of England" and was widely seen as a central inspiration of the Fourth Amendment in the United States.

While the term "general investigative warrant" has its attractions and its adherents (this is the term used, for example, by Watt J. in *R. v. Hayman Motors Ltd.*, [1998] O.J. No. 747 (Ont. Gen. Div.)), the statutory, and more common, designation "general warrant" is used here.

[38] *An Act to amend the Criminal Code, the Crown Liability and Proceedings Act and the Radiocommunication Act*, S.C. 1993, c. 40.

of Canada[39] and provincial Court of Appeal[40] decisions addressing constitutional and statutory limitations on certain investigative techniques.[41] These judgments had underscored the need for judicial pre-authorization for police activities that interfered with privacy interests, and had entrenched a broad and purposive understanding of the scope of s. 8's protection against unreasonable search and seizure.

At the same time these cases interpreted existing warrant-granting powers relatively narrowly. The result was a general trend in the jurisprudence of the late 1980s and early 1990s to identify situations in which there was a constitutional requirement to obtain a warrant, while at the same time holding that no existing statutory provision was sufficiently broad to allow a judicial officer to provide the form of authorization that the police should have sought.

The general warrant was Parliament's direct response to this trend. As the Federal Court of Appeal[42] has said of s. 487.01,

> This provision of the *Criminal Code* was enacted, as recognized by the appellant, in order *to fill any potential "gap" in the ability of peace officers to obtain prior judicial authorization* of a search or seizure in accordance with *Hunter*.[43] [emphasis added]

The sweeping language of s. 487.01 justifies the wide reading the power has been given. The authorization elements of the section provide:

> **487.01** (1) **Information for general warrant** – A provincial court judge, a judge of a superior court of criminal jurisdiction or a judge as defined in section 552 may issue a warrant in writing authorizing a peace officer to, subject to this section, use any device or investigative technique or procedure or do any thing described in the warrant that would, if not authorized, constitute an unreasonable search or seizure in respect of a person or a person's property if

---

[39] *R. v. Wong* (1990), 60 C.C.C. (3d) 460, 1 C.R. (4th) 1 (S.C.C.) (requirement and non-availability of warrant for video surveillance); *R. v. Duarte* (1990), 53 C.C.C. (3d) 1, 74 C.R. (3d) 281 (S.C.C.) (requirement and limited availability of authorization for consent interception of private communications); *R. v. Wise* (1992), 70 C.C.C. (3d) 193, 11 C.R. (4th) 253 (S.C.C.) (requirement and non-availability of warrant for tracking device installation and monitoring).

[40] For example, *R. v. Fegan* (1993), 80 C.C.C. (3d) 356, 21 C.R. (4th) 65 (Ont. C.A.) (possible requirement for warrant to install non-consensual dialled number recorder (DNR)).

[41] See, generally, the discussion of the Ontario Court of Appeal in *R. v. Noseworthy* (1997), 116 C.C.C. (3d) 376, 43 C.R.R. (2d) 313 at pp. 380-381 [C.C.C.], para. 12, reversing (1995), 101 C.C.C. (3d) 447, 1995 CarswellOnt 4283 (Ont. Gen. Div.).

[42] In *Schreiber v. Canada (Attorney-General)* (1997), 114 C.C.C. (3d) 97, 6 C.R. (5th) 314 (Fed. C.A.) at p. 125 [C.C.C.], reversed on other grounds (1998), 124 C.C.C. (3d) 129, 16 C.R. (5th) 1 (S.C.C.).

[43] Ibid. (Fed. C.A.), at p. 125 [C.C.C.]

(a) the judge is satisfied by information on oath in writing that there are reasonable grounds to believe that an offence against this or any other Act of Parliament has been or will be committed and that information concerning the offence will be obtained through the use of the technique, procedure or device or the doing of the thing;

(b) the judge is satisfied that it is in the best interests of the administration of justice to issue the warrant; and

(c) there is no other provision in this or any other Act of Parliament that would provide for a warrant, authorization or order permitting the technique, procedure or device to be used or the thing to be done.

Section 487.01(2) to (7) provide a number of limits on the operation of the broad plenary words of s. 487.01(1) (some of which are discussed below), particularly with respect to intrusions on "bodily integrity" and some instances of the use of video surveillance.[44] Beyond these relatively modest, and reasonable, limitations, s. 487.01 authorizes virtually any investigative technique.

The section has not been significantly altered since its original enactment. The only meaningful change came in 1997 to provide for covert entries and delayed notice to targets[45] (as part of other changes to the *Criminal Code* to enhance the ability of police to combat outlaw biker gangs and other criminal organizations).

(A) Background to Assistance Orders – Section 487.02

Section 487.02 was added to the *Criminal Code* with s. 487.01 in 1993. In its present form it provides:

> **487.02 Assistance order** – Where an authorization is given under section 184.2, 184.3, 186 or 188, a warrant is issued under this Act or an order is made under subsection 492.2(2), the judge or justice who gives the authorization, issues the warrant or makes the order may order any person to provide assistance, where the person's assistance may reasonably be considered to be required to give effect to the authorization, warrant or order.[46]

---

[44] Section **487.01(2)** prohibits the use of techniques which "[interfere] with the bodily integrity of any person"; s. **487.01(3)** calls for "such terms and conditions as the judge considers advisable to ensure that any search or seizure authorized by the warrant is reasonable in the circumstances." Section **487.01(4)** and **(5)** deal with the use of video surveillance and the incorporation of Part VI (interception of private communications) provisions in certain video surveillance situations. Section **487.01(5.1)** and **(5.2)** (added in the 1997 "anti-biker" amendments; see below) deal with covert entry and delayed notice. Section **487.01(6)** and **(7)** deal respectively with inter-provincial execution and the application of the telewarrant provisions.

[45] *An Act to amend the Criminal Code (criminal organizations) and to amend other Acts in consequence*, S.C. 1997, c. 23, s. 13.

[46] Section 487.02 was enacted by S.C. 1993, c. 40, s. 15 and amended by S.C. 1997, c. 18, s. 43.

Prior to 1993 there was no specific provision to authorize orders requiring or permitting the assistance of non-peace officers in the execution of search warrants or other orders.[47] Warrants under s. 487 could, however, be directed to non-peace officers who would then be permitted, but not required, to provide assistance to the police executing the warrant.[48]

Many investigative techniques, however, are only feasible with the assistance of third parties, not all of whom are friendly to the objectives of officers of the law. Moreover, many other techniques can be made far less invasive if third parties are called upon to provide assistance. Assistance orders allow courts to ensure that warrants and authorizations can be executed effectively, and with a minimum of intrusion on the privacy interests of the subject of the search activity.

Section 487.02 was originally enacted to provide for assistance orders in the execution of certain Part VI (interception of private communications) authorizations and general warrants.[49] The section was subsequently amended[50] to its present wording to permit the making of assistance orders in support of *any* warrant issued pursuant to the *Criminal Code*.

(B) *Parliamentary Debates and Committee Hearings*

Remarkably little mention was made of the general warrant and assistance order powers in either the debates or committee hearings on this package of amendments. The focus of discussion at the time seems to have been the modifications to Part VI of the *Criminal Code* (interception of private communications), which made up the bulk of the amending statute. None of the comments from the government in the House of Commons offer significant assistance in the interpretation of the sections under consideration here.[51]

---

[47] Prior to the changes in 1993, section 487 warrants could be directed to "a person named therein or a peace officer" (R.S.C. 1985, c. 27 (1st Supp.), s. 68). No individual officer needed to be named, and the practice was to direct the warrant to "the peace officers of the [police force] and other peace officers in the Province of Ontario." Where voluntary citizen searchers were to be engaged to assist the police, the direction of the warrant would go on to say "and to Jane Smith, Forensic Accountant" or language to like effect.

[48] Non-peace officers who are merely "assisting" the police appear to be permitted without further specific judicial intervention: *Re Old Rex Cafe* (1972), 7 C.C.C. (2d) 279, 19 C.R.N.S. 333 (N.W.T. Terr. Ct.).

[49] The original assistance order provisions related to Part VI authorizations under ss. 184.2, 184.3, 186, 188; to general warrants, s. 487.01; and to number recorders under ss. 492.2(1), 492.2(2).

[50] *An Act to amend the Criminal Code and certain other Acts*, S.C. 1997, c. 18, s. 43.

[51] Some comments about the general warrant or assistance order were made during the debates on Bill C-109 (S.C. 1993, c. 40): *H.C. Debates* (February 26, 1993) at p. 16564; (March 8, 1993) at p. 16650; (March 8, 1993) at p. 52; (May 3, 1993) at p. 18840; (May 3, 1993) at p. 19929; *Senate Debates* (May 6, 1993) at pp. 3224-3225; (May 27, 1993) at p. 3279; (June 21, 1993) at p. 3598. Also, the Honourable Pierre Blais, then Minister of Justice and Attorney General of Canada, characterized the provisions and defended their parameters during committee proceedings: Senate, *Legal and Constitutional Affairs* 48 (June 15, 1993) at pp. 14 and

(b) The Types of Techniques to be Authorized under Section 487.01

(i) *Internal Limitations*

As mentioned, s. 487.01 contains certain internal limitations intended to provide modest curbs on the otherwise untrammelled authority it conveys to judges to issue warrants. These are discussed here.

(A) *Bodily Integrity (Section 487.01(2))*

Section 487.01(2) provides that the general warrant-granting power created by s. 487.01 "shall [not] be construed as to permit interference with the bodily integrity of any person." This provision was particularly significant in the days prior to the enactment of s. 487.05 (DNA warrants). There was considerable debate in the jurisprudence and literature with respect to whether the various techniques for the seizure of DNA (hair pulling, buccal swab, blood) could be authorized in light of the bodily integrity limitation.[52]

A number of different views that have been advanced about this expression. The exact parameters of what is to be included in "bodily integrity" is, of course, important because that will provide an outer limit for the type of physical searches contemplated by the section. The *Oxford English Dictionary* definition of "bodily" includes the following:

> 1. Of the nature of body, corporeal, material, physical; as opposed to *spiritual* . . . .
>
> 2. Of or belonging to the body or physical nature of man. *bodily fear*: alarm for one's physical safety, apprehension of physical harm . . . .

That same reference work defines "integrity," in part, in the following terms:

> 1. The condition of having no part or element taken away or wanting; undivided or unbroken state; material wholeness, completeness, entirety . . . Something undivided; an integral whole . . . .

---

16. Although more extensive discussions took place with the witnesses during committee proceedings at both levels than occurred during the debates, neither committee suggested any amendments in their reports (*H.C. Debates* (April 1, 1993) at p. 17903; *Senate Debates* (June 16, 1993) at p. 3530.

[52] Among a number of cases, reference might be made to *R. v. Campbell, supra*, note 27, per Trafford J. (allowing blood); and *R. v. Hutchinson* (1995), 98 C.C.C. (3d) 221, 1995 CarswellOnt 1267 (Ont. Gen. Div.) (not allowing blood or buccal swabs, but allowing scalp hair plucking because that technique did not interfere with bodily integrity). See also R. Pomerance, " 'Body' of Evidence," *supra*, note 11. Finally, see as well the comments of the Alberta Court of Appeal in *R. v. Love* (1995), 102 C.C.C. (3d) 393, 1995 CarswellAlta 798 (Alta. C.A.) at p. 401 [C.C.C.], leave to appeal refused (1996), 105 C.C.C. (3d) vi (note), [1996] 2 S.C.R. viii (S.C.C.).

2. The condition of not being marred or violated; unimpaired or uncorrupted condition; original perfect state; soundness.

Some cases have used the expression bodily integrity, both in the search and seizure context, and in other areas. In one case (overturned for other reasons), seizure and inspection of urine was said to amount to a breach of the subject's bodily integrity;[53] in another, rectal searches were said to invade bodily integrity.[54] The different ways in which the expression has been used in the cases are not necessarily determinative of a reading of s. 487.01(3); the scope of this limiting section will only be determined as cases dealing with the expression *in this context* begin to be litigated.

The other aspect of "bodily integrity" that seems clear in quality (if not degree) is the notion that no physical harm be occasioned in the execution of the warrant. Thus, while surgery to remove a bullet from a suspect would not "seize" any living tissue, it would necessitate an interference with the physical body of the subject.[55] *Quaere* whether this provision could be used for non-intrusive medical techniques, for example, X-rays or ultrasounds to gather information about a non-cooperative victim or from a target?[56]

Two cases have looked at this expression with differing results. In *Campbell*,[57] the Court considered a pre-DNA warrant bodily sample seizure authorized under s. 487.01. Justice Trafford observed that, "given the scope of the terms 'unreasonable search and seizure' s. 487.01 has potential application to many investigative techniques relating to a person's body."[58] He concluded

---

[53] *Jackson v. Joyceville Penitentiary (Disciplinary Tribunal)* (1990), 55 C.C.C. (3d) 50, 75 C.R. (3d) 174 (Fed. T.D.).

[54] *R. v. Greffe* (1990), 55 C.C.C. (3d) 161, 75 C.R. (3d) 257 (S.C.C.).

[55] This is probably the more difficult aspect of "bodily integrity." Some issue might arise with respect to the question of whether the exemption prohibits modestly invasive "harvests," for example, mouth swabs to gather saliva for dead cells.

[56] X-raying was offered up as a possible s. 487.01 technique in *R. v. Oluwa* (1996), 107 C.C.C. (3d) 236, 49 C.R. (4th) 40 (B.C.C.A.) at pp. 252–253 [C.C.C.], para. 55, additional reasons (1996), 110 C.C.C. (3d) 95, 1996 CarswellBC 1785 (B.C.C.A.).

[57] *R. v. Campbell, supra,* note 27. See also *R. v. Beamish* (1996), 144 Nfld. & P.E.I.R. 338, 1996 CarswellPEI 88, [1996] P.E.I.J. No. 86 (T.D.).

[58] *R. v. Campbell, supra,* note 27, at para. 19. Trafford J. then went on to consider the balancing influence of the "bodily integrity" limitation on this power. His list of techniques which will require scrutiny under this provision is useful, however:

    (a)   The taking of hand, foot and palm prints;

    (b)   The inspection of the body for bruises, wounds and tattoos;

    (c)   The removal of bandages;

    (d)   The removal of dried blood or other bodily fluids from the surface of the skin;

    (e)   The washing of the hands or other parts of the body for the purposes of detecting the presence of gunshot residues, soil or other substances foreign to the body;

    (f)   The scraping of finger nails;

    (g)   The removal of dentures;

    (h)   The examination of the rectal or vaginal areas of the body for the purposes of

that the very limited invasion associated with taking blood by sterile lancet was so insignificant that it could not amount to an "interference" with bodily integrity. The second case, *Hutchinson*,[59] held that blood samples and buccal swabs were invasions of bodily integrity, but authorized hair plucking. The existence of the DNA warrant suggests that, at least where the objective is to obtain genetic information, bodily searches are removed from the ambit of general warrants by operation of s. 487.01(1)(c) (see the discussion below under the heading (e)(iv), "Techniques with Scheduled Offences").

Other techniques such as searching, even strip searching, a person would seem to be permissible (and as a person is not a building, receptacle or place, only a general warrant could authorize such a search).[60]

(B) *Video Surveillance*

Two subsections limit the availability of, or impose conditions upon, the use of video surveillance. These provide:

487.01 (4) **Video surveillance** – A warrant issued under subsection (1) that authorizes a peace officer to observe, by means of a television camera or other similar electronic device, any person who is engaged in activity in circumstances in which the person has a reasonable expectation of privacy shall contain such terms and conditions as the judge considers advisable to ensure that the privacy of the person or of any other person is respected as much as possible.

(5) **Other provisions to apply** – The definition "offence" in section 183 and sections 183.1, 184.2, 184.3 and 185 to 188.2, subsection 189(5), and sections 190, 193 and 194 to 196 apply, with such modifications as the circumstances require, to a warrant referred to in subsection (4) as though references in those provisions to interceptions of private communications were read as references to observations by peace officers by means of television cameras or similar electronic devices of activities in circumstances in which persons had reasonable expectations of privacy.[61]

---

      removing contraband;
  (i) The administration of enemas or emetics;
  (j) The taking of dental impressions;
  (k) The surgical removal of items such as bullets from the body.

[59] *R. v. Hutchinson, supra*, note 52.
[60] "Bed pan vigils" (which involve police waiting for a detainee to defecate), for example, do not involve any intrusion on bodily integrity: *R. v. Monney* (1999), 133 C.C.C. (3d) 129, 24 C.R. (5th) 97 (S.C.C.).
[61] As amended S.C. 1993, c. 40, s. 15; 1997, c. 18, s. 42; 1997, c. 23, s. 13.

The first subsection mandates the use of appropriate minimization clauses to ensure that video surveillance is used in a fashion which is carefully tailored to the justifying state interest.[62]

Section 487.01(5) incorporates by reference a number of provisions usually reserved for interceptions of private communications. These limitations only apply to general warrants involving video surveillance in situations *where such surveillance trenches on situations in which a person has a reasonable expectation of privacy*. This incorporation operates to:

1. limit the offences for which such investigative techniques are available to offences listed in the s. 183 definition of offence;
2. provide a regime for the authorization of consent video surveillance (ss. 183.1, 184.2);
3. provide for the use of "tele-authorizations" for such consent surveillance (s. 184.3);
4. set out further pre-requisites for an authorization including the provisions related to other investigative means (s. 185);
5. require sealing of information to obtain video warrants and to provide a scheme for the disclosure of such material in appropriate cases (ss. 187 to 190).

The net effect on video surveillance is to complicate the entire process so that, where it involves an interference with a reasonable expectation of privacy, it will involve a substantial amount of work in respect of a pre-authorization.[63]

It should be noted, however, that these strictures *only apply if the video equipment is to be used to capture images of persons engaged in conduct where they would have an expectation of privacy*. It is possible to imagine circum-

---

[62] Consider *United States v. Mesa-Rincon*, 911 F.2d 1433 (10th Cir. 1990), for examples of possible minimization clauses.

[63] On the question of reasonable expectation of privacy in respect of video surveillance, consider the judgment of the Quebec Court of Appeal in *R. v. Elzein* (1993), 82 C.C.C. (3d) 455, 1993 CarswellQue 213 (Que. C.A.), leave to appeal refused (1993), 84 C.C.C. (3d) vi (note), 166 N.R. 79 (note) (S.C.C.), where the Court concluded, after referring to *R. v. Wong, supra*, note 39, and *R. v. Duarte, supra*, note 39, that the photographing of the accused was not a search. Chevalier J. (ad hoc), for the Court of Appeal, said (at p. 466 [C.C.C.] [translation]):

> The videotaping and photographing were carried out from outside the areas where certain activities in which the appellant was involved took place, which premises were in addition commercial places and therefore accessible to all who came by. A person who enters or exits from a business establishment cannot reasonably expect that his actions will be protected by the privacy principle and I can not see how the fact that a person, whether or not a police officer, photographs him while he is carrying out this activity infringes the right that he may have to enjoy the privacy of those premises.

A similar proposition is put forward in *R. v. Bryntwick*, 2002 CarswellOnt 3106, [2002] O.J. No. 3618 (S.C.J.). See also *United States v. Cuevas-Sanchez*, 821 F.2d 248 (5th Cir. 1987) on the American approach to expectations of privacy in video situations.

stances where judicial pre-authorization of some sort is necessary even if the creation of the video image is not by itself a search. For example, investigators might seek to place a surreptitious video monitor in a location controlled by the target or an affiliated third party to record "non-private" activity (such as the comings and goings at a public location). Clandestine access to the location might be authorized by a s. 487.01 warrant without trenching on the concerns set out in ss. 487.01(4) and (5).

(C) *Covert Entry*

The last internal limitation was included to provide some statutory guidance for terms and conditions for general warrants which authorize covert entry. Section 487.01(5.1) and (5.2) combine to require and authorize notice to the subject of the intrusion at some time within up to three years of the search. While the sections do not specifically authorize a covert entry, it is obvious that such was contemplated by Parliament.[64]

(ii) *"A Flexible Range of Investigative Procedures"*

Section 487.01's "general warrant" provides a failsafe provision to ensure that almost any investigative technique is available to appropriate state actors. It is useful to examine the catalogue of techniques that have found favour with the courts, either on review when challenged (whether at trial or by way of prerogative writ) or which have been issued.

There have been few appellate considerations of s. 487.01. In *Noseworthy*,[65] the Ontario Court of Appeal looked at the section in the context of a challenge to a general warrant that authorized a search at some future time following some contingent event (a form of warrant sometimes called an "anticipatory warrant"). In that case the police had been ordered to return certain articles to the target of their investigation. In anticipation of complying with the order to

---

[64] Section 487.01(5.1) and (5.2), as enacted by S.C. 1997, c. 23, s. 13, provide:

> **487.01 (5.1) Notice after covert entry** – A warrant issued under subsection (1) that authorizes a peace officer to enter and search a place covertly shall require, as part of the terms and conditions referred to in subsection (3), that notice of the entry and search be given within any time after the execution of the warrant that the judge considers reasonable in the circumstances.

> **(5.2) Extension for period of giving notice** – Where the judge who issues a warrant under subsection (1) or any other judge having jurisdiction to issue such a warrant is, on the basis of an affidavit submitted in support of an application to vary the period within which the notice referred to in subsection (5.1) is to be given, is satisfied that the interests of justice warrant the granting of the application, the judge may grant an extension, or a subsequent extension, of the period, but no extension may exceed three years.

[65] *R. v. Noseworthy, supra,* note 41.

return the material, they obtained a general warrant which issued before the actual deadline to comply with the return order. The general warrant authorized the officers to "re-seize" the articles after they had complied with the order to return them to the target.

While a s. 487 warrant might permit a physical entry and seizure, it required that the things to be seized be at the place to be searched at the time the warrant was sought. The "present tense" requirement of s. 487 meant that authorization under that section was not possible.

The anticipatory warrant which had authorized the re-seizure was challenged by way of prerogative review. The judge conducting the review quashed the warrant. He took a narrow view of s. 487.01 and held that the "anticipatory warrant" was not authorized by the section because the underlying "technique" (physical seizure) was not within the scope of s. 487.01.[66] The reviewing judge concluded that the language in s. 487.01(1) which provided the authority to use "any device or investigative technique or procedure or do any thing" was to be read as an expression of a single concept limited to technological investigations involving surveillance. He said:

> In my view, this would be a rather sweeping interpretation to be given to s. 487.01(1) of the *Code*. I do not think that it is correct. I think that "any thing" must be read as being qualified by the preceding specific enumeration of "device" and "investigative technique or procedure", and in the context of the entire s. 487.01 and related amendments to the *Criminal Code* enacted by S.C. 1993, c. 40, such as ss. 492.1 (tracking devices) and 492.2 (telephone number recorders).
>
> This narrower interpretation is, in my view, reinforced by the language of para. (c) of s. 487.01(1), which provides that the issuing judge must be satisfied that there is no other provision of the *Code* (or any other Act of Parliament) "that would provide for a warrant . . . permitting the technique, procedure or device to be used or the thing to be done".
>
> A warrant for a search of a specified location for specified property unassociated with the use of any specified "device" or "investigative technique or procedure", may be issued under s. 487 of the *Code*. Anticipatory search warrants are not authorized under s. 487 of the *Code*. Had Parliament intended by the enactment of s. 487.01 to implement such an unrestricted approach to the issue of anticipatory search warrants as is suggested by the Crown in this case, the current language of s. 487 of the *Code* would surely have been amended at the same time to modify its restrictive language.[67]

The Ontario Court of Appeal reversed, saying that s. 487.01 was broad enough to embrace anticipatory warrants and other techniques. Justice Austin wrote:

---

[66] *R. v. Noseworthy* (Ont. Gen. Div.), *supra*, note 41.

[67] Ibid. (Ont. Gen. Div.), at p. 451 [C.C.C.].

[10] In my view, the interpretation employed by the motion judge is inconsistent with the purpose of the provision and with the legislative scheme in which it is enacted. That interpretation does not conform to the principles of statutory interpretation or enhance law enforcement or the protection of the values enunciated in the *Canadian Charter of Rights and Freedoms*.

[11] The following aspects of s. 487.01 are noteworthy:

(a) The power to issue warrants under the section is limited to provincial court judges and superior court judges. It is not extended to justices of the peace;

(b) An issuing judge is not bound by the strictures of other warrant provisions, but rather is governed by "the best interests of the administration of justice."

(c) Whereas s. 487 is limited to searching a building, receptacle or a place for a specified thing and to bringing that thing or reporting with respect to it to the court, s. 487.01 authorizes a court to issue a warrant to "use any device or investigative technique or procedure or do any thing described in the warrant." Thus, s. 487.01 is both more specific and more general than s. 487.

(d) The section authorizes warrants relating to offences not yet committed.

(e) Apart from its location in proximity to "device or investigative technique or procedure," there is nothing in the context to suggest that "any thing" should be read *ejusdem generis*. More specifically, "any thing" is not modified by the word "similar" or the phrase "of the same nature" or anything resembling them.

(f) Unlike s. 487, s. 487.01(3) and (4) provide that the judge may make the issuance of the warrant conditional upon such terms and conditions as she or he considers advisable.

(g) Section 487.01 does not provide simply for seizing things which are evidence, contraband or instrumentalities, but rather it provides for the doing of any thing which will yield information concerning an offence, thus paralleling the breadth of the informational privacy interests protected by s. 8 of the *Charter*. See *R. v. Plant*, [1993] 3 S.C.R. 281 at 296-297, 84 C.C.C. (3d) 203.[68]

Had there been any doubt, *Noseworthy* confirmed that the language of s. 487.01 (identifying the nature of the activity to be authorized) is to be given a broad reading consistent with the authorities dealing with the proper interpretation of warrant provisions. Most significantly, the Court held that the words "use any device or investigative technique or procedure or do any thing described in the warrant" are not to be read *ejusdem generis* but rather as discrete

---

[68] *R. v. Noseworthy* (Ont. C.A.), *supra*, note 41, at pp. 379–380 [C.C.C.].

and expansive bases for the issuance of a general warrant. In *R. v. Lauda*, the Court of Appeal further developed its reasoning from *Noseworthy*, saying:

> [24] Section 487.01 was introduced in 1993 and contains several novel features. Unlike a s. 487 warrant which can be issued by a justice of the peace, it can be issued by a superior court or provincial court judge only. Its purpose is described by Fontana in *The Law of Search and Seizure in Canada*, 4th ed. (Toronto: Butterworths, 1997) as follows at 257-8:
>
> > This new warrant is intended to fill an investigatory hiatus in that grey area where the distinction between investigation and search may be unclear and where warrantless surveillance would now be seen as a violating search under s. 8 of the *Charter*.
>
> In *R. v. Noseworthy* (1997), 33 O.R. (3d) 641, 116 C.C.C. (3d) 376, this court ascribed a broader purpose to s. 487.01. In considering its remedial character, the court stated that s. 487.01 provides *a flexible range of investigative procedures, ranging from various forms of surveillance to the search and seizure of tangible objects. . . .*[69] [emphasis added]

(iii) *Examples of Authorized Techniques*

Consistent with this broad approach a number of investigative techniques have been authorized or identified in the literature as appropriate practices for authorization within the scope of s. 487.01's broad grant of judicial power. The following techniques have been authorized:[70]

1. Permitting police (with the compelled assistance of Canada Post) to record postal information (sender and addressee address information) from mailable material delivered to post office box;[71]
2. Taking of DNA samples (pre- s. 487.05) by harvesting biological material from person of target of warrant, including (a) hair,[72] (b) blood,[73] and (c)

---

[69] *R. v. Lauda* (1998), 122 C.C.C. (3d) 74, 13 C.R. (5th) 20 (Ont. C.A.) at pp. 84–85 [C.C.C.], affirmed (1998), 129 C.C.C. (3d) 225, 20 C.R. (5th) 316 (S.C.C.). *Lauda* was not a general warrant case, but rather an instance (now commonly seen) of a court identifying a situation in which a warrant would be required and then indicating that s. 487.01 would provide the authority to grant such a warrant.

[70] These techniques are mentioned in the noted cases, though not always subject to meaningful consideration by the court.

[71] *Canada Post Corp. v. Canada (Attorney General)* (1995), 95 C.C.C. (3d) 568, 1995 CarswellOnt 1803 (Ont. Gen. Div.).

[72] *R. v. Hutchinson, supra,* note 52; *R. v. Beamish, supra,* note 57.

[73] Allowed in *R. v. Campbell, supra,* note 27, per Trafford J. But see *R. v. Hutchinson, supra,* note 52, where this process was not allowed. See also R. Pomerance, " 'Body' of Evidence,"

use of a buccal swab;[74]

3. Surreptitious entry into a storage locker to inspect and record contents (drugs) and to install alarm to notify police when accused re-entered space;[75]

4. Anticipatory searches to "re-seize" evidence that a court has ordered returned to target (where using a conventional s. 487 warrant would have been ineffective);[76]

5. The non-voluntary taking of dental impressions (pre-s. 487.092) from an accused;[77]

6. Review of records to locate information tending to assist police to identify other witnesses or complainants;[78]

7. Surreptitious entry to seize evidence without immediate notice to the accused that a warrant had been executed;[79]

8. Entry onto property to conduct a perimeter search, do additional surveillance, and to seize marijuana growing on site;[80]

9. Pre-planned preservation of dental matter extracted in the normal course

---

supra, note 11. See also the comments of the Alberta Court of Appeal in *R. v. Love, supra*, note 52, at p. 401 [C.C.C.].

[74] Consider the discussion below under heading (e)(iv), "Techniques with Scheduled Offences," for a consideration of the extent to which s. 487.01 might permit warrants to seize biological samples for offences not included in the schedule of offences in s. 487.04.

[75] *R. v. Russell*, 1999 CarswellBC 2199, [1999] B.C.J. No. 2245 (S.C.), warrant quashed on other grounds.

[76] *R. v. Noseworthy* (Ont. C.A.), *supra*, note 41. It should be noted that an important limit has been placed on "anticipatory searches" in *R. v. Brooks* (2003), 178 C.C.C. (3d) 361, 15 C.R. (6th) 319 (Ont. C.A.). There the Court of Appeal held that in order to meet the "no other warrant" requirement, the justice had to find that no other warrant would achieve the same evidence capture, not merely not authorize the particular approach to that task. In other words, if a conventional s. 487 warrant could, as a practical matter, be sought and executed in the normal course, then that should be done, even if an anticipatory warrant might be more convenient to officers.

[77] *R. v. Nguyen*, 1995 CarswellOnt 3182, [1995] O.J. No. 3586 (Ont. Gen. Div.), affirmed on unrelated grounds (2002), 161 C.C.C. (3d) 433, 48 C.R. (5th) 338 (Ont. C.A.). See also *R. v. Stillman* (1997), 196 N.B.R. (2d) 161, 1997 CarswellNB 620 (N.B.Q.B.).

[78] *Zamenzadeh v. Québec (Juge de la Cour du Québec)* (2000), 37 C.R. (5th) 194, 2000 CarswellQue 941 (Que. C.A.), the Court noting that the police might have used s. 487 to seize records, but that would be a different technique.

[79] *R. v. Kuitenen*, 45 C.R. (5th) 131, 2001 CarswellBC 1582, [2001] B.C.J. No. 1292 (S.C.), warrant quashed on other grounds; *R. v. Gatfield*, [2002] O.J. No. 166 (S.C.J.), where the Court said:

> [51] Section 487.01 allows for covert entry under a General Warrant. The police may maintain a long-term investigation without revealing their actions immediately. They may act covertly for an extended period of time without providing notice to the subject. However, the terms and conditions of the warrant must include that notice be given of it within a reasonable time after execution: see s. 487.01(5.1). The time is determined by the issuing court. Extensions may be granted: see 487.01(5.2).

[80] *R. v. Lauda* (Ont. C.A.), *supra*, note 69, at p. 85 [C.C.C.], para. 25.

OBSERVATIONS ON SOME SPECIALIZED WARRANTS

of treatment by prison dentist and subsequent seizure by police for DNA testing;[81]

10. Installation and monitoring of power meter on home;[82]

11. Use of Lumino chemical process on returned vehicle to detect traces of blood;[83]

12. Entry into subject's house to take photos and sketches of home (not in conjunction with execution of other process);[84]

13. Multiple entries into Department of Justice internal investigation unit offices over 12-month period to make copies of data contained on a computer system;[85]

14. Surreptitious audiotape and videotape recording of persons in situations where they have a reasonable expectation of privacy;[86]

15. Seizure of clothing worn by subject;[87]

16. Search for sentencing (dangerous offender) materials;[88]

17. Seizure of materials produced on compulsion of an assistance order (functional production order).[89]

Other cases have suggested, without specifically endorsing, techniques:

18. To provide for a request to other states to provide search assistance;[90]

19. To require X-rays of possible drug smugglers;[91]

---

[81] *R. v. Dorfer* (1996), 104 C.C.C. (3d) 528, 1996 CarswellBC 88 (B.C.C.A.), leave to appeal refused (1997), 41 C.R.R. (2d) 376 (note), 1996 S.C.C.A. 351 (S.C.C.).

[82] *R. v. Cristiensen*, [2001] A.J. No. 1515 (Prov. Ct.) at para. 23, holding authorization necessary and available.

[83] *R. v. Rochon* (2002), 167 C.C.C. (3d) 257 (translation), 2002 CarswellQue 1008 (Que. C.A.), leave to appeal refused (2002), 307 N.R. 196 (note), 2002 CarswellQue 2829 (S.C.C.), not considered on appeal.

[84] *R. v. Royer*, [1999] Q.J. No. 4711 (Prov. Ct.), not in issue in this case. (In *R. v. Gladwin* (1997), 116 C.C.C. (3d) 471, 1997 CarswellOnt 2183 (Ont. C.A.) at pp. 476–477 [C.C.C.], para. 15, leave to appeal refused (1997), 117 C.C.C. (3d) vi, 45 C.R.R. (2d) 376 (S.C.C.), the Ontario Court of Appeal appears to have approved of the use of photographs or videos to record the execution of an otherwise valid search warrant.)

[85] *Keating v. Nova Scotia (Attorney General)*, 194 N.S.R. (2d) 290, 2001 CarswellNS 206, [2001] N.S.J. No. 227 (N.S.S.C.), additional reasons (2001), 198 N.S.R. (2d) 110, 2001 CarswellNS 371 (N.S.S.C.), not in issue in this case.

[86] *R. v. Holtam* (2002), 165 C.C.C. (3d) 502, 2002 CarswellBC 1206 (B.C.C.A.) at pp. 520–523 [C.C.C.], paras. 34, 38, leave to appeal refused (2003), 317 N.R. 397 (note), 2003 CarswellBC 199 (S.C.C.). See also s. 487.01(4).

[87] *R. v. Kitaitchik* (2002), 166 C.C.C. (3d) 14, 95 C.R.R. (2d) 135 (Ont. C.A.); see also *R. v. Sam*, [2003] O.J. No. 819 (S.C.J.).

[88] *R. v. Ongley*, [2003] O.J. No. 3934 (S.C.J.).

[89] *R. v. National Post*, 19 C.R. (6th) 393, 2004 CarswellOnt 173, [2004] O.J. No. 178 (S.C.J.), additional reasons (2004), 236 D.L.R. (4th) 551, 2004 CarswellOnt 984 (Ont. S.C.J.); *Re General Warrant & Assistance Order* (April 4, 2003) (Ont. S.C.J.) (unsealed July 21, 2003).

[90] *Schreiber v. Canada (Attorney General)* (Fed. C.A.), *supra*, note 42, at pp. 125–126 [C.C.C.].

[91] *R. v. Oluwa*, *supra*, note 56, at pp. 252–253 [C.C.C.], para. 55.

20. Vehicle search under guise of routine traffic stop;[92]
21. To take over a repair garage (and alleged "chop-shop") to conduct prolonged search for possible stolen vehicles;[93]
22. To require interviews with prospective non-party witnesses.[94]

Justice Casey Hill, writing extra-judicially,[95] has noted a number of possible general warrant scenarios:

23. Police surveillance or observation post on private property;
24. Perimeter search on private property;
25. Marking private property;
26. Anticipatory searches;[96]
27. Use of forensic techniques at crime scenes;[97]
28. Canine entry, tracking or scenting on private property;
29. Vehicle searches;
30. Access onto computers (pre-s. 487(2.1)).

Other techniques that might be considered:

31. Audio testing (to determine whether an argument could be overheard as claimed by some witnesses);
32. Use of thermal imaging that is able to "see through" walls to gather detailed information about movements inside a home or other private building;[98]
33. Monitoring of factory-installed, or after-market, vehicle GPS systems.[99]

---

[92] *R. v. N. (H.H.)*, 284 A.R. 100, 2000 CarswellAlta 1270, 2000 ABPC 173 (Alta. Prov. Ct.), cited at footnote 21 in S. Coughlan, "General Warrants at the Crossroads: Limit or licence?" (2003) 10 C.R. (6th) 269.

[93] *R. v. Hayman Motors Ltd., supra*, note 37.

[94] Per McMurtry C.J.O. in *R. v. Inco Ltd.* (2001), 155 C.C.C. (3d) 383, 2001 CarswellOnt 1913 (Ont. C.A.) at pp. 400–401 [C.C.C.], paras. 37–38, leave to appeal refused (2002), 90 C.R.R. (2d) 376 (note), 2002 CarswellOnt 765 (S.C.C.) (also discussed below).

[95] C. Hill, "The General Investigative Search Warrant," chapter 1.8 in National Criminal Law Program, 1995 (Federation of Law Societies, 1995), at pp. 10 ff. See also Justice Hill's paper, "The New Search Warrants under Bill C-109" (June 1994) 2 Crown's Newsletter 1–41, prepared before his appointment to the bench.

[96] See *R. v. Noseworthy, supra*, note 41, where this technique is specifically approved of as authorized by s. 487.01. But see also *R. v. Brooks, supra*, note 76, for the limits on this use of s. 487.01.

[97] See also *R. v. Pichette* (2003), 175 C.C.C. (3d) 73 (translation), 11 C.R. (6th) 301, 2003 CarswellQue 21, [2003] Q.J. No. 20 (C.A.).

[98] As to when the use of such technology becomes a "search," see *R. v. Tessling* (October 29, 2004), Doc. 29670, 2004 CarswellOnt 4351, 2004 SCC 67 (S.C.C.), reversing (2003), 171 C.C.C. (3d) 361, 9 C.R. (6th) 36 (Ont. C.A.).

[99] See *State v. Jackson* (September 11, 2003), (Wash. Sup. Ct.).

The potential breadth of the language used in s. 487.01 is exemplified by the judgment of the Court of Appeal in *R. v. Inco Ltd.*[100] There the court commented on the range of activities which might be ordered pursuant to a warrant issued on the authority of provisions in two provincial statutes which are, in all material respects, identical to s. 487.01. Chief Justice McMurtry held that these sections could authorize an order requiring someone to participate in an interview with investigating authorities (compelled conduct which, it is submitted, goes far beyond what is contemplated by most warrant provisions). He said:

> [37] . . . In order to strengthen the enforcement powers under environmental legislation, . . . the OWRA [*Ontario Water Resources Act*, R.S.O. 1990, c. O.40] and the EPA [*Environmental Protection Act*, R.S.O. 1990, c. E.19] were both amended. . . . Among the amendments was the addition of the following provision, which is now found in s. 22.1(2) [en. S.O. 1998, c. 35, s. 58] of the OWRA and s. 163.1(2) [en. S.O. 1998, c. 35, s. 24] of the EPA:
>
> > On application without notice, a justice may issue an order in writing authorizing a provincial officer, subject to this section, to use any device, investigative technique or procedure or to do any thing described in the order if the justice is satisfied by evidence under oath that there are reasonable grounds to believe that an offence against this Act has been or will be committed and that information concerning the offence will be obtained through the use of the device, technique or procedure or the doing of the thing.
>
> [38] An IEB [Ministry of the Environment investigation and enforcement branch] officer who has reasonable and probable grounds to believe that an environmental offence has been committed can now apply for judicial authorization to conduct questioning sessions of the type that were authorized by the former s. 15(1)(n) of the OWRA (now s. 15(2)(*i*)) under the "investigative technique" umbrella.[101]

Similarly, in *Canadian Imperial Bank of Canada v. R.*,[102] the Court concluded that one application of s. 487.01 (in conjunction with s. 487.02) was perfectly consistent with the statute. There the Canadian Imperial Bank of Canada was the banker for a media outlet. The police sought two cancelled cheques which were alleged to be a link to a person breaching prison confidentiality laws. Locating the cheques would require a review of three months' worth of cancelled cheques drawn on the newspaper's accounts. The issuing

---

[100] *R. v. Inco Ltd., supra*, note 94.
[101] Ibid., at pp. 400–401 [C.C.C.].
[102] *Canadian Imperial Bank of Commerce v. R.*, 1997 CarswellOnt 5026, [1997] O.J. No. 5573 (Gen. Div.).

judge had issued the warrant and made an assistance order requiring the CIBC to locate the cheques and provide them to the police. The warrant and assistance order were upheld as being within the authority provided by the *Criminal Code* and as being consistent with the constitutional limitations of s. 8 of the *Charter*.

(c) The Types of Assistance Orders to be Authorized

Section 487.02 has been readily invoked by the courts to ensure that warrants and authorizations continue to be effective tools to gather evidence and information. This approach is, of course, consistent with the various interpretive mandates provided in respect of both the authorizing section and the orders made pursuant to those sections. Courts have used, or indicated a willingness to use, the section to require:

1. *Banks* to search for particular records within a large mass of records for a particular account[103] or to locate off-site records and provide them to police;[104]
2. *Canada Post* employees to identify and copy "cover information" from mailed material, and to keep their activities secret;[105]
3. *Department of Justice* lawyers to submit requests for foreign assistance in an investigation;[106]
4. *Automobile manufacturer/experts* to accompany police to assist in identification of stolen vehicles/parts;[107]
5. *Telephone companies* to provide "all necessary assistance" to install, maintain, monitor, and remove interception equipment;[108]
6. *Newspaper operators* to locate and prepare for seizure materials hidden off-site.[109]

(d) Preconditions to Issuance of General Warrants

(i) *Introduction*

Every warrant power can be considered in terms of the preconditions to authorization and the scope of the investigative authority granted to the state by the warrant if issued. The potential scope for state action has already been

---

[103] Ibid.
[104] *Re Canada (Department of National Revenue)*, [1998] O.J. No. 3517 (Prov. Div.).
[105] *Canada Post Corp. v. Canada (Attorney General)*, *supra*, note 71.
[106] *Schreiber v. Canada (Attorney General)* (Fed. C.A.), *supra*, note 42, at pp. 125–126 [C.C.C.].
[107] *R. v. Hayman Motors Ltd.*, *supra*, note 37.
[108] *R. v. Pham* (1997), 122 C.C.C. (3d) 90, 1997 CarswellBC 2839 (B.C.C.A.), leave to appeal refused [1998] 1 S.C.R. xiii (note) (S.C.C.).
[109] *R. v. National Post*, *supra*, note 89; *Re General Warrant & Assistance Order*, *supra*, note 89.

discussed. The preconditions to issuance – the statutory hurdles which must be passed before a warrant can properly be issued – are considered next.

The general warrant will issue upon a showing that there are reasonable grounds to believe:

1. An offence against the *Criminal Code* or other federal statute has been or will be committed; and that
2. Information concerning the offence will be obtained through the use of the technique, procedure or device or the doing of the thing;
3. The judge is satisfied that it is in the best interests of the administration of justice to issue the warrant; *and*
4. There is no other provision in this or any other Act of Parliament that would provide for a warrant, authorization or order permitting the technique, procedure or device to be used or the thing to be done.

(A) *Issuing Judicial Officer*

Only judges are authorized to issue general warrants.[110] This requirement of a legally trained judicial officer has been identified as a "noteworthy" element of the pre-authorization regime.[111] It is consistent with the wide-ranging and potentially intrusive nature of the warrant provided, and accords with Parliament's general tendency in recent years to reserve potentially invasive warrant powers for more senior members of the judiciary.[112]

(B) *Standard of Proof: "Reasonable grounds to believe"*

The constitutional and statutory standard for the issuance of a general warrant is a showing there are reasonable grounds (rooted in evidence and information acquired by the applicant so far) to believe that the preconditions for issuance exist. This well settled standard of proof asks the question, "Is the warrant applicant's belief a reasonable one, is it objectively justifiable?" The issuing judge is not asked to reach his or her own conclusion on whether he or she shares the belief, only to assess the *reasonableness* of the applicant's conclusion. This standard was helpfully articulated by Justice Hill in *R. v. Sanchez*:

> Mere suspicion, conjecture, hypothesis or "fishing expeditions" fall short of the minimally acceptable standard from both a common law and constitutional per-

---

[110] Section 487.01(1) limits the population of issuing judicial officers to a "provincial court judge, a judge of a superior court of criminal jurisdiction or a judge as defined in section 552 . . . ."

[111] *R. v. Noseworthy* (Ont. C.A.), *supra*, note 41, at p. 379 [C.C.C.], para. 11.

[112] DNA warrants (s. 487.05) are another example of warrants reserved to judges rather than justices of the peace.

spective. On the other hand, in addressing the requisite degree of certitude, *it must be recognized that reasonable grounds is not to be equated with proof beyond a reasonable doubt or a* prima facie *case:* . . . . *The appropriate standard of reasonable or credibly based probability envisions a practical, non-technical and common sense probability as to the existence of the facts and inferences asserted.*

Not only must the affiant subjectively or personally believe in the accuracy and credibility of the grounds of belief, but lawful issuance of a warrant also requires that the peace officer establish that, objectively, reasonable grounds in fact exist. *In other words, would a reasonable person, standing in the shoes of the police officer, have believed that the facts probably existed as asserted and have drawn the inferences therefrom submitted by the affiant* . . . . [113] [emphasis added]

(C) Information Concerning the Offence Will Be Obtained through the Technique

Hunter[114] articulates the basic precondition for establishing that the state's interest in law enforcement has surpassed the individual's interest in privacy in the context of conventional "search and seizure" activity: when there are reasonable grounds to believe that "there is evidence to be found at the place of the search."[115] This language does not track any specific warrant-granting provision. Indeed, various statutory formulations from before and after *Hunter* suggest that various approaches to the investigative "objective" (evidence versus a variety of species of "information") will vary depending on the nature of the intrusion proposed. Statutory standards include grounds to believe (or in some cases suspect) the following:

1. "[object of seizure] will afford *evidence*" (s. 487(1)(b) (conventional warrant));

2. "*anything* [that] . . . *will reveal* the whereabouts of a person who is believed to have committed an offence" (s. 487(1)(b) (warrant to find evidence of fugitive's location));

3. "*information concerning* the offence will be obtained by [the use of the authorized technique]" (s. 487.092(1)(a) (bodily impression warrants); s. 184.2(3) (consent intercepts));

4. "*information* that would *assist in the investigation* of the offence could be obtained" (s. 492.2(1) (number recorder));

---

[113] *R. v. Sanchez* (1994), 93 C.C.C. (3d) 357, 32 C.R. (4th) 269 (Ont. Gen. Div.) at p. 367 [C.C.C.]
[114] *Hunter v. Southam Inc., supra*, note 13.
[115] Ibid., at p. 115 [C.C.C.].

5. *"information* that is *relevant to the commission* of the offence . . . can be obtained" (s. 492.1(1) (tracking device));

6. *"information concerning the offence* will be obtained" (s. 487.01 (general warrant)). [emphasis added]

It is clear that the use of the expression "information" was intended to avoid the problems that might be associated with a potentially legalistic and complex term such as "evidence."[116] It recognizes that the state's compelling interest in advancing criminal investigations may often legitimately seek "information" as a stepping stone to evidence or other information. For example, police might seek to review files, without seizing them, to learn the identity of possible contacts for their investigation.[117]

(D) *The Best Interests of the Administration of Justice*

This precondition requires a judicial balancing of the state's legitimate interest in the swift, effective and complete investigation of all crime, against the countervailing rights of individual citizens to privacy. In the context of wiretap legislation (which included a similar requirement), Mr. Justice Martin of the Ontario Court of Appeal said:

> The prerequisite of the granting of [a wiretap] authorization that the judge be satisfied that, "it would be in the best interests of the administration of justice" to do so, embodies a broad concept. Although the term "in the best interests of the administration of justice" is incapable of precise definition it imports, in my view, in the context, two readily identifiable and mutually supportive components. The first component is that the judge must be satisfied that the granting of the authorization will *further* or *advance* the objectives of justice. The second component imports a balancing of the interests of law enforcement and the individual's interest in privacy.[118] [emphasis in original]

The same precondition appears in respect of DNA warrants,[119] DNA data bank orders[120] and impression warrants.[121] While not an explicit precondition for the issuance of other warrants (for example, it is not a precondition to the issuance of a s. 487 warrant), it is hard to imagine that such an order would be

---

[116] *Descôteaux v. Mierzwinski* (1982), 70 C.C.C. (2d) 385, 28 C.R. (3d) 289 (S.C.C.).
[117] *Zamenzadeh v. Québec (Juge de la Cour du Québec), supra,* note 78.
[118] *R. v. Finlay* (Ont. C.A.), *supra,* note 22, at p. 70 [C.C.C.].
[119] Section 487.05(1).
[120] Sections 487.051(1) and 487.052(1), discussed in *R. v. Hendry* (2001), 161 C.C.C. (3d) 275, 48 C.R. (5th) 310 (Ont. C.A.).
[121] Section 487.092(1).

made in the absence of a conclusion that it was in the best interests of the administration of justice to do so.

The importance of this discretion in the general warrant context, however, deserves this statutory emphasis. The open-ended language has the virtue of flexibility. But it creates a virtually unlimited potential for intrusive techniques to advance any criminal investigation. It is critical that the state make some showing that "the book is worth the candle," that the state objective to be achieved by the proposed invasion of privacy is proportional to the privacy interests being intruded upon. Whether expressed as a statutory term, or as an essential constitutional requirement, this discretion is a crucial component to any palatable search provision.

(E) *No Other Provision That Would Provide for a Warrant*

This requirement is intended to ensure that s. 487.01 is only used to supplement rather than supplant the existing warrant provisions. Where an existing power could authorize the investigative step in issue, the warrant applicant must have resort to that provision and satisfy the appropriate judicial officer that the relevant preconditions for issuance exist.

This does not mean that the technique must be completely novel. Physical seizures which, for one reason or another do not fall within s. 487's ambit, can be authorized. Anticipatory warrants, except for their "future tense" nature, are very similar to s. 487 warrants. Similarly, warrants which seek to seize articles to be located by others (who will be acting under assistance orders) are valid, even though the technique shares qualities with a s. 487 warrant.

This view accords with the judgments of courts reviewing and approving of general warrant and assistance order techniques in the *Canadian Imperial Bank of Commerce*[122] case, *Re General Warrant & Assistance Order*[123] and that which had been proposed in *Re Canada (Department of National Revenue)*.[124] As in *Noseworthy*, the technique involves a result not unlike that at the conclusion of a s. 487 warrant (the police possessing physical evidence of a crime) but it involves procedures that are distinct from those used under the authority of s. 487.

In *Brooks*,[125] the Court of Appeal for Ontario added an important gloss on *Noseworthy*. Anticipatory warrants that "pre-preauthorize" a technique that might otherwise be available do not meet the requirement that no other provision be available, unless the facts of the case make the other conventional warrant impractical. In other words, if a conventional warrant is legally available to achieve the same investigative objective (e.g., seizure of a particular

---

[122] *Canadian Imperial Bank of Canada v. R.*, *supra*, note 102.
[123] *Re General Warrant & Assistance Order*, *supra*, note 89.
[124] *Re Canada (Department of National Revenue)*, *supra*, note 104.
[125] *R. v. Brooks*, *supra*, note 76.

OBSERVATIONS ON SOME SPECIALIZED WARRANTS

item) and is practicable in the circumstances of the particular case, then that conventional warrant should be pursued rather than a s. 487.01 anticipatory general warrant. The anticipatory warrant in *Noseworthy* was justified by the fact that it would not be realistic to return the material and then apply for a warrant to reseize – the only realistic option was an anticipatory warrant.

(e) Specific Issues

(i) *"Rolled-up" Approach*

General warrants are frequently sought and issued as part of an overall investigative strategy that will seek to engage other forms of judicial pre-authorization. For example, an applicant may seek to have a Part VI order made in conjunction with a s. 487.01 warrant for video surveillance, together with the installation of a tracking device in the target's vehicle.

In such cases the police may well seek pre-authorization from a single judicial officer (assuming the judicial officer could properly make all orders sought). In *Re Criminal Code*, the Court observed:

> [5] The rolled-up approach to an application for related orders is a sensible way of assimilating the investigative data underlying the requests of the authorities for related orders. In the context of electronic surveillance, with related physical surveillance, a number of orders working in tandem frequently serve to secure the maximum benefits from each.
>
> [6] In circumstances where the rolled-up application is utilized, it is of course necessary that the statutory preconditions respecting each order be addressed in the affidavit/information in order to ensure compliance with the statute and the reasonableness requirements of s. 8 of the *Charter*.[126]

As a matter of law, a rolled-up application can be based on a single supporting affidavit that articulates the grounds for the issuance of the various orders sought. There is authority which suggests that the supporting material should take the form of an "information" (roughly in the form provided in Form 1).[127]

---

[126] *Re Criminal Code*, [1997] O.J. No. 4393 (Ont. Gen. Div.).

[127] Section 849 provides a very simple version of the s. 487 Information to Obtain:

INFORMATION TO OBTAIN A SEARCH WARRANT
Canada,
Province of .... ,
(*territorial division*).
    This is the information of A.B., of .... in the said (*territorial division*), (*occupation*), hereinafter called the informant, taken before me.
    The informant says that (*describe things to be searched for and offence in respect of which search is to be made*), and that he believes on reasonable grounds that the

There are any number of administrative protocols that govern the application process, which are usually drafted to conform to the needs of a particular judicial area.[128]

(ii) *The "Confirm or Deny" Warrant*

One especially ingenious, but constitutionally suspect, form of s. 487.01 warrant that has been proposed and issued on occasion (usually involving offences of possession of drugs or property obtained by crime) is the "confirm or deny" warrant. Such warrants authorize the police to enter a dwelling (sometimes surreptitiously) to confirm or deny the presence of the contraband articles (stolen goods or controlled substances). Generally these warrants are sought before the police have crystallized reasonable grounds to believe that the articles are at the place to be entered. They do, however, have grounds to believe that entering the house will provide them with "information concerning the offence" which they believe has been committed. The information in question is the confirmation or refutation of the theory that the contraband articles are at the location to be entered. Where entry confirms the presence of the articles the police then use that information to obtain either a s. 487 warrant or a *Controlled Drugs and Substances Act* s. 11 warrant.

These peculiar warrants are not the same as valid "sneak and peek" warrants that authorize entries to permit some record to be made of crimes in progress without taking down a criminal organization. A valid "sneak and peek" warrant is based on a reasonable belief that the evidence to be observed is at the place to be entered but the police, for legitimate investigative reasons, do not wish to conduct a conventional seizure of that evidence at the relevant time.

In the case of the questionable "confirm or deny" warrant the police seek to enter locations where they *cannot say whether evidence will be discovered*, on

---

said things, or some part of them, are in the (*dwelling-house, etc.*) of C.D., of ...... , in the said (*territorial division*). (*Here add the grounds of belief, whatever they may be.*)

Wherefore the informant prays that a search warrant may be granted to search the said (*dwelling-house, etc.*) for the said things.

Sworn before me this .... day of ...., A.D ...., at ....
(*Signature of Informant*)
....
A Justice of the Peace in and for ....

Two authorities – *Re Magar*, 1998 CarswellOnt 2429, [1998] O.J. No. 2495 (Ont. Prov. Div.) and *Re Canada (Department of National Revenue)*, *supra*, note 104 – combine to suggest that the "information on oath" required by s. 487.01 must include the substantive qualities of Form 1, and that one important element of such a form is that it is sworn before a Justice of the Peace rather than a Commissioner for taking oaths.

[128] See *Re Application for a General Warrant pursuant to S. 487.01 of the Criminal Code*, 2002 CarswellSask 70, 2002 SKPC 11, [2002] S.J. No. 54 (Prov. Ct.) for a review of judicial protocols and considerations that go into them.

the theory that finding out whether evidence is there or not, is "information" that should be available to the police for further investigative steps. It is, of course, possible to have the words of s. 487.01 surrender such an interpretation if sufficient brute force is applied. There is no other technique and there will be information in the form of the confirmation or refutation of the location as a place involved in crime. But such a tortured approach is problematic at best.

First, if the police lack the grounds to enter the location under s. 487, it is hard to see how it is in the best interests of the administration of justice to let them engage in the same entry to get grounds. The ambivalent state objective (uncertain whether it will inculpate or clear the location) is so vague or uncertain that it cannot justify the intrusion proposed.

Second, carried forward logically, such an approach would permit searches of any location which might be associated with criminality. Neighbourhoods with high crime rates might be entered and "swept" with such "confirm or deny" warrants. The prevalence of grow operations in some locations in Canada might justify entries into a number of homes to determine which of the houses on a street had the ubiquitous basement marijuana farm.

While such a warrant would be a powerful weapon for those involved in protecting the community from crime, it is difficult to imagine what privacy would look like if such warrants were readily available.

(iii) *Returns in General Warrant Cases*

Following the successful execution of a conventional search warrant the seizing officer is obliged to make a report to a justice. Section 489.1 requires "a peace officer [who] has seized anything under a warrant issued under this Act or under section 487.11 [statutory exigent circumstances] or 489 [statutory plain view] or otherwise in the execution of duties under this or any other Act of Parliament, the peace officer shall, as soon as is practicable, . . . return the thing seized, . . . and report to the justice. . . ." This is an expanded view of this requirement which was put in place in 1997.[129]

The historical reason for this provision is to provide for judicial supervision of property interests. Section 490 provides for a variety of procedures to deal with conflicting claims to seized property.

In a post-*Charter* world, a secondary purpose of this process is a form of judicial post-seizure supervision of non-property interests.

The general warrant provisions authorize techniques that will not necessarily involve any sort of physical seizure. In the absence of such a seizure there is no statutory process for judicial post-seizure supervision. It remains open, however, to a judge to require some form of return as a term or condition of a s. 487.01 warrant. Indeed, warrant applicants are well advised to incorporate

---

[129] *An Act to amend the Criminal Code and certain other Acts*, S.C. 1997, c. 18, s. 49.

customized return provisions in their proposed warrants to add to the overall reasonableness of any authorized technique.

(iv) *Techniques with Scheduled Offences*

By its terms the s. 487.01 general warrant is available to fill any authorization lacuna which may exist. The language in s. 487.01(1)(c), that

> there is no other provision in this or any other Act of Parliament that would provide for a warrant, authorization or order permitting the technique, procedure or device to be used or the thing to be done

is the principal limitation on the availability of the warrant. If no other authorization power is available, s. 487.01 steps in to fill the void.

A question arises whether this broad provision can be invoked to authorize the use of an existing technique in circumstances which fall outside of an existing, more specific, authorization regime.

For example, the DNA warrant regime authorizes particular techniques to gather biological material from the subject of an investigation.[130] But one of the preconditions for the issuance of a warrant authorizing this technique is the requirement that the offence under investigation be one of a number of "scheduled" offences (which is, in general, limited to serious personal injury offences).[131] DNA warrants are not available for the investigation of, for example, extortion.[132]

An officer who wishes to prove the connection between an accused and an envelope used to deliver an extortive message might want to obtain a buccal swab or blood sample to compare to the genetic material left on the moistened seal licked to close the envelope. At first blush, a literal reading of the section would seem to permit a s. 487.01 warrant in these circumstances. There is no doubt that "information concerning the offence will be obtained through the use of the [proposed] technique." As well, the limitation on the availability of

---

[130] The techniques authorized under the DNA regime are set out in s. 487.06, as amended to S.C. 2000, c. 10, s. 19:

> **487.06** (1) **Investigative procedures** – A peace officer or another person under the direction of a peace officer is authorized to take samples of bodily substances from a person by a warrant under section 487.05 or an order under section 487.051 or 487.052 or an authorization under section 487.055 or 487.091, by any of the following means:
>
> (a) the *plucking of individual hairs* from the person, including the root sheath;
> (b) the *taking of buccal swabs* by swabbing the lips, tongue and inside cheeks of the mouth to collect epithelial cells; or
> (c) the *taking of blood by pricking the skin* surface with a sterile lancet. [emphases added]

[131] Sections 487.05(1)(a) and 487.04.
[132] Section 346.

s. 487.05 warrants means that there would be "no other provision in this or any other Act of Parliament that would provide for a warrant . . . permitting the technique."

Such an interpretation of s. 487.01 would, however, seem to be inconsistent with Parliament's expressed intention that this invasive technique is only justified in cases involving certain identified offences. Applying this logic to other similar techniques, would permit, for example, using s. 487.01 to obtain wiretaps for offences not scheduled in s. 183. That result would be inconsistent with the long-settled intent behind Part VI and the regime for the authorization of interceptions of private communications. It would also be at odds with the interpretive principle which recognizes that specific legislative provisions "trump" general provisions.

A similar problem arises in the context of DNA warrants where the person to be tested is not an alleged party to the offence.[133] For example, in a case where the police require a genetic sample from an non-cooperating victim to confirm that blood found on the accused was from the victim, it is not possible to obtain a sample under s. 487.05. No other provision applies. Can s. 487.01 fill this "gap"? As attractive as that option may seem, it is difficult to square with the clear limits placed on genetic harvesting by the carefully considered (if poorly drafted) DNA regime.

(v) *Cover-ups and Distractions: Terms and Conditions*

Covert or surreptitious entries and seizures are a favourite technique under s. 487.01. As well, police sometimes seek to search without disclosing their true purpose.[134] Such investigative gambits permit the police to discover and preserve evidence and information while permitting a criminal enterprise to carry on. Police are able to build a more compelling case without "taking down" the targets of their probe.

General warrants have issued authorizing surreptitious entries and seizures of contraband and, by their terms and conditions, permitted the police to "stage" a break and enter to serve as a "cover" for what would otherwise have been discovered as a police search. The question arises whether such terms are within the scope of s. 487.01.

While the section does not specifically authorize such "cover-ups," one might make a compelling argument that such authority is a reasonable and necessary power to give effect to the clearly authorized covert entries. There is no doubt that covert entries will require some degree of subterfuge by the authorities. Terms which carefully prescribe how a staged break-in is to be

---

[133] Recall that s. 487.05(1)(c) requires that the person to be tested be "a party to the offence" that is being investigated.

[134] *R. v. N. (H.H.)*, *supra*, note 92 (s. 487.01 used to authorize vehicle search disguised as routine traffic stop), cited in S. Coughlan, "General Warrants at the Crossroads," *supra*, note 92.

achieved (damage to the point of entry, police obligation to repair, removal of "distracter" items besides objects of evidence, police attendance to take a "report" of the "break-in") are legitimate provided their purpose is to make the existing technique effective.

One might question how far such warrants can (or need to) go in light of ss. 25.1 to 25.4 and the regime now in place to govern the administrative authorization of the commission of certain acts that would normally amount to criminal offences.[135]

(f) No Provincial Offences

While a general warrant is available to investigate any federal offence, it is not available to advance an investigation into a breach of provincial statute.

4. Special Locations

(a) Law Offices after the Demise of Section 488.1

(i) *Introduction*

The Supreme Court of Canada has recently reviewed the law related to searches of law offices in the context of a successful challenge to the *Criminal Code* sections controlling such searches.[136] Section 488.1 set up a procedural regime for law office searches that required lawyers to claim privilege and name a client before privilege was engaged. Police were required to seal materials if such a request was made. The section then set up a procedure that required the subject of the search to make an application to the Court to get the material back and permitted the Crown to see the material if the Court thought that might assist in determining whether it should be privileged. It set up strict time limits and established a default position that failure to pursue the application in time would lead to material being turned over to the police.

The Court identified a number of problems with s. 488.1 of the *Criminal Code* (the section that had regulated law office searches since 1985). Those problems are summarized below:[137]

1. *The absence or inaction of the solicitor.*
   If no one was present at the lawyer's office, or if the lawyer was negligent or otherwise failed to claim privilege, then privilege would be lost. By

---

[135] See the provisions added by S.C. 2001, c. 32, s. 2 and, more generally, *R. v. Campbell* (1999), 133 C.C.C. (3d) 257, 24 C.R. (5th) 365 (S.C.C.).
[136] *R. v. Lavallee, Rackel & Heintz*, 167 C.C.C. (3d) 1, 3 C.R. (6th) 209, 2002 CarswellAlta 1818, 2002 SCC 61 (S.C.C.).
[137] Ibid., at pp. 230–233 [C.R.], paras. 27–33.

effectively putting the onus to the lawyer and providing for a default position for the disclosure of material, s. 488.1 unfairly exposed solicitor-client privileged material to release to the state.

2. *The naming of clients.*
   The section required the lawyer to name clients. Sometimes, however, even naming a client is a breach of privilege.

3. *The fact that notice is not given to the client.*
   Because s. 488.1 left it to the searched lawyer to name and notify the subject client, it was possible for a person to have their solicitor-client privilege breached without his or her knowledge.

4. *Its strict time limits.*
   The strict time limits of s. 488.1, and the default position which saw material disclosed if there was a breach of such limits, was unconstitutional. It permitted disclosure of potentially privileged materials without a judge ever considering the matter.

5. *An absence of discretion on the part of the judge determining the existence of solicitor client privilege.*
   The section was structured in a way that suggested that there was no discretion in the judge hearing an application to determine whether privilege existed in some situations.

6. *The possibility of the Attorney General's access prior to that judicial determination.*
   The section allowed the judge to permit the Crown to look at the materials before a decision about privilege had been made to assist in making submissions. In some cases this would result in privileged materials being seen by the Crown.

   The demise of s. 488.1 does not mean that the police cannot search a law office. It does mean, however, that the clarity that s. 488.1 had provided to the procedure is gone. The common law as restated in *Lavallee*[138] governs. In its judgment in that case the majority of the Supreme Court of Canada summarized the rules related to law office searches as follows:

   1. No search warrant can be issued with regards to documents that are known to be protected by solicitor-client privilege.
   2. Before searching a law office, the investigative authorities must satisfy the issuing justice that there exists no other reasonable alternative to the search.

---

[138] Ibid.

3. When allowing a law office to be searched, the issuing justice must be rigorously demanding so to afford maximum protection of solicitor-client confidentiality.

4. Except when the warrant specifically authorizes the immediate examination, copying and seizure of an identified document, all documents in possession of a lawyer must be sealed before being examined or removed from the lawyer's possession.

5. Every effort must be made to contact the lawyer and the client at the time of the execution of the search warrant. Where the lawyer or the client cannot be contacted, a representative of the Bar should be allowed to oversee the sealing and seizure of documents.

6. The investigative officer executing the warrant should report to the Justice of the Peace the efforts made to contact all potential privilege holders, who should then be given a reasonable opportunity to assert a claim of privilege and, if that claim is contested, to have the issue judicially decided.

7. If notification of potential privilege holders is not possible, the lawyer who had custody of the documents seized, or another lawyer appointed either by the Law Society or by the court, should examine the documents to determine whether a claim of privilege should be asserted, and should be given a reasonable opportunity to do so.

8. The Attorney General may make submissions on the issue of privilege, but should not be permitted to inspect the documents beforehand. The prosecuting authority can only inspect the documents if and when it is determined by a judge that the documents are not privileged.

9. Where sealed documents are found not to be privileged, they may be used in the normal course of the investigation.

10. Where documents are found to be privileged, they are to be returned immediately to the holder of the privilege, or to a person designated by the court.

Solicitor-client privilege is a rule of evidence, an important civil and legal right and a principle of fundamental justice in Canadian law. While the public has an interest in effective criminal investigation, it has no less an interest in maintaining the integrity of the solicitor-client relationship. Confidential communications to a lawyer represent an important exercise of the right to privacy, and they are central to the administration of justice in an adversarial system. Unjustified, or even accidental infringements of the privilege erode the public's confidence in the fairness of the criminal justice system. This is why all efforts must be made to protect such confidences.[139]

---

[139] Ibid., at pp. 240–241 [C.R.], para. 49.

(ii) The *Post*-Lavallee *Law Office Search*

Prior to seeking a law office search warrant, police would be well advised to consult with a Crown. These warrants have always been highly contentious and are now even more so.

A warrant application must show reasonable grounds to believe that the material to be seized is not subject to solicitor-client privilege. Not every communication between a lawyer and a client is privileged, nor is every document in a lawyer's file privileged. This being said, there is a practical (if not a legal) presumption that material in a law office is privileged and so the warrant applicant should address why the material sought is not covered by privilege. There are a number of possible reasons:

1. the material was created by or with, or was intended to be shared with, someone *outside* the solicitor-client relationship;[140]
2. the solicitor-client relationship existed to permit or facilitate the commission of a fraud or other crime;[141]
3. the documents are not part of a *bona fide* solicitor-client relationship (i.e., they relate to a business venture between the lawyer and another person who is not seeking legal advice).

As well, a warrant applicant should satisfy the court that the things to be seized are not reasonably available from any other source. Often it will be necessary to seize materials from a law office to place knowledge in a particular party's hands, or to obtain originals for forensic study. Both reasons would be a basis for seizure, even if the content of the things to be seized were available in copies in other locations.

The presence of a member of the Law Society to supervise the search will be essential if there is any reason to believe that the lawyer being searched will not be there, or if the lawyer being searched is implicated in any sort of wrongdoing. Normally the best course is to contact the Law Society beforehand and ask for the name of the appropriate person to identify in an assistance order. Such an order provides the Law Society with the legal authority (indeed, obligation) to attend and assist.

A warrant to search a law office post-*Lavallee* should include the following conditions:

1. The search will be conducted, if possible, in the presence of a partner with the firm, offering the least intrusion into the normal operating practices of the offices during the business hours of the offices.

---

[140] *R. v. Dunbar* (1982), 68 C.C.C. (2d) 13, 28 C.R. (3d) 324 (Ont. C.A.).
[141] *Borden & Elliot v. R.* (1975), 30 C.C.C. (2d) 337, 70 D.L.R. (3d) 579 (Ont. C.A.) at p. 588 [D.L.R.].

2. If no partner of the firm is present upon the attendance of the police, no search will commence for at least thirty minutes after the peace officers have announced their reason for attendance or until a solicitor is present – whichever occurs first.

3. Pursuant to the Assistance Order made this day [Law Society representative] of the [Law Society] shall attend for the execution of the warrant and take whatever steps are required to supervise the execution of the warrant and assert any relevant claim of privilege not made by the solicitors whose offices are being searched.

4. All and any documents to be seized will be immediately sealed and initialed by the seizing peace officer, without further examination or copying. Any overseeing solicitor or the [Law Society representative] will be given the opportunity to initial all seized documents.

5. Any and all documents seized in their packaged and unexamined state will be taken forthwith or as soon as practicable to the Sheriff [or other official] and shall be stored there to be dealt with as the Superior Court may order.

6. A copy of the warrant to search will be presented upon arrival of police and deposited with the legal office at the conclusion of the search.

The assistance order under s. 487.02 for the law society representative might appear in these terms:

> WHEREAS, it appears upon the Information of [Detective Constable] that the assistance of [Law Society representative] is necessary to ensure the proper execution of this Search Warrant.
>
> This, THEREFORE is to authorize and require, pursuant to section 487.02 of the *Criminal Code*, that
>
> [Law Society representative] provide such assistance as is set out in this Assistance Order and to take such steps as are necessary to assist in the execution of the Warrant to which this Assistance Order is attached on [date for execution].

(b) Media Outlets

It is not uncommon for media organizations (newspaper, radio and television reporters) to witness and record evidence of offences, both criminal and regulatory. In such cases it may be appropriate for an investigator to obtain a warrant to search for and seize material from the identified media organization. Because of the important place of freedom of expression in our society, however, special provisions should be made in the case of such searches.[142] Like all search warrant applications, an application for a warrant to search for and seize material from a media organization requires the investigator to satisfy

---

[142] *R. v. Canadian Broadcasting Corp.* (2001), 42 C.R. (5th) 290, 2001 CarswellOnt 538 (Ont. C.A.), leave to appeal refused (2001), 276 N.R. 398 (note), 2001 CarswellOnt 3075 (S.C.C.).

the justice of the peace that the state's interest in the investigation of wrong-doing is superior to the interests of the subject of the search in privacy. Freedom of expression and the need to foster a free press suggest restraint (both by the investigator and the issuing justice) in the pursuit of material from media organizations dedicated to the collection and dissemination of information. These searches are fraught with legal pitfalls – the investigator considering such a search would be well advised to consult legal counsel in advance.

In two 1993 cases, the Supreme Court of Canada set down helpful and clear rules to govern such warrant applications. In *Canadian Broadcasting Corp. v. New Brunswick (Attorney General)*[143] and *Canadian Broadcasting Corp. v. Lessard,*[144] the Court looked at searches of television stations for videotaped evidence of criminal conduct at a labour demonstration. Mr. Justice Cory summarized the position of the Court on the procedure to be adopted in such cases in these terms:

> It may be helpful to summarize the factors to be considered by a justice of the peace on an application to obtain a warrant to search the premises of a news media organization, together with those factors which may be pertinent to a court reviewing the issuance of a search warrant.

> (1) It is essential that all the requirements set out in s. 487(1)(*b*) of the *Criminal Code* for the issuance of a search warrant be met.

> (2) Once the statutory conditions have been met, the justice of the peace should consider all of the circumstances in determining whether to exercise his or her discretion to issue a warrant.

> (3) The justice of the peace should ensure that a balance is struck between the competing interests of the state in the investigation and prosecution of crimes and the right to privacy of the media in the course of their news gathering and news dissemination. It must be borne in mind that the media play a vital role in the functioning of a democratic society. Generally speaking, the news media will not be implicated in the crime under investigation. They are truly an innocent third party. This is a particularly important factor to be considered in attempting to strike an appropriate balance, including the consideration of imposing conditions on that warrant.

> (4) The affidavit in support of the application must contain sufficient detail to enable the justice of the peace to properly exercise his or her discretion as to the issuance of a search warrant.

> (5) Although it is not a constitutional requirement, the affidavit material should ordinarily disclose whether there are alternative sources from

---

[143] *Canadian Broadcasting Corp. v. New Brunswick (Attorney General)* (1991), 67 C.C.C. (3d) 544, 9 C.R. (4th) 192 (S.C.C.).

[144] *Canadian Broadcasting Corp. v. Lessard* (1991), 67 C.C.C. (3d) 517, 9 C.R. (4th) 133 (S.C.C.).

which the information may reasonably be obtained and, if there is an alternative source, that it has been investigated and all reasonable efforts to obtain the information have been exhausted.

(6) If the information sought has been disseminated by the media in whole or in part, this will be a factor which will favour the issuing of the search warrant.

(7) If a justice of the peace determines that a warrant should be issued for the search of media premises, consideration should then be given to the imposition of some conditions on its implementation, so that the media organization will not be unduly impeded in the publishing or dissemination of the news.

(8) If, subsequent to the issuing of a search warrant, it comes to light the authorities failed to disclose pertinent information that could well have affected the decision to issue the warrant, this may result in a finding that the warrant was invalid.

(9) Similarly, if the search itself is unreasonably conducted, this may render the search invalid.[145]

Where a warrant is sought in relation to premises ordinarily occupied by a media organization (as an innocent third party), the justice of the peace should be provided with the information necessary to enable him or her to exercise discretion in relation to: (i) whether to issue the warrant; and (ii) what special terms to attach to the execution to the warrant. Such terms should be directed at minimizing the impact of the search on the general operations of the organization and, more particularly, on the operations of the organization *qua* media organization.

For example, the warrant authorizing the search for, and seizure of, material generated by a number of Toronto media organizations following the riots in Toronto in May 1992 included the following special terms endorsed upon the warrant following the suggestion of the informant:

1. The police officer(s) executing the search warrant shall serve a copy of the information to obtain this search warrant and a copy of the warrant at the premises subject to the search.

---

[145] *Canadian Broadcasting Corp. v. New Brunswick (Attorney General)*, *supra*, note 143, at pp. 560–561 [C.C.C.]. Courts are not reluctant to strike down such warrants where they fail to meet the general preconditions for authorization: *Canadian Broadcasting Corp. v. British Columbia* (1994), 32 C.R. (4th) 256, [1994] B.C.J. No. 1543 (B.C. S.C.) and *Canadian Broadcasting Corp. v. Newfoundland* (1994), 119 Nfld. & P.E.I.R. 140, 370 A.P.R. 140 (Nfld. T.D.). Note especially the comments of the Court in *Canadian Broadcasting Corp. v. Newfoundland* with respect to the imposition of terms and conditions. The Court noted that the absence of such terms was not, by itself, a ground to quash the warrant, but stressed that the issuing justice had not been told of any special reason for the imposition of such terms.

2. The police officer(s) possessing the original copy of the warrant to search shall thereafter request surrender or production of the things to be searched for and seized as described [in the warrant].

3. Thereafter the police officer(s) executing this search warrant shall provide a period of time, of not less that [sic] 3 hours in duration, to permit voluntary production of the things to be searched for.

4. Failing production of the said things to be searched for, the police officer(s) executing this search warrant shall search the premises of place for things described in this warrant, seize same and carry them away to be dealt with according to law. In searching, the police shall interfere as little as possible with the operations of the place being searched and avoid, to the extent possible, examining any notes, documents, records or lists unconnected with securing the location of the things subject to seizure.

5. In the event that anyone on [the day fixed for the execution of the warrant] at the place to be searched, following upon voluntary production and seizure by the police or following upon search and seizure by the police, requests that the things subject to seizure be sealed the police officer(s) executing this search warrant shall:

    (A) without making copies of said material suitably seal the things seized in a package and identify the package,

    (B) record on the package the identity of the person requesting sealing of the things and any reason advanced for the said sealing,

    (C) place the package in the custody of the office of the clerk of the Ontario Court (Provincial Division) at 60 Queen Street West, Toronto.

6. Where no application has been made to this Court within fourteen days of seizure for the continued sealing and return of any things sealed pursuant to paragraph 5 of the police officer(s) executing the search warrant may obtain release of the sealed package from the clerk's office and access its contents.

7. Where an application is made to this Court, on notice of the Attorney General of Ontario, within fourteen days of seizure for the continued sealing and the return of things seized, the Court will, upon hearing the parties establish such procedure and hold such hearing as may be within its jurisdiction respecting said things.

These conditions provide a simple and fair balance between the right of the press to conduct their constitutionally significant information gathering/distribution function, with the equally legitimate need to allow investigators effectively to investigate and prosecute wrongdoing.

(i) *Conditions to Ensure Proper Execution*

There is a duty on the issuing judicial officer to add conditions to prevent any serious impediment to the proper functioning of the media outlet subject to the search in question. If conditions cannot prevent impeding media functions, then the warrant should only issue as a last resort.[146]

(ii) *The Possibility of* Inter Partes *Hearings*

The media are often aware that the police will be seeking a warrant, though they may not know the details of the application. They will almost always seek to have notice of the application so that they can attend and make submission to the judicial officer considering the warrant. The authorities are clear that there is a strong presumption that warrant applications are *ex parte*.[147]

That said, in some situations the court has accepted that notice might be appropriate. That possibility is "remote in the extreme" but the court could "not foreclose, at least in theory, the possibility that in some instances," the justice should provide notice.[148]

Where a media outlet requests notice, the applicant should normally decline but agree to place any correspondence or other material from the subject of the proposed search before the court on the application.

(c) Hospitals and Doctors' Offices

(i) *Regular Medical Records*

Some earlier authority suggested that special rules attached to the seizure of medical records.[149] Later cases seemed to hold that ordinary medical records are seizable on the basis of a s. 487 warrant without special endorsement or particular pleading[150] (unless provincial legislation suggests some other additional process).[151]

However, at least one court has found a need for special endorsements where the police seek to seize third-party health records. In *R. v. Serendip Physiotherapy*, the Court held where the police seek to seize health records from non-targets a "seize and seal" process was mandatory:

[68] If the Justice of the Peace determines that the documents sought are health records and that there may be a privacy interest of a patient at risk if the records

[146] *R. v. Canadian Broadcasting Corp.*, *supra*, note 142, at p. 307 [C.R.], paras. 66–67.

[147] *R. v. F. (S.)*, *supra*, note 12; *R. v. Canadian Broadcasting Corp.*, *supra*, note 142.

[148] *R. v. Canadian Broadcasting Corp.*, *supra*, note 142, at p. 293 [C.R.].

[149] *R. v. Worth* (1989), 54 C.C.C. (3d) 215, 1989 CarswellOnt 858, [1989] O.J. No. 1301 (Ont. H.C.), affirmed (1989), 54 C.C.C. (3d) 215 at 223, 1989 CarswellOnt 2347, [1989] O.J. No. 2450 (Ont. C.A.).

[150] *R. v. O'Connor* (1995), 103 C.C.C. (3d) 1, 44 C.R. (4th) 1 (S.C.C.).

[151] *R. v. French* (1977), 37 C.C.C. (2d) 201, 1977 CarswellOnt 1011 (Ont. C.A.) at pp. 213–214 [C.C.C], affirmed (1979), 47 C.C.C. (2d) 411, [1980] 1 S.C.R. 158 (S.C.C.); *R. v. McArthur* (June 1, 1987) (Ont. C.A.) at p. 14; *R. v. Waterford Hospital* (1983), 6 C.C.C. (3d) 481, 35 C.R. (3d) 348 (Nfld. C.A.).

are seized, then the Justice of the Peace should proceed in accordance with these guidelines:

(a) The warrant should require that the records be sealed immediately upon seizure and remain sealed until a judicial officer holds a hearing. The records must not be read by the police until a judicial officer can make a determination as outlined below. . . .

(b) Where it is practically feasible to give notice, the Justice of the Peace should require the applicant, after the execution of the warrant, to give notice to those in possession of the records and to those who have a privacy interest in the records to permit them to make submissions as to the balancing of the competing interests . . . .

(c) The applicant and those persons receiving notice should be afforded an opportunity to make submissions to the judicial officer who is to make the decision about disclosure after the search warrant is executed.

(d) The judicial officer must make a decision as to whether and to what extent to require disclosure after balancing the competing interests of the police need to investigate crime and a patient's right to privacy. In making this determination the judicial officer should consider these factors:

   (i) Is the record likely to be relevant to the alleged crime? . . .

   (ii) The extent to which the records are necessary for the police to investigate a crime. . . .

   (iii) The probative value of the record.

   (iv) The nature and extent of the reasonable expectation of privacy vested in that record.

   (v) The potential prejudice to the privacy of the person who is the subject of the record.

(e) The judicial officer should consider examining the records to determine whether and to what extent they should be disclosed. . . .

(f) The judicial officer should consider restricting disclosure and mitigating the invasion of privacy by imposing conditions.[152]

It is difficult to reconcile the rule in *Serendip Physiotherapy* with other well established search warrant principles. The only area where post-seizure *inter partes* hearings are considered mandatory is law office searches, but special status given to solicitor-client privilege readily distinguishes such locations. The Crown has appealed the decision in *Serendip Physiotherapy* to the Court of Appeal.[153]

---

[152] *R. v. Serendip Physiotherapy Clinic* (2003), 175 C.C.C. (3d) 474 (Ont. S.C.J.) at pp. 487–488 [C.C.C.], para. 68.

[153] Ontario Court of Appeal Doc. 40275.

(ii) *Psychiatric Records*

The position with respect to psychiatric records is less clear. There is authority suggesting that the appropriate course is to follow a procedure mirroring that used in the law office and media outlet context.[154]

5. Mail Searches

Mail being delivered by Canada Post enjoys a peculiar elevated status under the *Canada Post Corporation Act*.[155] The Act makes it an offence to "open. . . delay or detain" mail unless "expressly authorized" to do so under that statute (apparently ousting the *Criminal Code* authority under s. 487).[156] "Mail" is limited to "mailable matter from the time it is posted to the time it is delivered to the addressee. . .".[157] Mail is "delivered" once it is placed in the post box, or post office box to which it is addressed.[158] This odd conundrum might be addressed using a general warrant (to seize the material after it has been delivered and thereby ceases to be "mail"), but care should be taken in the drafting of such a warrant.[159]

6. *"Feeney* Warrants" – Section 529 and 529.1 Warrants and Related Orders

The judgment of the Supreme Court of Canada in *Feeney*[160] held that police require search warrants to enter dwelling houses to give effect to a routine power of arrest or apprehension. This struck down the old common law rule, which had provided a relatively unrestrained power of entry whenever a power of arrest existed.[161]

In response to the new need for a warrant, Parliament put in place ss. 529 to 529.4, which create a mini-code for the consideration of "entry to arrest" activity, both warranted and warrantless.

There are two forms of judicial order available under this regime – the s. 529 endorsement and the freestanding entry order. Section 529 provides for a

---

[154] See *R. v. L. (J.)*, [2000] O.J. No. 2796 (S.C.J.) (a judgment that may have been removed from the Quicklaw database temporarily because of a publication ban pending trial); and *R. v. O. (J.)*, [1996] O.J. No. 4799 (Gen. Div.).

[155] *Canada Post Corporation Act*, R.S.C. 1985, c. C-10.

[156] Ibid., s. 48.

[157] Ibid., s. 2(1).

[158] Ibid., s. 2(2).

[159] *Canada Post Corp. v. Canada (Attorney General)* (1995), 95 C.C.C. (3d) 568, 1995 CarswellOnt 1803 (Ont. Gen. Div.).

[160] *R. v. Feeney* (1997), 115 C.C.C. (3d) 129, 7 C.R. (5th) 101 (S.C.C.), reconsideration granted [1997] 2 S.C.R. 117 (S.C.C.).

[161] *R. v. Landry* (1986), 25 C.C.C. (3d) 1, 50 C.R. (3d) 55 (S.C.C.).

special endorsement on the back of a conventional arrest warrant. The endorsement is made at the time that the arrest warrant is issued. It is based on some written application by the officer seeking the arrest warrant. The preconditions for the making of the s. 529 endorsement (beyond the basis for the issuance of the arrest warrant itself) is simply a showing of reasonable grounds to believe that the person to be arrested "is or will be present in the dwelling-house."

The freestanding entry order under s. 529.1 is intended to deal with those situations in which the possible dwelling house location of the target is not known at the time the arrest warrant is issued, or where there is a power to arrest without warrant. The s. 529.1 order requires reasonable grounds to believe that:

1. there is a valid *federal* power of arrest or apprehension in place;
2. the person to be arrested is or will be present in the dwelling to be entered.

7. Telewarrants

Section 487.1 (which creates the telewarrant authority) does not actually create a free-standing warrant-granting power, but rather provides an alternative process for the consideration of warrants authorized elsewhere.[162]

The regime does not relieve the applicant from any of the substantive requirements for the issuance of the particular warrant; all the preconditions for the issuance must be demonstrated to the same degree. The section provides a mechanism to allow each officer to apply without physically attending before a justice. Where geography, schedules or judicial scarcity would otherwise make a warrant unavailable or impracticable, telewarrants step in.

The judiciary controls whether, and how, this regime is to work. Section 487.1(1) permits applications to "a justice *designated for the purpose* by the chief judge of the provincial court" [emphasis added]. This has permitted courts to control when such warrants are available. In Ontario, for example, telewarrants have been available only since 1997. They are only available through a written facsimile process which is tightly controlled by a detailed protocol.[163] Prior to the protocol no justices were designated by the chief justice.

One key difference between conventional warrants and telewarrants is the additional requirement in s. 487.1 that the officers swear that it is "impracticable" to obtain a warrant through a conventional "in person" application. There must be some good reason why this process is being used in place of the usual, local and direct route. Urgency, or the geographic unavailability of

---

[162] Other warrant powers which could lawfully be issued by telewarrant are s. 487.01 (general warrants), s. 256 (blood warrants), bodily impression warrants (s. 487.092), s. 529.1 (*Feeney* warrants to enter and arrest), *Controlled Drugs and Substances Act* s. 11 warrants.

[163] S. Howell, "The Telewarrant Centre," unpublished paper delivered at *Preparing Search Warrant Materials* (Collingwood, Ontario, November 2001).

a justice, are common reasons – but these must be spelled out in the Information to Obtain if they are to have any sway with the court.

In one case,[164] the British Columbia Court of Appeal held that "impracticable" in this section took on the same meaning as in s. 254(3) of the *Code*: "The question here is one of impracticality, not impossibility . . . [I]mpractical connotes a degree of reason and involves some regard for practice." The officer must believe that, as a practical matter, it is unlikely that he or she will be able to apply for a warrant using normal warrant avenues within the time available before the object of seizure is moved, destroyed or otherwise placed beyond the reach of the court.

8. *Mutual Legal Assistance in Criminal Matters Act* Requests

In recent years, the growing "international flavour" of all forms of misconduct has highlighted the usefulness of international cooperation in the war on crime. Canada has entered into a number of treaties which provide for the legal basis for mutual legal assistance in criminal matters. Pursuant to domestic legislation,[165] Canada will gather evidence for foreign authorities and in return they will gather evidence needed by Canadian investigators.

Orders are available from judges on a showing similar to that required for a conventional domestic warrant. Before any evidence is sent out of Canada there must be an *inter partes* hearing.[166]

9. Statutory Production Orders – Sections 487.012 and 487.013

In 2004 the *Criminal Code* was amended to create two new warrant-granting powers. These new powers authorized two orders requiring the production of documents or data relevant to criminal investigations. Section 487.012 created a general document "production order" which requires the subject to produce existing data. These documents are then seized by the police.[167] The preconditions for the issuance of the production order require reasonable grounds to *believe* that the documents will afford evidence of a criminal offence (the same standard as in s. 487). It is important to note that no person who is the subject

---

[164] *R v. Pedersen* (2004), 2 M.V.R. (5th) 1, 2004 CarswellBC 232, [2004] B.C.J. No. 229 (C.A.) at para. 21, quoting *R. v. Salmon* (1999), 141 C.C.C. (3d) 207, 1999 CarswellBC 2830 (B.C.C.A.), leave to appeal refused (2001), 156 Man. R. (2d) 320 (note), 2001 CarswellBC 93 (S.C.C.).

[165] *Mutual Legal Assistance in Criminal Matters Act*, R.S.C. 1985, c. 30 (4th Supp.).

[166] The Act and its operation are explained in P. Downes, "A Primer on Search and Seizure in the Mutual Legal Assistance Context," Proceedings, Third Symposium on Issues in Search and Seizure Law in Canada (Osgoode Hall Professional Development, 2003); and R.J. Currie, "Search Warrants Under the *Mutual Legal Assistance in Criminal Matters Act*" (2004) 12 C.R. (6th) 275–295.

[167] See Chapter 15, "Checklists," for the checklist for these provisions.

of the investigation in question can be ordered to produce[168] and any person who does produce a document under such an order enjoys a use immunity against it being used against them.[169]

A less expansive order is available to require certain financial institutions and other commercial entities[170] to produce basic account information. They must tell police the account number of a person named in the order or the name of a person whose account number is specified in the order, as well as providing the status and type of the account, and the date on which it was opened or closed. This financial institutions' production order is available upon a reasonable suspicion standard.[171]

[168] Section 487.012(1), enacted S.C. 2004, c. 3, s. 7, in force September 15, 2004.

[169] Section 487.016, enacted S.C. 2004, c. 3, s. 7, in force September 15, 2004.

[170] As defined in the *Bank Act*, S.C. 1991, c. 46, or an entity described in s. 5 of the *Proceeds of Crime (Money Laundering) and Terrorist Financing Act*, S.C. 2000, c. 17.

[171] Section 487.013(4).

11

Specific Procedural Issues

1. Sealing a Warrant and Related Material

(a) Common Law Power and Its Limits

Normally a search warrant (and the supporting material) is a public court document.[1] At common law, the court has an inherent power to control its own records. Prior to 1997 this was the only basis for the making of such orders.[2] In May of that year the *Criminal Code* was amended to codify the rules relating to the sealing of search warrant applications and related material. The common law position had left it unclear whether justices of the peace had the power to seal and required applicants to be aware of the idiosyncrasies of local practice to seek the order.

(b) Codified Power in Section 487.3

Parliament intervened and introduced a clear statutory basis for the making of sealing orders. The provisions are set out as follows:

> **487.3 (1) Order denying access to information used to obtain a warrant or production order** – A judge or justice may, on application made at the time of issuing a warrant under this or any other Act of Parliament or a production order under section 487.012 or 487.013, or of granting an authorization to enter a dwelling-house under section 529 or an authorization under section 529.4 or at

---

[1] *Nova Scotia (Attorney General) v. MacIntyre* (1982), 65 C.C.C. (2d) 129, 26 C.R. (3d) 193 (S.C.C.).

[2] *Ontario (Attorney General) v. Yanover* (1982), 68 C.C.C. (2d) 151, 26 C.R. (3d) 216 (Ont. Prov. Ct.); *R. v. Gerol* (1982), 69 C.C.C. (2d) 232 (Ont. Prov. Ct.); *Henderson v. Jolicoeur* (1983), 9 C.C.C. (3d) 79 (Ont. H.C.); *R. v. Jany* (1983), 9 C.C.C. (3d) 349, 1983 CarswellBC 795 (B.C. S.C.); *R. v. Rideout* (1986), 31 C.C.C. (3d) 211, 185 A.P.R. 160 (Nfld. T.D.); *R. v. Flahiff* (1998), 123 C.C.C. (3d) 79, 17 C.R. (5d) 94 (Que. C.A.), leave to appeal refused (1998), [1998] S.C.C.A. No. 87, 232 N.R. 197 (note) (S.C.C.); *Vickery v. Nova Scotia (Supreme Court)*, 64 C.C.C. (3d) 65, [1991] 1 S.C.R. 671 (S.C.C.); *Dagenais v. Canadian Broadcasting Corp.* (1994), 94 C.C.C. (3d) 289, 34 C.R. (4th) 269 (S.C.C); *Re Ontario (Commission on Proceedings involving Guy Paul Morin)* (1997), 113 C.C.C. (3d) 31, 6 C.R. (5th) 137 (Ont. C.A.).

any time thereafter, make an order prohibiting access to and the disclosure of any information relating to the warrant, production order or authorization on the ground that

(a) the ends of justice would be subverted by the disclosure for one of the reasons referred to in subsection (2) or the information might be used for an improper purpose; and

(b) the ground referred to in paragraph (a) outweighs in importance the access to the information.

(2) **Reasons** – For the purposes of paragraph (1)(a), an order may be made under subsection (1) on the ground that the ends of justice would be subverted by the disclosure

(a) if disclosure of the information would
 (i) compromise the identity of a confidential informant,
 (ii) compromise the nature and extent of an ongoing investigation,
 (iii) endanger a person engaged in particular intelligence-gathering techniques and thereby prejudice future investigations in which similar techniques would be used, or
 (iv) prejudice the interests of an innocent person; and
(b) for any other sufficient reason.

(3) **Procedure** – Where an order is made under subsection (1), all documents relating to the application shall, subject to any terms and conditions that the justice or judge considers desirable in the circumstances, including, without limiting the generality of the foregoing, any term or condition concerning the duration of the prohibition, partial disclosure of a document, deletion of any information or the occurrence of a condition, be placed in a packet and sealed by the justice or judge immediately on determination of the application, and that packet shall be kept in the custody of the court in a place to which the public has no access or in any other place that the justice or judge may authorize and shall not be dealt with except in accordance with the terms and conditions specified in the order or as varied under subsection (4).

(4) **Application for variance of order** – An application to terminate the order or vary any of its terms and conditions may be made to the justice or judge who made the order or a judge of the court before which any proceedings arising out of the investigation in relation to which the warrant or production order was obtained may be held.[3]

---

[3] As amended by S.C. 1997, c. 23, s. 14; 1997, c. 39, s. 1; 2004, c. 3, s. 8.

(c) When Should a Sealing Order Be Considered?

Section 487.3 identifies four examples of when a sealing order might be justified.

Confidential Informers: Clearly a sealing order should be considered if the Information to Obtain contains information tending to, or potentially tending to, identify the confidential informer or tipster. The police have an affirmative legal duty to take steps to protect the privileged status of such an informer's identity.[4] It is likely that if a charge is laid, the Information to Obtain will be unsealed and subject to editing.

Great care should be taken in dealing with informer privilege before and after a charge. The court should proceed with caution when considering such requests for sealing/editing. "If there is any doubt as to whether disclosure would reveal that identity, disclosure should not be made."[5] This may require "blanket non-disclosure" to ensure that the privilege is properly respected.

Care should be taken to "draft around" future editing problems by, for example, placing potentially identifying material in an appendix and sealing it separately.

Ongoing Investigations: Warrants are, of course, used during the currency of continuing investigations. Investigators will have a number of reasons for wishing to keep information about the progress of their investigation out of the public realm while they continue to investigate. These include preventing the dissemination of (a) confidential "holdback" information, (b) information concerning which witnesses have spoken to the police, (c) the contents of what witnesses have told the police, (d) the success, or failure, of forensic examinations, (e) whether a co-accused is cooperating with the police, and (f) any information included in the warrant application that might impair the future progress of the case.

Where the "integrity of the investigation" is the basis for a sealing order request, there is a particular premium on the police explaining why sealing is necessary. It is important to remember that a sealing order is not intended to simply give the police a "leg up." "[A]ccess to court documents cannot be denied solely because maintaining the secrecy of those proceedings would give

---

[4] See the discussion of this in Chapter 9, Specific Drafting Challenges, under heading 3, "The Informer and the Tipster."

[5] *Toronto Star Newspapers Ltd. v. Ontario* (2003), 178 C.C.C. (3d) 349, 17 C.R. (6th) 392 (Ont. C.A.), leave to appeal granted (2004), 112 C.R.R. (2d) 376n, 2004 CarswellOnt 1762 (S.C.C.), at p. 359 [C.C.C.], para. 28, citing *R. v. Leipert* (1997), 112 C.C.C. (3d) 385, 4 C.R. (5th) 259 (S.C.C.).

the police an advantage in the conduct of their investigation."[6] In order to succeed on this basis the Information to Obtain must show that early disclosure of material contained in an information to obtain a search warrant will significantly impair the ability of the police to obtain accurate statements from potential witnesses or otherwise prevent them from effectively investigating the crime in issue. Where, for example, the Information to Obtain contains numerous details that are otherwise secret, or refers to the progress of an investigation (e.g., who has been interviewed, or who has been cooperating with the police), then it may be possible to justify a time-limited sealing order.

Intelligence-gathering: Clearly, ongoing investigative activity can be compromised by disclosure. Techniques, even if not "secret" in the sense of being completely confidential within the police community, become less effective when they become widely known. As well, the specific application of such techniques to a particular case, or within a particular jurisdiction, can undermine the effectiveness of such practices.[7]

For example, if a warrant application includes reference to ongoing (or as yet undisclosed) wiretaps, it will normally be appropriate to seal the warrant.

Innocent Third Parties: An Information to Obtain will sometimes of necessity contain information that would not normally be public. For example, an Information in a sexual assault investigation will usually have to name the victim and any relationship he or she has to the subject of the investigation. Or in an incest investigation, a child of the union may be identified. In either case it would be appropriate to seal the Information to Obtain. If charges are laid these individuals will likely have the benefit of a publication ban (although no such ban is available for information in an Information to Obtain).

Intercepted Private Communications: Where a warrant application includes reference to the content of intercepted private communications, s. 193 of the *Code* requires that steps be taken to seal or edit out that material. This is a function of the general secrecy policy related to wiretaps rather than investigative integrity.[8]

---

[6] Ibid., at p. 359 [C.C.C.], para. 27. While the court in *Toronto Star* did not find the particular sealing order was justified on this basis, it did accept that investigative integrity could properly form the basis for sealing.

[7] *R. v. E. (O.N.)* (2001), 158 C.C.C. (3d) 478, 47 C.R. (5th) 89 (S.C.C.); *R. v. Mentuck* (2001), 158 C.C.C. (3d) 449, 47 C.R. (5th) 63 (S.C.C.).

[8] *National Post Co. v. Ontario* (2003), 176 C.C.C. (3d) 432, 2003 CarswellOnt 2134 (S.C.J.), leave to appeal refused (2004), 2004 CarswellOnt 1620 (S.C.C.).

(d) Insufficient Reasons

Police seeking an order under s. 487.3 are obliged to set out the grounds for concluding that the information in the warrant application would be misused. It is not enough to "parrot" the words of the section. Normally the officer seeking such an order will be required to identify why the circumstances of the particular warrant require an order preventing the public from having access to the material after the warrant has been executed.[9]

Also, the basis for the request must be more than mere "embarrassment" to the investigators or to third parties. For example, the victim of a fraud who feels foolish and embarrassed is not a proper basis for a sealing application.

(e) Review of Sealing Orders

A sealing order can be varied or terminated by the justice or judge who made the original order, or by a judge of a court that could hear any charge arising from the offence under investigation (whether or not a charge has been laid).[10]

2. Material in the Hands of a Regulatory Investigator

Where material is in the hands of a regulatory investigator and the police wish to appropriate it for use in a criminal investigation, they must ensure that the rules applicable to a criminal investigation govern the gathering of evidence for the criminal investigation. That is, they must take care not to acquire evidence on the back of regulatory "super powers" of investigation. Normally the process by which to do this is to have the police develop their own reasonable grounds to believe, independent of the evidence from the regulatory agency. On the basis of those grounds they can then obtain a s. 487 warrant to seize the material in the hands of the regulator.[11]

---

[9] In *Toronto Star Newspapers Ltd. v. Ontario, supra*, note 5, at pp. 358–359 [C.C.C.], para. 26, Justice Doherty pointed out the need for "case-specific" reasons based on the circumstances of the case. General propositions about the desirability of investigative secrecy at large are not sufficient. See also *R. v. Eurocopter Canada Ltd.* (2003), 180 C.C.C. (3d) 15, 2003 CarswellOnt 4472 (Ont. S.C.J.).

[10] *Phillips v. Vancouver Sun* (2004), 182 C.C.C. (3d) 483, 19 C.R. (6th) 55, 2004 CarswellBC 32, [2004] B.C.J. No. 14 (B.C.C.A.).

[11] *R. v. Colarusso* (1994), 87 C.C.C. (3d) 193, 26 C.R. (4th) 289 (S.C.C.).

3. Assistance Orders

Assistance orders are a relatively recent phenomenon of the *Criminal Code*.[12] An assistance order *requires* the person named in the order to provide the assistance identified in the order. Such orders must be drafted to ensure:

- The person who is commanded to act is clearly identified, either by name or by virtue of some office they occupy (for example, "Jason Smith, or any other person occupying the position of system administrator").
- The nature of the assistance is clearly described.
- Reasonable terms and conditions are imposed to ensure that the assistance required does not operate unfairly in relation to the assistor (this does not mean that the assistance order cannot impose some burden on the named party, only that it ought not to be oppressive).
- The order should not normally name a possible target of the investigation (although it appears that a target can be named, but he or she will be given the benefit of some later use immunity for anything learned from their assistance).[13]

The potential use of these assistance orders is discussed in more detail in the context of the s. 487.01 general warrant power in Chapter 10, under heading 3, "General Warrants and Assistance Orders – Sections 487.01 and 487.02."

4. Multiple Warrants and Successive Applications

There is nothing to prevent a police officer from making successive applications for warrants on the same location where earlier warrants have been refused. Clearly the warrant applicant must make full disclosure of the fact of the earlier applications and the refusals. Normally the subsequent application should only be made on the basis of further and better materials than those presented to the initial judicial officer (either redrafted to improve the presentation, or based on additional material not presented to the initial judicial officer).[14]

---

[12] Introduced in 1993 with a variety of other warrant-related provisions. See also the discussion in Chapter 10, heading 3, on the relationship between general warrants and assistance orders.

[13] *R. v. S. (R.J.)* (1995), 96 C.C.C. (3d) 1, 36 C.R. (4th) 1 (S.C.C.). This is codified now for production orders under ss. 487.012 and 487.013.

[14] *R. v. Eng* (1995), 56 B.C.A.C. 18, 1995 CarswellBC 1702, [1995] B.C.J. No. 329 (B.C.C.A.) at paras. 47–53; *R. v. Colbourne* (2001), 157 C.C.C. (3d) 273, 2001 CarswellOnt 3337, [2001] O.J. No. 3620 (Ont. C.A.). But see *R. v. Chang* (2003), 180 C.C.C. (3d) 330, 2003 CarswellAlta 1473 (Ont. C.A.), leave to appeal refused (2004), 114 C.R.R. (2d) 188 (note), 2004 CarswellAlta 507 (S.C.C.).

12

Execution Issues Related to Warrant Drafting

1. Timing of Execution

(a) Introduction

The *Criminal Code* has no provision for the expiry of a s. 487 warrant, but a warrant should be executed while the judicial pre-authorization remains meaningful. This will vary depending on the circumstances of the case, including whether the subject of the search is an innocent third-party custodian of the material for seizure. A warrant will, in the ordinary course, set a date for its execution within a day or two of the swearing of the Information to Obtain. This makes sense when one recalls that the warrant is to search for something that is believed to be at the place to be searched at the time when the warrant is issued and that, depending on the case, circumstances may change. An officer seeking a warrant should suggest a reasonable time within which the warrant is to be executed.[1] Ontario's *Provincial Offences Act*[2] provides that warrants issued under the authority of this statute must be endorsed with an expiry date and that such date shall not be more than 15 days after the date of issue.

(b) The "In-and-Out" Rule

There is no statutory requirement that police enter, search, and depart within any time endorsed on the warrant. The so-called "in-and-out" issue may, however, arise depending on the wording used in the particular warrant. In *Pars Oriental Rug v. Canada (Attorney General)*,[3] the British Columbia Su-

---

[1] Indeed, most justices will insist on such a limitation where the subject of the search has not indicated a request to have a broad period within which the warrant might be executed to minimize the trouble caused to an innocent third-party custodian of evidence.

[2] *Provincial Offences Act*, R.S.O. 1990, c. P.33, s. 158(2).

[3] *Pars Oriental Rug v. Canada (Attorney General)* (1988), 18 C.E.R. 6, 1988 CarswellBC 1324 (B.C. S.C. [In Chambers]).

preme Court agreed with the defence submission that the ambiguous language in the concluding words of the standard form warrant in use at the time did in fact set a "departure time." The Court's problem arose not from any statutory requirement, but rather from questionable drafting in the form used for the warrant. Indeed, the Court noted that the French language version of Form 1 made it clear that the authority conferred in such a warrant did not necessarily include a departure requirement.

A contrary conclusion was expressed by the Ontario Court of Appeal in *Woodall*.[4] The Court there affirmed a trial judgment that had found no constitutional violation in an entry at 8:48 p.m. (where the warrant "expired" at 9:00 p.m.). This trial judge had found that "the search warrant first obtained on August 7 . . . did not lapse at 9:00 p.m. that night, and remained operative and cloaking all activity conducted until the police finally left the premises with the thus lawfully seized articles on August 9th . . . ."[5] Similarly, in *Cardinal*,[6] the British Columbia Supreme Court held that, on the language of the particular warrant, the time frame spelled out mandated *entry* but not exit.

(c) Night Execution

488. Execution of search warrant – A warrant issued under section 487 or 487.1 shall be executed by day, unless

    (a) the justice is satisfied that there are reasonable grounds for it to be executed by night;

    (b) the reasonable grounds are included in the information; and

    (c) the warrant authorizes that it be executed by night.[7]

This section limits the time of day for the execution of a warrant. Time is, of course, measured according to local time.[8] If an investigator wishes to have the justice endorse the warrant with some different time for execution, the Information to Obtain should set out the reasons for such a departure from the norm. It is important to remember that such an endorsement is a significant extension on an already intrusive state act and a failure to justify it in the

---

[4] *R. v. Woodall*, [1993] O.J. No. 4001 (Ont. C.A.), affirming [1991] O.J. No. 3563. See S.C. Hill, "When Does Authority to Search Expire" (1994) 2 S.S.L.R. 139. *Contra*: see *Pars Oriental Rug v. Canada (Attorney General)*, *supra*, note 3. See also the American authorities: *People v. Vara*, 499 N.Y.S.2d 296 (U.S.N.Y.A.D. 1986); *United States v. Burgard*, 551 F.2d 190 (1977); *United States v. Joseph*, 278 F.2d 504 (1960); and *United States v. Forsythe*, 560 F.2d 1127 (1977).

[5] *R. v. Woodall* (1991), *supra*, note 4, at para. 61.

[6] *R. v. Cardinal*, 2003 CarswellBC 2795, [2003] B.C.J. No. 2598 (S.C.).

[7] As amended by R.S.C. 1985, c. 27 (1st Supp.), s. 70; S.C. 1997, c. 18, s. 47.

[8] For example, in Ontario, see generally, Rule 3.01(2), *Rules of Civil Procedure* (cf. *Timmerman v. Central Guaranty Trust Co.* (1992), 23 R.P.R. (2d) 237, 8 O.R. (3d) 669 (Ont. Gen. Div.)), and the federal *Interpretation Act*, R.S.C. 1985, c. I-21.

application materials might result in the warrant being quashed. A situation of urgency might necessitate immediate execution of the warrant, as might the need to enter with notice to the holder of the property, but without notice to some other party.[9]

Warrants are presumptively to be executed "by day."[10] Day is defined as the period between 6 a.m. and 9 p.m. If a s. 487 warrant[11] is to be executed outside this time frame the officer is obliged to describe his or her reasons for requesting this extraordinary power. A night search is only to be used in "exceptional circumstances."[12]

In general, there must be some reason that requires that the warrant be executed before morning. This reason might include concern that criminal activity is ongoing or that evidence will be destroyed or obscured if action is not taken before day.[13]

(d) The "One Search" Rule

In the absence of some unusual special endorsement, a search warrant authorizes only one entry onto the property described in the warrant. Once the police have ended their search, either by finding all the articles described in the warrant, or by satisfying themselves that those articles are not on the premises, their authority under the warrant ends.[14] Similarly, if police end their search and completely retire from the premises, whether their search is done or not, they cannot re-enter on the authority of the original warrant.[15] Individual officers may come and go, however, so long as there is at least one searcher continuing the execution of the warrant at the place to be searched.

A search warrant, by its terms, normally authorizes police to enter and seize the evidence they seek on a particular day or days, but such a limitation is not

---

[9] On the question of covert entries, regard must be had to the general warrant provision and the special terms and conditions required by s. 487.01(5.1), discussed below.

[10] Section 488 (see note 7, *supra*).

[11] The statutory rule and definition of day only apply to s. 487 (and s. 487.1) warrants. Common law and constitutional reasonableness standards, however, would suggest limits on time of entry and a requirement that night entries be justified: *R. v. Duncan* (2002), 2002 CarswellMan 397, 2002 MBQB 240 (Man. Q.B.), affirmed (2004), 2004 CarswellMan 341, 2004 MBCA 64 (Man. C.A.).

[12] *R. v. Sutherland* (2000), 150 C.C.C. (3d) 231, 39 C.R. (5th) 310 (Ont. C.A.) at p. 241 [C.C.C.], para. 25.

[13] *R. v. Peddle* (1997), 157 Nfld. & P.E.I.R. 54, 1997 CarswellNfld 312 (Nfld. T.D.) (justified where search for drugs which might be sold at any time); *R. v. Charlie* (1992), [1992] Y.J. No. 97 (Y.T. Terr. Ct.) (not justified for routine search for stolen goods); *R. v. Sutherland*, *supra*, note 12 (not justified for routine search for stolen goods); *Gooding v. United States*, 94 S.Ct. 1780, 416 U.S. 430 (U.S.S.C. 1974), quoted with approval in *Sutherland*.

[14] *R. v. Moran* (1987), 36 C.C.C. (3d) 225, 1987 CarswellOnt 1116, [1987] O.J. No. 794 (Ont. C.A.) at pp. 247–248 [C.C.C.], leave to appeal refused [1988] 1 S.C.R. xi (S.C.C.).

[15] *R. v. Finlay* (1985), 23 C.C.C. (3d) 48, 48 C.R. (3d) 341 (Ont. C.A.) at p. 63 [C.C.C.], leave to appeal refused 50 C.R. (3d) xxv, [1986] 1 S.C.R. ix (S.C.C.).

required in every case *per se* (though reasonableness will normally suggest that such a term be included).

(e) Extended Execution Periods

There is nothing necessarily wrong with a warrant that permits execution within a relatively broad window of time.[16] As Fontana observes, "the time period over which a warrant extends must be reasonable. What is reasonable will depend on the circumstances of the case."[17] In any event, a warrant that authorizes execution "at any time" is unreasonable.[18] As well, while s. 488 requires a warrant to be specially endorsed if it is to be "executed" at "night," this would seem to relate to the time of entry, rather than any portion of the time when the warrant authorizes police presence at the place.[19]

However, even a warrant that authorizes a broad window for execution only authorizes single entry, and is spent upon that entry.[20]

2. Dynamic or "No Knock" Entries

The realities of the investigation of crime mean that there will be cases in which the police will be justified in using extraordinary methods in entering a place to be searched. Normally a warrant is to be executed, especially at a dwelling house, by the police attending at the normal entrance to the place, knocking on the door and announcing to those at the place their purpose and authority (i.e., that they are there to execute a search warrant).[21] It is, in the overwhelming majority of cases, this normal process that will govern.

In some cases, however, the police will be able to show reasonable grounds to believe that the execution of the warrant will be frustrated, or that officer safety may be compromised, if this normal process of execution is used. In such a case the police can seek, and the judicial officer may grant, an endorsement permitting the warrant to be executed in a manner that departs from the presumed process of announcement and entry.[22]

---

[16] *R. v. Coull* (1986), 33 C.C.C. (3d) 186, 1986 CarswellBC 681 (B.C. C.A.) at pp. 189–190 [C.C.C.].

[17] J. A. Fontana, *The Law of Search and Seizure in Canada*, 4th ed. (Toronto: Butterworths, 1997) at p. 14.

[18] *R. v. Malik*, 2002 CarswellBC 3634, 2002 BCSC 1731 (B.C.S.C.).

[19] The effect of any other reading is to require the police to get a s. 488 endorsement whenever they may be at a place for even a brief period after 9 p.m.

[20] *R. v. Coull, supra*, note 16; *R. v. Adams* (1980), 70 Cr. App. R. 149, [1980] Q.B. 575 (Eng. C.A.) at p. 155 [Cr. App. R.]; *R. v. Finlay, supra*, note 15, at p. 63 [C.C.C.].

[21] *R. v. Delong* (1989), 47 C.C.C. (3d) 402, 69 C.R. (3d) 147 (Ont. C.A.).

[22] *R. v. Genest* (1989), 45 C.C.C. (3d) 385, 67 C.R. (3d) 224 (S.C.C.).

The language of s. 529.4 of the *Criminal Code*[23] provides a helpful bench-mark for when such an endorsement might be made as part of a discretionary order associated with any other warrant. It provides:

> **529.4** (1) **Omitting announcement before entry** – A judge or justice who authorizes a peace officer to enter a dwelling-house under section 529 or 529.1 [i.e., issues a "*Feeney*" warrant or entry order], or any judge or justice, may authorize the peace officer to enter the dwelling-house without prior announce-ment if the judge or justice is satisfied by information on oath that there are reasonable grounds to believe that prior announcement of the entry would
>
> (a) expose the peace officer or any other person to imminent bodily harm or death; or
> (b) result in the imminent loss or imminent destruction of evidence relating to the commission of an indictable offence.[24]

Before an order can properly issue for such an entry the belief in the danger to officers must be shown to be based on reasonable grounds. This standard should be assessed with a measure of deference to legitimate police safety concerns and experience.[25]

Where a "no knock" warrant has issued without a proper basis, the quality of intrusion is significantly more serious than would otherwise have taken place. Exclusion of any evidence obtained may be the proper remedy.[26]

3. Out-of-Province Warrants – "Backing"

A justice of the peace can issue a search warrant for execution anywhere in Canada. However, where a s. 487 warrant is to be executed in a territorial division or province outside the issuing judicial officer's geographic jurisdic-tion, the warrant must first be endorsed by a judicial officer in the second jurisdiction. This requirement, imposed by s. 487(2), is met by the judicial officer in the execution jurisdiction endorsing his or her approval in the lan-guage of Form 28[27] as follows:

---

[23] Dealing with entry without announcement in the context of *Feeney* warrants (so-called after *R. v. Feeney* (1997), 115 C.C.C. (3d) 129, 7 C.R. (5th) 101 (S.C.C.)) (s. 529.1) and entry orders (s. 529.2).
[24] Section 529.4, as amended by S.C. 1997, c. 39, s. 2.
[25] *R. v. Godoy* (1997), 115 C.C.C. (3d) 272, 7 C.R. (5th) 216 (Ont. C.A.).
[26] *R. v. Schedel* (2003), 175 C.C.C. (3d) 193, 12 C.R. (6th) 207, 2003 CarswellBC 1519, [2003] B.C.J. No. 1430 (C.A.).
[27] See s. 849 of the *Criminal Code*.

Pursuant to application this day made to me, I hereby authorize the execution of this warrant, within the said (*territorial division*).

Dated this .... day of .... A.D ...., at ....

....

A Justice of the Peace in and for

....[28]

In the case of general warrants (s. 487.01), DNA evidence warrants (s. 487.05), tracking device warrants (s. 492.1), and number recorder warrants (s. 492.2), the provisions of s. 487.03 apply. These require an endorsement (in no particular form, though Form 28 would suffice) approving the execution of the warrant where:

1. it may reasonably be expected that the warrant is to be executed in another province; *and*
2. the execution of the warrant will require
    (a) entry into or on property in another province; *or*
    (b) an assistance order under s. 487.02 to compel someone in the second province to perform some act.

It is not clear what function is performed by the "backing" judicial officer. There would appear to be no real judicial function, but rather a "ministerial" or administrative function in receiving and being aware of the execution of the warrant in question.[29]

4. Photographing and Videotaping During Execution

A conventional search warrant authorizes an entry into a particular place to search for and seize certain things that have a physical existence. It does not authorize a trespass intended to facilitate an observation.[30] This said, it will frequently be the case that the police will wish to use still or video photography to record the execution of a s. 487 search warrant. In some jurisdictions warrant applicants will sometimes refer to their intention to make a video record in their Information to Obtain. Such a reference is not a request for permission from the judicial officer to use such a technique, but merely a part of the making of full, frank and fair disclosure to the judicial officer. Unless the

---

[28] As amended by R.S.C. 1985, c. 27 (1st Supp.), s. 184(12).

[29] *R v. Benz* (1986), 27 C.C.C. (3d) 454, 51 C.R. (3d) 363, 1986 CarswellOnt 114 (Ont. C.A.). See also *Jones v. Grace* (1889), 17 O.R. 681, [1889] O.J. No. 225 (Ont. C.A.); *Re Ciment Indépendant Inc. and R.* (1985), 21 C.C.C. (3d) 429, 47 C.R. (3d) 83, 1985 CarswellQue 14 (Que. C.A.).

[30] *Re Bell Telephone Co.* (1947), 89 C.C.C. 196, 4 C.R. 162 (Ont. H.C.) at p. 200 [C.C.C.].

warrant includes a reference to videotaping, the technique being authorized remains a conventional warrant.

When used as an "electronic notebook," this use of technology would seem to be acceptable and can be seen as a necessarily implied power in the warrant. In one case, the Ontario Court of Appeal confirmed this *limited* use of video technology:

> [15] . . . [W]ith respect to the complaint that the police officers made a videotape recording during the course of the executing of the warrant, O'Driscoll J. was satisfied that they were entitled to do so as an adjunct to the search. In our opinion the audio/videotape was nothing more than a record of the search and seizure that would be admissible if required to show how and where the search was conducted. The videotaping was not covert nor was it directed to obtaining inculpatory evidence relating to the predicate offences underlying the warrant. As such, it is distinguishable from cases where covert police video surveillance in circumstances where there is an expectation of privacy have been held to be unlawful: see *R. v. Wong* (1990), 60 C.C.C. (3d) 460 (S.C.C.).[31]

Where the videotaping will involve some additional intrusion on the subject's expectation of privacy – beyond that already contemplated by the execution of the warrant – some additional authority will be required (for example, a s. 487.01 general warrant).

5. Extraneous or Unnecessary Intrusions

Anything that extends or prolongs the nature of the intrusion on a citizen's privacy in a material way must be justified to the usual *Hunter*[32] standard. Extraneous or unnecessary intrusions added onto an otherwise valid search may render the process invalid. For example, inviting a television crew to "ride along" on a warrant execution renders the execution unreasonable.[33]

---

[31] *R. v. Gladwin* (1997), 116 C.C.C. (3d) 471, 1997 CarswellOnt 2183 (Ont. C.A.) at pp. 476–477 [C.C.C.], leave to appeal refused (1997), 117 C.C.C. (3d) vi, 45 C.R.R. (2d) 376 (note) (S.C.C.).

[32] *Hunter v. Southam Inc.* (1984), 14 C.C.C. (3d) 97, 41 C.R. (3d) 97 (S.C.C.).

[33] *R. v. West* (1997), 122 C.C.C. (3d) 218, 12 C.R. (5th) 106 (B.C.C.A.). See also *R. v. Derksen* (2000), 196 Sask. R. 121, [2001] 3 W.W.R. 364 (Q.B.). The U.S. Supreme Court took the same view in *Wilson v. Layne*, 526 U.S. 603 (1999).

13

Post-Execution Issues

1. Introduction – Judicial Supervision After Authorization

The *Criminal Code* includes a code of procedure to ensure judicial super-vision of evidence and property seized by police. These provisions probably do not engage *Charter* s. 8 concerns (s. 8 being spent with the lawful execution of the seizure power).[1] They do, nonetheless, create important statutory duties governing the conduct of those who purport to act pursuant to *Criminal Code* seizure powers. Moreover, they provide a useful and practical code to govern the disposition of things seized by the police.

Defence counsel are properly vigilant in reviewing the manner in which police deal with property seized from those under investigation. How an officer deals with his or her duties under ss. 489.1 and 490 is often indicative of the degree of professionalism overall. Whether or not one concludes that s. 8 is directly engaged by a defect in the report process, it is clear that there is a statutory requirement to make the report. As one author has noted: "While in most cases [a breach of s. 490] will, in and of itself, not be serious enough to warrant exclusion of the seized items, it may well be used as an additional factor tipping the balance towards exclusion in cases where there are other problems with the search and seizure."[2]

2. Report to a Justice

(a) The Need for a Report for Every Seizure Covered by Section 489.1

Section 489.1 is clear that a report to a justice (sometimes called "a return") is required in all cases where something has been seized by a peace officer

---

[1] *R v. Nelson* (1986), 32 C.C.C. (3d) 44, 1986 CarswellSask 259 (Sask. C.A.), leave to appeal refused (April 6, 1987), Doc. 20229 (S.C.C.); *R. v. Church of Scientology (No. 6)* (1987), 31 C.C.C. (3d) 449, 30 C.R.R. 238 (Ont. C.A.), leave to appeal refused [1987] 1 S.C.R. vii, 33 C.R.R. 384 (note) (S.C.C.); *Barnable P.C.J. v. R.* (1986), 27 C.C.C. (3d) 565, 178 A.P.R. 112 (Nfld. T.D.) (for an earlier, countervailing view, see *R. v. Guiller* (1985), 25 C.R.R. 273, 1985 CarswellOnt 1731 (Ont. Dist. Ct.).

[2] J. Di Luca, "The Report to a Justice: The Forgotten Corner of Search and Seizure Law" (April, 2002) *For the Defence* at p. 20.

197

"under a warrant issued under [the *Criminal Code*] or under section 487.11 [statutory exigent circumstances] or 489 [statutory plain view] or otherwise in the execution of duties under [the *Criminal Code*] or any other" federal statute. The report or return brings the seized articles under the regime established by s. 490. It ensures judicial supervision of things seized pursuant to statutory authority.

Even if charges had been laid and s. 490 did not require continued detention orders, nothing in s. 489.1 or s. 490 exempts the seizing officer from making the report.

The language of s. 489.1 is very broad. The section refers to warranted, plain view and exigent seizures, as well as seizures in the execution of other federal duties. This would arguably excuse from returns material seized pursuant to statutory duties created by provincial statute, including provincially constituted police agencies (which would include all municipal services in provinces, and the provincial services in Ontario, Quebec, and Newfoundland and Labrador. The RCMP, created by federal statute, look to federal legislation[3] for their existence and for their status as constables (and the related duties and powers to act). There is a compelling argument to be made that everything seized by an RCMP peace officer is subject to s. 489.1.

(b) Consent Searches

We frequently speak of "consent searches" or "consent seizures," but this language is not entirely accurate. The authorities suggest, however, that when police officers take something from someone with their permission, they are not engaged in any sort of seizure activity at all.[4] Rather, a police officer who engages in a "consent seizure" is simply receiving evidence from a member of the public. There is no reason for any judicial supervision. The language of s. 489.1 does not stretch this far. As such, no return is needed.

(c) Other Warrantless Searches

As noted, whether a statutory duty to make a return exists depends on the authority for the police seizure. If that authority is a federal warrant or statutory power of seizure, then a return is required. If the power is warrantless, and the officer is not generally created under, or generally governed by, a federal statute, s. 489.1 does not apply.

---

[3] *Royal Canadian Mounted Police Act*, R.S.C. 1985, c. R-10.
[4] *R. v. Wills* (1992), 70 C.C.C. (3d) 529, 12 C.R. (4th) 58 (Ont. C.A.).

(d) Banking Documents: Originals and Copies – *Canada Evidence Act* – Section 29(7)

Section 29(7) of the *Canada Evidence Act* relieves an officer who seizes *copies* of banking records from participating in the ongoing judicial supervision normally required of things seized under warrant. The section provides, among other things, that, "section 490 of the *Criminal Code* does not apply in respect *of the copies* of those books or records obtained under a warrant referred to in this section" [emphasis added].[5] This is consistent with s. 490's principal role in managing proprietary rights, a role with only limited relevance where copies have been seized.

It should be noted, however, that s. 29(7) does not relieve against the initial report to a justice required by s. 489.1 of the *Criminal Code*.

(e) Production Orders – Sections 487.012 and 487.013

Documents produced pursuant to s. 487.012[6] production orders (but *not* s. 487.013[7] production orders) will be subject to the return and detention orders regime.[8]

3. Detention Orders – Section 490

(a) Table Summarizing Detention Orders

The *Criminal Code* established a regime to control how police deal with property they have seized pursuant to federal statutory powers. The regime is summarized in the table below.

Summary of Time Frame and Standard for Continued Detention			
Time Frame	*Section*	*Standard for Detention*	*Court*
Initial report (as soon as is practicable)[9]	489.1	required in virtually all cases involving a power of seizure rooted in federal law (including all *Criminal Code* warrants)	to issuing justice or other justice in same territorial division

---

[5] *Canada Evidence Act*, R.S.C. 1985, c. C-5, s. 29(7), as amended by S.C. 1994, c. 44, s. 90(2).
[6] Sections 487.012 and 498.013 were enacted by S.C. 2004, c. 3, s. 7, in force September 15, 2004.
[7] See note 6, *supra*.
[8] See section 487.012(6).
[9] The words "as soon as practicable" have been interpreted to mean "within a reasonably prompt

Summary of Time Frame and Standard for Continued Detention			
Time Frame	*Section*	*Standard for Detention*	*Court*
First three months after seizure	490(1)	"required for the purposes of any investigation or a preliminary inquiry, trial or other proceeding"	to issuing justice or other justice in same territorial division
Three months and a day to 12 months from date of seizure	490(2)(a)	"having regard to the nature of the investigation, its further detention for a specified period is warranted"	to issuing justice or other justice in same territorial division
Anything more than 12 months	490(3)(a)	"having regard to the complex nature of the investigation, that the further detention of the thing seized is warranted for a specified period"	judge of the superior court
For any time after a charge has been laid	490(2)(b) 490(3)(b)	"proceedings [have been] instituted in which the thing detained may be required"	N/A
Consents (for any period of time *after* the initial report)	490(3.1)	"if the lawful owner or person who is lawfully entitled to possession of the thing seized consents in writing to its detention for that period"	N/A

(b) The Initial Detention Order

Section 490(1) begins the scheme of post-seizure judicial supervision by requiring a justice to order the return of the articles unless "the prosecutor, or the peace officer or other person having custody of the thing seized, satisfies the justice that the detention of the thing seized is *required for the purposes of*

time," not "as soon as possible": see *R. v. Ashby* (1980), 57 C.C.C. (2d) 348, 9 M.V.R. 158, 1980 CarswellOnt 28 (Ont. C.A.), leave to appeal refused (1981), 37 N.R. 393 (S.C.C.); *R. v. Phillips* (1988), 42 C.C.C. (3d) 150, 64 C.R. (3d) 154, 1988 CarswellOnt 65 (Ont. C.A.); *R. v. Letford* (2000), 150 C.C.C. (3d) 225, 51 O.R. (3d) 737 (C.A.); and *R. v. Purdon* (1989), 52 C.C.C. (3d) 270, 19 M.V.R. (2d) 129 (Alta. C.A.).

any investigation or a preliminary inquiry, trial or other proceeding."[10] The initial detention order can be for up to 3 months *from the date of the seizure* (and not 3 months from the date of the order), but the justice could make an order for a shorter period if reasons existed to do so.

(c) Where a Charge Is Laid (or Other "Proceedings Instituted")

Where a charge is laid and the articles seized, the post-seizure supervision regime in s. 490 ceases to apply, though the police may be required to show that "proceedings [have been] instituted in which the thing detained may be required." This language enjoys broad scope and would permit the retention of things needed to defend against anticipated *Charter* applications (even where the seized things were not themselves evidence of the offence itself).[11]

(d) Subsequent Orders

(i) *Three to Twelve Months*

An article seized can be detained for up to three months from the date of the seizure pursuant to the initial detention order under s. 490(1). Under s. 490(2) the justice of the peace can make a further order for the detention of the things seized if the justice is "satisfied that, *having regard to the nature of the investigation, its further detention for a specified period is warranted* and the justice so orders" [emphasis added]. An application for a detention order in excess of three months (where no charge has been laid) is to be made *on notice to the person from whom the things were seized.*[12] While the initial detention order is normally (but not always) granted without significant inquiry, the s. 490(2) applications (and even more so, the s. 490(3) applications) are not infrequently contested. Officers should prepare supporting material (affidavit or statement of officer depending on local practice) setting out why the nature of the investigation would mandate a further detention.

(ii) *More Than Twelve Months*

Section 490(3) deals with the relatively unusual situation of a seizure of evidence where charges remain unlaid after 12 months. The provision requires an application, on notice to the person from whom the things were seized, in

---

[10] Section 490, as amended to S.C. 1997, c. 18, s. 50.

[11] *R. v. Church of Scientology of Toronto* (1991), 63 C.C.C. (3d) 328, 49 O.A.C. 13 (Ont. C.A.), leave to appeal refused (1991), 5 C.R.R. (2d) 384n (S.C.C.) permitting the Crown to retain documents not evidence of the offence but potentially relevant to the Crown's response to a defence complaint of "overseizure."

[12] Section 490(2) requires the making of a summary application to the justice "after three clear days notice thereof to the person from whom the thing detained was seized."

the superior court. The standard to be met is a showing on the materials filed (normally including a complete and thorough affidavit from the officer-in-charge or his or her superior detailing the circumstances of the investigation) that "having regard to the complex nature of the investigation, that the further detention of the thing seized is warranted for a specified period."

Crown counsel or a barrister representing the police must attend on the application in the superior court. Such applications are frequently contested, especially where the things seized have some arguable value (for example, business records or equipment) to the person from whom they were seized. It is important for the police and the Crown on such applications to ensure that the materials address the "complex nature of the investigation" as the basis for the continued detention of the things seized.[13]

(e) Consent to Detention Following a Warranted Search

Often non-target third parties are willing to allow the police to retain things they have seized under lawful authority. Section 490(3.1) removes the requirement for subsequent detention orders "if the lawful owner or person who is lawfully entitled to possession of the thing seized consents in writing to its detention for that period."

(f) Lapsed Orders

Where an order has lapsed – that is, where the officer has over-held the seized things without obtaining the necessary extension or laying a charge – s. 490(9.1) offers some relief. It permits an application to remedy the lapse to be made to a judicial officer who would have had jurisdiction to make the order if brought in time. In order to succeed the applicant must satisfy the court that "the continued detention of the thing might reasonably be required" for the purposes of a preliminary inquiry, trial or other proceeding and "that it is in the interests of justice to do so."

(g) No Constitutional Challenges at Detention Hearings

The purpose of a hearing under s. 490(2) or (3) is very limited and is not the proper forum for the litigation of a *Charter* challenge to the underlying seizure.[14]

---

[13] The defence will sometimes argue – successfully – that the reason the case remains open is not the complex nature of the investigation but the failure of the police to adequately resource the investigative team. See, for example, *Re Moyer* (1995), 95 C.C.C. (3d) 174, 1994 CarswellOnt 1831 (Ont. Gen. Div.).

[14] *R. v. Raponi* (2004), 185 C.C.C. (3d) 338, 2004 CarswellAlta 943 (S.C.C.).

14

Possible Language for Specific Situations

1. Introduction

A warrant applicant should be careful whenever using precedents, whatever the source. Precedents or templates can perpetuate errors just as easily as they can suggest helpful wording. The courts have repeatedly cautioned officers against "reliance on ritualistic phrases" that often comes from excessive reliance on precedent materials.[1] Judicial officers who see such standard wording will, quite properly, consider carefully whether the use of such customary language is a proper, helpful and tested expression of an idea or factual matter that is often repeated, or is instead the ill-considered boiler-plate language inserted by an unthinking applicant who simply copied out material from another document.

These proposed wordings are offered with some trepidation because of the courts' repeated caution against excessive use of pattern warrant applications. The need to think about the application of the suggested language to the circumstances of the particular case should be underscored. These suggested wordings are a start to the writing process, not a substitute for the hard labour of writing an individualized warrant application.

2. Possible Wordings

(a) Introducing the Warrant Applicant/Informant

It is appropriate, indeed necessary, for the warrant applicant to introduce himself or herself to the judicial officer. The judicial officer can properly show deference to the inferences drawn by the warrant applicant based on his or her

---

[1] See *R. v. Branton* (2001), 154 C.C.C. (3d) 139, 44 C.R. (5th) 275 (Ont. C.A.) at p. 153 [C.C.C.], para. 30, and the discussion above in Chapter 4, General Drafting Approaches, under heading 4, "Using Precedents."

expertise.[2] If this is to be done, the applicant has to let the judicial officer know what expertise he or she has:

A. Introduction of Affiant
1. I have been a member of the Royal Canadian Mounted Police for 8 years, presently holding the rank of Corporal. For the past 4 years I have been assigned to the Commercial Crime Section at the Wawa Detachment. In that time I have participated in the investigation of 12 large commercial frauds. I have been the Officer-in-Charge of 3 of these investigations. I am the Officer-in-Charge of the investigation giving rise to this warrant application. In addition to the training provided to all police officers, I have taken the following in service programs:
 – computer investigative techniques (Canadian Police College)
 – advanced computer investigative techniques (Canadian Police College)
 – *etc.*

(b) Introducing an Overview, Cast of Characters or Other Organizational Aid

The overview and other organizational aids have no formal basis for inclusion in the warrant. They should be introduced in a way that makes their limited, but important, function clear:

B. Organization of This Information to Obtain
1. This Information to Obtain sets out the results of a complex and continuing investigation into the affairs of a criminal organization. In order to assist in the presentation of my grounds for belief, I have included in this Information to Obtain an Overview, a "Cast of Characters" and headings subdividing my grounds for belief.

(c) Where the Subject of the Search Has Requested Notice

The subject of search generally has no right to attend on the warrant application – it is an *ex parte* proceeding. Where the subject seeks notice the applicant should bring that fact to the attention of the judicial officer, together with any relevant material (correspondence, etc.):

C. Notice to the Subject
1. Three days ago I was contacted by John Bar, counsel for the subject of this investigation. He indicated that he expected that we would be seeking a DNA warrant under s. 487.05. I did not tell Mr. Bar whether he was correct. He indicated that he wanted to be given notice of any such application and that he intended to appear and make submissions to the provincial judge hearing the application. I

---

[2] *R. v. Sanchez* (1994), 93 C.C.C. (3d) 357, 32 C.R. (4th) 269 (Ont. Gen. Div.).

told Mr. Bar that I did not believe I had a duty to give him notice and that I likely would not give him notice. I did, however, tell Mr. Bar that I would bring his desire for notice and an opportunity to appear to the attention of the judicial officer considering this warrant application. He wrote to me later that day reiterating his desire for notice and to attend. I have appended to this my Information to Obtain a true copy of his letter and marked it as "Exhibit A."

(d) Where There Has Been a Previous Warrant Application

Obviously, if there has been a previous application that fact must be disclosed to the present judicial officer. The reason for the refusal should be disclosed if known:

> D. Previous Applications
> 8. On December 7, five days ago, I made an earlier application for a warrant similar to this one to Her Worship Justice of the Peace Opal. At that time Her Worship refused to issue the warrant as sought indicating in a brief written endorsement on the face of the warrant materials "Refused – no grounds to believe things to be seized are at location to be searched." A copy of the draft warrant and Information to Obtain presented to Justice of the Peace Opal are appended as Exhibit "B" to my present Information to Obtain. The contents of that Information to Obtain are still true and I incorporate them by reference in my present Information to Obtain. Since that time I have done further investigation to show that the things to be seized are at the location to be searched, the substance of which is set out below.

This language has the effect of incorporating the earlier Information to Obtain into the present Information to Obtain, and updating it with the new evidence intended to address the problem identified by the initial judicial officer considering the warrant.

3. Language to Deal with Unnamed Sources[3]

(a) The Tipster

The "tipster" presents particular challenges to the drafter because his or her identity is, by definition, unknown to the police. Tipster information must be presented in such a way that it does not give away the identity of the source. But because the police do not know the source, great care must be taken with any information about the "tip" – the police will not necessarily know what

---

[3] See above, Chapter 9, Specific Drafting Challenges, under heading 3, "The Informer and the Tipster," for discussion of some of the issues related to such sources.

information would tend to identify the informer.[4] This must be balanced against the officer's general duty to make full, frank and fair disclosure to the issuing justice.

1. In the course of this investigation I have received information from a "tipster" (an individual who has provided information to the police without disclosing their identity to the police). I do not know this person's identity and therefore cannot attest to their general credibility. As well, because I do not know the source's identity, I cannot say what information might tend to identify them. I have not provided details of the information this source provided (in the sense of exact quotes of what they said to police) because I cannot be sure what information might tend to identify them.

2. This information was provided to me in the following circumstances: [*set out the circumstances: for example, anonymous call to police information line, or information provided through established "tipline" such as CrimeStoppers. If the tipster will receive some reward if information is accurate (as is usually the case with CrimeStoppers) indicate that as a factor tending to bolster the credibility of the information*].

3. The substance of the information provided by the tipster is: John Smith was responsible for the theft of three new snow machines from Jimmy's Snowmobile Shoppe in Cold Bay. He stole them two nights ago (January 2) and has them under a tarpaulin behind his house north of town.

4. The information provided by the tipster has been confirmed in the following respects (as detailed in my further grounds for belief set out below in paragraphs 8 to 15):

   (a) There was a theft of snow machines from Jimmy's Snowmobile Shoppe the same night as the tipster identifies (see paragraphs 8 to 10, below).
   (b) John Smith has a criminal record which includes two counts of theft over and one count of possession of stolen property (see paragraph 11, below). I have spoken to the officer in charge of investigation leading to the possession of stolen property conviction and he reports that the conviction related to a stolen snow machine.

---

[4] In *R. v. Leipert* (1997), 112 C.C.C. (3d) 385, 4 C.R. (5th) 259 (S.C.C.) at p. 393 [C.C.C.], the Supreme Court of Canada acknowledged this concern, observing:

> [16] . . . Since the informer whom the privilege is designed to protect and his or her circumstances are unknown, it is often difficult to predict with certainty what information might allow the accused to identify the informer. A detail as innocuous as the time of the telephone call may be sufficient to permit identification. In such circumstances, courts must exercise great care not to unwittingly deprive informers of the privilege which the law accords to them.

(c) This morning my colleague Constable Jones attended at John Smith's house to serve a subpoena to a witness on him. At that time he noted a large tarpaulin covering an object or objects big enough to be two or three snow machines. (see paragraphs 12 to 14, below).

(d) The theft at Jimmy's was not reported in the press (see paragraph 15, below).

(b) The Experienced Informer for Hire

The experienced informer will usually be well known to the drafting officer, or to another officer able to provide information concerning the informer's background. The challenge is to fully and fairly portray the informer "warts and all," without openly giving away his or her identity. This can be done by avoiding specifics and, where necessary, alerting the judicial officer to possible problems in the informer's evidence and inviting the judicial officer to take the most skeptical view of the issue. Consider the case of an informer who provides information for pay on a regular basis.

1. In the course of this investigation I have received information from a confidential informer, referred to here as "*C.I. One.*" This individual provided information to me upon my promise that I would keep *C.I. One*'s identity a secret. As such *C.I. One* enjoys informer privilege and I am obliged to present the information he/she has given me in a way that makes full, frank and fair disclosure while being mindful of my duty to protect *C.I. One*'s identity. In order to accomplish this I have presented relevant and material elements of *C.I. One*'s background but avoided specifics which might tend to identify him/her.

2. *C.I. One* has a substantial criminal record including offences of dishonesty. His/Her evidence should therefore be reviewed with extreme caution. Notwithstanding the concern this record might cause, I believe *C.I. One* to be a credible source for the following reasons:

(a) *C.I. One* has provided information to me on more than 10 occasions in the past. That information has been accurate on all but one occasion. On that one occasion *C.I. One*'s information was not accurate and I cannot say whether *C.I. One* was mistaken or was lying to me.

(b) *C.I. One* is a paid informer. If the information provided is not accurate he/she will not be paid. If *C.I. One* regularly provides inaccurate information his/her employment by the police would cease.

(c) To the best of my knowledge *C.I. One* has no motive to fabricate information in relation to this transaction (I do not, however, have an exhaustive knowledge of *C.I. One*'s possible motives).

(d) At the present time *C.I. One* has no outstanding charges. It should be noted, however, that *C.I. One* continues to consort with criminals and may be involved in criminal activity not known to the police. He/she may perceive the possibility of some future benefit in providing helpful information at this time.

(c) The Citizen Informer

The citizen informer is normally a "one-time" source who does not wish to be identified for one of any number of reasons (fear for safety, a desire not to "get involved," etc.). Regardless of the reason, the individual's wish to enjoy informer privilege must be respected. Great care must be taken with any informer, but especially the citizen informer, for he or she will usually be in a relationship of some duration with the target of the investigation (spouse, family member, longtime friend). Warrant applicants should carefully consider whether such an informer should be mentioned at all.

4. Language to Deal with Unconstitutionally Obtained Evidence

Sometimes it is apparent to the drafting officer that there has been an obvious constitutional breach during the investigation. This should normally be confirmed with Crown counsel as soon as possible (so that the misstep can be corrected if possible, and so that all subsequent investigation can take place without being tainted). The law is clear that unconstitutionally obtained evidence cannot provide the basis for later investigative steps. That is, one cannot use illegally obtained evidence to advance a warrant application.

> E. Constitutional Breaches – Information Not Relied Upon
> 1. I am aware of my duty to make full, frank and fair disclosure to the justice considering this search warrant application. This duty includes disclosing all material information even if I do not rely upon such information. During this investigation it appears that some information or evidence has been gathered in a way that may breach the *Charter* rights of the target of the investigation, Al Jones. I am including this information here only to fulfil my duty to make full, frank and fair disclosure. I do not rely upon the evidence summarized under this heading to establish my reasonable grounds for belief.

15

Checklists

1. Introduction

No checklist can itemize every step in the process of either reviewing or preparing a warrant application. These checklists seek to identify the principal areas for consideration by warrant writers and those who determine whether the particular warrant should be issued. Most of what is noted here has been discussed above in more detail. These checklists are intended as a "handier" reference and memory aid.

I should point out that the checklists are intended to capture the highpoints of best practice. The fact that a point is mentioned here does not necessarily mean that it must be mentioned or dealt with in order for the warrant to meet the minimum standards set out in either the *Criminal Code* or the *Charter*. Rather, these checklists attempt to reflect the various matters that good, conscientious judicial officers and warrant applicants will turn their minds to when performing their respective roles in the warrant process.

The checklists are set out under the following headings:

2. Checklists – General
3. Specific Warrant Checklists
4. Special Procedural Steps
5. Statutory Warrantless Search Powers

2. Checklists – General

(a) General Checklist for Judicial Officers

1. **Statutory Authority – *"Read to the Section"***
   a. Locate and review the statutory provision which authorizes judicial officer to issue the warrant sought.
   b. On the face of the materials, has the warrant applicant brought this application to the appropriate court and appropriate judicial officer for the warrant/order sought? Note especially the common errors:
      – justices of the peace not authorized to issue general warrants (s. 487.01);
      – superior court judges and justices of the peace not authorized to issue DNA warrants (s. 487.05).

2. **Formal Validity**
   a. Information to Obtain complies with s. 849 (forms requirement).
   b. Information has been sworn.
   c. Draft warrant is in the correct form with appropriate recitals.
   d. Submission complies with any applicable protocol.

3. **Facial Validity**
   (Section 487 – modify for other warrant powers; see section-specific checklists later in this chapter.)
   a. Description of the place to be searched (fellow officer test):
      i. Reasons for believing that the things to be seized are at the location to be searched, including (where justified):
         A. outbuildings (unattached garage, shed, outhouse),
         B. motor vehicles on the property,
         C. computer systems on the scene (s. 487(2.1)).
      ii. Description is reasonably precise and, if not associated with municipal address, otherwise unambiguously identifies place.
   b. Description of the things to be seized (fellow officer test):
      i. nexus or connection between thing and offence (i.e., why it will afford evidence, including evidence relevant to a defence) is explained;
      ii. descriptions of individual items are reasonably particular;
      iii. class descriptions (and associated "basket clauses") are precise, limited and justified.
   c. Description of the offence under investigation (identify the transaction):

    i. Information to Obtain identifies a transaction (rather than simply a *Criminal Code* section);

    ii. Information to Obtain sets out grounds to believe in all of the elements of the offence.

4. **Does the Information to Obtain Contain Reasonable Grounds to Believe (or Suspect as the Case May Be) Each of the Preconditions for the Issuance of the Warrant?**[1]

For example, in the case of a s. 487 conventional warrant, are there reasonable grounds to believe:

a. an offence (or offences) against the *Criminal Code* or other federal statute has been committed;[2]

b. the things to be seized are to be found in an identified building, receptacle or place at the time the warrant is being issued;

c. the thing to be seized has a physical existence (i.e., it is not an intangible);

d. the thing to be seized:

    i. will afford evidence with respect to the commission of the offence;

    ii. is something on or in respect of which the offence was committed;

    iii. will reveal the whereabouts of a person who is believed to have committed the offence; *or*

    iv. is any offence-related property (as defined in s. 2 of the *Criminal Code*).

5. **Special Locations**

a. Does the application seek authority to search a special location:

    i. law office,

    ii. media outlet,

    iii. psychiatric records,

    iv. third-party health records?

b. If so, does the Information to Obtain make out the necessary basis to overcome that special interest?[3]

c. Does the draft warrant include necessary terms and conditions (if not, judicial officer should add)?

---

[1] The conditions for the issuance of the most common warrants are set out below in checklists for each of these warrants.

[2] Section 487(1)(a) and (c) suggests intended or suspected commission, but these powers are constitutionally suspect and only rarely necessary. Of course, a completed offence includes the inchoate offences of conspiracy and attempt.

[3] See Chapter 10, Observations on Some Specialized Warrants, under heading 4, "Special Locations."

6. **Tipsters/Confidential Informers**

    Information from unnamed sources – to be considered on a *totality of the circumstances* basis:

    a. Has the officer indicated whether the source is *credible*:
        i.   does the tipster/confidential informer have a "track record" of providing accurate, or usually accurate, information;
        ii. has the officer set out *why* he or she considers the source to be credible?

    b. Is the information provided by the tipster/confidential informer *compelling*:
        i.   is it first-hand information,
        ii.   is it detailed information about the offence,
        iii. does it have a "ring of truth" in the sense of being a story that "makes sense"?

    c. Is the information provided by the tipster/confidential informer corroborated by other police investigation?

    d. *Overall* – Does the totality of the circumstances permit a conclusion that reasonable grounds exist?

7. **"Three Questions" Reading**

    a. Does the application allow the warrant applicant to determine:
        i.   what the applicant knows,
        ii.   how the applicant knows it,
        iii. why that information matters?

        (although an answer for the "why" question is not fatal if the warrant applicant otherwise demonstrates reasonable grounds).

8. **Ancillary Orders**

    a. Does the Information to Obtain (or other sworn material before the court) permit the granting of any of the ancillary orders or endorsements sought:
        i.   night execution (where warrant to authorize execution *to begin* between 9 p.m. and 6 a.m.) (s. 488),
        ii.   surreptitious entry (s. 487.01),
        iii. assistance order (s. 487.02),
        iv.   sealing order (s. 487.3),
        v.   dynamic entry/"no knock" entry.

9. **Discretion**[4]

a. Even if the necessary preconditions for the issuance of the warrant exist, is there some *exceptional* circumstance which might suggest that the issuance of the warrant is not in the best interests of the administration of justice? For example:

   i. the seriousness of the proposed intrusion is far greater than the seriousness of the offence being investigated;

   ii. the value of the evidence to be seized is slight and the invasion of privacy is drastic;

   iii. there have been serious constitutional breaches in the course of the investigation and judicial authorization should be withheld.

---

[4] It should be noted that while there is a discretion to withhold a warrant where the preconditions for issuance exist, it should be exercised only in truly extraordinary cases. In general the judicial officer's principal function is to ensure that the preconditions to issuance exist at an objective level. See *Re Criminal Code*, [2002] O.J. No. 3804 (Ont. C.J.), endorsement of Mr. Justice Horkins of the Ontario Court, dated September 17, 2002, where His Honour stated:

> Prior to issuing the warrant I sought and received submissions from Crown counsel with respect to my initial concern that this was an application for an *ex post facto* authorization of a past seizure. Crown counsels' submissions were to the effect that: the application as currently framed meets the threshold requirements of s. 487 and that the Court therefore has jurisdiction to issue the warrant as currently sought. All that remains is the issue of judicial discretion, as s. 487 states, a justice *may* issue a warrant. The Crown submits that this is not a case where the discretion not to issue an otherwise justified warrant ought to be exercised. I agree and issue the warrant on that basis.
>
> This application is clearly brought by the police to regularize their possession of evidence which was initially seized under apparently exigent circumstances and in a good faith belief that the immediate seizure was necessary in order to preserve the evidence. The discretion not to sign a warrant which meets the 487 requirements should be reserved for situations in which the Court does not wish to condone egregious conduct leading up to the 487 grounds. I have no basis before me to make any such conclusion.

See also the discussion in L. Paikin, *The Issuance of Search Warrants*, Study Paper, Law Reform Commission of Canada (Ottawa: 1981).

(b) General Checklist for Warrant Applicants

1. **Research and Preparation – "Write to the Section"**
   a. Review and analyze the statutory provision that authorizes the judicial officer to issue the warrant being sought. Identify:
      i. the statutory preconditions to issuance for this warrant, and
      ii. the standard required for this warrant.
   b. Review and comply with any applicable judicial protocol or explain non-compliance in Information to Obtain.

2. **Research and Preparation – Full Disclosure**
   a. Comprehensive knowledge of the facts of the investigation;
   b. Lead investigators are aware of duty of full disclosure and they have confirmed that warrant writer is aware of all relevant and material facts.

3. **Correct Warrant Sought**
   a. Does the warrant being sought authorize the investigative technique proposed?
   b. Common error:
      i. Using s. 487, which only authorizes seizure of tangible, existing evidence, instead of s. 487.01 for intangibles and information or to conduct other tests.

4. **Formatting**
   a. Page numbering.
   b. Paragraph numbering.
   c. Consistent use of fonts, margins, etc.

5. **Headings**
   a. Introductions, overview.
   b. Cast of characters.
   c. Use of headings to identify key preconditions.
   d. Use of headings to break up narrative of investigation.
   e. Conclusion and order requested.

6. **Facial Validity**
   (Section 487 – modify for other warrant powers; see section-specific checklists later in this chapter.)
   a. Description of the place to be searched (fellow officer test):
      i. Reasons for believing that the things to be seized are at the location to be searched, including (where justified):
         A. outbuildings (unattached garage, shed, outhouse),

      B. motor vehicles on the property,

      C. computer systems on the scene (s. 487(2.1)).

  ii. description is reasonably precise and, if not associated with municipal address, otherwise unambiguously identifies place.

b. Description of the things to be seized (fellow officer test):

  i. nexus or connection between thing and offence (i.e., why it will afford evidence) is explained;

  ii. descriptions of individual items are reasonably particular;

  iii. class descriptions (and associated "basket clauses") are precise, limited and justified.

c. Description of the offence under investigation (identify the transaction):

  i. Information to Obtain identifies a transaction (rather than simply a *Criminal Code* section);

  ii. Information to Obtain sets out grounds to believe in all of the elements of the offence.

d. If warrant is to authorize search of computers for data, form of warrant complies with s. 487(2.1).[5]

7. **Does the Information to Obtain Contain Reasonable Grounds to Believe (or Suspect as the Case May Be) Each of the Preconditions for the Issuance of the Warrant?**[6]

For example, in the case of a s. 487 conventional warrant, are there reasonable grounds to believe:

a. an offence (or offences) against the *Criminal Code* or other federal statute has been committed;[7]

b. the things to be seized are to be found in an identified building, receptacle or place at the time the warrant is being issued;

c. the thing to be seized has a physical existence;

d. the thing to be seized:

  i. will afford evidence with respect to the commission of the offence,

  ii. is something on or in respect of which the offence was committed,

  iii. will reveal the whereabouts of a person who is believed to have committed the offence, *or*

---

[5] See Chapter 8, Computers and Search Warrants.

[6] The preconditions for the issuance of the most common warrants are set out below in checklists for each of these warrants.

[7] Section 487(1)(a) and (c) suggests intended or suspected commission, but these powers are constitutionally suspect and only rarely necessary. Of course, a completed offence includes the inchoate offences of conspiracy and attempt.

iv. is any offence-related property (as defined in s. 2 of the *Criminal Code*).

8. **Notice to the Target**
   a. If the subject of the search or his or her counsel has indicated a desire to have notice of the warrant application,
      i. the materials include reference to the fact of the request and any record of that request (for example, correspondence on the issue);
      ii. the warrant applicant has conferred with the Crown.

9. **Content**
   Does it:
   a. comply with the rule against narrative?[8]
   b. provide full, frank and fair disclosure of all relevant and material evidence (including evidence that might run against the officer's theory)?
   c. provide disclosure of any unconstitutional pre-activity?
   d. provide disclosure of any earlier applications that were refused and the reasons for such refusal?

10. **"Three Questions" Writing**
    a. Does the warrant application consistently answer the three questions:
       i. what does the officer know?
       ii. how does the officer know it?[9]
       iii. why does the information matter?

11. **Consistency and Completeness**
    a. Place to be searched in the warrant and in the Information to Obtain are the same.
    b. The warrant and the Information to Obtain identify the same offences for investigation.

12. **Tipster/Confidential Informers**
    a. Any tipster/confidential informer information has been pre-

---

[8] See the discussion above in Chapter 4, General Drafting Approaches, under heading 8, "The 'Rule Against Narrative'."

[9] This requires the officer to trace information back to the original source. It is not enough to "source" to another officer who has gathered information, unless the warrant applicant notes the source used by that other officer. In this sense the officer must ask "Is this my knowledge or something I have been told? If it is information provided by some other source, how does that source know?" Each layer of hearsay is permitted, provided it is set out, until the root of the information is clear.

sented in a way that will not tend to disclose the identity of the source.

b. If at all uncertain, an application to seal the warrant should be sought.

c. Tipster/confidential informer information has been considered in the totality of circumstances with regard to:
   i.   *credibility* of the source (officer's reasons for thinking this person is believable),
   ii. *compelling* nature of the information (level of detail, source of knowledge),
   iii. *corroboration* of the material information from tipster/confidential informer from other investigative sources.

13. **Special Endorsements/Orders**
   (Special endorsements/orders are sought where necessary with appropriate supporting materials.)
   a. night execution (after 9 p.m. and before 6 a.m.);
   b. out-of-province execution;
   c. surreptitious entry;
   d. sealing order;
   e. assistance order (to have non-peace officer assist in execution);
   f. dynamic entry/"no knock" entry.

14. **Warrant/Information to Obtain Reconciled**
   a. The warrant and the Information to Obtain refer to the same
      i.   offence under investigation;
      ii. things to be seized;
      iii. place to be searched.

15. **Proofreading**
   If warrant writer is not the principal investigator, then the principal investigator should
   a. review the warrant application to ensure full, frank, and fair disclosure;
   b. spell-check on computer;
   c. have the warrant application proofread by colleague or associate for spelling and grammar;
   d. have the warrant application proofread by someone unfamiliar with investigation for comments on organization and effectiveness of presentation.

16. **Legal Advice**
   a. Legal review by Crown counsel to determine

  i.   if necessary reasonable grounds to believe (or suspect) have
       been demonstrated;
  ii. if investigative technique in question can be authorized as
       requested;
  iii. whether other legal alternatives are available.

17. **If a Warrant Relates to a Special Location (Law Office, Medical
    Outlet, Psychiatric Facility)**
    a. Crown counsel should review first.
    b. Have other sources been considered?
    c. Have special conditions (sealing upon request) been included?

3. Specific Warrant Checklists

(a) Section 487 – Conventional Search Warrant

1. **Issuing Judicial Officer(s):** Justice of the Peace[10]

2. **Form Requirements:** Written Information on oath in Form 1[11]

3. **Telewarrant Authorized by Statute?:** Yes (s. 487.1(1))

4. **Standard for Issuance:** Reasonable grounds to believe

5. **Preconditions to Issuance:**
    a. An offence (or offences) against the *Criminal Code* or other federal statute has been committed;[12]
    b. the things to be seized are to be found in an identified building, receptacle or place at the time the warrant is being issued;
    c. the thing to be seized has a physical existence; and
    d. the thing to be seized:
        i.   will afford evidence with respect to the commission of the offence,
        ii. is something on or in respect of which the offence was committed,
        iii. will reveal the whereabouts of a person who is believed to have committed the offence, *or*
        iv. is any offence-related property (as defined in s. 2 of the *Criminal Code*).

6. **Investigative Activity Authorized:**
    A warrant issued to the peace officer or public officer to enter the building, receptacle or place to search for and seize the things identified in the warrant.

    (The warrant is presumptively executed "by day" (between 6 a.m. and 9 p.m.) unless the Information to Obtain sets out a basis for night execution and the issuing justice makes a special endorsement authorizing a night entry.)

---

[10] Note: includes most other judicial officers by virtue of statutory provisions which make them justices of the peace *ex officio*. See above in Chapter 3, Understanding Warrant Provisions, under heading 4, "Which Judicial Officer Is Authorized to Issue?"

[11] As prescribed in s. 849 of the *Criminal Code*, with reasonable modification permitted in preprinted forms.

[12] Section 487(1)(a) and (c) suggests intended or suspected commission, but these powers are constitutionally suspect and only rarely necessary. Of course, a completed offence includes the inchoate offences of conspiracy and attempt.

If the warrant authorizes the search of a *computer system for data*, the officers may:

a. use (or cause to be used) any computer system at the building or place to search any data contained in or available to the computer system;

b. reproduce (or cause to be reproduced) any data in the form of a print-out or other intelligible output;

c. seize the print-out or other output for examination or copying; and

d. use (or cause to be used) any copying equipment at the place to make copies of the data.

(b) Section 487.01 – General Warrant

1. **Issuing Judicial Officer(s):** Provincial court judge, judge of a superior court of criminal jurisdiction or judge as defined in s. 552[13]

2. **Form Requirements:** Information on oath in writing (no Form 1 requirement, but a Form 1 modified to suit the case is recommended)

3. **Telewarrant Authorized by Statute?:** Yes (s. 487.01(7))[14]

4. **Standard for Issuance:** Reasonable grounds to believe

5. **Preconditions to Issuance:**
   a. An offence against the *Criminal Code* or other federal statute has been or will be committed.
   b. Information concerning the offence will be obtained through the use of the technique, procedure or device or the doing of the thing.
   c. The judge is satisfied that it is in the best interests of the administration of justice to issue the warrant.
   d. There is no other provision in the *Code* or any other federal statute that would provide for a warrant, authorization or order permitting the technique, procedure or device to be used or the thing to be done.

---

[13] Section 552 defines a judge as follows (as amended to S.C. 2002, c. 7, s. 145):

"judge" means,
  (a) in the Province of Ontario, a judge of the superior court of criminal jurisdiction of the Province,
  (b) in the Province of Quebec, a judge of the Court of Quebec,
  (c) in the Province of Nova Scotia, a judge of the superior court of criminal jurisdiction of the Province,
  (d) in the Province of New Brunswick, a judge of the Court of Queen's Bench,
  (e) in the Province of British Columbia, the Chief Justice or a puisne judge of the Supreme Court,
  (f) in the Provinces of Prince Edward Island and Newfoundland, a judge of the Supreme Court,
  (g) in the Province of Manitoba, the Chief Justice, or a puisne judge of the Court of Queen's Bench,
  (h) in the Provinces of Saskatchewan and Alberta, a judge of the superior court of criminal jurisdiction of the province,
  (i) in Yukon and the Northwest Territories, a judge of the Supreme Court, and
  (j) in Nunavut, a judge of the Nunavut Court of Justice.

[14] Note that in order to be able to take advantage of the telewarrant system there must be a judicial protocol in place which makes an appropriate judicial officer available. Not all provinces have such a system in place. In Ontario, for example, only justices of the peace are available for telewarrants and as such s. 487.01 warrants cannot be considered.

Additional Considerations:

e.   Terms and conditions tending to limit the scope of the intrusion should be included.

f.   The technique to be authorized cannot interfere with anyone's bodily integrity.

g.   If the technique involves video surveillance of anyone in circumstances where they have a reasonable expectation of privacy, large portions of Part VI (interception of private communications) apply.

h.   Covert entries require the notice period to be identified.

Important Note Respecting Video Surveillance:

Where the proposed investigative technique includes the use of surreptitious video surveillance in circumstances where the subjects of the surveillance have a reasonable expectation of privacy, then the general warrant application must conform to most of the strict conditions for the issuance of a Part VI interception of private communications authorization (s. 487.01(5)).

6.   **Investigative Activity Authorized:**

A general warrant may authorize a peace officer to use any device or investigative technique or procedure or do any thing described in the warrant that would, if not authorized, constitute an unreasonable search or seizure in respect of a person or a person's property. Ordinarily the warrant should include terms and conditions to minimize the impact of the technique on the privacy interests of anyone affected by the use of the technique authorized by the order.

A general warrant *cannot* authorize an investigative technique that "[interferes] with the bodily integrity of any person."[15]

---

[15] See Chapter 10 for examples of techniques authorized by general warrant.

(c) Section 487.05 – DNA Warrant (Investigative)

1. **Issuing Judicial Officer(s):** Provincial judge

2. **Form Requirements:** Information on oath, in writing, using Form 5.01; warrant in Form 5.02

3. **Telewarrant Authorized by Statute?:** Yes (s. 487.05(3))[16]

4. **Standard for Issuance:** Reasonable grounds to believe

5. **Preconditions to Issuance:**
   a. That a designated offence (see s. 487.04) has been committed;
   b. That a bodily substance has been found or obtained:
      i. at the place where the offence was committed,
      ii. on or within the body of the victim of the offence,
      iii. on anything worn or carried by the victim at the time when the offence was committed, *or*
      iv. on or within the body of any person or thing or at any place associated with the commission of the offence;
   c. that the person the police want to test was a party to the offence; and
   d. that forensic DNA analysis of a bodily substance from that person will provide evidence about whether the found bodily substance was from the person to be sampled; *and*
   e. it is in the best interests of the administration of justice to issue the warrant.

6. **Investigative Activity Authorized:**
   A warrant in Form 5.02 authorizing the taking, from that person, for the purpose of forensic DNA analysis, of any number of samples of one or more bodily substances that is reasonably required for the purpose of DNA testing by means of
   a. plucking individual hairs from the person, including the root sheath;
   b. taking a buccal swab (swabbing the lips, tongue and inside cheeks of the mouth to collect epithelial cells); or
   c. taking blood by pricking the skin surface with a sterile lancet.

---

[16] But note, only where a judge (as opposed to a justice) has been designated under s. 487.1. As well, given the nature of most DNA-based investigations, and the fact that, by definition, such evidence is always available, it is unlikely that an officer could meet the impracticability requirement in s. 487.1(1).

Note: A special post-execution regime is prescribed by ss. 487.07 to 487.09.

(d) Section 487.092 – Bodily Impression Warrant

1. **Issuing Judicial Officer(s):** Justice of the Peace

2. **Form Requirements:** Information on oath, in writing (no Form 1 requirement, but a Form 1 modified to suit the case is recommended)

3. **Telewarrant Authorized by Statute?:** Yes (s. 487.091(4))

4. **Standard for Issuance:** Reasonable grounds to believe

5. **Preconditions to Issuance:**
   a. An offence against the *Criminal Code* or other federal statute has been committed; and
   b. information concerning the offence will be obtained if the police have access to a print or bodily impression of the person to be printed; and
   c. it is in the best interests of the administration of justice to issue the warrant.

6. **Investigative Activity Authorized:**
   A warrant in writing authorizing a peace officer to do anything (or cause anything to be done under the officer's direction) that is authorized in the warrant in order to obtain a
   a. hand print,
   b. fingerprint,
   c. footprint,
   d. foot impression,
   e. teeth impression, or
   f. other print or impression of the body or any part of the body of a named person.

(e) Section 487.012 – General Production Order

1. **Issuing Judicial Officer(s):** Justice of the Peace or Judge

2. **Form Requirements:** Information on oath in writing (no specific form required but Form 1 modified for the circumstances would be appropriate)

3. **Telewarrant Authorized by Statute?:** No

4. **Standard for Issuance:** Reasonable grounds to believe

5. **Preconditions to Issuance:**
    a. A *Criminal Code* or other federally created offence has been committed.
    b. The documents or data[17] to be produced will afford evidence respecting the commission of the offence.
    c. The documents or data to be produced are in the possession of or under the control of the person who is the subject of the order.

6. **Investigative Activity Authorized:**
    An order requiring any person named in the order (who *cannot* be a subject of the investigation) to
    a. produce documents (or certified copies supported by affidavits) or data that they possess or control;
    b. prepare a document based on documents or data already in existence, and produce that created document.
    The order shall require the subject to produce the documents or data to a named peace officer (or named public officer with federal law enforcement duties) at a place, within a time, and in a form set out in the order.

Note: Section 487.012(4) provides for terms and conditions, including terms to preserve any possible solicitor-client privilege. Section 487.015 provides for a procedure to challenge a production order. For production orders from *financial institutions*, see s. 487.013.

---

[17] Section 487.011 defines "data" as having the same meaning as appears in s. 342.1(2) and "document" as "any medium on which is recorded or marked anything that is capable of being read or understood by a person or a computer system or other device."

(f) Section 487.013 – Financial or Commercial Information Production Orders

1. **Issuing Judicial Officer(s):** Justice of the Peace or Judge

2. **Form Requirements:** Information on oath in writing (no specific form required but Form 1 modified for the circumstances would be appropriate)

3. **Telewarrant Authorized by Statute?:** No

4. **Standard for Issuance:** Reasonable grounds to suspect

5. **Preconditions to Issuance:**
   a. A *Criminal Code* or other federally created offence has been committed.
   b. The information to be produced will assist in the investigation of that offence.
   c. The information is under the possession or control of the subject of the order.

6. **Investigative Activity Authorized:**
   An order requiring a financial institution[18] to produce in writing
   a. the account number of a person named in the order;
   b. the name of a person whose account number is in the order; and
   c. the status and type of account and the date on which it was opened or closed.

Note: Section 487.013(5) provides for terms and conditions, including terms to preserve any possible solicitor-client privilege. Section 487.015 provides for a procedure to challenge a production order. For general production orders, see s. 487.012.

---

[18] Section 487.013(1) refers to "a financial institution, as defined in section 2 of the *Bank Act* [S.C. 1991, c. 46], or a person or entity referred to in section 5 of the *Proceeds of Crime (Money Laundering) and Terrorist Financing Act* [S.C. 2000, c. 17] . . . ."

(g) Section 492.1 – Tracking Device Warrant

1. **Issuing Judicial Officer(s):** Justice

2. **Form Requirements:** Information to Obtain in writing (no Form 1 requirement, but a Form 1 modified to suit the case is recommended)

3. **Telewarrant Authorized by Statute:** No[19]

4. **Standard for Issuance:** Reasonable grounds to suspect

5. **Preconditions to Issuance:**
   a. An offence under the *Criminal Code* or other federal statute has been or will be committed; and
   b. information that is relevant to the commission of the offence, including the whereabouts of any person, can be obtained through the use of a tracking device.

6. **Investigative Activity Authorized:**
   A warrant authorizing a peace officer or a public officer whose duties include the enforcement of federal law to
   • install,
   • maintain, and
   • remove
   a tracking device in or on any thing, including a thing carried, used or worn by any person, and to
   • monitor, or
   • to have monitored
   a tracking device installed in or on any thing.

---

[19] But note that s. 487.11 authorizes use of this power in exigent circumstances. See the checklist for s. 487.11 below under heading 5, "Statutory Warrantless Search Powers."

(h) Section 492.2 – Number Recorder Warrant

1. **Issuing Judicial Officer(s):** Justice of the Peace

2. **Form Requirements:** Information to Obtain in writing (no Form 1 requirement, but a Form 1 modified to suit the case is recommended)

3. **Telewarrant Authorized by Statute:** No

4. **Standard for Issuance:** Reasonable grounds to suspect[20]

5. **Preconditions to Issuance:**
    a. An offence under the *Criminal Code* or other federal law has been or will be committed;
    b. information that would assist in the investigation of the offence could be obtained through the use of a number recorder.

6. **Investigative Activity Authorized:**
    A warrant authorizing a peace officer or a public officer to
    *   install,
    *   maintain, and
    *   remove
    a number recorder in relation to any telephone or telephone line, and
    *   to monitor, or
    *   to have monitored
    the number recorder.

    As well, subsection 492.2(2) authorizes a justice to order that any person or body that lawfully possesses records of telephone calls originating from, or received or intended to be received at, any telephone give the records or a copy of the records to a person named in the order.

---

[20] But see *R. v. Nguyen* (2004), 20 C.R. (6th) 151, 2004 CarswellBC 279, 2004 BCSC 76 (B.C.S.C.), additional reasons to (2004), 20 C.R. (6th) 135, 2004 CarswellBC 280 (B.C.S.C.), further additional reasons (2004), 20 C.R. (6th) 146, 2004 CarswellBC 281 (B.C.S.C.), finding that this threshold was too low and reading in a "reasonable grounds to believe" standard. *Nguyen* has not yet been followed by any court outside of British Columbia.

(i) Section 529 – Entry Order on Arrest Warrant (*Feeney* Endorsement)

1. **Issuing Judicial Officer(s):** Judge[21] or justice

2. **Form Requirements:** Information on oath in writing (no Form 1 requirement, but must be in writing)

3. **Telewarrant Authorized by Statute:** Yes (s. 529.5)

4. **Standard for Issuance:** Reasonable grounds to believe

5. **Preconditions to Issuance:**
   a. Order takes the form of endorsement on the back of arrest warrant so fact of valid arrest warrant is necessary.
   b. The person is or will be present in the dwelling-house.

6. **Investigative Activity Authorized:**
   An endorsement on an arrest warrant granting additional power to authorize a peace officer to enter a dwelling-house described in the warrant for the purpose of arresting or apprehending the person.
   Officer executing such a warrant and using entry power must have reasonable grounds to believe person to be arrested is in dwelling house immediately before executing warrant (s. 529(2)).

---

[21] Section 493 defines "judge" (as amended to S.C. 2002, c. 7, s. 143) for the purposes of Part XVI as:

"judge" means
(a) in the Province of Ontario, a judge of the superior court of criminal jurisdiction of the Province,
(b) in the Province of Quebec, a judge of the superior court of criminal jurisdiction of the province or three judges of the Court of Quebec,
(c) [Repealed, 1992, c. 51, s. 37.]
(d) in the Provinces of Nova Scotia, New Brunswick, Manitoba, British Columbia, Prince Edward Island, Saskatchewan, Alberta and Newfoundland, a judge of the superior court of criminal jurisdiction of the Province,
(e) in Yukon and the Northwest Territories, a judge of the Supreme Court, and
(f) in Nunavut, a judge of the Nunavut Court of Justice; . . ."

(j) Section 529.1 – Warrant to Enter Dwelling and Arrest (*Feeney* Warrant)

1. **Issuing Judicial Officer(s):** Judge[22] or justice

2. **Form Requirements:** "Information on oath" – *no writing requirement* but some record of application must be made

3. **Telewarrant Authorized by Statute:** Yes (s. 529.5)

4. **Standard for Issuance:** Reasonable grounds to believe

5. **Preconditions to Issuance:**
   a. At the time the s. 529.1 entry warrant is sought one of the following applies:
      i. a warrant referred to in the *Criminal Code* or other federal statute to arrest or apprehend the person is in force anywhere in Canada;
      ii. grounds exist to arrest the person without warrant under s. 495(1)(a) or (b) of the *Criminal Code*; or
      iii. grounds exist to arrest or apprehend without warrant the person under some federal statute besides the *Criminal Code*;
      and
   b. the person *is* or *will be* present in the dwelling-house to be named in the warrant.

6. **Investigative Activity Authorized:**
   A warrant in Form 7.1 authorizing a peace officer to enter a dwelling-house described in the warrant for the purpose of arresting or apprehending a person identified or identifiable by the warrant.

---

[22] See previous note.

(k) *Controlled Drugs and Substances Act* (CDSA)[23] – Section 11

1. **Issuing Judicial Officer(s):** Justice of the Peace

2. **Form Requirements:** Information on oath (no explicit writing requirement)

3. **Telewarrant Authorized by Statute?:** Yes (CDSA s. 11(2))

4. **Standard for Issuance:** Reasonable grounds to believe

5. **Preconditions to Issuance:**
    a. One of the following things is (present tense) in the place to be searched:
        i.   a controlled substance or precursor in respect of which the CDSA has been contravened;
        ii.   any thing in which a controlled substance or precursor in respect of which the CDSA has been contravened is contained or concealed;
        iii. offence-related property; or
        iv.   any thing that will afford evidence in respect of an offence under the CDSA.

6. **Investigative Activity Authorized:**
    A warrant authorizing a peace officer, at any time, to search the place for any such controlled substance, precursor, property or thing and to seize it.

---

[23] S.C. 1996, c. 19.

(l) Section 117.04 – Firearms Warrant[24]

1. **Issuing Judicial Officer(s):** Justice

2. **Form Requirements:** "An application" (implicit that it is to be on sworn evidence, but no Form 1 requirement)

3. **Telewarrant Authorized by Statute:** No[25]

4. **Standard for Issuance:** Reasonable grounds to believe

5. **Preconditions to Issuance:**
   a. An application by a police officer respecting a subject person.
   b. The person possesses, in a building, receptacle or place, one or more of the following:
      i. a weapon,
      ii. prohibited device,
      iii. ammunition,
      iv. prohibited ammunition, or
      v. an explosive substance.
   c. It is not desirable in the interests of safety of
      i. the subject person, *or*
      ii. anyone else,
      for the subject person to possess any
      i. weapon,
      ii. prohibited device,
      iii. ammunition,
      iv. prohibited ammunition, *or*
      v. explosive substance.

6. **Investigative Activity Authorized:**
   A warrant authorizing a peace officer to search for and seize any such thing, and any authorization, licence or registration certificate relating to any such thing, that is held by or in the possession of the person.

---

[24] Section 117.04, as amended on April 22, 2004, S.C. 2004, c. 12, s. 3.
[25] But see the exigent search power provided in s. 117.02; see checklist below.

(m) Section 256 – Blood Warrant

1. **Issuing Judicial Officer(s):** Justice of the Peace

2. **Form Requirements:** Information to Obtain in Form 1

3. **Telewarrant Authorized by Statute?:** Yes (s. 256(1))

4. **Standard for Issuance:** Reasonable grounds to believe

5. **Preconditions to Issuance:**
   a. A person has committed, as a result of the consumption of alcohol or a drug, an offence under s. 253 (impaired/over 80);
   b. the offence was within the preceding 4 hours;
   c. the person was involved in an accident resulting in
      i. the death of another person, *or*
      ii. bodily harm to himself or herself or to any other person;
   d. a *qualified medical practitioner* ("qualified medical practitioner" means a person duly qualified by provincial law to practise medicine[26]) is of the opinion that
      i. the person is unable to consent to the taking of samples of his or her blood,
      ii. by reason of any physical or mental condition of the person that resulted from the consumption of alcohol or a drug, the accident or any other occurrence related to or resulting from the accident, *and*
      iii the taking of samples of blood from the person would not endanger the life or health of the person.

6. **Investigative Activity Authorized:**
   A warrant requiring a qualified medical practitioner to take, or to cause to be taken, by a qualified technician (designated by the Attorney General) under the direction of the qualified medical practitioner, the samples of the blood of the person that in the opinion of the person taking the samples are necessary to enable a proper analysis to be made in order to determine the concentration, if any, of alcohol or drugs in the person's blood.

---

[26] Section 254.

4. Special Procedural Steps

(a) Section 487.02 – Assistance Orders

1. **Judicial Officer(s) Who Can Make Order:** Any judicial officer who could have issued the warrant (or order) that requires assistance. Available in conjunction with orders under s. 184.2 (consent intercept), s. 184.3 (urgent situation intercept), s. 186 (authorization to intercept private communications), s. 188 (emergency authorization), s. 492.2(2) (number recorder information or toll record) or whenever a *warrant* is issued under the *Criminal Code*.

2. **Form Requirements:** None – application can be made at time of issuance or at any later time

3. **Telewarrant Authorized by Statute?:** Depends on warrant being issued and "assisted"

4. **Standard for Making of Order:** None stated, presumably reasonable grounds to believe or balance of probabilities

5. **Preconditions to Making of Order:**
    Where the person's assistance may reasonably be considered to be required to give effect to the authorization, warrant or order.

6. **Order Authorized:**
    An order requiring any person named in the order (or precisely described by their position or title) to provide assistance necessary to give effect to the authorization, warrant or order.

(b) Section 487.3 – Sealing Orders

1. **Judicial Officer(s) Who Can Make Order:** Any judicial officer who could have issued the warrant or made the order to be sealed

2. **Form Requirements:** None. Application can be made at time of issuance or at any later time

3. **Telewarrant Authorized by Statute?:** Possibly available on same basis as warrant being issued

4. **Standard for Making of Order:** Balance of probabilities

5. **Preconditions to Making of Order:**
   Order to be made after balancing two competing sets of interests:
   a. *in favour of sealing*:
      i. if unrestricted access to the warrant materials would
         A. compromise the identity of a confidential informant,
         B. compromise the nature and extent of an ongoing investigation,
         C. endanger a person engaged in particular intelligence-gathering techniques and thereby prejudice future investigations in which similar techniques would be used, or
         D. prejudice the interests of an innocent person; or
      ii. if there is "any other sufficient reason";
   b. *against sealing*:
      i. the general importance of access to the information based on the "open courts" presumption in favour of public documents being available.

6. **Order Authorized:**
   Order requiring:
   a. all documents relating to the application be placed in a packet and sealed by the justice or judge immediately on determination of the application;
   b. that packet shall be kept in the custody of the court in a place to which the public has no access or in any other place that the justice or judge may authorize;
   c. the order may contain any terms and conditions, including but not limited to, any term or condition concerning
      i. the duration of the prohibition (the order may contain a "sunset clause," which automatically terminates the order after a specified period (e.g., "6 months from date of order"),

   ii. partial disclosure of a document (permitting parts of a document to be seen (e.g., seal one-half of Information to Obtain, but releasing warrant and other one-half of Information to Obtain),

  iii. deletion of any information, or

  iv. the occurrence of a condition (order terminates after passage of a fixed period of time (e.g., 6 months or on laying of charges or need for Crown to make disclosure).

5. Statutory Warrantless Search Powers

(a) Section 487.11 – Exigent Circumstances

1. **Issuing Judicial Officer(s):** None

2. **Form Requirements:** None

3. **Telewarrant Authorized by Statute?:** N/A

4. **Standard to Invoke Warrantless Power:** Reasonable grounds to believe if invoking s. 487 investigative technique; reasonable grounds to suspect if invoking s. 492.1 technique

5. **Preconditions to Invoke Power:**
    a. Available to peace officer or public officer with federal enforcement duties.[27]
    b. The investigative technique to be invoked is potentially available under s. 487 (conventional warrant) or s. 492.1 (tracking device order).
    c. The preconditions for the issuance of the s. 487 or s. 492.1 warrant exist.
    d. By reason of exigent circumstances it would be impracticable to obtain a warrant.

6. **Investigative Activity Authorized:**
    The officer is authorized to exercise any of the powers described in the warrant provision that applies.

---

[27] Section 487(1) (as amended to S.C. 1999, c. 5, s. 16) refers to "a public officer who has been appointed or designated to administer or enforce a federal or provincial law and whose duties include the enforcement of this Act or any other Act of Parliament."

(b) Section 117.02(1) – Exigent Seizure of Evidence of Weapons Offences

1. **Issuing Judicial Officer(s):** None

2. **Form Requirements:** None

3. **Telewarrant Authorized by Statute?:** N/A

4. **Standard to Invoke Warrantless Power:** Reasonable grounds to believe

5. **Preconditions to Invoke Power:**
    a. That a weapon, an imitation firearm, a prohibited device, any ammunition, any prohibited ammunition or an explosive substance was used in the commission of an offence; *or*
    b. that an offence is being committed, or has been committed, under any provision of this Act that involves, or the subject-matter of which is, a firearm, an imitation firearm, a cross-bow, a prohibited weapon, a restricted weapon, a prohibited device, ammunition, prohibited ammunition or an explosive substance;
    and
    c. evidence of the offence is likely to be found
        i.   on a person,
        ii.   in a vehicle, or
        iii   in any place or premises,
        iv.   *but not* in a dwelling-house;
    d. the conditions for obtaining a s. 487 warrant exist (see above for 487 grounds);
    but
    e. by reason of exigent circumstances, it would not be practicable to obtain a warrant.

6. **Investigative Activity Authorized:**
    To search, without warrant, the person, vehicle, place or premises, and seize any thing by means of or in relation to which that peace officer believes on reasonable grounds the offence is being committed or has been committed.

(c) Section 117.04(2) – Exigent Public Safety Seizure of Weapons[28]

1. **Issuing Judicial Officer(s):** None

2. **Form Requirements:** None

3. **Telewarrant Authorized by Statute?:** N/A

4. **Standard to Invoke Warrantless Power:** Reasonable grounds to believe

5. **Preconditions to Invoke Power:**
    a. A peace officer is satisfied that there are reasonable grounds to believe that it is not desirable, in the interests of the safety of the person or any other person, for the person to possess any weapon, prohibited device, ammunition, prohibited ammunition or explosive substance;
    b. the grounds for obtaining a warrant under s. 117.04(1) exist; but
    c. by reason of a possible danger to the safety of that person or any other person, it would not be practicable to obtain a warrant.

6. **Investigative Activity Authorized:**
    A warrantless search for and seizure of any weapon, prohibited device, ammunition, prohibited ammunition or explosive substance, and any authorization, licence or registration certificate relating to any such thing, that is held by or in the possession of the person.

---

[28] Section 117.04 was amended on April 22, 2004, S.C. 2004, c. 12, s. 3, to deal with the defects noted in *R. v. Hurrell* (2002), 166 C.C.C. (3d) 343, 4 C.R. (6th) 169 (Ont. C.A.), leave to appeal to S.C.C. abandoned (April 26, 2004), Doc. 29376 (S.C.C.).

(d) Section 529.3 – Exigent Entry to Dwelling House to Arrest or Apprehend

1. **Issuing Judicial Officer(s):** None

2. **Form Requirements:** None

3. **Telewarrant Authorized by Statute?:** N/A

4. **Standard to Invoke Warrantless Power:**
   a. Reasonable grounds to believe power of arrest or apprehension in respect of target;
   plus
   b. reasonable grounds to believe if exigency relates to *destruction of evidence* (s. 529.3(2)(b));
   c. reasonable grounds to suspect if exigency relates to *need to prevent bodily harm or death* (s. 529.3(2)(a));
   d. other basis for grounding exigent circumstances.[29]

5. **Preconditions to Invoke Power:**
   For both powers:
   a. reasonable grounds to believe the accused is arrestable because:
      i. a warrant referred to in the *Criminal Code* or other federal statute to arrest or apprehend the person is in force anywhere in Canada; *or*
      ii. grounds exist to arrest the person without warrant under ss. 495(1)(a) or (b) of the *Criminal Code*; *or*
      iii. grounds exist to arrest or apprehend without warrant the person under some federal statute besides the *Criminal Code*;
      and
      iv. the person is or will be present in the dwelling-house to be entered;
      and
   b. where the exigency is to *prevent imminent bodily harm or death* – s. 529.3(2)(a), grounds to *suspect*
      v. entry into the dwelling-house is necessary to prevent imminent bodily harm or death to any person;

---

[29] The section provides a partial definition of exigent circumstances, being reasonable belief in destruction of evidence or reasonable suspicion in harm or death. It is possible that other exigencies may exist at different standards: consider *R. v. Golub* (1997), 117 C.C.C. (3d) 193, 9 C.R. (5th) 98 (Ont. C.A.), leave to appeal refused (1998), 128 C.C.C. (3d) vi (S.C.C.).

    c.   where the exigency is to *prevent the destruction of evidence –*
       529.3(2)(b), grounds to *believe*

        vi. evidence relating to the commission of an indictable offence
            is present in the dwelling-house and that entry into the
            dwelling-house is necessary to prevent the imminent loss
            or imminent destruction of the evidence.

6.   **Investigative Activity Authorized:**
    The officer is authorized to enter the dwelling house to give effect
    to the power of arrest or apprehension in question.

(e) *Controlled Drugs and Substances Act* (CDSA) – Section 11(7) – Exigent Drug Searches

1. **Issuing Judicial Officer(s):** None

2. **Form Requirements:** None

3. **Telewarrant Authorized by Statute?:** N/A

4. **Standard to Invoke Warrantless Power:** Reasonable grounds to believe

5. **Preconditions to Invoke Power:**
   a. The conditions for obtaining a CDSA s. 11 warrant exist,
   b. but by reason of exigent circumstances it would be impracticable to obtain one.

6. **Investigative Activity Authorized:**
   The officer is authorized exercise any of the following powers
   a. search the place for any such controlled substance, precursor, property or thing and to seize it;
   b. search the person at the scene of the search for the controlled substance, precursor, property or thing and seize it;
   c. seize
      i. any controlled substance or precursor in respect of which the peace officer believes on reasonable grounds that this Act has been contravened,
      ii. any thing that the peace officer believes on reasonable grounds to contain or conceal a controlled substance or precursor referred to in paragraph (i),
      iii any thing that the peace officer believes on reasonable grounds is offence-related property, or
      iv. any thing that the peace officer believes on reasonable grounds will afford evidence in respect of an offence under this Act.

Appendices

Appendix I
Key *Criminal Code* Search Warrant Provisions

PART I — GENERAL

. . . .

Protection of Persons Administering and Enforcing the Law

25. (1) Protection of persons acting under authority—Every one who is required or authorized by law to do anything in the administration or enforcement of the law

    (a) as a private person,

    (b) as a peace officer or public officer,

    (c) in aid of a peace officer or public officer, or

    (d) by virtue of his office,

is, if he acts on reasonable grounds, justified in doing what he is required or authorized to do and in using as much force as is necessary for that purpose.

(2) Idem—Where a person is required or authorized by law to execute a process or to carry out a sentence, that person or any person who assists him is, if that person acts in good faith, justified in executing the process or in carrying out the sentence notwithstanding that the process or sentence is defective or that it was issued or imposed without jurisdiction or in excess of jurisdiction.

(3) When not protected—Subject to subsections (4) and (5), a person is not justified for the purposes of subsection (1) in using force that is intended or is likely to cause death or grievous bodily harm unless the person believes on reasonable grounds that it is necessary for the self-preservation of the person or the preservation of any one under that person's protection from death or grievous bodily harm.

(4) When protected—A peace officer, and every person lawfully assisting the peace officer, is justified in using force that is intended or is likely to cause death or grievous bodily harm to a person to be arrested, if

(a) the peace officer is proceeding lawfully to arrest, with or without warrant, the person to be arrested;

(b) the offence for which the person is to be arrested is one for which that person may be arrested without warrant;

(c) the person to be arrested takes flight to avoid arrest;

(d) the peace officer or other person using the force believes on reasonable grounds that the force is necessary for the purpose of protecting the peace officer, the person lawfully assisting the peace officer or any other person from imminent or future death or grievous bodily harm; and

(e) the flight cannot be prevented by reasonable means in a less violent manner.

(5) Power in case of escape from penitentiary—A peace officer is justified in using force that is intended or is likely to cause death or grievous bodily harm against an inmate who is escaping from a penitentiary within the meaning of subsection 2(1) of the *Corrections and Conditional Release Act*, if

(a) the peace officer believes on reasonable grounds that any of the inmates of the penitentiary pose a threat of death or grievous bodily harm to the peace officer or any other person; and

(b) the escape cannot be prevented by reasonable means in a less violent manner.

1994, c. 12, s. 1.

. . . .

PART VIII — OFFENCES AGAINST THE PERSON AND REPUTATION

. . . .

Motor Vehicles, Vessels and Aircraft

. . . .

256. (1) Warrants to obtain blood samples—Subject to subsection (2), if a justice is satisfied, on an information on oath in Form 1 or on an information on oath submitted to the justice under section 487.1 by telephone or other means of telecommunication, that there are reasonable grounds to believe that

(a) a person has, within the preceding four hours, committed, as a result of the consumption of alcohol or a drug, an offence under section 253 and the person was involved in an accident resulting in the death of another person or in bodily harm to himself or herself or to any other person, and

(b) a qualified medical practitioner is of the opinion that

(i) by reason of any physical or mental condition of the person that resulted from the consumption of alcohol or a drug, the accident or any other occurrence related to or resulting from the accident, the person is unable to consent to the taking of samples of his or her blood, and

(ii) the taking of samples of blood from the person would not endanger the life or health of the person,

the justice may issue a warrant authorizing a peace officer to require a qualified medical practitioner to take, or to cause to be taken by a qualified technician under the direction of the qualified medical practitioner, the samples of the blood of the person that in the opinion of the person taking the samples are necessary to enable a proper analysis to be made in order to determine the concentration, if any, of alcohol or drugs in the person's blood.

(2) Form—A warrant issued pursuant to subsection (1) may be in Form 5 or 5.1 varied to suit the case.

(3) Information on oath—Notwithstanding paragraphs 487.1(4)(*b*) and (*c*), an information on oath submitted by telephone or other means of telecommunication for the purposes of this section shall include, instead of the statements referred to in those paragraphs, a statement setting out the offence alleged to have been committed and identifying the person from whom blood samples are to be taken.

(4) Duration of warrant—Samples of blood may be taken from a person pursuant to a warrant issued pursuant to subsection (1) only during such time as a qualified medical practitioner is satisfied that the conditions referred to in subparagraphs (1)(*b*)(i) and (ii) continue to exist in respect of that person.

(5) Facsimile to person—Where a warrant issued pursuant to subsection (1) is executed, the peace officer shall, as soon as practicable thereafter, give a copy or, in the case of a warrant issued by telephone or other means of telecommunication, a facsimile of the warrant to the person from whom the blood samples were taken.

R.S.C. 1985, c. 27 (1st Supp.), s. 36; 1992, c. 1, s. 58(1) (Sched. I, item 5); 1994, c. 44, s. 13; 2000, c. 25, s. 3.

. . . .

PART XV — SPECIAL PROCEDURE AND POWERS

General Powers of Certain Officials

. . . .

487. **(1) Information for search warrant**—A justice who is satisfied by information on oath in Form 1 that there are reasonable grounds to believe that there is in a building, receptacle or place

(a) anything on or in respect of which any offence against this Act or any other Act of Parliament has been or is suspected to have been committed,

(b) anything that there are reasonable grounds to believe will afford evidence with respect to the commission of an offence, or will reveal the whereabouts of a person who is believed to have committed an offence, against this Act or any other Act of Parliament,

(c) anything that there are reasonable grounds to believe is intended to be used for the purpose of committing any offence against the person for which a person may be arrested without warrant, or

(c.1) any offence-related property,

may at any time issue a warrant authorizing a peace officer or a public officer who has been appointed or designated to administer or enforce a federal or provincial law and whose duties include the enforcement of this Act or any other Act of Parliament and who is named in the warrant

(d) to search the building, receptacle or place for any such thing and to seize it, and

(e) subject to any other Act of Parliament, to, as soon as practicable, bring the thing seized before, or make a report in respect thereof to, the justice or some other justice for the same territorial division in accordance with section 489.1.

(2) Endorsement of search warrant—Where the building, receptacle, or place in which anything mentioned in subsection (1) is believed to be is in any other territorial division, the justice may issue his warrant in like form modified according to the circumstances, and the warrant may be executed in the other territorial division after it has been endorsed, in Form 28, by a justice having jurisdiction in that territorial division.

(2.1) Operation of computer system and copying equipment—A person authorized under this section to search a computer system in a building or place for data may

(a) use or cause to be used any computer system at the building or place to search any data contained in or available to the computer system;

(b) reproduce or cause to be reproduced any data in the form of a print-out or other intelligible output;

(c) seize the print-out or other output for examination or copying; and

(d) use or cause to be used any copying equipment at the place to make copies of the data.

(2.2) Duty of person in possession or control—Every person who is in possession or control of any building or place in respect of which a search is carried out under this section shall, on presentation of the warrant, permit the person carrying out the search

(a) to use or cause to be used any computer system at the building or place in order to search any data contained in or available to the computer system for data that the person is authorized by this section to search for;

(b) to obtain a hard copy of the data and to seize it; and

(c) to use or cause to be used any copying equipment at the place to make copies of the data.

(3) Form—A search warrant issued under this section may be in the form set out as Form 5 in Part XXVIII, varied to suit the case.

(4) Effect of endorsement—An endorsement that is made on a warrant as provided for in subsection (2) is sufficient authority to the peace officers or public officers to whom it was originally directed, and to all peace officers within the jurisdiction of the justice by whom it is endorsed, to execute the warrant and to deal with the things seized in accordance with section 489.1 or as otherwise provided by law.
R.S.C. 1985, c. 27 (1st Supp.), s. 68; 1994, c. 44, s. 36; 1997, c. 18, s. 41; 1997, c. 23, s. 12; 1999, c. 5, s. 16.

487.01 (1) Information for general warrant—A provincial court judge, a judge of a superior court of criminal jurisdiction or a judge as defined in section 552 may issue a warrant in writing authorizing a peace officer to, subject to this section, use any device or investigative technique or procedure or do any thing described in the warrant that would, if not authorized, constitute an unreasonable search or seizure in respect of a person or a person's property if

(a) the judge is satisfied by information on oath in writing that there are reasonable grounds to believe that an offence against this or any other Act of Parliament has been or will be committed and that information concerning the offence will be obtained through the use of the technique, procedure or device or the doing of the thing;

(b) the judge is satisfied that it is in the best interests of the administration of justice to issue the warrant; and

(c) there is no other provision in this or any other Act of Parliament that would provide for a warrant, authorization or order permitting the technique, procedure or device to be used or the thing to be done.

(2) Limitation—Nothing in subsection (1) shall be construed as to permit interference with the bodily integrity of any person.

(3) Search or seizure to be reasonable—A warrant issued under subsection (1) shall contain such terms and conditions as the judge considers advisable to ensure that any search or seizure authorized by the warrant is reasonable in the circumstances.

(4) Video surveillance—A warrant issued under subsection (1) that authorizes a peace officer to observe, by means of a television camera or other similar electronic device, any person who is engaged in activity in circumstances in which the person has a reasonable expectation of privacy shall contain such terms and conditions as the judge considers advisable to ensure that the privacy of the person or of any other person is respected as much as possible.

(5) Other provisions to apply—The definition "offence" in section 183 and sections 183.1, 184.2, 184.3 and 185 to 188.2, subsection 189(5), and sections 190, 193 and 194 to 196 apply, with such modifications as the circumstances require, to a warrant referred to in subsection (4) as though references in those provisions to interceptions of private communications were read as references to observations by peace officers by means of television cameras or similar electronic devices of activities in circumstances in which persons had reasonable expectations of privacy.

(5.1) Notice after covert entry—A warrant issued under subsection (1) that authorizes a peace officer to enter and search a place covertly shall require, as part of the terms and conditions referred to in subsection (3), that notice of the entry and search be given within any time after the execution of the warrant that the judge considers reasonable in the circumstances.

(5.2) Extension of period for giving notice—Where the judge who issues a warrant under subsection (1) or any other judge having jurisdiction to issue such a warrant is, on the basis of an affidavit submitted in support of an application to vary the period within which the notice referred to in subsection (5.1) is to be given, is satisfied that the interests of justice warrant the granting of the application, the judge may grant an extension, or a subsequent extension, of the period, but no extension may exceed three years.

(6) Provisions to apply—Subsections 487(2) and (4) apply, with such modifications as the circumstances require, to a warrant issued under subsection (1).

(7) Telewarrant provisions to apply—Where a peace officer believes that it would be impracticable to appear personally before a judge to make an application for a warrant under this section, a warrant may be issued under this section on an information submitted by telephone or other means of telecommunication and, for that purpose, section 487.1 applies, with such modifications as the circumstances require, to the warrant.

1993, c. 40, s. 15; 1997, c. 18, s. 42; 1997, c. 23, s. 13.

487.011 Definitions—The following definitions apply in sections 487.012 to 487.017.

"data" has the same meaning as in subsection 342.1(2). *("données")*

"document" means any medium on which is recorded or marked anything that is capable of being read or understood by a person or a computer system or other device. *("document")*

2004, c. 3, s. 7.

487.012 (1) Production order—A justice or judge may order a person, other than a person under investigation for an offence referred to in paragraph (3)(*a*),

(a) to produce documents, or copies of them certified by affidavit to be true copies, or to produce data; or

(b) to prepare a document based on documents or data already in existence and produce it.

(2) Production to peace officer—The order shall require the documents or data to be produced within the time, at the place and in the form specified and given

(a) to a peace officer named in the order; or

(b) to a public officer named in the order, who has been appointed or designated to administer or enforce a federal or provincial law and whose duties include the enforcement of this or any other Act of Parliament.

(3) Conditions for issuance of order—Before making an order, the justice or judge must be satisfied, on the basis of an *ex parte* application containing information on oath in writing, that there are reasonable grounds to believe that

   (a) an offence against this Act or any other Act of Parliament has been or is suspected to have been committed;

   (b) the documents or data will afford evidence respecting the commission of the offence; and

   (c) the person who is subject to the order has possession or control of the documents or data.

(4) Terms and conditions—The order may contain any terms and conditions that the justice or judge considers advisable in the circumstances, including terms and conditions to protect a privileged communication between a lawyer and their client or, in the province of Quebec, between a lawyer or a notary and their client.

(5) Power to revoke, renew or vary order—The justice or judge who made the order, or a judge of the same territorial division, may revoke, renew or vary the order on an *ex parte* application made by the peace officer or public officer named in the order.

(6) Application—Sections 489.1 and 490 apply, with any modifications that the circumstances require, in respect of documents or data produced under this section.

(7) Probative force of copies—Every copy of a document produced under this section, on proof by affidavit that it is a true copy, is admissible in evidence in proceedings under this or any other Act of Parliament and has the same probative force as the original document would have if it had been proved in the ordinary way.

(8) Return of copies—Copies of documents produced under this section need not be returned.

2004, c. 3, s. 7.

487.013 (1) Production order—financial or commercial information—A justice or judge may order a financial institution, as defined in section 2 of the *Bank Act*, or a person or entity referred to in section 5 of the *Proceeds of Crime (Money Laundering) and Terrorist Financing Act*, unless they are under investigation for an offence referred to in paragraph (4)(*a*), to produce in writing the account number of a person named in the order or the name of a person whose account number is specified in the order, the status and type of the account, and the date on which it was opened or closed.

(2) Identification of person named in the order—For the purpose of confirming the identity of the person named in the order or whose account number is specified in the order, the production order may require the financial institution, person or entity to produce that person's date of birth, current address and any previous addresses.

(3) Production to peace officer—The order shall require the information to be produced within the time, at the place and in the form specified and given

(a) to a peace officer named in the order; or

(b) to a public officer named in the order, who has been appointed or designated to administer or enforce a federal or provincial law and whose duties include the enforcement of this or any other Act of Parliament.

(4) Conditions for issuance of order—Before making an order, the justice or judge must be satisfied, on the basis of an *ex parte* application containing information on oath in writing, that there are reasonable grounds to suspect that

(a) an offence against this Act or any other Act of Parliament has been or will be committed;

(b) the information will assist in the investigation of the offence; and

(c) the institution, person or entity that is subject to the order has possession or control of the information.

(5) Terms and conditions—The order may contain any terms and conditions that the justice or judge considers advisable in the circumstances, including terms and conditions to protect a privileged communication between a lawyer and their client or, in the province of Quebec, between a lawyer or a notary and their client.

(6) Power to revoke, renew or vary order—The justice or judge who made the order, or a judge of the same territorial division, may revoke, renew or vary the order on an *ex parte* application made by the peace officer or public officer named in the order.

2004, c. 3, s. 7.

487.014 (1) Power of peace officer—For greater certainty, no production order is necessary for a peace officer or public officer enforcing or administering this or any other Act of Parliament to ask a person to voluntarily provide to the officer documents, data or information that the person is not prohibited by law from disclosing.

(2) Application of section 25—A person who provides documents, data or information in the circumstances referred to in subsection (1) is deemed to be authorized to do so for the purposes of section 25.

2004, c. 3, s. 7.

487.015 (1) Application for exemption—A person named in an order made under section 487.012 and a financial institution, person or entity named in an order made under section 487.013 may, before the order expires, apply in writing to the judge who issued the order, or a judge of the same territorial division as the judge or justice who issued the order, for an exemption from the requirement to produce any document, data or information referred to in the order.

(2) Notice—A person, financial institution or entity may only make an application under subsection (1) if they give notice of their intention to do so to the peace officer or public officer named in the order, within 30 days after it is made.

(3) Order suspended—The execution of a production order is suspended in respect of any document, data or information referred to in the application for exemption until a final decision is made in respect of the application.

(4) Exemption—The judge may grant the exemption if satisfied that

(a) the document, data or information would disclose information that is privileged or otherwise protected from disclosure by law;

(b) it is unreasonable to require the applicant to produce the document, data or information; or

(c) the document, data or information is not in the possession or control of the applicant.

2004, c. 3, s. 7.

487.016 Self-incrimination—No person is excused from complying with an order made under section 487.012 or 487.013 on the ground that the document, data or information referred to in the order may tend to incriminate them or subject them to any proceeding or penalty, but no document prepared by an individual under paragraph 487.012(1)(*b*) may be used or received in evidence against that individual in any criminal proceedings subsequently instituted against them, other than a prosecution under section 132, 136 or 137.

2004, c. 3, s. 7.

487.017 Offence—A financial institution, person or entity who does not comply with a production order made under section 487.012 or 487.013 is guilty of an offence and liable on summary conviction to a fine not exceeding $250,000 or imprisonment for a term not exceeding six months, or to both.

2004, c. 3, s. 7.

487.02 Assistance order—Where an authorization is given under section 184.2, 184.3, 186 or 188, a warrant is issued under this Act or an order is made under subsection 492.2(2), the judge or justice who gives the authorization, issues the warrant or makes the order may order any person to provide assistance, where the person's assistance may reasonably be considered to be required to give effect to the authorization, warrant or order.

1993, c. 40, s. 15; 1997, c. 18, s. 43.

487.03 (1) Execution in another province—Where

(a) a warrant is issued under section 487.01, 487.05 or 492.1 or subsection 492.2(1) in one province,

(b) it may reasonably be expected that the warrant is to be executed in another province, and

(c) the execution of the warrant would require entry into or on the property of any person in the other province or would require that an order be made under section 487.02 with respect to any person in that other province,

a judge or justice, as the case may be, in the other province may, on application, endorse the warrant and the warrant, after being so endorsed, has the same force in that other province as though it had originally been issued in that other province.

(2) Execution in another province — taking of bodily substances—When an order or authorization referred to in section 487.051, 487.052, 487.055 or 487.091 is made or granted, and it may reasonably be expected to be executed in another province, a provincial court judge of that province may, on application, endorse the order or authorization in Form 28.1. Once the order or authorization is endorsed, it has the same force in that province as though it had originally been issued there.

1993, c. 40, s. 15; 1995, c. 27, s. 1; 2000, c. 10, s. 13.

Forensic DNA Analysis

487.04 Definitions—In this section and sections 487.05 to 487.09,

"adult" has the meaning assigned by subsection 2(1) of the *Youth Criminal Justice Act*;

"designated offence" means a primary designated offence or a secondary designated offence;

"DNA" means deoxyribonucleic acid;

"forensic DNA analysis"

(a) in relation to a bodily substance that is taken from a person in execution of a warrant under section 487.05, means forensic DNA analysis of the bodily substance and the comparison of the results of that analysis with the results of the analysis of the DNA in the bodily substance referred to in paragraph 487.05(1)(*b*), and includes any incidental tests associated with that analysis, and

(b) in relation to a bodily substance that is provided voluntarily in the course of an investigation of a designated offence or taken from a person in execution of an order under section 487.051 or 487.052 or under an authorization under section 487.055 or 487.091, or a bodily substance referred to in paragraph 487.05(1)(*b*), means forensic DNA analysis of the bodily substance;

"primary designated offence" means

(a) an offence under any of the following provisions, namely,

(i) section 75 (piratical acts),

(i.01) section 76 (hijacking),

(i.02) section 77 (endangering safety of aircraft or airport),

(i.03) section 78.1 (seizing control of ship or fixed platform),

(i.04) subsection 81(1) (using explosives),

(i.05) section 83.18 (participation in activity of terrorist group),

(i.06) section 83.19 (facilitating terrorist activity),

(i.07) section 83.2 (commission of offence for terrorist group),

(i.08) section 83.21 (instructing to carry out activity for terrorist group),

(i.09) section 83.22 (instructing to carry out terrorist activity),

(i.1) section 83.23 (harbouring or concealing),

(i.11) section 151 (sexual interference),

(ii) section 152 (invitation to sexual touching),

(iii) section 153 (sexual exploitation),

(iv) section 155 (incest),

(v) subsection 212(4) (offence in relation to juvenile prostitution),

(vi) section 233 (infanticide),

(vii) section 235 (murder),

(viii) section 236 (manslaughter),

(ix) section 244 (causing bodily harm with intent),

(x) section 267 (assault with a weapon or causing bodily harm),

(xi) section 268 (aggravated assault),

(xii) section 269 (unlawfully causing bodily harm),

(xiii) section 271 (sexual assault),

(xiv) section 272 (sexual assault with a weapon, threats to a third party or causing bodily harm),

(xv) section 273 (aggravated sexual assault),

(xvi) section 279 (kidnapping),

(xvii) section 279.1 (hostage taking),

(xviii) section 431 (attack on premises, residence or transport of internationally protected person),

(xix) section 431.1 (attack on premises, accommodation or transport of United Nations or associated personnel), and

(xx) subsection 431.2(2) (explosive or other lethal device),

(b) an offence under any of the following provisions of the *Criminal Code*, chapter C-34 of the Revised Statutes of Canada, 1970, as they read from time to time before January 4, 1983, namely,

(i) section 144 (rape),

(ii) section 146 (sexual intercourse with female under fourteen and between fourteen and sixteen), and

(iii) section 148 (sexual intercourse with feeble-minded, etc.),

(c) an offence under paragraph 153(1)(a) (sexual intercourse with step-daughter, etc.) of the *Criminal Code*, chapter C-34 of the Revised Statutes of Canada, 1970, as it read from time to time before January 1, 1988,

(c.1) an offence under any of the following provisions of the *Security of Information Act*, namely,

(i) section 6 (approaching, entering, etc., a prohibited place),

(ii) subsection 20(1) (threats or violence), and

(iii) subsection 21(1) (harbouring or concealing), and

(d) an attempt to commit or, other than for the purposes of subsection 487.05(1), a conspiracy to commit an offence referred to in any of paragraphs (*a*) to (*c*);

"provincial court judge", in relation to a young person, includes a youth justice court judge within the meaning of subsection 2(1) of the *Youth Criminal Justice Act*;

"secondary designated offence" means

(a) an offence under any of the following provisions, namely,

(i) [Repealed 2001, c. 41, s. 17(4).]

(ii) [Repealed 2001, c. 41, s. 17(4).]

(iii) [Repealed 2001, c. 41, s. 17(4).]

(iv) [Repealed 2001, c. 41, s. 17(4).]

(v) [Repealed 2001, c. 41, s. 17(4).]

(vi) subsection 160(3) (bestiality in the presence of or by child),

(vii) section 163.1 (child pornography),

(viii) section 170 (parent or guardian procuring sexual activity),

(ix) section 173 (indecent acts),

(x) section 220 (causing death by criminal negligence),

(xi) section 221 (causing bodily harm by criminal negligence),

(xii) subsection 249(3) (dangerous operation causing bodily harm),

(xiii) subsection 249(4) (dangerous operation causing death),

(xiv) section 252 (failure to stop at scene of accident),

(xv) subsection 255(2) (impaired driving causing bodily harm),

(xvi) subsection 255(3) (impaired driving causing death),

(xvii) section 266 (assault),

(xviii) section 269.1 (torture),

(xix) paragraph 270(1)(a) (assaulting a peace officer),

(xx) [Repealed 2001, c. 41, s. 17(5).]

(xxi) section 344 (robbery),

(xxii) subsection 348(1) (breaking and entering with intent, committing offence or breaking out),

(xxiii) subsection 430(2) (mischief that causes actual danger to life),

(xxiv) section 433 (arson — disregard for human life), and

(xxv) section 434.1 (arson — own property),

(b) an offence under any of the following provisions of the *Criminal Code*, as they read from time to time before July 1, 1990, namely,

(i) section 433 (arson), and

(ii) section 434 (setting fire to other substance), and

(c) an attempt to commit or, other than for the purposes of subsection 487.05(1), a conspiracy to commit an offence referred to in paragraph (*a*) or (*b*);

"young person" has the meaning assigned by subsection 2(1) of the *Youth Criminal Justice Act.*
1995, c. 27, s. 1; 1998, c. 37, s. 15; 2001, c. 41, s. 17; 2002, c. 1, s. 175.

487.05 (1) Information for warrant to take bodily substances for forensic DNA analysis—A provincial court judge who on *ex parte* application made in Form 5.01 is satisfied by information on oath that there are reasonable grounds to believe

(a) that a designated offence has been committed,

(b) that a bodily substance has been found or obtained

(i) at the place where the offence was committed,

(ii) on or within the body of the victim of the offence,

(iii) on anything worn or carried by the victim at the time when the offence was committed, or

(iv) on or within the body of any person or thing or at any place associated with the commission of the offence,

(c) that a person was a party to the offence, and

(d) that forensic DNA analysis of a bodily substance from the person will provide evidence about whether the bodily substance referred to in paragraph (b) was from that person

and who is satisfied that it is in the best interests of the administration of justice to do so may issue a warrant in Form 5.02 authorizing the taking, from that person, for the purpose of forensic DNA analysis, of any number of samples of one or more bodily substances that is reasonably required for that purpose, by means of the investigative procedures described in subsection 487.06(1).

(2) Criteria—In considering whether to issue the warrant, the provincial court judge shall have regard to all relevant matters, including

(a) the nature of the designated offence and the circumstances of its commission; and

(b) whether there is

(i) a peace officer who is able, by virtue of training or experience, to take samples of bodily substances from the person, by means of the investigative procedures described in subsection 487.06(1), or

(ii) another person who is able, by virtue of training or experience, to take, under the direction of a peace officer, samples of bodily substances from the person, by means of those investigative procedures.

(3) Telewarrant—Where a peace officer believes that it would be impracticable to appear personally before a judge to make an application for a warrant under this section, a warrant may be issued under this section on an information submitted by telephone or other means of telecommunication and, for that purpose, section 487.1 applies, with such modifications as the circumstances require, to the warrant.

1995, c. 27, s. 1; 1997, c. 18, s. 44; 1998, c. 37, s. 16.

. . . .

487.06 (1) Investigative procedures—A peace officer or another person under the direction of a peace officer is authorized to take samples of bodily substances from a person by a warrant under section 487.05 or an order under section 487.051 or 487.052 or an authorization under section 487.055 or 487.091, by any of the following means:

(a) the plucking of individual hairs from the person, including the root sheath;

(b) the taking of buccal swabs by swabbing the lips, tongue and inside cheeks of the mouth to collect epithelial cells; or

(c) the taking of blood by pricking the skin surface with a sterile lancet.

(2) Terms and conditions—The warrant, order or authorization shall include any terms and conditions that the provincial court judge or court, as the case may be, considers advisable to ensure that the taking of the samples authorized by the warrant, order or authorization is reasonable in the circumstances.

(3) Fingerprints—A peace officer, or any person acting under a peace officer's direction, who is authorized to take samples of bodily substances from a person by an order under section 487.051 or 487.052 or an authorization under section 487.055 or 487.091 may take fingerprints from the person for the purpose of the *DNA Identification Act.*

1995, c. 27, s. 1; 1998, c. 37, s. 18; 2000, c. 10, s. 19.

487.07 (1) Duty to inform—Before taking samples of bodily substances from a person, or causing samples of bodily substances to be taken from a person under the direction of a peace officer, in execution of a warrant under section 487.05 or an order under section 487.051 or 487.052 or under an authorization under section 487.055 or 487.091, the peace officer shall inform the person from whom the samples are to be taken of

(a) the contents of the warrant, order or authorization;

(b) the nature of the investigative procedures by means of which the samples are to be taken;

(c) the purpose of taking the samples;

(d) the authority of the peace officer and any other person under the direction of the peace officer to use as much force as is necessary for the purpose of taking the samples; and

(d.1) [Repealed 2000, c. 10, s. 20(2).]

(e) in the case of samples of bodily substances taken in execution of a warrant,

(i) the possibility that the results of forensic DNA analysis may be used in evidence, and

(ii) if the sample is taken from a young person, the rights of the young person under subsection (4).

(2) Detention of person—A person from whom samples of bodily substances are to be taken may

(a) be detained for that purpose for a period that is reasonable in the circumstances; and

(b) be required to accompany a peace officer for that purpose.

(3) Respect of privacy—A peace officer who takes samples of bodily substances from a person, or a person who takes such samples under the direction of a peace officer, shall ensure that the person's privacy is respected in a manner that is reasonable in the circumstances.

(4) Execution of warrant against young person—A young person against whom a warrant is executed has, in addition to any other rights arising from his or her detention under the warrant,

>(a) the right to a reasonable opportunity to consult with, and

>(b) the right to have the warrant executed in the presence of

counsel and a parent or, in the absence of a parent, an adult relative or, in the absence of a parent and an adult relative, any other appropriate adult chosen by the young person.

(5) Waiver of rights of young person—A young person may waive his or her rights under subsection (4) but any such waiver

>(a) must be recorded on audio tape or video tape or otherwise; or

>(b) must be made in writing and contain a statement signed by the young person that he or she has been informed of the right being waived.
>>1995, c. 27, ss. 1, 3; 1998, c. 37, s. 19; 2000, c. 10, s. 20.

. . . .

487.08 (1) Use of bodily substances—warrant—No person shall use bodily substances that are taken in execution of a warrant under section 487.05 or under section 196.12 of the *National Defence Act* except to use them for the purpose of forensic DNA analysis in the course of an investigation of a designated offence.

(1.1) Use of bodily substances—order, authorization—No person shall use bodily substances that are taken in execution of an order under section 487.051 or 487.052, under an authorization under section 487.055 or 487.091, in execution of an order under section 196.14 or 196.15 of the *National Defence Act*, or under an authorization under section 196.24 of that Act except

>(a) to use them for the purpose of forensic DNA analysis; or

>(b) to transmit any portions of samples of those bodily substances that are not used in forensic DNA analysis to the Commissioner of the Royal Canadian Mounted Police under subsection 487.071(2).

(2) Use of results—warrant—No person shall use the results of forensic DNA analysis of bodily substances that are taken in execution of a warrant under section 487.05 or under section 196.12 of the *National Defence Act* except

(a) in the course of an investigation of the designated offence or any other designated offence in respect of which a warrant was issued or a bodily substance was found in the circumstances described in paragraph 487.05(1)(*b*) or in paragraph 196.12(1)(*b*) of the *National Defence Act*; or

(b) in any proceeding for such an offence.

(2.1) Use of results—order, authorization—No person shall use the results of forensic DNA analysis of bodily substances that are taken in execution of an order under section 487.051 or 487.052 or under an authorization under section 487.055 or 487.091, or in execution of an order under section 196.14 or 196.15 of the *National Defence Act*, or under an authorization under section 196.24 of that Act, except to transmit them to the Commissioner of the Royal Canadian Mounted Police.

(3) Offence—Every person who contravenes subsection (1) or (2) is guilty of an offence punishable on summary conviction.

(4) Offence—Every person who contravenes subsection (1.1) or (2.1)

(a) is guilty of an indictable offence and liable to imprisonment for a term not exceeding two years; or

(b) is guilty of an offence punishable on summary conviction and liable to a fine not exceeding $2,000 or to imprisonment for a term not exceeding six months, or to both.

1995, c. 27, s. 1; 1998, c. 37, s. 21; 2000, c. 10, s. 22.

487.09 (1) Destruction of bodily substances, etc.—warrant—Subject to subsection (2), bodily substances that are taken from a person in execution of a warrant under section 487.05 and the results of forensic DNA analysis shall be destroyed or, in the case of results in electronic form, access to those results shall be permanently removed, without delay after

(a) the results of that analysis establish that the bodily substance referred to in paragraph 487.05(1)(b) was not from that person;

(b) the person is finally acquitted of the designated offence and any other offence in respect of the same transaction; or

(c) the expiration of one year after

(i) the person is discharged after a preliminary inquiry into the designated offence or any other offence in respect of the same transaction,

(ii) the dismissal, for any reason other than acquittal, or the withdrawal of any information charging the person with the designated offence or any other offence in respect of the same transaction, or

(iii) any proceeding against the person for the offence or any other offence in respect of the same transaction is stayed under section 579 or under that section as applied by section 572 or 795,

unless during that year a new information is laid or an indictment is preferred charging the person with the designated offence or any other offence in respect of the same transaction or the proceeding is recommenced.

(2) Exception—A provincial court judge may order that the bodily substances that are taken from a person and the results of forensic DNA analysis not be destroyed during any period that the provincial court judge considers appropriate if the provincial court judge is satisfied that the bodily substances or results might reasonably be required in an investigation or prosecution of the person for another designated offence or of another person for the designated offence or any other offence in respect of the same transaction.

(3) Destruction of bodily substances, etc. voluntarily given—Bodily substances that are provided voluntarily by a person and the results of forensic DNA analysis shall be destroyed or, in the case of results in electronic form, access to those results shall be permanently removed, without delay after the results of that analysis establish that the bodily substance referred to in paragraph 487.05(1)(b) was not from that person.

1995, c. 27, s. 1; 1998, c. 37, s. 22.

. . . .

487.092 (1) Information for impression warrant—A justice may issue a warrant in writing authorizing a peace officer to do any thing, or cause any thing to be done under the direction of the peace officer, described in the warrant in order to obtain any handprint, fingerprint, footprint, foot impression, teeth impression or other print or impression of the body or any part of the body in respect of a person if the justice is satisfied

(a) by information on oath in writing that there are reasonable grounds to believe that an offence against this or any other Act of Parliament has been committed and that information concerning the offence will be obtained by the print or impression; and

(b) that it is in the best interests of the administration of justice to issue the warrant.

(2) Search or seizure to be reasonable—A warrant issued under subsection (1) shall contain such terms and conditions as the justice considers advisable to ensure that any search or seizure authorized by the warrant is reasonable in the circumstances.

(3) Provisions to apply—Subsections 487(2) and (4) apply, with such modifications as the circumstances require, to a warrant issued under subsection (1).

(4) Telewarrant—Where a peace officer believes that it would be impracticable to appear personally before a justice to make an application for a warrant under this section, a warrant may be issued under this section on an information submitted by telephone or other means of telecommunication and, for that purpose, section 487.1 applies, with such modifications as the circumstances require, to the warrant.

1997, c. 18, s. 45; 1998, c. 37, s. 23.

[Editor's Note: This section was originally enacted as s. 487.091 by 1997, c. 18, s. 45 and was renumbered as s. 487.092 by 1998, c. 37, s. 23.]

Other Provisions respecting Search Warrants
[Heading added 1995, c. 27, s. 1]

487.1 (1) Telewarrants—Where a peace officer believes that an indictable offence has been committed and that it would be impracticable to appear personally before a justice to make application for a warrant in accordance with section 256 or 487, the peace officer may submit an information on oath by telephone or other means of telecommunication to a justice designated for the purpose by the chief judge of the provincial court having jurisdiction in the matter.

(2) Information on oath and record—An information submitted by telephone or other means of telecommunication, other than a means of telecommunication that produces a writing, shall be on oath and shall be recorded verbatim by the justice, who shall, as soon as practicable, cause to be filed, with the clerk of the court for the territorial division in which the warrant is intended for execution, the record or a transcription of it, certified by the justice as to time, date and contents.

(2.1) Information submitted by other means of telecommunication—The justice who receives an information submitted by a means of telecommunication that produces a writing shall, as soon as practicable, cause to be filed, with the clerk of the court for the territorial division in which the warrant is intended for execution, the information certified by the justice as to time and date of receipt.

(3) Administration of oath—For the purposes of subsection (2), an oath may be administered by telephone or other means of telecommunication.

(3.1) Alternative to oath—A peace officer who uses a means of telecommunication referred to in subsection (2.1) may, instead of swearing an oath, make a statement in writing stating that all matters contained in the information are true to his or her knowledge and belief and such a statement is deemed to be a statement made under oath.

(4) Contents of information—An information submitted by telephone or other means of telecommunication shall include

(a) a statement of the circumstances that make it impracticable for the peace officer to appear personally before a justice;

(b) a statement of the indictable offence alleged, the place or premises to be searched and the items alleged to be liable to seizure;

(c) a statement of the peace officer's grounds for believing that items liable to seizure in respect of the offence alleged will be found in the place or premises to be searched; and

(d) a statement as to any prior application for a warrant under this section or any other search warrant, in respect of the same matter, of which the peace officer has knowledge.

(5) Issuing warrant—A justice referred to in subsection (1) who is satisfied that an information submitted by telephone or other means of telecommunication

(a) is in respect of an indictable offence and conforms to the requirements of subsection (4),

(b) discloses reasonable grounds for dispensing with an information presented personally and in writing, and

(c) discloses reasonable grounds, in accordance with subsection 256(1) or paragraph 487(1)(*a*), (*b*) or (*c*), as the case may be, for the issuance of a warrant in respect of an indictable offence,

may issue a warrant to a peace officer conferring the same authority respecting search and seizure as may be conferred by a warrant issued by a justice before whom the peace officer appears personally pursuant to subsection 256(1) or

487(1), as the case may be, and may require that the warrant be executed within such period as the justice may order.

(6) Formalities respecting warrant and facsimiles—Where a justice issues a warrant by telephone or other means of telecommunication, other than a means of telecommunication that produces a writing,

(a) the justice shall complete and sign the warrant in Form 5.1, noting on its face the time, date and place of issuance;

(b) the peace officer, on the direction of the justice, shall complete, in duplicate, a facsimile of the warrant in Form 5.1, noting on its face the name of the issuing justice and the time, date and place of issuance; and

(c) the justice shall, as soon as practicable after the warrant has been issued, cause the warrant to be filed with the clerk of the court for the territorial division in which the warrant is intended for execution.

(6.1) Issuance of warrant where telecommunication produces writing—Where a justice issues a warrant by a means of telecommunication that produces a writing,

(a) the justice shall complete and sign the warrant in Form 5.1, noting on its face the time, date and place of issuance;

(b) the justice shall transmit the warrant by the means of telecommunication to the peace officer who submitted the information and the copy of the warrant received by the peace officer is deemed to be a facsimile within the meaning of paragraph (6)(*b*);

(c) the peace officer shall procure another facsimile of the warrant; and

(d) the justice shall, as soon as practicable after the warrant has been issued, cause the warrant to be filed with the clerk of the court for the territorial division in which the warrant is intended for execution.

(7) Providing facsimile—A peace officer who executes a warrant issued by telephone or other means of telecommunication, other than a warrant issued pursuant to subsection 256(1), shall, before entering the place or premises to be searched or as soon as practicable thereafter, give a facsimile of the warrant to any person present and ostensibly in control of the place or premises.

(8) Affixing facsimile—A peace officer who, in any unoccupied place or premises, executes a warrant issued by telephone or other means of telecommunication, other than a warrant issued pursuant to subsection 256(1), shall, on entering the place or premises or as soon as practicable thereafter, cause a facsimile of the warrant to be suitably affixed in a prominent place within the place or premises.

(9) Report of peace officer—A peace officer to whom a warrant is issued by telephone or other means of telecommunication shall file a written report with the clerk of the court for the territorial division in which the warrant was intended for execution as soon as practicable but within a period not exceeding seven days after the warrant has been executed, which report shall include

(a) a statement of the time and date the warrant was executed or, if the warrant was not executed, a statement of the reasons why it was not executed;

(b) a statement of the things, if any, that were seized pursuant to the warrant and the location where they are being held; and

(c) a statement of the things, if any, that were seized in addition to the things mentioned in the warrant and the location where they are being held, together with a statement of the peace officer's grounds for believing that those additional things had been obtained by, or used in, the commission of an offence.

(10) Bringing before justice—The clerk of the court shall, as soon as practicable, cause the report, together with the information and the warrant to which it pertains, to be brought before a justice to be dealt with, in respect of the things seized referred to in the report, in the same manner as if the things were seized pursuant to a warrant issued, on an information presented personally by a peace officer, by that justice or another justice for the same territorial division.

(11) Proof of authorization—In any proceeding in which it is material for a court to be satisfied that a search or seizure was authorized by a warrant issued by telephone or other means of telecommunication, the absence of the information or warrant, signed by the justice and carrying on its face a notation of the time, date and place of issuance, is, in the absence of evidence to the contrary, proof that the search or seizure was not authorized by a warrant issued by telephone or other means of telecommunication.

(12) Duplicates and facsimiles acceptable—A duplicate or a facsimile of an information or a warrant has the same probative force as the original for the purposes of subsection (11).
R.S.C. 1985, c. 27 (1st Supp.), s. 69; 1992, c. 1, s. 58(1) (Sched. I, items 9, 18); 1994, c. 44, s. 37.

487.11 Where warrant not necessary—A peace officer, or a public officer who has been appointed or designated to administer or enforce any federal or provincial law and whose duties include the enforcement of this or any other Act of Parliament, may, in the course of his or her duties, exercise any of the powers described in subsection 487(1) or 492.1(1) without a warrant if the conditions for obtaining a warrant exist but by reason of exigent circumstances it would be impracticable to obtain a warrant.

1997, c. 18, s. 46.

487.2 (1) Restriction on publicity—[unconstitutional][1]

(2) Definition of "newspaper"—In this section, **"newspaper"** has the same meaning as in section 297.

R.S.C. 1985, c. 27 (1st Supp.), s. 69.

487.3 (1) Order denying access to information used to obtain a warrant or production order—A judge or justice may, on application made at the time of issuing a warrant under this or any other Act of Parliament or a production order under section 487.012 or 487.013, or of granting an authorization to enter a dwelling-house under section 529 or an authorization under section 529.4 or at any time thereafter, make an order prohibiting access to and the disclosure of any information relating to the warrant, production order or authorization on the ground that

(a) the ends of justice would be subverted by the disclosure for one of the reasons referred to in subsection (2) or the information might be used for an improper purpose; and

(b) the ground referred to in paragraph (a) outweighs in importance the access to the information.

(2) Reasons—For the purposes of paragraph (1)(a), an order may be made under subsection (1) on the ground that the ends of justice would be subverted by the disclosure

(a) if disclosure of the information would

(i) compromise the identity of a confidential informant,

(ii) compromise the nature and extent of an ongoing investigation,

(iii) endanger a person engaged in particular intelligence-gathering techniques and thereby prejudice future investigations in which similar techniques would be used, or

---

[1] *Canadian Newspapers Co. v. Canada (Attorney General)* (1986), 28 C.C.C. (3d) 379, 31 D.L.R. (4th) 601 (Man. Q.B.); *Canadian Newspapers Co. v. Canada (Attorney General)* (1986), 29 C.C.C. (3d) 109, 53 C.R. (3d) 203 (Ont. H.C.), additional reasons at (1986), 27 C.R.R. 52, 32 D.L.R. (4th) 292 at 304 (Ont. H.C.); *Thibault v. Demers* (2001), 153 C.C.C. (3d) 217, 43 C.R. (5th) 161 (Que. C.A.), leave to appeal refused (2001), 282 N.R. 198 (note) (S.C.C.).

(iv) prejudice the interests of an innocent person; and

(b) for any other sufficient reason.

(3) Procedure—Where an order is made under subsection (1), all documents relating to the application shall, subject to any terms and conditions that the justice or judge considers desirable in the circumstances, including, without limiting the generality of the foregoing, any term or condition concerning the duration of the prohibition, partial disclosure of a document, deletion of any information or the occurrence of a condition, be placed in a packet and sealed by the justice or judge immediately on determination of the application, and that packet shall be kept in the custody of the court in a place to which the public has no access or in any other place that the justice or judge may authorize and shall not be dealt with except in accordance with the terms and conditions specified in the order or as varied under subsection (4).

(4) Application for variance of order—An application to terminate the order or vary any of its terms and conditions may be made to the justice or judge who made the order or a judge of the court before which any proceedings arising out of the investigation in relation to which the warrant or production order was obtained may be held.

1997, c. 23, s. 14; 1997, c. 39, s. 1; 2004, c. 3, s. 8.

488. Execution of search warrant—A warrant issued under section 487 or 487.1 shall be executed by day, unless

(a) the justice is satisfied that there are reasonable grounds for it to be executed by night;

(b) the reasonable grounds are included in the information; and

(c) the warrant authorizes that it be executed by night.

R.S.C. 1985, c. 27 (1st Supp.), s. 70; 1997, c. 18, s. 47.

488.1 (1) Definitions—In this section,[2]

"custodian" means a person in whose custody a package is placed pursuant to subsection (2);

"document", for the purposes of this section, has the same meaning as in section 321;

"judge" means a judge of a superior court of criminal jurisdiction of the province where the seizure was made;

---

[2] This section is unconstitutional – see discussion in Chapter 10, Observations on Some Specialized Warrants, under heading 4, "Special Locations."

"lawyer" means, in the Province of Quebec, an advocate, lawyer or notary and, in any other province, a barrister or solicitor;

"officer" means a peace officer or public officer.

(2) Examination or seizure of certain documents where privilege claimed—Where an officer acting under the authority of this or any other Act of Parliament is about to examine, copy or seize a document in the possession of a lawyer who claims that a named client of his has a solicitor-client privilege in respect of that document, the officer shall, without examining or making copies of the document,

> (a) seize the document and place it in a package and suitably seal and identify the package; and

> (b) place the package in the custody of the sheriff of the district or county in which the seizure was made or, if there is agreement in writing that a specified person act as custodian, in the custody of that person.

(3) Application to judge—Where a document has been seized and placed in custody under subsection (2), the Attorney General or the client or the lawyer on behalf of the client, may

> (a) within fourteen days from the day the document was so placed in custody, apply, on two days notice of motion to all other persons entitled to make application, to a judge for an order

>> (i) appointing a place and a day, not later than twenty-one days after the date of the order, for the determination of the question whether the document should be disclosed, and

>> (ii) requiring the custodian to produce the document to the judge at that time and place;

> (b) serve a copy of the order on all other persons entitled to make application and on the custodian within six days of the date on which it was made; and

> (c) if he has proceeded as authorized by paragraph (*b*), apply, at the appointed time and place, for an order determining the question.

(4) Disposition of application—On an application under paragraph (3)(*c*), the judge

> (a) may, if the judge considers it necessary to determine the question whether the document should be disclosed, inspect the document;

(b) where the judge is of the opinion that it would materially assist him in deciding whether or not the document is privileged, may allow the Attorney General to inspect the document;

(c) shall allow the Attorney General and the person who objects to the disclosure of the document to make representations; and

(d) shall determine the question summarily and,

(i) if the judge is of the opinion that the document should not be disclosed, ensure that it is repackaged and resealed and order the custodian to deliver the document to the lawyer who claimed the solicitor-client privilege or to the client, or

(ii) if the judge is of the opinion that the document should be disclosed, order the custodian to deliver the document to the officer who seized the document or some other person designated by the Attorney General, subject to such restrictions or conditions as the judge deems appropriate,

and shall, at the same time, deliver concise reasons for the determination in which the nature of the document is described without divulging the details thereof.

(5) Privilege continues—Where the judge determines pursuant to paragraph (4)(*d*) that a solicitor-client privilege exists in respect of a document, whether or not the judge has, pursuant to paragraph (4)(*b*), allowed the Attorney General to inspect the document, the document remains privileged and inadmissible as evidence unless the client consents to its admission in evidence or the privilege is otherwise lost.

(6) Order to custodian to deliver—Where a document has been seized and placed in custody under subsection (2) and a judge, on the application of the Attorney General, is satisfied that no application has been made under paragraph (3)(*a*) or that following such an application no further application has been made under paragraph (3)(*c*), the judge shall order the custodian to deliver the document to the officer who seized the document or to some other person designated by the Attorney General.

(7) Application to another judge—Where the judge to whom an application has been made under paragraph (3)(*c*) cannot act or continue to act under this section for any reason, subsequent applications under that paragraph may be made to another judge.

(8) Prohibition—No officer shall examine, make copies of or seize any document without affording a reasonable opportunity for a claim of solicitor-client privilege to be made under subsection (2).

(9) Authority to make copies—At any time while a document is in the custody of a custodian under this section, a judge may, on an *ex parte* application of a person claiming a solicitor-client privilege under this section, authorize that person to examine the document or make a copy of it in the presence of the custodian or the judge, but any such authorization shall contain provisions to ensure that the document is repackaged and that the package is resealed without alteration or damage.

(10) Hearing in private—An application under paragraph (3)(*c*) shall be heard in private.

(11) Exception—This section does not apply in circumstances where a claim of solicitor-client privilege may be made under the *Income Tax Act* or under the *Proceeds of Crime (Money Laundering) and Terrorist Financing Act.*
R.S.C. 1985, c. 27 (1st Supp.), s. 71; 2000, c. 17, s. 89; 2001, c. 41, s. 80.

489. (1) Seizure of things not specified—Every person who executes a warrant may seize, in addition to the things mentioned in the warrant, any thing that the person believes on reasonable grounds

(a) has been obtained by the commission of an offence against this or any other Act of Parliament;

(b) has been used in the commission of an offence against this or any other Act of Parliament; or

(c) will afford evidence in respect of an offence against this or any other Act of Parliament.

(2) Seizure without warrant—Every peace officer, and every public officer who has been appointed or designated to administer or enforce any federal or provincial law and whose duties include the enforcement of this or any other Act of Parliament, who is lawfully present in a place pursuant to a warrant or otherwise in the execution of duties may, without a warrant, seize any thing that the officer believes on reasonable grounds

(a) has been obtained by the commission of an offence against this or any Act of Parliament;

(b) has been used in the commission of an offence against this or any other Act of Parliament; or

(c) will afford evidence in respect of an offence against this or any other Act of Parliament.

R.S.C. 1985, c. 27 (1st Supp.), s. 72; R.S.C. 1985, c. 42 (4th Supp.), s. 3; 1993, c. 40, s. 16; 1997, c. 18, s. 48.

489.1 (1) Restitution of property or report by peace officer—Subject to this or any other Act of Parliament, where a peace officer has seized anything under a warrant issued under this Act or under section 487.11 or 489 or otherwise in the execution of duties under this or any other Act of Parliament, the peace officer shall, as soon as is practicable,

(a) where the peace officer is satisfied,

(i) that there is no dispute as to who is lawfully entitled to possession of the thing seized, and

(ii) that the continued detention of the thing seized is not required for the purposes of any investigation or a preliminary inquiry, trial or other proceeding,

return the thing seized, on being issued a receipt therefor, to the person lawfully entitled to its possession and report to the justice who issued the warrant or some other justice for the same territorial division or, if no warrant was issued, a justice having jurisdiction in respect of the matter, that he has done so; or

(b) where the peace officer is not satisfied as described in subparagraphs (a)(i) and (ii),

(i) bring the thing seized before the justice referred to in paragraph (a), or

(ii) report to the justice that he has seized the thing and is detaining it or causing it to be detained

to be dealt with by the justice in accordance with subsection 490(1).

(2) Idem—Subject to this or any other Act of Parliament, where a person, other than a peace officer, has seized anything under a warrant issued under this Act or under section 487.11 or 489 or otherwise in the execution of duties under this or any other Act of Parliament, that person shall, as soon as is practicable,

(a) bring the thing seized before the justice who issued the warrant, or some other justice for the same territorial division or, if no warrant was issued, before a justice having jurisdiction in respect of the matter, or

(b) report to the justice referred to in paragraph (a) that he has seized the thing and is detaining it or causing it to be detained, to be dealt with by the justice in accordance with subsection 490(1).

(3) Form—A report to a justice under this section shall be in the form set out as Form 5.2 in Part XXVIII, varied to suit the case and shall include, in the case of a report in respect of a warrant issued by telephone or other means of telecommunication, the statements referred to in subsection 487.1(9).

R.S.C. 1985, c. 27 (1st Supp.), s. 72; 1993, c. 40, s. 17; 1997, c. 18, s. 49.

490. (1) Detention of things seized—Subject to this or any other Act of Parliament, where, pursuant to paragraph 489.1(1)(*b*) or subsection 489.1(2), anything that has been seized is brought before a justice or a report in respect of anything seized is made to a justice, the justice shall,

(a) where the lawful owner or person who is lawfully entitled to possession of the thing seized is known, order it to be returned to that owner or person, unless the prosecutor, or the peace officer or other person having custody of the thing seized, satisfies the justice that the detention of the thing seized is required for the purposes of any investigation or a preliminary inquiry, trial or other proceeding; or

(b) where the prosecutor, or the peace officer or other person having custody of the thing seized, satisfies the justice that the thing seized should be detained for a reason set out in paragraph (*a*), detain the thing seized or order that it be detained, taking reasonable care to ensure that it is preserved until the conclusion of any investigation or until it is required to be produced for the purposes of a preliminary inquiry, trial or other proceeding.

(2) Further detention—Nothing shall be detained under the authority of paragraph (1)(*b*) for a period of more than three months after the day of the seizure, or any longer period that ends when an application made under paragraph (*a*) is decided, unless

(a) a justice, on the making of a summary application to him after three clear days notice thereof to the person from whom the thing detained was seized, is satisfied that, having regard to the nature of the investigation, its further detention for a specified period is warranted and the justice so orders; or

(b) proceedings are instituted in which the thing detained may be required.

(3) Idem—More than one order for further detention may be made under paragraph (2)(*a*) but the cumulative period of detention shall not exceed one year from the day of the seizure, or any longer period that ends when an application made under paragraph (*a*) is decided, unless

(a) a judge of a superior court of criminal jurisdiction or a judge as defined in section 552, on the making of a summary application to him after three clear days notice thereof to the person from whom the thing detained was seized, is satisfied, having regard to the complex nature of the investigation, that the further detention of the thing seized is warranted for a specified period and subject to such other conditions as the judge considers just, and the judge so orders; or

(b) proceedings are instituted in which the thing detained may be required.

(3.1) Detention without application where consent—A thing may be detained under paragraph (1)(*b*) for any period, whether or not an application for an order under subsection (2) or (3) is made, if the lawful owner or person who is lawfully entitled to possession of the thing seized consents in writing to its detention for that period.

(4) When accused ordered to stand trial—When an accused has been ordered to stand trial, the justice shall forward anything detained pursuant to subsections (1) to (3) to the clerk of the court to which the accused has been ordered to stand trial to be detained by the clerk of the court and disposed of as the court directs.

(5) Where continued detention no longer required—Where at any time before the expiration of the periods of detention provided for or ordered under subsections (1) to (3) in respect of anything seized, the prosecutor, or the peace officer or other person having custody of the thing seized, determines that the continued detention of the thing seized is no longer required for any purpose mentioned in subsection (1) or (4), the prosecutor, peace officer or other person shall apply to

(a) a judge of a superior court of criminal jurisdiction or a judge as defined in section 552, where a judge ordered its detention under subsection (3), or

(b) a justice, in any other case,

who shall, after affording the person from whom the thing was seized or the person who claims to be the lawful owner thereof or person entitled to its possession, if known, an opportunity to establish that he is lawfully entitled to the possession thereof, make an order in respect of the property under subsection (9).

(6) Idem—Where the periods of detention provided for or ordered under subsections (1) to (3) in respect of anything seized have expired and proceedings have not been instituted in which the thing detained may be required, the prosecutor, peace officer or other person shall apply to a judge or justice referred to in paragraph (5)(*a*) or (*b*) in the circumstances set out in that paragraph, for an order in respect of the property under subsection (9) or (9.1).

(7) Application for order of return—A person from whom anything has been seized may, after the expiration of the periods of detention provided for or ordered under subsections (1) to (3) and on three clear days notice to the Attorney General, apply summarily to

(a) a judge of a superior court of criminal jurisdiction or a judge as defined in section 552, where a judge ordered the detention of the thing seized under subsection (3), or

(b) a justice, in any other case,

for an order under paragraph (9)(*c*) that the thing seized be returned to the applicant.

(8) Exception—A judge of a superior court of criminal jurisdiction or a judge as defined in section 552, where a judge ordered the detention of the thing seized under subsection (3), or a justice, in any other case, may allow an application to be made under subsection (7) prior to the expiration of the periods referred to therein where he is satisfied that hardship will result unless such application is so allowed.

(9) Disposal of things seized—Subject to this or any other Act of Parliament, if

(a) a judge referred to in subsection (7), where a judge ordered the detention of anything seized under subsection (3), or

(b) a justice, in any other case,

is satisfied that the periods of detention provided for or ordered under subsections (1) to (3) in respect of anything seized have expired and proceedings have not been instituted in which the thing detained may be required or, where such periods have not expired, that the continued detention of the thing seized will not be required for any purpose mentioned in subsection (1) or (4), he shall

(c) if possession of it by the person from whom it was seized is lawful, order it to be returned to that person, or

(d) if possession of it by the person from whom it was seized is unlawful and the lawful owner or person who is lawfully entitled to its possession is known, order it to be returned to the lawful owner or to the person who is lawfully entitled to its possession, and may, if possession of it by the person from whom it was seized is unlawful, or if it was seized when it was not in the possession of any person, and the lawful owner or person who is lawfully entitled to its possession is not known, order it to be forfeited to Her Majesty, to be disposed of as the Attorney General directs, or otherwise dealt with in accordance with the law.

(9.1) Exception—Notwithstanding subsection (9), a judge or justice referred to in paragraph (9)(*a*) or (*b*) may, if the periods of detention provided for or ordered under subsections (1) to (3) in respect of a thing seized have expired but proceedings have not been instituted in which the thing may be required, order that the thing continue to be detained for such period as the judge or justice considers necessary if the judge or justice is satisfied

(a) that the continued detention of the thing might reasonably be required for a purpose mentioned in subsection (1) or (4); and

(b) that it is in the interests of justice to do so.

(10) Application by lawful owner—Subject to this or any other Act of Parliament, a person, other than a person who may make an application under subsection (7), who claims to be the lawful owner or person lawfully entitled to possession of anything seized and brought before or reported to a justice under section 489.1 may, at any time, on three clear days notice to the Attorney General and the person from whom the thing was seized, apply summarily to

(a) a judge referred to in subsection (7), where a judge ordered the detention of the thing seized under subsection (3), or

(b) a justice, in any other case,

for an order that the thing detained be returned to the applicant.

(11) Order—Subject to this or any other Act of Parliament, on an application under subsection (10), where a judge or justice is satisfied that

(a) the applicant is the lawful owner or lawfully entitled to possession of the thing seized, and

(b) the periods of detention provided for or ordered under subsections (1) to (3) in respect of the thing seized have expired and proceedings have not been instituted in which the thing detained may be required or, where such periods have not expired, that the continued detention of the thing seized will not be required for any purpose mentioned in subsection (1) or (4),

the judge or justice shall order that

(c) the thing seized be returned to the applicant; or

(d) except as otherwise provided by law, where, pursuant to subsection (9), the thing seized was forfeited, sold or otherwise dealt with in such a manner that it cannot be returned to the applicant, the applicant be paid the proceeds of sale or the value of the thing seized.

(12) Detention pending appeal, etc.—Notwithstanding anything in this section, nothing shall be returned, forfeited or disposed of under this section pending any application made, or appeal taken, thereunder in respect of the thing or proceeding in which the right of seizure thereof is questioned or within thirty days after an order in respect of the thing is made under this section.

(13) Copies of documents returned—The Attorney General, the prosecutor or the peace officer or other person having custody of a document seized may, before bringing it before a justice or complying with an order that the document be returned, forfeited or otherwise dealt with under subsection (1), (9) or (11), make or cause to be made, and may retain, a copy of the document.

(14) Probative force—Every copy made under subsection (13) that is certified as a true copy by the Attorney General, the person who made the copy or the person in whose presence the copy was made is admissible in evidence and, in the absence of evidence to the contrary, has the same probative force as the original document would have if it had been proved in the ordinary way.

(15) Access to anything seized—Where anything is detained pursuant to subsections (1) to (3.1), a judge of a superior court of criminal jurisdiction, a judge as defined in section 552 or a provincial court judge may, on summary application on behalf of a person who has an interest in what is detained, after three clear days notice to the Attorney General, order that the person by or on whose behalf the application is made be permitted to examine anything so detained.

(16) Conditions—An order that is made under subsection (15) shall be made on such terms as appear to the judge to be necessary or desirable to ensure that anything in respect of which the order is made is safeguarded and preserved for any purpose for which it may subsequently be required.

(17) Appeal—A person who feels aggrieved by an order made under subsection (8), (9), (9.1) or (11) may appeal from the order to the appeal court, as defined in section 812, and for the purposes of the appeal the provisions of sections 814 to 828 apply with such modifications as the circumstances require.

(18) Waiver of notice—Any person to whom three days notice must be given under paragraph (2)(*a*) or (3)(*a*) or subsection (7), (10) or (15) may agree that the application for which the notice is given be made before the expiration of the three days.

R.S.C. 1985, c. 27 (1st Supp.), s. 73; 1994, c. 44, s. 38; 1997, c. 18, s. 50.

490.01 Perishable things—Where any thing seized pursuant to this Act is perishable or likely to depreciate rapidly, the person who seized the thing or any other person having custody of the thing

(a) may return it to its lawful owner or the person who is lawfully entitled to possession of it; or

(b) where, on *ex parte* application to a justice, the justice so authorizes, may

(i) dispose of it and give the proceeds of disposition to the lawful owner of the thing seized, if the lawful owner was not a party to an offence in relation to the thing or, if the identity of that lawful owner cannot be reasonably ascertained, the proceeds of disposition are forfeited to Her Majesty, or

(ii) destroy it.

1997, c. 18, s. 51; 1999, c. 5, s. 17.

. . . .

Forfeiture of Offence-related Property

. . . .

492.1 (1) Information for tracking warrant—A justice who is satisfied by information on oath in writing that there are reasonable grounds to suspect that an offence under this or any other Act of Parliament has been or will be committed and that information that is relevant to the commission of the offence, including the whereabouts of any person, can be obtained through the use of a tracking device, may at any time issue a warrant authorizing a peace officer or a public officer who has been appointed or designated to administer or enforce a federal or provincial law and whose duties include the enforcement of this Act or any other Act of Parliament and who is named in the warrant

(a) to install, maintain and remove a tracking device in or on any thing, including a thing carried, used or worn by any person; and

(b) to monitor, or to have monitored, a tracking device installed in or on any thing.

(2) Time limit for warrant—A warrant issued under subsection (1) is valid for the period, not exceeding sixty days, mentioned in it.

(3) Further warrants—A justice may issue further warrants under this section.

(4) Definition of "tracking device"—For the purposes of this section, "**tracking device**" means any device that, when installed in or on any thing, may be used to help ascertain, by electronic or other means, the location of any thing or person.

(5) Removal after expiry of warrant—On *ex parte* application in writing supported by affidavit, the justice who issued a warrant under subsection (1) or a further warrant under subsection (3) or any other justice having jurisdiction to issue such warrants may authorize that the tracking device be covertly removed after the expiry of the warrant

    (a) under any terms or conditions that the justice considers advisable in the public interest; and

    (b) during any specified period of not more than sixty days.

1993, c. 40, s. 18; 1999, c. 5, s. 18.

492.2 (1) Information re number recorder—A justice who is satisfied by information on oath in writing that there are reasonable grounds to suspect that an offence under this or any other Act of Parliament has been or will be committed and that information that would assist in the investigation of the offence could be obtained through the use of a number recorder, may at any time issue a warrant authorizing a peace officer or a public officer who has been appointed or designated to administer or enforce a federal or provincial law and whose duties include the enforcement of this Act or any other Act of Parliament and who is named in the warrant

    (a) to install, maintain and remove a number recorder in relation to any telephone or telephone line; and

    (b) to monitor, or to have monitored, the number recorder.

(2) Order re telephone records—When the circumstances referred to in subsection (1) exist, a justice may order that any person or body that lawfully possesses records of telephone calls originated from, or received or intended to be received at, any telephone give the records, or a copy of the records, to a person named in the order.

(3) Other provisions to apply—Subsections 492.1(2) and (3) apply to warrants and orders issued under this section, with such modifications as the circumstances require.

(4) Definition of "number recorder"—For the purposes of this section, **"number recorder"** means any device that can be used to record or identify the telephone number or location of the telephone from which a telephone call originates, or at which it is received or is intended to be received.

1993, c. 40, s. 18; 1999, c. 5, s. 19.

PART XVI — COMPELLING APPEARANCE OF AN ACCUSED BEFORE A JUSTICE AND INTERIM RELEASE

. . . .

Powers to Enter Dwelling-houses to Carry out Arrests
[Heading added 1997, c. 39, s. 2]

529. (1) Including authorization to enter in warrant of arrest—A warrant to arrest or apprehend a person issued by a judge or justice under this or any other Act of Parliament may authorize a peace officer, subject to subsection (2), to enter a dwelling-house described in the warrant for the purpose of arresting or apprehending the person if the judge or justice is satisfied by information on oath in writing that there are reasonable grounds to believe that the person is or will be present in the dwelling house.

(2) Execution—An authorization to enter a dwelling-house granted under subsection (1) is subject to the condition that the peace officer may not enter the dwelling-house unless the peace officer has, immediately before entering the dwelling-house, reasonable grounds to believe that the person to be arrested or apprehended is present in the dwelling-house.

1997, c. 39, s. 2.

529.1 Warrant to enter dwelling-house—A judge or justice may issue a warrant in Form 7.1 authorizing a peace officer to enter a dwelling-house described in the warrant for the purpose of arresting or apprehending a person identified or identifiable by the warrant if the judge or justice is satisfied by information on oath that there are reasonable grounds to believe that the person is or will be present in the dwelling-house and that

(a) a warrant referred to in this or any other Act of Parliament to arrest or apprehend the person is in force anywhere in Canada;

(b) grounds exist to arrest the person without warrant under paragraph 495(1)(a) or (b) or section 672.91; or

(c) grounds exist to arrest or apprehend without warrant the person under an Act of Parliament, other than this Act.

1997, c. 39, s. 2; 2002, c. 13, s. 23.

529.2 Reasonable terms and conditions—Subject to section 529.4, the judge or justice shall include in a warrant referred to in section 529 or 529.1 any terms and conditions that the judge or justice considers advisable to ensure that the entry into the dwelling-house is reasonable in the circumstances.

1997, c. 39, s. 2.

529.3 (1) Authority to enter dwelling without warrant—Without limiting or restricting any power a peace officer may have to enter a dwelling-house under this or any other Act or law, the peace officer may enter the dwelling-house for the purpose of arresting or apprehending a person, without a warrant referred to in section 529 or 529.1 authorizing the entry, if the peace officer has reasonable grounds to believe that the person is present in the dwelling-house, and the conditions for obtaining a warrant under section 529.1 exist but by reason of exigent circumstances it would be impracticable to obtain a warrant.

(2) Exigent circumstances—For the purposes of subsection (1), exigent circumstances include circumstances in which the peace officer

(a) has reasonable grounds to suspect that entry into the dwelling-house is necessary to prevent imminent bodily harm or death to any person; or

(b) has reasonable grounds to believe that evidence relating to the commission of an indictable offence is present in the dwelling-house and that entry into the dwelling-house is necessary to prevent the imminent loss or imminent destruction of evidence.

1997, c. 39, s. 2.

529.4 (1) Omitting announcement before entry—A judge or justice who authorizes a peace officer to enter a dwelling-house under section 529 or 529.1, or any judge or justice, may authorize the peace officer to enter the dwelling-house without prior announcement if the judge or justice is satisfied by information on oath that there are reasonable grounds to believe that prior announcement of the entry would

(a) expose the peace officer or any other person to imminent bodily harm or death; or

(b) result in the imminent loss or imminent destruction of evidence relating to the commission of an indictable offence.

(2) Execution of authorization—An authorization under this section is subject to the condition that the peace officer may not enter the dwelling-house without prior announcement despite being authorized to do so unless the peace officer has, immediately before entering the dwelling-house,

> (a) reasonable grounds to suspect that prior announcement of the entry would expose the peace officer or any other person to imminent bodily harm or death; or

> (b) reasonable grounds to believe that prior announcement of the entry would result in the imminent loss or imminent destruction of evidence relating to the commission of an indictable offence.

(3) Exception—A peace officer who enters a dwelling-house without a warrant under section 529.3 may not enter the dwelling-house without prior announcement unless the peace officer has, immediately before entering the dwelling-house,

> (a) reasonable grounds to suspect that prior announcement of the entry would expose the peace officer or any other person to imminent bodily harm or death; or

> (b) reasonable grounds to believe that prior announcement of the entry would result in the imminent loss or imminent destruction of evidence relating to the commission of an indictable offence.

1997, c. 39, s. 2.

529.5 Telewarrant—If a peace officer believes that it would be impracticable in the circumstances to appear personally before a judge or justice to make an application for a warrant under section 529.1 or an authorization under section 529 or 529.4, the warrant or authorization may be issued on an information submitted by telephone or other means of telecommunication and, for that purpose, section 487.1 applies, with any modifications that the circumstances require, to the warrant or authorization.

1997, c. 39, s. 2.

. . . .

Appendix II
Criminal Code Forms for Warrants (Section 849)

1. Introduction

Section 849 deals with forms prescribed under the *Criminal Code*. It provides that the text of the forms provided by the statute may be changed "to suit the case" and that "forms to the like effect are deemed to be good, valid and sufficient in the circumstances for which they are provided."[3]

The forms prescribed by s. 849 are, invariably, the barest minimum that the *Criminal Code* will tolerate. All jurisdictions, and most police agencies, have pre-printed forms which elaborate on the skeletal forms provided here. They provide a starting point, not a finished product.

Form 1 — Information to Obtain A Search Warrant

(Section 487)

Canada,
Province of ....,
(*territorial division*).

This is the information of A.B., of ...., in the said (*territorial division*), (*occupation*), hereinafter called the informant, taken before me.

The informant says that (*describe things to be searched for and offence in respect of which search is to be made*), and that he believes on reasonable grounds that the said things, or some part of them, are in the (*dwelling-house, etc.*) of C.D., of ...., in the said (*territorial division*). (*Here add the grounds of belief, whatever they may be*).

Wherefore the informant prays that a search warrant may be granted to search the said (*dwelling-house, etc.*) for the said things.

Sworn before me this
.... day of

.........., A.D. ...., ...

at ....   (*Signature of Informant*)

....
A Justice of the Peace in and for

---

[3] Section 849(1).

285

. . . .

Form 5 — Warrant to Search

(Section 487)

Canada,
Province of ....,
(*territorial division*).

To the peace officers in the said (*territorial division*) or to the (*named public officers*):

Whereas it appears on the oath of A.B., of .... that there are reasonable grounds for believing that (*describe things to be searched for and offence in respect of which search is to be made*) are in .... at.........., hereinafter called the premises;

This is, therefore, to authorize and require you between the hours of (*as the justice may direct*) to enter into the said premises and to search for the said things and to bring them before me or some other justice.

Dated this .... day of .... A.D. ...., at ....

....

A Justice of the Peace in and for

....

1999, c. 5, s. 45.

Form 5.01 — Information to Obtain a Warrant to take Bodily Substances for Forensic DNA Analysis

(Subsection 487.05(1))

Canada,
Province of ....,
(*territorial division*)

This is the information of (*name of peace officer*), (*occupation*), of .... in the said (*territorial division*), hereinafter called the informant, taken before me.

The informant says that he or she has reasonable grounds to believe

(a) that (*offence*), a designated offence within the meaning of section 487.04 of the *Criminal Code*, has been committed;

(b) that a bodily substance has been found

(i) at the place where the offence was committed,

(ii) on or within the body of the victim of the offence,

(iii) on anything worn or carried by the victim at the time when the offence was committed, or

(iv) on or within the body of any person or thing or at any place associated with the commission of the offence;

(c) that (*name of person*) was a party to the offence; and

(d) that forensic DNA analysis of a bodily substance from (*name of person*) will provide evidence about whether the bodily substance referred to in paragraph (*b*) was from that person.

The reasonable grounds are:

The informant therefore requests that a warrant be issued authorizing the taking from (*name of person*) of the number of samples of bodily substances that are reasonably required for forensic DNA analysis, provided that the person taking the samples is able by virtue of training or experience to take them by means of the investigative procedures described in subsection 487.06(1) of the *Criminal Code* and provided that, if the person taking the samples is not a peace officer, he or she take the samples under the direction of a peace officer.

Sworn to before me

this ....day of.........,

A.D. ...., at ....

....

(*Signature of informant*)

....

(*Signature of provincial court judge*)

1998, c. 37, s. 24.

Form 5.02 — Warrant Authorizing the Taking of Bodily Substances for Forensic DNA Analysis

(Subsection 487.05(1))

Canada,

Province of ....,
(*territorial division*)

To the peace officers in (*territorial division*):

Whereas it appears on the oath of (*name of peace officer*) of .... in the said (*territorial division*), that there are reasonable grounds to believe

(a) that (*offence*), a designated offence within the meaning of section 487.04 of the *Criminal Code*, has been committed,

(b) that a bodily substance has been found

(i) at the place where the offence was committed,

(ii) on or within the body of the victim of the offence,

(iii) on anything worn or carried by the victim at the time when the offence was committed, or

(iv) on or within the body of any person or thing or at any place associated with the commission of the offence,

(c) that (*name of person*) was a party to the offence, and

(d) that forensic DNA analysis of a bodily substance from (*name of person*) will provide evidence about whether the bodily substance referred to in paragraph (b) was from that person;

And whereas I am satisfied that it is in the best interests of the administration of justice to issue this warrant;

This is therefore to authorize and require you to take from (*name of person*) or cause to be taken by a person acting under your direction, the number of samples of bodily substances that are reasonably required for forensic DNA analysis, provided that the person taking the samples is able by virtue of training or experience to take them by means of the investigative procedures described in subsection 487.06(1) of the *Criminal Code* and provided that, if the person taking the samples is not a peace officer, he or she take the samples under the direction of a peace officer. This warrant is subject to the following terms and conditions that I consider advisable to ensure that the taking of the samples is reasonable in the circumstances:

Dated this ...... day of ....

A.D. ...., at ....

....

(*Signature of provincial court judge*)

1998, c. 37, s. 24.

. . . .

Form 5.07 — Report to a Provincial Court Judge or the Court

(Subsection 487.057(1))

Canada,
Province of ....,
(*territorial division*)

[ ] To (*name of judge*), a judge of the provincial court who issued a warrant under section 487.05 or granted an authorization under section 487.055 or 487.091 of the *Criminal Code* or to another judge of that court:

[ ] To the court from which an order under section 487.051 or 487.052 of the *Criminal Code* was made:

I, (*name of peace officer*), have (*state here whether you have acted in execution of a warrant under section 487.05 or an order under section 487.051 or 487.052, or under an authorization under section 487.055 or 487.091*) of the *Criminal Code*.

I have (*state here whether you have taken the samples yourself or caused them to be taken under your direction*) from (*name of offender*) the number of samples of bodily substances that I believe are reasonably required for forensic DNA analysis, in accordance with (*state whether the taking of the samples was under the warrant issued or an authorization granted by the judge or another judge of the court or an order made by the court*).

The samples were taken at .... a.m./p.m. on the .... day of .... A.D. ......

I (*or state the name of the person who took the samples*) was able by virtue of training or experience to take the following samples from (*name of offender*) in accordance with subsection 487.06(1) of the *Criminal Code* and did so take them:

[ ] individual hairs, including the root sheath

[ ] epithelial cells taken by swabbing the lips, tongue or inside cheeks of the mouth

[ ] blood taken by pricking the skin surface with a sterile lancet

Any terms or conditions in the (*warrant, order or authorization*) have been complied with.

Dated this ...... day of ....

A.D. ...., at ....

....

(*Signature of peace officer*)

1998, c. 37, s. 24.

. . . .

Form 5.1 — Warrant To Search

(Section 487.1)

Canada,
Province of [*specify province*].

To A.B. and other peace officers in the [*territorial division in which the warrant is intended for execution*]:

Whereas it appears on the oath of A.B., a peace officer in the [*territorial division in which the warrant is intended for execution*], that there are reasonable grounds for dispensing with an information presented personally and in writing; and that there are reasonable grounds for believing that the following things

[*describe things to be searched for*]

relevant to the investigation of the following indictable offence

[*describe offence in respect of which search is to be made*]

are to be found in the following place or premises

[*describe place or premises to be searched*]:

This is, therefore, to authorize you to enter the said place or premises between the hours of [*as the justice may direct*] and to search for and seize the said things and to report thereon as soon as practicable but within a period not exceeding seven days after the execution of the warrant to the clerk of the court for the [*territorial division in which the warrant is intended for execution*].

Issued at [*time*] on the [*day*] of [*month*] A.D. [*year*], at [*place*].

....

A Judge of the Provincial Court in and for the Province of [*specify province)*].

To the Occupant: This search warrant was issued by telephone or other means of telecommunication. If you wish to know the basis on which this warrant was issued, you may apply to the clerk of the court for the territorial division in which the warrant was executed, at [*address*], to obtain a copy of the information on oath.

You may obtain from the clerk of the court a copy of the report filed by the peace officer who executed this warrant. That report will indicate the things, if any, that were seized and the location where they are being held.

R.S.C. 1985, c. 27 (1st Supp.), s. 184(3),
R.S.C. 1985, c. 1 (4th Supp.), s. 17.

Form 5.2 — Report To A Justice

(Section 489.1)

Canada
Province of ....,
[*territorial division*).

To the justice who issued a warrant to the undersigned pursuant to section 256, 487 or 487.1 of the *Criminal Code* (*or another justice for the same territorial division or, if no warrant was issued, any justice having jurisdiction in respect of the matter*).

I, (*name of the peace officer or other person*) have (*state here whether you have acted under a warrant issued pursuant to section 256, 487 or 487.1 of the Criminal Code or under section 489 of the Criminal Code or otherwise in the execution of duties under the Criminal Code or other Act of Parliament to be specified*)

1. searched the premises situated at ....; and

2. seized the following things and dealt with them as follows:

Property Seized (describe each thing seized)	Disposition (state, in respect of each thing seized, whether
	(a) it was returned to the person lawfully entitled to its possession, in which case the receipt therefor shall be attached hereto, or

> *(b)* *it is being detained to be dealt with according to law, and the location and manner in which, or where applicable, the person by whom it is being detained).*

1. ....

2. ....

3. ....

4. ....

In the case of a warrant issued by telephone or other means of telecommunication, the statements referred to in subsection 487.1(9) of the *Criminal Code* shall be specified in the report.

Dated this .... day of .... A.D. ...., at ....

....
Signature of peace
officer or other
person

R.S.C. 1985, c. 27 (1st Supp.), s. 184(3).

Form 5.3 — Report To A Judge of Property Seized

(Section 462.32)

Canada
Province of ....,
(territorial division).

To a judge of the court from which the warrant was issued (*specify court*):

I, (*name of the peace officer or other person*) have acted under a warrant issued under section 462.32 of the *Criminal Code* and have

1. searched the premises situated at ....; and

2. seized the following property:

Property Seized (describe each item of property	Location (state, in respect of each item of property seized, the location where it is

seized)   *being detained).*

1. ....

2. ....

3. ....

4. ....

Dated this .... day of .... A.D. ....., at

....

....

Signature of peace
officer or other
person

R.S.C. 1985, c. 42 (4th Supp.), s. 6.

. . . .

Form 7.1 — Warrant to Enter Dwelling-House

(Section 529.1)

Canada,
Province of ....,
(*territorial division*).

To the peace officers in the said (*territorial division*):

This warrant is issued in respect of the arrest of A.B., or a person with the following description (   ), of ...., (*occupation*).

Whereas there are reasonable grounds to believe:*

(a) a warrant referred to in this or any other Act of Parliament to arrest or apprehend the person is in force anywhere in Canada;

(b) grounds exist to arrest the person without warrant under paragraph 495(1)(a) or (b) or section 672.91 of the *CriminalCode*; or

(c) grounds exist to arrest or apprehend without warrant the person under an Act of Parliament, other than this Act;

And whereas there are reasonable grounds to believe that the person is or will be present in (*here describe dwelling-house*);

This warrant is issued to authorize you to enter the dwelling-house for the purpose of arresting or apprehending the person.

Dated this .... day of .... A.D. ...., at ....

....

Judge, Clerk of the Court,
Provincial Court Judge or Justice

_____

Initial applicable recital.

1997, c. 39, s. 3; 2002, c. 13, s. 85.

. . . .

Form 28 — Endorsement of Warrant

(Sections 487 and 528)

Canada,
Province of ....,
(*territorial division*).

Pursuant to application this day made to me, I hereby authorize the arrest of the accused (*or* defendant) (*or* execution of this warrant, in the case of a warrant issued pursuant to section 487), within the said (*territorial division*).

Dated this .... day of .... A.D. ...., at ....

....

....

A Justice of the Peace in and for

....

R.S.C. 1985, c. 27 (1st Supp.), s. 184(12).

Index

PROVINCIAL OFFENCES ACT
(ONTARIO), 96, 189

PSYCHIATRIC RECORDS, 39-40, 179

REGULATORY INVESTIGATIONS
• searches, 3, 21, 52
• seizure of materials from, 129-132, 187

REPORT TO JUSTICE
• banking documents, and, 199
• consent searches, and, 198
• forms, 291-292
• general warrant cases, in, 166-167
• generally, 197
• need for, 197-198
• production orders, 199
• warrantless searches, and, 198

RETURN *see* **REPORT TO JUSTICE**

"ROLLED-UP" APPLICATIONS, 60, 63, 129, 164-165

SCHOOL SEARCHES, 9

SEALING ORDERS
• checklist, 236-237
• common law power, 183
• generally, 60
• legislative power, 183-184
• reasons
•• sufficiency, 187
• review of, 187
• when appropriate, 184-186

"SNEAK AND PEEK" WARRANTS, 165

"SNIFFER-DOGS," 15

SOURCING, 46

STATE AGENCY, 18

SUCCESSIVE APPLICATIONS, 188

TELEWARRANTS, 50, 68-71, 180-181, 290-291

"THREE QUESTIONS APPROACH," 78-79

TIPSTERS
• assessing reliability, 24, 121-125, 127
• generally, 120
• nomenclature, 120-121, 205-208
• privilege
•• exception, 128
•• nature and scope, 125-127
• protecting, 127-128
• safety concerns, 126-128

TRACKING DEVICE WARRANT
• checklist, 228
• standard of proof, 20, 55-56
• use as search, 8, 15, 144
• warrant requirement, 144

VIDEO SURVEILLANCE, 7, 8, 149-151, 156, 194-195, 222

WARRANTLESS SEARCH POWERS, STATUTORY
• exigent circumstances, 238
• exigent drug searches, 243
• exigent entry to dwelling house to arrest or apprehend, 241-242
• exigent public safety seizure of weapons, 240
• exigent seizure of evidence of weapons offences, 239

YOUTH CRIMINAL JUSTICE ACT, 140